She-wolf

She-wolf
A cultural history of female werewolves

edited by Hannah Priest

Manchester University Press

Copyright © Manchester University Press 2015

While copyright in the volume as a whole is vested in Manchester University Press, copyright in individual chapters belongs to their respective authors, and no chapter may be reproduced wholly or in part without the express permission in writing of both author and publisher.

Published by Manchester University Press
Altrincham Street, Manchester M1 7JA, UK
www.manchesteruniversitypress.co.uk

British Library Cataloguing-in-Publication Data is available

ISBN 978 0 7190 8934 3 *hardback*
ISBN 978 1 5261 1689 5 *paperback*

First published by Manchester University Press in hardback 2015

This edition first published 2018

The publisher has no responsibility for the persistence or accuracy of URLs for any external or third-party internet websites referred to in this book, and does not guarantee that any content on such websites is, or will remain, accurate or appropriate.

Printed by Lightning Source

Contents

	Notes on contributors	*page* vii
1	Introduction: a history of female werewolves *Hannah Priest*	1
2	Estonian werewolf legends collected from the island of Saaremaa *Merili Metsvahi*	24
3	'She transformed into a werewolf, devouring and killing two children': trials of she-werewolves in early modern French Burgundy *Rolf Schulte*	41
4	Participatory lycanthropy: female werewolves in *Werewolf: The Apocalypse* *Jay Cate*	59
5	Fur girls and wolf women: fur, hair and subversive female lycanthropy *Jazmina Cininas*	77
6	Female werewolf as monstrous other in Honoré Beaugrand's 'The Werewolves' *Shannon Scott*	96
7	'The complex and antagonistic forces that constitute one soul': conflict between societal expectations and individual desires in Clemence Housman's *The Werewolf* and Rosamund Marriott Watson's 'A Ballad of the Were-wolf' *Carys Crossen*	111
8	I was a teenage she-wolf: boobs, blood and sacrifice *Hannah Priest*	129
9	The case of the cut-off hand: Angela Carter's werewolves in historical perspective *Willem de Blécourt*	148
10	The she-wolves of horror cinema *Peter Hutchings*	166
11	*Ginger Snaps*: the monstrous feminine as *femme animale* *Barbara Creed*	180

12 *Dans Ma Peau*: shape-shifting and subjectivity 196
    Laura Wilson

    Select bibliography 211
    Index 221

Notes on contributors

Willem de Blécourt studied anthropology at the University of Amsterdam. He is an Honorary Research Fellow at the Huizinga Institute, and has published extensively on witchcraft and magical practice in European culture. He is the author of *Werewolves* (2005), and the editor of *Beyond the Witch Trials* (2004) and *Witchcraft Continued* (2005).

Jay Cate is the pen-name of a collective of writers, researchers and gamers based in the UK. Between them they have (undergraduate and postgraduate) degrees in English Literature, Molecular Biology, Information Systems and Social Work. Some work, some study, some play and some write; the final product is a collaboration.

Jazmina Cininas is an Australian artist, arts writer, curator and academic at RMIT University, Melbourne, where she recently completed her PhD, titled 'The Girlie Werewolf Hall of Fame: Historical and Contemporary Figurations of the Female Lycanthrope'. Jazmina's evolving portrait gallery of reduction linocuts, the Girlie Werewolf Project, has been exhibited throughout Australia and the world, and her work is included in many major Australian and international collections. She has also presented papers on various aspects of female lycanthropy at international conferences in Australia, the USA, Hungary and the UK.

Barbara Creed is Professor of Screen Studies at the University of Melbourne. She has spoken and written extensively in Australia and overseas on feminist film theory, horror, gender, evolutionary theory and popular culture. Her books include the acclaimed *The Monstrous-Feminine: Film, Feminism, Psychoanalysis* (1993); *Media Matrix: Sexing the New Reality* (2003); *Phallic Panic: Film, Horror and the Primal Uncanny* (2005); and *Darwin's Screens: Evolutionary Aesthetics, Time and Sexual Display in the Cinema* (2009). She has been the recipient of five Australian Research Council Grants. In 2006 she became a Fellow of the Academy of the Humanities in Australia. Her current research and publications are in the area of human animal studies and she is the director of HRAE, the Human Rights and Animal Ethics Research Network.

Carys Crossen was awarded her PhD in English and American Studies by the University of Manchester in 2011. She currently teaches at the same university, and her research interests include the Gothic, Victorian literature, feminist theory, monster theory and anything with werewolves. Her publications include a book chapter on celibate male vampires, a forthcoming book contribution on Gothic fairy tales and a forthcoming article for *Horror Studies* on the issue of education with Stephenie Meyer's Twilight saga.

Peter Hutchings is Professor of Film Studies at Northumbria University. He is the author of *Hammer and Beyond: The British Horror Film* (1994); *Terence Fisher* (2001); *The British Film Guide to Dracula* (2006); *The Horror Film* (2004) and *The Historical Dictionary of Horror Cinema* (2008) as well as co-editor of *The Film Studies Reader* (2000). He has also published numerous journal articles and book chapters on horror cinema, British film and television, science fiction cinema and television, and the thriller.

Merili Metsvahi is a senior researcher at the Department of Estonian and Comparative Folklore, University of Tartu, Estonia. In 2000, she completed her MA thesis on the werewolf image in Estonian and Livonian legends and witchcraft trials at the University of Tartu. In 2007 she was awarded her PhD for the individual-centred study 'Individual, Memory and Creativity: Ksenia Müürsepp's Mental World from a Folklorist's Perspective' at the University of Tartu. She has co-edited a textbook of folklore (with Ülo Valk), *Regisvärsist natinaljadeni. Sissejuhatus rahvaluulesse* (2005) and a special issue of *Journal of Ethnology and Folkloristics* (7:2, 2013). In addition to her dissertation she has published more than thirty articles and participated in numerous international conferences. She teaches courses on Estonian folk belief and folklore fieldwork at the University of Tartu, and has given lectures at universities in Hungary, Lithuania, India, Turkey and Greece. Her research interests are women in Estonian folklore, storytelling and Estonian folktales.

Hannah Priest is an Honorary Research Fellow at Swansea University, attached to the Centre for Medieval and Early Modern Research. She has published a number of articles on medieval and contemporary popular culture, with a particular focus on the intersections of sex, violence and the monstrous, including chapters in Glennis Byron and Dale Townshend (eds), *The Gothic World* (2013), Anne Kirkham and Cordelia Warr (eds), *Wounds in the Middle Ages* (2014) and Deborah Mutch (ed.), *The Modern Vampire and Humanity* (2013). As Hannah Kate, she is a short story writer and poet, and is the editor of *Wolf-Girls: Dark Tales of Teeth, Claws and Lycogyny* (2012).

Rolf Schulte is a Fellow at the University of Kiel in Germany. His research and publications centre on witch hunts in the early modern periods, as well as nineteenth- and twentieth-century German and European history.

His publications in English include *Man as Witch: Male Witches in Central Europe* (2009); *Witchcraft in Sub-Saharan Africa: Witches, Witch-Hunts and Magical Imaginaries/Hexenverfolgung und magische Vorstellungswelten im modernen Afrika* (2008) (co-edited with B. Schmidt); 'Men as Accused Witches in the Holy Roman Empire', in Alison Rowlands (ed.), *Witchcraft and Masculinities in Early Modern Europe* (2008).

Shannon Scott is an adjunct professor of English at the University of St Thomas and St Catherine University in St Paul, Minnesota. She is the co-editor of *Terrifying Transformations: An Anthology of Victorian Werewolf Fiction, 1838–1896* (2012). She has presented her essays on werewolves in nineteenth-century literature at the University of North Carolina, Roehampton University and the MMLA conference in Chicago. She has taught the course, Werewolves in World Literature, where students were heard to howl at the moon during an intermission of the film *The Wolf Man* (1941). She is currently working on her first novel.

Laura Wilson was awarded her PhD in 2013 by the University of Manchester with her project 'Physical Spectatorship and the Contemporary Mutilation Film'. This is due for publication in 2015. She is currently an independent researcher continuing research into physicality and cinema, with a focus on how embodied responses shape analyses of representations of gender and race in film.

1

Introduction: a history of female werewolves

Hannah Priest

A cultural history of werewolves

The werewolf is an inherently contradictory creature.

There is a relatively common narrative explaining the prevalence of werewolves in European and Euro-American popular culture: once, long ago, our ancestors lived alongside wolves. The savage *canis lupus* was a constant threat to the cave-dwelling *homo sapiens*, who feared this ferocious predator more than any other. When early humans emerged, blinking, from their caves and began to hunt and gather, the wolf dogged their every step – a shadowy and ancient enemy. And yet, these humans held a grudging respect for the wolf; they began to glorify its speed and ruthlessness, to desire some appropriation of its power for themselves. Almost cultishly, they worshipped the wolf, but, for the most part, when the lupine enemy stalked, they cowered like lambs to the proverbial slaughter. Some of our ancestors were lucky: they met with wolves who were gentler, who approached proto-settlements and were amenable to companionship. These wolves were domesticated and became the ancestors of today's pet dogs. However, even companion animals hold traces of the savagery of their kin. People told stories of the wolf, created mythologies and folklore – and the shadows of these tales are still with us in contemporary narratives of the werewolf.

This opening paragraph is intentionally poetic and hyperbolic, as it reflects the sustained romanticisation of this persistent werewolf origin myth. In popular reference books, it is reproduced with frequency. In his book, *Werewolves*, for instance, Bob Curran writes:

> Arguably, the wolf is mankind's oldest foe, with an enmity that goes back almost into pre-human times. It was with the wolf that our distant ancestors competed for game and with whom they probably fought in the primal forests of an early world. And it may also be that the wolf won over the proto-men, for they were quick, strong and cunning, probably more able to chase and hunt down food than our heavy and lumbering forebears and even better at defending their territory than the early men. ... In every way, it seemed to be a fearsome and successful hunting and killing machine, better than anything our

ancient ancestors could produce. Is it any wonder then, that early man both hated and feared the wolf?[1]

Similarly, in the introduction to Brian Frost's *The Essential Guide to Werewolf Literature*, we find the claim that werewolf legends are 'immeasurably old and can be traced back to the earliest records of civilization'.[2] Even in more scholarly studies, we can see versions of this story. Leslie Sconduto, for example, begins her examination of werewolves in medieval and early modern literature with a poetic nod to the lycanthropy origin myth:

> Through the mists of time, we catch fleeting glimpses of the first werewolves, as if they were illuminated only momentarily by the light of a full moon partially obscured by clouds on a carefully constructed Hollywood sound stage.[3]

Walter Burkert's anthropological study of Ancient Greek ritual offers another, though more specified and localised, version of this. In outlining mythic sacrificial rites relating to werewolves and wolves, he writes that these must be taken as 'especially ancient', as they reflect 'the ideology of the predatory animal pack at its sacrificial meal, and this in spite of the fact that cooking in a kettle, a clearly cultural achievement, is an essential part of the rite'.[4]

Burkert's introduction to Greek wolf rituals is significant, as it offers the possibility of another narrative of the werewolf – and one which will be of central concern to this volume. The 'ideology of the predatory animal pack' notwithstanding, the rites that Burkert outlines require and involve important elements that are 'clearly a cultural achievement'. The werewolf, here, is revealed, not through mythologies of the pre- or proto-human, but through human culture, invention and ritualised social practice. Though the origins of the werewolf are romantically imagined as belonging to prehistory, the narrative of the werewolf is inextricably bound to historical circumstance, civilisation and literature. Even when, as Sconduto suggests, we feel we are getting a 'fleeting glimpse' through the 'mists of time', we are equally aware that we are actually looking at a 'carefully constructed' stage. Moreover, this stage is always a product of the culture that produced it – whether Ancient Greek myth or Hollywood cinema – and to understand the werewolf requires an engagement, not only with a sense of underlying 'ideology', but also with specific details of context. In her influential study of werewolf fiction, Chantal Bourgault du Coudray asserts that 'material relating to the werewolf in every period has been informed by prevailing cultural values and dominant ways of knowing or speaking about the world'.[5] The chapters in this volume reflect this way of approaching the figure of the werewolf, directly addressing the cultural values, tastes and ideologies that have informed various representations of the werewolf over the course of several centuries.

A note on terminology is needed here. This volume focuses on the figure of the werewolf, which is understood as a being that transforms between human and lupine forms, though this may occasionally be a symbolic rather than physical transformation, or (less frequently) a hybridised human/wolf.

The history of the werewolf is also understood to be a product of European (and, later, colonial) culture, though 'European' here is used as a negotiable and historicised classification.[6] That is not to deny the long histories of shape-shifters in other cultures – including other mythologies of lupine transformation – nor to deny fruitful readings of the werewolf against other hybridised or transformative monsters. However, the werewolf is a particular category of shape-shifting, with a coherent history of representation and construction and a specific geography of cultural production. In fact, as several chapters in this volume suggest, the history of the werewolf can be read as a revealing reflection of the development of 'prevailing cultural values and dominant ways of knowing or speaking about the world' that shape our conceptualisation of European and colonial identities.

Nevertheless, despite this volume's focus on cultural history and territorial specificity, I do not advocate a wholesale dismissal of the romantic lycanthropy origin myth. This mythic and universalising narrative has some use in a discussion of female werewolves – particularly since the female of the species is often entirely excluded from such stories. The myth becomes significant, not in its 'truth' (or otherwise), but in its reception and development at various points in history. For the purposes of this volume, the use of this narrative in gendering werewolves is of vital importance.

The gendering of werewolves

In most presentations of the lycanthropy origin myth, the presence of the female is, if not erased entirely, then at least obscured. Curran's presentation of the myth uses the universal 'man' in place of 'human', as does Frost's suggestion of a 'common ancestry' shared by 'man and wolves'.[7] As Rolf Schulte outlines in Chapter 3 of this volume, the word 'werewolf' and its French equivalent 'loup garou' are likely derived from words for 'wolf' and 'man', thus offering etymological evidence of a traditional gendering of the monster.[8]

Ideologically, the focus on hunting, savagery and aggression in the origin myth aligns the werewolf with behaviours and ideals more commonly associated with masculine identity positions in European cultural history. When used in popular discourse as generalised terms for prehistoric humans, 'hunters' and 'gatherers' are gendered male and female respectively. The werewolf origin myth is a story of the 'hunters', rather than the 'gatherers', and this is reflected in not only the gendering of the werewolf, but also in the specific traits of 'masculine' and 'feminine' that are constructed and affirmed in werewolf texts.

This generalised gendering of the 'hunter' werewolf is certainly revealed in numerous texts – from the savage hunters of Marie de France's twelfth-century poem *Bisclavret*, in which all werewolves (bar the protagonist) stalk the forest looking for human prey, to the ferocious beast that haunts the Yorkshire Moors in John Landis's 1980 film *An American Werewolf in London* – all of which present lycanthropy as an exclusively male condition. It also accounts for the late medieval literary fascination with the 'sympathetic werewolf', as the 'hunter' wolf is recognised as an avatar for the noble courtly hunters of medieval romance. It should be remembered that Marie's Bisclavret, though trapped in lupine form by his perfidious wife, begins his reintegration with human society when he encounters a royal *hunting* party: the werewolf is rejected by the party's dogs, but accepted by the hunters themselves.[9] This identification is also reflected in the rhetoric surrounding the historical hunting of wolves in various parts of medieval Europe, with the bounties attached to dead wolves and the high status of 'specialist' wolf-hunters revealing a consistent characterisation of the wolf as the greatest adversary a *man* could face.[10]

This mythic ideation of wolves is undoubtedly reflected across the millennia of presenting sympathetic and non-sympathetic male werewolves. However, I would suggest that the cultural (and culturally specific) history of werewolves also has implications on the dominant gendering of the creature. In his study of human interactions with wolves, Garry Marvin argues that the 'problem of the wolf for humans' comes at a concrete, rather than mythologised, point in human history.[11] The wolf was transformed from 'a large carnivore' to a direct antagonist between 6,000 and 10,000 years ago, when human beings began to domesticate animals:

> With domestication a new class of animals emerged that was not the result of neutral processes of evolution but rather a combination of natural and cultural processes, shaped and maintained for specifically human purposes. Two of the complex relationships between humans and animals in the context of domestication are important here: mutual dependency and ownership. ... Their owners therefore made an investment in these animals, which entered into their economies and so into their social and cultural worlds.[12]

The wolf becomes, then, not a threat to individual humans or a competitor for prey, but rather a threat to domesticated animals. As agriculture and economies developed, this might be better characterised as a threat to property and investment.

The literary and folkloric history of werewolves, based on what survives today, has been produced almost entirely in societies that have posited property ownership and economic independence as predominantly male privileges in both the cultural imaginary and legal practice. The wolf is a threat, not just to the primal male hunter, but also to the monetised male landowner, seeking to protect his 'social and cultural worlds' and his 'investment' from a destructive, external force. Read in this light, the male werewolf is a double threat – an external force combined with an internal identification – which serves to undermine the stability of masculine economic privilege. It is symptomatic of an anxiety of property ownership and status: the wolf that is destroying a man's livelihood might well turn out to be the man himself.

This economic lycanthropic narrative of property ownership and threat appears to exclude the female werewolf in much the same way as the mythic narrative of the primal hunter. Indeed, this is potentially evidenced by counterpoints produced by cultures with different economic traditions. As Merili Metsvahi's Chapter 2 attests, the island of Saaremaa, an area of Estonia with matrilineal property inheritance and female land ownership throughout the late Middle Ages and into early modernity, produced more folktales about female werewolves than any other European territory.

The discourses introduced here – the etymological, the mythic and the economic – are all present in the dominant presentation of the werewolf as male monster. Different iterations of lycanthropy might privilege one or the other, but the traces of all three are visible throughout the cultural history of the male werewolf. It might seem, initially, that the female werewolf can only ever be read as a deliberate subversion or rejection of this. And, it must be admitted, this is occasionally the case in constructions of the female lycanthrope, where texts reveal the female werewolf simply as a 'surprise' that confounds expectations based on conventional gendering.[13]

However, just as cultural narratives of the human male reveal, despite (and through) their erasure of the female, a space for an 'other' narrative, so too do we find space for the female werewolf. The female narrative draws on many of the same cultural assumptions and values as that of the male, but it often represents and reflects on these with a different focus. Moreover, the narrative of the female werewolf combines aspects of the lycanthropy origin myth with mythic and cultural narratives of womanhood: if the werewolf is an inherently contradictory creature, so too is a woman. The specificities of these contradictions will be explored throughout this collection, with the chapters exploring particular moments of the female werewolf narrative to reveal a variety of cultural assumptions, narrative tropes and putative archetypes of femaleness and femininity.

The textual history of female werewolves

The female werewolf enters literature around 3,000 years later than her male counterpart.[14] Although the literature and myth of antiquity presented numerous female monsters that were human/animal hybrids or transformative female bodies, the concept of a woman who could transform into a wolf first appears in literary form in Gerald of Wales's twelfth-century *Topographia Hiberniae*, an account of the author's travels following the Norman invasion of Ireland. In the second part of his narrative, Gerald tells the story of a priest who spends the night on the borders of Meath. The priest encounters a wolf, who is miraculously able to speak. The wolf explains:

> We are natives of Ossory. From there every seven years, because of the imprecation of a certain saint, namely the abbot Natalis, two persons, a man and a woman, are compelled to go into exile not only from their territory but

also from their bodily shape. They put off the form of man completely and put on the form of wolf. When the seven years are up, and if they have survived, two others take their place in the same way, and the first pair return to their former country and nature.

My companion in this pilgrimage is not far from here and is seriously ill. Please give her in her last hour the solace of the priesthood in bringing to her the revelation of the divine mercy.[15]

The priest then visits the dying she-wolf, who also requests the last rites:

To remove all doubt he [the male werewolf] pulled all the skin off the she-wolf from the head down to the navel, folding it back with his paw as if it were a hand. And immediately the shape of an old woman, clear to be seen, appeared. At that, the priest, more through terror than reason, communicated her as she had earnestly demanded, and she then devoutly received the sacrament. Afterwards, the skin which had been removed by the he-wolf resumed its former position.[16]

In the context of medieval werewolf narratives, Gerald's account of the werewolves of Ossory is unusual in a number of ways. The werewolves' speech, the revelation of human skin beneath the fur, and the careful situation of the transformation within the acceptable limits of Christian doctrine are all distinctive to Gerald's account. Moreover, as Sconduto points out, the tale 'is also unique for its Christian setting in which it presents a pair of werewolves whose metamorphosis has been inflicted on them as expiation for communal sin'.[17]

For this introduction, the significant characteristic of Gerald's tale is that it includes a female werewolf. Moreover, brief as Gerald's story may be, the werewolves of Ossory episode introduces some key features that resonate with post-medieval presentations of female werewolves. Firstly, the werewolves exist as a bonded pair – unlike other twelfth-century (male) werewolves, this female werewolf exists as part of a social unit. Secondly, there is a focus on bodily appearance and its mutability. Elsewhere in medieval literature, the corporeality of werewolf transformation is elided or denied; the transformation from human to werewolf (and, more importantly, from werewolf back to human) is associated more with the removal and recovery of clothes than with shifts in bodily form.[18] Gerald's text offers something different: for his female werewolf, the body *is* the clothing, and a graphic image of corporeal dissonance is offered.[19]

Finally, the woman who is revealed beneath the wolf is 'old'. Sconduto suggests that the age of the woman works as 'a metaphor for her humanity that has remained unchanged'.[20] However, the woman is depicted, not just as an image of unchanging humanity, but also as an example of ageing femininity. Again, there is a dissonance here. The male and female coupling initially implies a heterosexual pair bond, but the woman's age situates her as the non-sexual, non-fertile feminine. Similarly, though the Christianity of the woman is affirmed through her receiving the Eucharist from the priest, a shadow of monstrosity hangs over her and her companion's status as communal 'scapegoats'.

The she-wolf of Ossory is the only female werewolf found in medieval literature. Indeed, the female werewolf remains a 'surprising absentee' from literature until 1839 and the publication of Frederick Marryat's *The Phantom Ship*.[21] In the intervening years, however, the female werewolf was a recurrent presence in other cultural productions, particularly church tracts, Inquisition handbooks and folktales. The early modern period saw the development of a theological correlation between witchcraft and lycanthropy, both in theory and in legal practice, occasionally explicitly gendering both as female.[22] In addition to this, symbolic conceptualisations of the she-wolf became attached to various narratives of female leadership, national identity and modes of feminine aggression and assertiveness. In the Middle Ages, the symbolism of the she-wolf is a separate discourse to that of the werewolf, but the two intersect at various points. The she-wolf as contradictory and ambiguous symbol of female political power, with the potential for physical violence, questionable or promiscuous sexuality and an intrinsic connection to the formation of national identity, can be seen most clearly in the narratives surrounding the lupine totem of Rome.[23] It also informs discourses of medieval queenship, most notably concerning Isabella, consort of Edward II of England.[24]

Through such non-literary iterations, the narrative of the female werewolf developed, integrating narratives of the werewolf with (often negative) tropes of femininity, class and culture and blending the traditions of various European cultures with Classical narratives of the monstrous (and virtuous) female. By the time Marryat's Gothic white wolf Christina emerged in the nineteenth century as a seductive, homicidal and ultimately doomed female lycanthrope, the she-wolf had become a distillation of disparate and (often) contradictory cultural values. Moreover, although Gerald's Ossory werewolves are a fairly evenly matched pair, the female werewolf that enters supernatural fiction can be read as radically distinct from her male counterparts.

Just over eight hundred years after Gerald of Wales composed his *Topographia Hiberniae*, Atom Books published Lisi Harrison's novel *Monster High*. This book is, in a characteristically late-capitalist way, a novelisation of a range of toys. The Monster High dolls, produced by Mattel, are a collection of teenage anthropomorphic 'monsters', with posable limbs, dressable hair, and a range of accessories and possessions available for purchase and collection. While the dolls themselves are simply plastic models with 'profiles', outfits and accessories, Harrison's book offers a story and character development. The novel takes place in Salem, Oregon, where monsters (or RADs – 'Regular Attribute Dodgers' – as they call themselves) have taken refuge. The 'RAD' of interest here is Claudine (or Clawdeen) Wolf, the female werewolf of the toy range.[25]

Clawdeen Wolf is – according to marketing materials – 'a wolf in chic clothing'. She hates gym (because she cannot wear her platform heels) and loves 'shopping and flirting with boys'.[26] Her description continues:

> My hair is worthy of a shampoo commercial and that's just what grows on my legs. Plucking and shaving is definitely a full time job but that's a small price to pay for being scarily fabulous.[27]

Harrison's novel takes this description as its foundation, but develops a more sustained characterisation.

Monster High follows the parallel experiences of two new girls at Merston High. The first is Melody Carver, a human (or 'normie' as the monsters call them) girl who has experienced bullying related to her physical appearance at her old school. Her father, a plastic surgeon, has 'corrected' her face. The second new girl is Frankie Stein, the newly created and green-skinned 'daughter' of Viktor and Viveka Stein. Both Frankie and Melody are desperate to make friends at their new school, but both encounter problems with 'fitting in'.

The female werewolf is introduced as a student *before* any revelation of her monstrous nature, as Melody and a boy named Jackson enter the school cafeteria:

> Two attractive alternative girls, consumed by their own conversation, tried to squeeze past them. The Shakira-looking one, who had auburn curls and a tray stacked with Kobe beef sliders, made it by Jackson. ... 'Untrue!' barked the girl with the sliders. ... The barker wore purple leggings and a black bomber jacket lined in fur the same color as her hair.[28]

The second description offers further physical details:

> Claudine turned away from the window. 'Hey,' she said, tearing open a bag of organic turkey jerky. Her looks – yellowish-brown eyes, a mess of auburn curls, long manicured fingernails painted bronze – were just as striking as Cleo's [a mummy] but in a more wild, feral way. Her style, however, seemed tamer: all-American with a touch of old-world Hollywood glamour.[29]

While readers familiar with the toy range will know what Clawdeen's appearance signifies, the novel has not yet revealed that the girl is a werewolf. In fact, apart from Frankie, readers not told whether any of the characters at the school are 'RADs'. Nevertheless, there are substantial clues as to Clawdeen's nature. She is often seen eating meat, unlike the rest of the characters who are remarkably picky about food. Not only this, but Clawdeen eats large quantities of meat and eats impatiently; her tray is 'stacked' with beef sliders and she 'tears' into the bag of jerky. Perhaps a bigger clue is Clawdeen's fur, which she is always seen wearing and which is the same colour as her hair – later on in the novel it is revealed that this is because it *is* her hair. This fur is accentuated by her 'mess' of curls and 'wild, feral eyes'.

Another aspect of characterisation key to the presentation of Clawdeen is her 'pack'. Apart from Frankie's creators/parents, Clawdeen's family is the only monster family presented in any detail. She has a large group of overprotective brothers, who are leery, hairy and self-consciously hypermasculine. Clawdeen is both resentful of their protectiveness and mindful of the need to stay loyal to them, echoing other twenty-first-century texts in which a teenage werewolf exists as the lone female in an otherwise exclusively male lycanthropic pack.[30]

What is curious in the *Monster High* novel and toy range is that any question of full lupine transformation is avoided. Clawdeen appears to be more a hybrid half-wolf, half-woman than a young woman who transforms into a wolf. She has a pelt while clearly in 'human' form, which allows her to hide her lycanthropy by getting body waxes at an expensive beauty salon. At no point is it suggested that she, or her brothers, will undergo a complete bodily transformation, nor that she will pose any particular threat to human beings should this happen.

Monster High may seem an odd choice of text to offer as comparison with Gerald of Wales's *Topographia Hiberniae*; however, this juxtaposition offers a significant introduction to the way in which the cultural history of the female werewolf can be understood. On the one hand, these two texts are starkly different, both in form, purpose, composition and circulation. On the other, there are interesting (and, perhaps, unexpected) points of similarity that are indicative of a broader history of representation and interpretation of femininity and female lycanthropy.

Both texts presented here are products of their time, and reveal contemporaneous cultural assumptions and values with little or no ingenuousness. Gerald of Wales's *Topographia* is a text produced by a member of an invading nation with the purpose of narrating and delineating the history and customs of the invaded. The werewolves of Ossory episode is part of a series of depictions of monstrous and primitive creatures, with the overriding narration being one of impartial, but superior, observer. The werewolves can thus be contextualised as belonging to a list of curiosities, revealing not only animalistic human bodies but also indigenous rituals, which, though ostensibly Christian, are barbaric and potentially unjust. *Monster High* is also written with an unequivocal purpose – the marketing of a range of commercial products. Clawdeen's presentation is thus situated within a narrative of consumption, materiality and narcissistic desire.

The idiosyncrasies of the two texts are illuminated by this understanding of their context and purpose. Gerald's female werewolf does not undergo a 'true' transformation, as to do so would contradict underlying Christian theological ideas of metamorphosis.[31] The removal of the wolf skin in order to receive the Eucharist elevates the visiting priest to an upholder of hegemonic Christian authority over localised pseudo-religious barbarism. Conversely, Clawdeen Wolf's lack of 'true' transformation privileges late capitalist ideation of consumer culture: though she does not undergo a full lupine metamorphosis, she is able to remove her pelt (and 'transform' herself) because she and her peers are able to afford to pay for an 'exclusive' spa.

The fact that this is presented alongside a female character who has been 'transformed' by her plastic surgeon father affirms this.

Nevertheless, there are similarities between these two werewolves. Issues of corporeality and the non-normative female body arise. Both texts offer, though in different ways and to differing degrees, a depiction of the female body that, while not explicitly monstrous, has an uneasy emphasis on potentially abject features. Gerald's werewolf has an 'old' body; Harrison's Clawdeen has excessive body hair. Additionally, both these female werewolves are fundamentally aligned with a social unit – Gerald's female lycanthrope has a male partner, and Clawdeen has a group of siblings. Neither of these female werewolves is a predatory 'hunter', and, while they are excluded from 'normal' society, this exclusion is a shared experience. These are tropes that recur throughout the cultural history of female werewolves.

The domesticated werewolf

As noted, the history of the female werewolf is not a linear one. It is impossible to chart a progression or development from early texts to later ones. Nevertheless, given the comparison in the previous section, it is possible to identify recurrent motifs and traditions within texts of divergent media, composition and genre.

As is apparent from both the *Topographia Hiberniae* and *Monster High*, the social unit is a key feature of many representations of the female werewolf. In contemporary texts, this is most commonly depicted as a 'pack' to which the female werewolf belongs.[32] Where no 'pack' exists, female werewolves are frequently constructed through their identity within a pre-existing or newly formed social group, particularly through those with familial or pseudo-familial associations.[33]

For example, the first series of the UK television series *Being Human* (2008–13) features a (male) werewolf, George, who shares a house with a vampire and a ghost. In this text, werewolves are 'made', rather than 'born', following the twentieth-century cinematic convention of transmission of lycanthropy through a contagious bite. George is presented as being desirous of social and domestic security and, eventually, paternity, and much of series one is concerned with the preservation of George's 'humanity', in contrast to the apparently hopeless case of the vampire Mitchell.[34] However, George is alone as a werewolf, despite a brief visit from his 'sire' in the second episode.[35] He only truly achieves a 'social unit' when he infects his girlfriend Nina with lycanthropy in the final episode of the first series.

For the female werewolf, however, this process of socialisation works the other way around. As a human, Nina is presented initially as somewhat unfriendly and aloof. She is resistant to George's advances, before revealing the scars of an abusive childhood and a narrative of isolation and self-reliance.[36] Once infected with lycanthropy, however, Nina attains a role as part of the *Being Human* household, though she temporarily leaves George after discovering his complicity in covering up a vampiric murder. In the third series, the werewolf pack is extended as a result of Nina's pregnancy and the arrival of two other werewolves – McNair and Tom – allowing Nina to come to terms with her impending motherhood. Though she is at first resistant to maternity as a result of a poor relationship with her own mother, she comes to accept it as her relationship with George develops and Tom and McNair begin to act like 'overzealous midwives'.[37] Lycanthropy, in this text, is what enables the female to become part of a social unit; at the same time, it is the female who allows the lycanthropic social unit to come into existence in the first place.[38] This emphasising of female-centred pack structures is evident even in texts where the female is presented (and even defined) as resistant to socialisation and desirous of isolation. In both Martin Millar's *Lonely Werewolf Girl* and Thomas Emson's *Maneater*, the protagonists resist imposed social groupings in favour of a solitary lifestyle; however, both novels see the female werewolf form a new social group over the course of the narrative, based on shared experiences and companionship.[39] Jay Cate's Chapter 4 on the feminisation of werewolves in a twenty-first-century role-playing game explores this association of the pack with female werewolves, suggesting that the socialisation of werewolves privileges idealised feminine characteristics of communication and negotiation over the predatory and solitary aggression found in literary traditions of presenting male werewolves.

While the prominence of the pack in contemporary fiction is undeniable, there are tensions surrounding the social unit that surface in female werewolf fiction. As I suggested in the opening section of this introduction, the cultural history of the werewolf can be read through the history of property ownership and domestication. While male werewolves (like wolves) are often figured as an external threat to male property, female werewolves (like women) are more likely to be imagined as trapped *within* this economic and societal structuring. The attack of the werewolf, in both cases, is an attack to the heart of masculine-defined and patriarchal society – but while the male werewolf attempts to disrupt from without, the female werewolf is often trying to break out.

In 2009, Columbian singer-songwriter Shakira released a song entitled 'She Wolf'. The accompanying music video makes clear visual reference to various tropes of lycanthropy. Lithe, near-nude, contorting female flesh both demands and threatens the male gaze. Hints of violence are offered and diffused by sexualised, vibrant femininity. Reference is made to the problematic associations of female werewolves to both the *vagina dentata* and the female reproductive cycle – associations explored by Barbara Creed in her consideration of *Ginger Snaps* (2000, dir. John Fawcett) – by having the singer dance around in a red-lined cave-like set, which is highly suggestive of a vagina.

However, it is the opening lyrics that most clearly set out the version of female lycanthropy being evoked in the song's title: 'A domesticated girl, that's all you ask of me,/ Darling it's no joke, this is lycanthropy.' Thus 'domestication' stands in sharp contrast to 'lycanthropy'. The video plays on this; the 'domesticated' (perhaps even 'wifely') woman, lying in a pristine white double bed with her unaware male partner, rises and enters the closet. This unleashes a side of the woman that stands in stark distinction to the 'homely'. The song continues: 'I've been devoting myself to you Monday to Monday, Friday to Friday,/ Not getting enough retribution or incentives to keep me at it.' The frame of reference here is the workplace, underlined by the female voice likening herself to a 'coffee machine' that has been 'abused'. Thus, 'lycanthropy' is an alternative to the patriarchal control of both the home and the contemporary workplace. Unlike in Alan Moore's graphic story 'The Curse', in which a beleaguered and menstruating housewife turns her lycanthropic rage against her husband, ripping him to pieces in their family home, Shakira's 'She Wolf' is revealed to be a fantasy, and at the close of the video the singer returns to the clean white sheets of the marital bed; however, the song's repeated refrain of 'there's a she-wolf in your closet' implies a regularity with which this figure will emerge.[40]

And, indeed, the lycanthropic threat to domesticity is a frequent feature of female werewolf fiction. As Carys Crossen examines in Chapter 7, female writers of the late nineteenth century employed this trope in their presentation of female werewolves. In Rosamund Marriott Watson's 'A Ballad of the Were-wolf' this threat is not just an escape from the home and into the wild, but a confrontation with her husband and the implied murder of her children. This suggestion of lycanthropic infanticide parallels the first piece of female werewolf 'fiction' – distinct from those writings with didactic or instructional purposes – Marryat's narrative from *The Phantom Ship*, in which the lycanthropic Christina (in the guise of a large white wolf) murders her husband's children and later desecrates a grave in order to devour the flesh of her victim.[41]

In turn, this evokes the image of the early modern werewolf panics discussed in Schulte's chapter, particularly the story of Perrenette Gandillon. While Schulte explores in detail the historical circumstances of the Gandillon case, with reference to both ecclesiastical and legal developments in the region of Jura at the time, there is a popularised version of the tale, based on the outline given in Sabine Baring-Gould's 1865 work *The Book of Were-Wolves*, which surfaces in various contemporary cultural productions. Baring-Gould describes the case thus:

> Pernette Gandillon was a poor girl in the Jura, who in 1598 ran about the country on all fours, in the belief that she was a wolf. One day as she was ranging the country in a fit of lycanthropic madness, she came upon two children who were plucking wild strawberries. Filled with a sudden passion for blood, she flew at the little girl and would have brought her down, had not her brother, a lad of four years old, defended her lustily with a knife. Pernette, however, wrenched the weapon from his tiny hand, flung him down and gashed

his throat, so that he died of the wound. Pernette was torn to pieces by the people in their rage and horror.[42]

The story of Perrenette Gandillon may not be the most well-known werewolf story, but it has been referenced by recent popular culture in interesting ways. The heroine's family in Annette Curtis Klause's 1997 teen werewolf novel *Blood and Chocolate* has the surname Gandillon, for instance. The card game *Werewolf* – a variant on the party game *Mafia* – in which players are dealt cards marked 'villager' or 'werewolf' and must act on this secret identity, also contains an echo of the Gandillon case. The game is played in 'night' rounds and 'day' rounds. The aim of the game for the werewolves is to wait until nightfall and secretly 'turn' villagers; the aim of the game for the villagers is, during each 'day' round, to choose a player to be 'lynched' as a werewolf – without really knowing if they were actually a werewolf or just acting suspiciously like one. The infanticide element of the Gandillon tale has also entered contemporary popular culture as a dark 'stereotype' of the female werewolf, and its shadow can be seen even in texts with sympathetic and non-murderous heroines. In Carrie Vaughn's Kitty Norville series of novels, the eponymous heroine is a modern, urban werewolf who tries to balance her lycanthropic side with a career in radio, a developing love life and a series of life-threatening clashes with vampires and other supernatural creatures. Kitty is presented as intelligent, moral and principled, and frequently risks her own safety to protect people she cares about or people she considers vulnerable. However, when she agrees to take part in a Senate hearing regarding the existence of supernatural creatures, she assumes that the first question directed at her will be: 'Eaten any babies lately, Ms Norville?'[43]

For all her worry about infanticidal stereotypes, Kitty makes a sustained attempt at engaging with domesticity throughout Vaughn's fiction. She balances a career, a home life and a love life, remains in contact with her human family and even marries her lycanthropic lover. However, while she may not eat babies, Kitty is unable to give birth; whether she desires it or not, she is unable to fully identify with the 'normal' domestic female.

The sterility of the female werewolf could be posited as a development of the 'attack' this figure often poses to domestication. Vaughn's Kitty Norville series may not feature any infanticide, but miscarriage is presented as a clear and unavoidable consequence of female lycanthropy. In *Kitty and the Silver Bullet*, the protagonist discovers that, not only will she not be able to bear children, she may well have experienced multiple miscarriages without realising. When another werewolf suggests that female lycanthropes simply cannot get pregnant in the first place, Kitty is forced to explain the 'reality':

> 'You're wrong. We can get pregnant. The pregnancy doesn't survive shape-shifting. You might never even know it.'
> She gaped at me, astonished, like I'd slapped her. How many woozy, crampy mornings was she looking back on? How many times had she just written it off to an odd cycle?[44]

The impossibility of lycanthropic pregnancy is a feature of a number of texts about female werewolves; this focus on reproductive biology is generally not found in narratives of male werewolves, where the emphasis (where it exists at all) is more commonly on paternity as a social role, rather than a biological function.[45] *Being Human*'s Nina's pregnancy is in fact unusual in its viability; in the US version *Being Human* (2011–), Norah (Nina's counterpart) miscarries within the first few months of pregnancy, when the foetus begins an *in utero* werewolf transformation.[46] As I discuss Chapter 8 on young adult fiction, Stephenie Meyer's Twilight series includes a female werewolf whose lycanthropy is explicitly associated with being prematurely 'menopausal', signalling a supernatural sterility that, while not as visceral as the repeated miscarriages described in Vaughn's series, is just as much an involuntary rejection of maternity and family life.[47] As Kitty Norville reflects, after infection with lycanthropy, '[t]here'd never be a golden retriever in the backyard'.[48]

Hypersexuality and masculinisation

While the female werewolf's threat to domesticity is either violent and confrontational or tragic and irreversible in the texts mentioned above, elsewhere she poses a more insidious threat. In the season four episode of *Buffy the Vampire Slayer* (1997–2003) entitled 'Wild at Heart', male werewolf Oz, happily and 'domestically' in a relationship with the human girl Willow, encounters a singer named Veruca.[49] From her first appearance on screen earlier in the series, Veruca is the polar opposite of Willow: she is confident, confrontational, seductive and sexual.[50] Although Vercua's lycanthropy is not revealed until the 'Wild at Heart' episode, her sexual appeal (particularly to Oz) is figured as feral and potent. Eventually, Oz discovers that Veruca is a werewolf; she admits that she was able to discern his nature without being told. Veruca encourages Oz to eschew the monthly precautions he has been taking to prevent any harm being caused by his transformation, and they ultimately have sex. This destroys Oz's relationship with Willow, and leads to his self-imposed exile from Sunnydale. Veruca's disruption of the status quo – effected through her hypersexualised and 'wild' lycanthropy – also has consequences for the characterisation of Willow, setting into motion a narrative that will see this character transform into a stronger, more wilful woman, who will embrace lesbianism, witchcraft and, on one occasion, a desire to bring about the apocalypse. There are also implications for Buffy, as Willow's attempts to deal with Oz and Veruca's betrayal involve her casting a spell that causes Buffy to 'fall in love' with the antagonistic vampire Spike.[51] This foreshadows the darker and more 'feral' presentation of Buffy's sexuality in the sixth season, when she enters into a violent and self-destructive relationship with Spike.[52] While Veruca only appears in three episodes of *Buffy*, her impact can be discerned, arguably, for the remainder of the show's narrative.

The characterisation of Veruca can be compared to that of Marryat's Christina – whose seductive appearance blinds her husband to her murderous double-life – but also to Mattel's Clawdeen Wolf – the only Monster High doll to list 'flirting' as a 'hobby'. The overt sexualisation of the female werewolf has been a common trope of fiction since Victorian literature, but, as with many aspects of female werewolf fiction, has a history that predates this. As Barbara Creed explores in Chapter 11, the presentation of female sexuality and corporeality as animalistic and 'feral' finds its *locus classicus* in the Inquisition handbooks of the early modern witch-hunts, particularly in the *Malleus Maleficarum*. However the hypersexualised female werewolf, perhaps, finds its most developed expression (thus far) in the cinema, television and fiction of the late twentieth and early twenty-first centuries, where traditions of animalistic female nature combine with medieval notions of the perfidious female, Victorian Gothic tropes of the supernatural seductress, the film noir's *femme fatale* and anxieties surrounding 'sex-positive' post-feminism.

Buffy's Veruca is an extreme – and explicitly sexual – example of this presentation of the female werewolf, but my reference to Clawdeen Wolf indicates that this sexualisation can be found, albeit in a 'sanitised' form, in texts intended for younger audiences. Moreover, considerations of these 'sanitised' texts reveal the ways in which the sexuality of the female werewolf is not only a reflection of a transhistorical notion of feral and animalistic femininity, but also a tool that may be employed in context-specific cautionary tales.

The Disney Channel's television show, *Wizards of Waverly Place* (2007–12) features a female werewolf in the episode 'Beware Wolf'.[53] The series' narrative premise revolves around a family of 'wizards' in New York, with particular focus on the magical training of their children Justin and Alex. 'Beware Wolf' begins with Justin announcing that he is going on a blind date with a girl he has met on 'WizFace' (the social networking site for wizards).[54] His family warn him not to do it, as the last girl he met on WizFace turned out to be a centaur, foreshadowing the introduction of lycanthropy with another 'monstrous' female hybrid. Nevertheless, a knock on the door reveals Isabella – an apparently 'cute' and normal young woman. Isabella and Justin immediately hit it off, but the young woman is not what she seems. When Justin leaves the room, she takes Alex's jumper in her mouth and plays with it. Later, she laps water out of a glass, and exhibits other behaviours associated with a domestic dog. Isabella, it is revealed, is a werewolf. And when Justin kisses her, he becomes a werewolf too.

The lycanthropy episode of *Wizards of Waverly Place* is played for laughs, as most of the series is, and has nothing that could be described as 'explicit' sexual content. And yet, there is something about Isabella that allows us to read her alongside *Buffy*'s Veruca and Marryat's Christina. For example, note that this text presents lycanthropy as being transmitted through a contagious kiss, rather than a bite. Although the kiss is a chaste peck on the cheek, the implication is that, as soon as Justin accepts a less than platonic relationship with the she-wolf, he is lost, just as *Buffy*'s Oz was before him. It should be remembered that Isabella was first encountered by Justin as he looked through the 'World Wide Wiz-Web' for girls who wanted to *date* boys, suggesting that, for all her puppy-like submissiveness, Isabella had been proactively seeking a non-platonic male companion. This is underlined by the final lesson that Justin learns in the episode. Having been told expressly by his parents not to contact girls on WizFace, he is forced to admit that they are right before his father will give him the cure for lycanthropy. He is mocked by his whole family and repeatedly told that the girls he will meet on social networking sites will not be what they seem. This lesson can be read as a rather unsubtle warning to the intended audience about the perils of modern communication channels, with 'WizFace' being an obvious reference to Facebook; however, that the vehicle chosen to deliver this message is the female werewolf speaks to the Victorian and post-Victorian tradition of epitomising alluring but dangerous female sexuality in the body of the female lycanthrope. *Wizards of Waverly Place*'s combination of contemporary cautionary tale with transhistorical modes of representation is reminiscent of Honoré Beaugrand's short story 'The Werewolves', examined by Shannon Scott in Chapter 6. In Beaugrand's narrative, a context-specific warning – caution against intermarriage between French colonial soldiers and Native Canadian women – is embodied in La-Linotte-Qui-Chante, a distillation of European anxieties regarding the feminine, the indigenous and the monstrous.

The dangerous (hyper)sexuality and attractiveness of the female werewolf can be read as a form of hyperfeminisation, particularly given the consistent focus on (exaggerated) female corporeality and, from Victorian supernatural fiction onwards, feminine clothing and adornment. However, while the female werewolf is often constructed as hyperfeminised, this gendering is problematised by a parallel history of characterising the lycanthrope through masculine or non-normative feminine traits. Elizabeth Clark names this as the 'masculine-female-grotesque', though she is referring specifically to the 'cinematic monster' with this term.[55]

Body hair may be an obvious example of this, though this is a recent concern of female werewolf fiction, with texts from before the 1970s rarely addressing it directly. In her introduction to *The Last Taboo: Women and Body Hair*, Karín Lesnik-Oberstein suggests that the visibility of female body hair 'does indeed reveal femininity as that which hides within itself the potentially masculine', and continues: 'This revelation of the masculine in the feminine is impermissible – and thus its "madness" – and precisely this emphasises the threat that is posed by a female body not constituting itself as "absolute" other.'[56] Jazmina Cininas's Chapter 5 explores a historical fascination with hirsute women and the relationship we can read between such hirsutism and the female werewolf, exploring the ways in which excess body hair can function as a challenge to both species and gender boundaries.

Lycanthropic growth of additional body hair is handled in a variety of texts. On the whole, few female werewolf texts suggest that the lycanthrope has more hair when in human form. *Ginger Snaps* is a notable exception to this, and the film offers a darkly comedic parallel between Ginger's werewolf 'fur' and puberty-related 'hair that wasn't there before'. Mattel's Clawdeen Wolf also has excess hair during her 'everyday' life – this is the 'fur' that she wears, and which she has removed at the 'exclusive spa'. It is telling that both Ginger and Clawdeen turn to commercial hair removal processes – the shop-bought razor and the beauty salon – to deal with this side-effect of lycanthropy.[57] This reinforces the 'impermissible' nature of female body hair, as the tools for its removal are made readily available to fifteen- and sixteen-year-old girls. Additionally, the fact that both Clawdeen and Ginger's excess hair is specifically on their legs and chest – areas of the body on which male hirsutism is permitted and, in some cases, celebrated – suggests that their bodily excess can be read as a potential 'revelation of the masculine in the feminine', though as Cininas argues in her examination of Justine Larbalestier's novel *Liar*, exploitations of gender anxieties in such texts are often situated within 'an extended range of contested boundary transgressions', including those of species and racial integrity.[58]

Although body hair is a relatively infrequent marker of the masculinisation of the female werewolf, we can read its presence alongside other examples of revealing the 'masculine in the feminine'. Hypersexualised werewolves, for example, may be the epitome of feminine allure and seductiveness, but this frequently threatens to spill over into more typically masculine displays of sexual assertiveness. From Marryat's Christina and Clemence Housman's White Fell to *Buffy*'s Veruca, the female werewolf is often ruthless in her pursuit of a man, and ferocious if rebuffed. In recent fiction, this depiction of the 'alpha female' is taken even further, suggesting a non-normative feminine sexuality that appropriates, not only the ideals of the masculine, but potentially the corporeality of the male.

In L.L. Raand's Midnight Hunters series – books in the increasingly popular category of lesbian werewolf erotica – werewolves are highly sexualised beings:

> Physical contact – touch, sexual release – was essential to Were physical and emotional well-being, and the more dominant the Were, the greater the need. Without a physical outlet for their intrinsically high levels of endorphins and adrenergic hormones, especially if augmented by stress, the delicate balance between beast and reason broke down. Unrelenting sex frenzy could push Weres to become feral, and going feral was a death sentence.[59]

Sexual activity, here, is the mechanism that allows a werewolf to balance 'beast' and 'reason', an ostensible rejection of conventional presentation of female sexualities as inherently irrational and bestial. While the Weres in Raand's fiction are both male and female, and are bisexual in their partner choices, the narrative follows alpha Sylvan Mir's relationship with the human Drake McKennan, and the developing sexual relationship between these two women. All of the sexual behaviour described in the novel is between women – any heterosexual sex occurs 'off-stage'. This presentation of active lesbian sexuality is a recent development in popular culture; it is also a new departure in werewolf fiction, disavowing Caitlin Giacopasi's (generally accurate) claim that '[w]erewolves can be oversexed, but only if they are heterosexual'.[60] The alpha wolf's choice of a homosexual relationship is neither taboo nor 'unnatural' in the world of this novel, and, significantly, it does not preclude breeding.

After Drake is transformed into a werewolf, the new details of her physiognomy are explained to her by another female lycanthrope, with particular emphasis placed on sexual and reproductive characteristics:

> 'Early in the development of our species, all Weres, including females, had a cartilaginous core in the phallus,' Elena said. 'The dominant females still have a very thin remnant. Feel lower, at the base. You'll have to press hard.'
>
> Drake palpitated two olive-sized oval masses buried deep beneath her clitoris. ... 'What are they?'
>
> 'Sex glands,' Elena said.[61]

The protagonists of *The Midnight Hunt* have androgynous names and 'dominant' personalities. And yet it would be wrong to read them as transgender, or even as unproblematically 'butch lesbian'.[62] Their unorthodox genitalia in fact reflects the complexity of gender in portrayals of the alpha female – albeit in an extreme and eroticised form. Their 'phallus' undoubtedly integrates something of the normative male body into their corporeality, enabling penetrative sex and impregnation; however, this 'very thin remnant' is part of the clitoris, and this fact is repeated throughout the book. Raand's lesbian werewolves potentially 'reveal the masculine', but always 'in the feminine', existing as an exaggerated (and, possibly, redemptive) form of the sexual assertion and excessive corporeality of the female werewolf from Victorian fiction onwards. Nevertheless, these sexually 'liberated' lesbian werewolves carry an echo of earlier representations of the female monster as masculinised, grotesque and, arguably, a genetic throwback.

The she-wolf narrative in context(s)

This introduction is intended to give some overview of the narrative of the female werewolf. I have presented some of the dominant tropes and modes of presentation found in female werewolf fiction, film and television. These are by no means the only media that present the female werewolf, but the texts I have discussed give glimpses into the complex and non-linear nature of the narrative.

Each of the chapters that follow takes a more specific and localised approach, revealing historical, literary, cinematic and folkloric contexts for iterations of the female lycanthrope. As is revealed, all of the texts under consideration by the contributors can be read both as reflections of the cultural assumptions and values associated with the circumstance of their production, and as interpretations of longer (and broader) traditions.

Some chapters take particular texts as the object of study; for instance, Carys Crossen's Chapter 7 focuses on two late Victorian narratives, revealing the ways in which dominant ideologies of femininity and the female writer might be reimagined through the representation of the female werewolf, and Shannon Scott's examination of Honoré Beaugrand's 'The Werewolves' in Chapter 6 offers fruitful discussion of the female werewolf's integration into colonial discourse and narrative. My own Chapter 8 examines twenty-first-century young adult paranormal romance texts, considering the ways in which such texts associate lycanthropy with contemporary idealisations and constructions of the post-adolescent female. Other chapters consider patterns of presentation across specific media: Peter Hutchings in Chapter 10 explores presentations of body-centred violence in film, drawing parallels between female werewolves and other violent females in horror cinema, and Barbara Creed in Chapter 11 examines cinematic representations of the *femme animale* with an exploration of how this conceptualisation of the feminine might inform a reading of *Ginger Snaps*.

Other chapters in the collection discuss historical context and non-literary/cinematic iterations of female lycanthropy. The collection opens with Merili Metsvahi's examination in Chapter 2 of folkloric records of the island of Saaremaa, Estonia, a territory in which, unusually, there are more folktales of female werewolves than male. Metsvahi offers a discussion of this anomaly, with reference to the particular history and geography of the area, but also with attention given to the effects of Christianisation on the folklore of the island. This is followed by Rolf Schulte's analysis of the early modern Burgundian werewolf trials in Chapter 3, drawing on contemporaneous ecclesiastical and political circumstance to explain the relative frequency with which female werewolves were accused and tried in this particular area of France.

Willem de Blécourt's Chapter 9 takes a particular motif common to several werewolf narratives – the 'severed paw' which, although removed as a paw from the werewolf, is revealed as a human hand post-mortem – and examines its significance in the light of both folkloric and literary histories. De Blécourt's chapter reveals important connections between narratives of lycanthropy and narratives of incest and shame, while also unsettling the privileging of 'oral histories' in recent criticism of contemporary werewolf fictions. In Chapter 5, Jazmina Cininas similarly focuses on a specific aspect of the female werewolf – excessive body hair – and discusses the display of, and fascination with, hirsute women in early modern Europe. Cininas uses this historical evidence to read contemporary texts featuring both female werewolves and female body hair in terms of monstrosity, humanity and gender.

As is apparent from the range of approaches taken in these chapters, a consideration of the female werewolf necessarily intersects with other conceptualisations of femininity and monstrosity. In the final chapter of the book, Laura Wilson uses this as a starting point for discussion of a film that does not contain a female werewolf, but rather a self-harming and self-abjectifying woman. Wilson's analysis of *Dans Ma Peau* as a lycanthropic film, albeit one without a werewolf, illuminates the ways in which tropes of the female werewolf can be used to understand and interpret feminine corporeality more broadly. Conversely, Jay Cate's examination of the role-playing game, *Werewolf: The Apocalypse* in Chapter 4, addresses the opposite problem to Wilson's chapter: how is it possible to read the female werewolf in a narrative that may not contain any female characters? Cate explores tropes and strategies of feminisation evident in *Werewolf: The Apocalypse* to reveal an almost unique disavowal of the masculine werewolf in favour of traditions of presenting the female werewolf.

Aspects of female lycanthropy discussed in this introduction are revealed in the various texts and contexts under consideration and, as stated, connections and parallels are found that are often unexpected and transhistorical. Nevertheless, each of the examined narratives is revealed to be a reflection of, or a resistance to, the dominant cultural values of its time of production. What emerges is a narrative of the female werewolf that is at once universal and culturally specific, coherent and fragmentary.

The female werewolf is an inherently contradictory creature.

Notes

1. Bob Curran, *Werewolves: A Field Guide to Shapeshifters, Lycanthropes, and Man-Beasts* (Franklin Lakes, NJ: New Page Books, 2009), 17–18.
2. Brian Frost, *The Essential Guide to Werewolf Literature* (Madison: University of Wisconsin Press, 2003), 3–4.
3. Leslie A. Sconduto, *Metamorphoses of the Werewolf: A Literary Study From Antiquity Through the Renaissance* (Jefferson, NC: McFarland and Co., 2008), 7.
4. Walter Burkert, *Homo Necans: The Anthropology of Ancient Greek Sacrificial Ritual and Myth*, Peter Bing (trans.) (Berkeley and Los Angeles: University of California Press, 1983), 83.
5. Chantal Bourgault du Coudray, *The Curse of the Werewolf: Fantasy, Horror and the Beast Within* (London and New York: I.B. Tauris, 2006), 2.
6. I favour 'European' over 'Western' here. Both terms are problematic. The former gives primacy to medieval, Christian conceptualisations of the world, inflected through modern geographical and political boundaries. The latter aligns Western Europe with the modern concept of 'First World' nations, while potentially excluding histories of Eastern and (on occasion) Northern Europe. For a cultural history of werewolves, the historical conceptualisation of Europe is, perhaps, a more apt territorial delineation.
7. Frost, *Essential Guide to Werewolf Literature*, 4.

8   An alternative etymology has been proposed for 'werewolf', based on doubts that 'were-' is derived from Old English, which derives the first part of the word from the Norse 'varg-r' meaning 'wolf'. See *Oxford English Dictionary*, 'werewolf'.
9   See Marie de France, 'Bisclavret', in Karl Warnke (ed.), *Lais de Marie de France* (Paris Librairie Générale Française, 1990), 117–34.
10 For a brief outline of medieval wolf-hunting, see Garry Marvin, *Wolf* (London: Reaktion Books, 2012), 81–4. Marvin goes on to discuss colonial attempts at eradicating the wolf from North America; these later programmes of wolf-hunting are explored in greater detail by S.K. Robisch in *Wolves and the Wolf Myth in American Literature* (Reno, NV: University of Nevada Press, 2009).
11 Marvin, *Wolf*, 35.
12 *Ibid.*, 35–6.
13 A good example of this can be found in the short film, *The Furred Man* (2010, dir. Paul Williams). A hapless camper is terrorised by a werewolf who has killed a number of people. (Male) police officers suspect the camper himself is responsible for the deaths, but reluctantly agree to investigate his claims. They leave the man in the care of an unassuming female police officer, much to his relief. However, the woman is then revealed to be the werewolf in a 'twist' ending.
14 I am following an accepted timeline here, which claims the Akkadian *Epic of Gilgamesh* (c. 1700 BC) as the first example of werewolf literature. See, for example, Sconduto, *Metamorphoses of the Werewolf*, 7.
15 Gerald of Wales, *The History and Topography of Ireland*, John O'Meara (trans.) (London: Penguin, 1982), 70.
16 *Ibid.*, 71–2.
17 Sconduto, *Metamorphoses of the Werewolf*, 29.
18 I have written elsewhere on the association of late medieval werewolf transformation with clothing and disguise. See Hannah Priest, '"Bogeysliche as a Boye": Performing Sexuality in *William of Palerne*', in Robert Rouse and Cory Rushton (eds), *Sexual Culture in Late Medieval Britain* (Cambridge: D.S. Brewer, 2014).
19 Caroline Walker Bynum argues that the 'wolf' in Gerald's narrative is 'a skin or garment overclothing the human', and relates this to the animal-skin disguises found in the romance narrative, *Guillaume de Palerne*. I would suggest, rather, that the pulling back of the skin by the he-wolf of Ossory is a more corporeal and visceral act than the temporary disguises (worn specifically over clothing, rather than human skin) in *Guillaume*. See Caroline Walker Bynum, *Metamorphosis and Identity* (Brooklyn, NY: Zone Books, 2001), 108.
20 Sconduto, *Metamorphoses of the Werewolf*, 29.
21 'Surprising absentee' is taken from Frost, *Essential Guide to Werewolf Literature*, 59.
22 See, for example, Heinrich Kramer and James Sprenger, *The Malleus Maleficarum*, Montague Summers (trans.) (New York: Dover Publications, 1971).
23 See Christina Mazzoni, *She-Wolf: The Story of a Roman Icon* (Cambridge: Cambridge University Press, 2010).
24 See Alison Weir, *Isabella: She-Wolf of France, Queen of England* (London: Vintage, 2012); Helen Castor *She-Wolves: The Women Who Ruled England Before Elizabeth* (London: Faber and Faber, 2011).
25 My analysis of *Monster High* is based on a lengthier discussion of the character of Clawdeen Wolf that I posted in two articles on my blog. See 'If Barbie Was a

Werewolf' (21 August 2010), http://shewolf-manchester.blogspot.co.uk/2010/08/if-barbie-was-werewolf.html; 'Monster High vs. Sweet Valley High' (3 April 2012), http://shewolf-manchester.blogspot.co.uk/2012/04/monster-high-vs-sweet-valley-high.html. Accessed 19 August 2014.
26 See www.monsterhigh.com/en-us/characters/clawdeen-wolf. Accessed 21 August 2010.
27 *Ibid.*
28 Lisi Harrison, *Monster High* (London: Atom Books, 2010), 53–4.
29 *Ibid.*, 83.
30 See, for example, Leah Clearwater in Stephenie Meyer's Twilight series. My own chapter in this collection explores Leah's resentment and loyalty in detail.
31 For discussion of this, see Sconduto, *Metamorphoses of the Werewolf*, 29–30; Bynum, *Metamorphosis and Identity*, 107–8.
32 The concept of the werewolf pack is, of course, based on (imagined) wolf pack formation, though this aspect of lupine behaviour is often romanticised, misunderstood or exaggerated in fiction. See Robisch, *Wolves and the Wolf Myth*, 20, 94–103.
33 On the familial connotations of the werewolf pack in contemporary popular culture, see my article 'Pack versus Coven: Guardianship of Tribal Memory in Vampire versus Werewolf Narratives', in Simon Bacon and Katarzyna Bronk (eds), *Undead Memory: Vampires and Human Memory in Popular Culture* (New York: Peter Lang, 2014.
34 *Ibid.*
35 'Tully', *Being Human* 1:2 (2008).
36 See 'Ghost Town', *Being Human* 1:3 (2008).
37 'The Pack', *Being Human* 3:4 (2011).
38 *Being Human* posits the missing female element of McNair and Tom's incomplete pack as a necessary and nurturing balance to the nomadic 'warrior' lifestyle. See 'The Pack'; McNair is explicitly described as 'warrior' in 'Though the Heavens Fall', *Being Human* 3:7 (2011).
39 See Martin Millar, *Lonely Werewolf Girl* (London: Piatkus, 2010); Thomas Emson, *Maneater* (London: Snowbooks, 2008).
40 See Alan Moore, 'The Curse', *Swamp Thing* 40 (September 1985).
41 Frederick Marryat, 'The White Wolf of the Hartz Mountains', in Alexis Easley and Shannon Scott (eds), *Terrifying Transformations: An Anthology of Victorian Werewolf Fiction* (Kansas City: Valancourt Books, 2013), 23–41.
42 Sabine Baring-Gould, *The Book of Were-Wolves* (1865; Forgotten Books, 2008), 43.
43 Carrie Vaughn, *Kitty Goes to Washington* (London: Gollancz, 2008), 85.
44 Carrie Vaughn, *Kitty and the Silver Bullet* (London: Gollancz, 2008), 263.
45 See, for example, *The Wolfman* (2010, dir. Joe Johnston).
46 'A Funny Thing Happened on the Way to Me Killing You', *Being Human* (US) 1:13 (2011).
47 Two recent werewolf texts might be offered as counterexamples to Meyer's menopausal werewolf. In both Catherine Lundoff's novel *Silver Moon* and Helen Cross's short story 'Fur', lycanthropy is presented as a side effect of the menopause, in a positive and celebratory way. The 'change of life' allows the protagonists to reinvent themselves as assertive and self-determining individuals, in a way that they could not as women of child-bearing age. Tellingly, however, both texts end with a rejection of heterosexual domesticity; Cross's protagonist

simply leaves her husband without explanation or excuse, while Lundoff's heroine tentatively embarks on a lesbian relationship after accepting her ex-husband's offer to buy up her share of their former family home. See Catherine Lundoff, *Silver Moon* (Maple Shade NJ: Lethe Press, 2012); Helen Cross, 'Fur', in Hannah Kate (ed.), *Wolf-Girls: Dark Tales of Teeth, Claws and Lycogyny* (Manchester: Hic Dragones, 2012), 219–26.
48 Vaughn, *Kitty Goes to Washington*, 245. The 'golden retriever' here is emblematic of '[m]arriage, children, tract housing on the prairie … What all the other girls were doing.' (244)
49 'Wild at Heart', *Buffy the Vampire Slayer* 4:6 (1999).
50 Veruca's first appearance is in 'Living Conditions', *Buffy the Vampire Slayer* 4:2 (1999), and she also briefly appears in 'Beer Bad', 4:5 (1999). Though Oz is aware of her in these earlier appearances, Veruca's first (and only) interaction comes in 'Wild at Heart'.
51 'Something Blue', *Buffy the Vampire Slayer* 4:9 (1999).
52 'Smashed', *Buffy the Vampire Slayer* 6:9 (2001). On this aspect of the series narrative, see Lynne Y. Edwards, Elizabeth L. Rambo and James B. South (eds), *Buffy Goes Dark* (Jefferson, NC: McFarland, 2008).
53 I am grateful to my student, Amy Ninian, for bringing this episode to my attention.
54 'Beware Wolf', *Wizards of Waverly Place* 2:2 (2008).
55 Elizabeth M. Clark, '"Hairy Thuggish Women": Female Werewolves, Gender, and the Hoped-For Monster', MA dissertation (Georgetown University, 2008).
56 Karín Lesnik-Oberstein (ed.), *The Last Taboo: Women and Body Hair* (Manchester: Manchester University Press, 2006), 11.
57 See also, Carrie Vaughn, *Kitty and the Dead Man's Hand* (London: Gollancz, 2009), 9. The reference to leg-shaving here is comedic, and may not reflect Kitty's corporeal reality.
58 Larbalestier's protagonist Micah is mixed-race, and Cininas discusses the intersections of race and gender in her consideration of this character. Her claim here is strengthened by the fact that Clawdeen Wolf has 'brown skin' and is commonly read as African-American, and that anxieties about Canadian racial and national identities have been identified in readings of *Ginger Snaps*. See Sunnie Rothenburger, '"Welcome to Civilization": Colonialism, the Gothic, and Canada's Self-Protective Irony in the *Ginger Snaps* Werewolf Trilogy', *Journal of Canadian Studies*, 44:3 (2010): 96–117.
59 L.L. Raand, *The Midnight Hunt* (Valley Falls, NY: Bold Stokes Books, 2010), 41.
60 Caitlin B. Giacopasi, 'The Werewolf Pride Movement: A Step Back from Queer Medieval Tradition', MA dissertation (Seton Hall University, 2011), http://scholarship.shu.edu/theses/4. Accessed 20 November 2011.
61 Raand, *The Midnight Hunt*, 139–40.
62 On the recent (occasionally conflicting) cultural histories of these terms, see Judith Halberstam, *Female Masculinity* (Durham, NC and London: Duke University Press, 1998).

2
Estonian werewolf legends collected from the island of Saaremaa

Merili Metsvahi
Translated (including quotations from primary and secondary sources) by Ene-Reet Soovik

Introduction

Collecting folklore has played a significant role in the history of the Estonian nation and state, helping to build an Estonian identity – one of the preconditions for the emergence of an independent state. The collection that started at the beginning of the nineteenth century resulted in folklore archives in Estonia, a country with a population of 1.34 million, that are considered to be the third largest in the world after the Irish and Finnish archives. The existence of the Estonian Folklore Archives (EFA) has, to a great degree, determined the development of the study of Estonian folklore in the twentieth and twenty-first centuries.

The archives contain approximately 1,400 texts on the topic of werewolves. This article discusses the werewolf texts collected on the island of Saaremaa (historically, Ösel), which comprise about one-seventh of the full corpus. Saaremaa has been chosen, firstly, because virtually all types of Estonian werewolf legend have been told there; and, secondly, for the reason that there are more tales about women as werewolves on Saaremaa in comparison with the rest of Estonia.

Saaremaa, Estonia's largest island, is situated in the Baltic Sea. Its territory is 2,673 square kilometres, and the length of the island's coastline is 854 kilometres.[1] At the beginning of the nineteenth century, 40 to 50 per cent of the territory of Saaremaa was covered in woodland; by the end of the 1930s, 7 per cent of the island was wooded. Today, woods, alvars, wooded meadows, former fields and pastures overgrown with bushes cover the greater part of the island again.[2] The data on woodland are relevant here as tales of werewolves are more likely to spread in wooded locations where wolves live. Indeed, wolves (*Canis lupus*) used to live on Saaremaa in earlier times and live there even now.[3]

Beliefs and tales about werewolves in Estonia throughout history

Estonia is notorious for its connection with werewolf stories. In 1555, Olaus Magnus wrote in his *Historia de gentibus septentrionalibus* about the extremely widespread belief in werewolves in Livonia. Oskar Loorits, the founder of the EFA and the grand old man of the study of Estonian folk belief, wrote in his *Grundzüge der estnischen Volksglaubens* that the high tide of belief in werewolves in Estonia, and in the whole Eastern Baltic region, had been in the sixteenth and seventeenth centuries.[4] Loorits grounded his claim in history and travel books, but also on the preserved records of witch trials that touch upon a belief in werewolves in Estonia and Livonia. All in all, data from about 150 witch trials have been preserved in Estonia; on eighteen occasions villagers (eighteen women and thirteen men) were accused of harming someone as werewolves.[5] In general, the records are brief and do not contain much information; for example, there are no records as thorough and rich in information as that of the trial of the Latvian peasant Thies near Riga in 1692.[6]

The largest body of material on werewolves can be found in the EFA; the majority of it is unpublished and can be accessed only as manuscript texts. The EFA includes approximately 1,400 texts about werewolves that cannot be classified as fairy tales, yet not all of them are legends in the strictest sense. Also, they include a number of short texts defining the notion of the werewolf that probably constitute answers to the folklore collectors' questions as to whether the respondents had heard anything about werewolves.

The texts about werewolves can be divided into two larger groups: firstly, those in which the werewolf turns into a wolf of its own accord, and, secondly, those in which people are turned into wolves against their own will by someone malicious (often a witch). The geographic origins of the recordings show that the first type of tales was told in Western Estonia, while the second type rather derives from Eastern Estonia. The latter legends are influenced by the lore of Slavonic peoples, while the werewolf tales from the islands are instead influenced by Scandinavian folklore. As a generalisation, it can be said that in the tales in which people turn into wolves on their own initiative they do it in order to kill domestic animals and get fresh meat, or else to be able to move around more quickly. In cases where someone has turned into a wolf willingly, they know how to regain their human shape again (with the exception of the tales in which someone imitates a werewolf character for fun or out of curiosity). In the tales in which people have been turned into wolves from malicious motives, they do not know how to become humans again and are doomed to live as wolves until they are retransformed into humans by chance.

The connection of werewolf tales with daily reality cannot be determined unequivocally. There are tales of particular shapeshifters who are named and whose activities are reported, as well as those about anonymous characters (such as the master of the farm and his hired farmhand). Considerably more stories belong to the latter type and such tales were considered mere entertainment in the period of folklore collecting. Although many of them were probably regarded as fictional, they can be used as sources of information on attitudes to and evaluations of social relations and other more general topics. On the basis of the tales about particular people turning into wolves, conclusions can be drawn not only about the social relations of the time, but also about the attitudes towards particular individuals and households.

In Estonian folktales both men and women can be werewolves, with the tales that represent female werewolves being slightly more numerous. Legend plots in which the werewolf engages in activities characteristic of women, such as giving birth and breastfeeding, are characteristic of Estonian folklore. It is interesting to mention that while the tale type 'The Girl as Wolf',[7] about a werewolf suckling her child, appears both as a fairy tale and a legend and is one of the most popular plots in the EFA, there appears to be no connection between werewolves and giving birth and breastfeeding in the lore of other countries.

In Loorits's opinion, the concept of the werewolf played no major role in the folk belief of Estonians, Latvians and Livonians.[8] I would like to claim that the suggestion is not valid, at least as regards Estonian folk belief. Nevertheless, the conception of the werewolf certainly did change over time and acquired different shades of meaning, gradually losing its importance as a living creature in folk belief. In analysing the tales today it seems more appropriate to speak not of the concept of the werewolf in general, but about particular werewolf tales that carry different meanings. The fact that even the folklore scholars of the early twenty-first century have succeeded in recording tales about werewolves that have motifs in common with the speeches of those accused of witchcraft in the seventeenth-century trials demonstrates that the concept of the werewolf has been a vital part of Estonian folk belief.[9] It is only when backed by belief that a motif can survive in folklore for so long.

Folktale collecting and werewolf legends from Saaremaa

From Saaremaa, where folklore collecting began even before the emergence of Estonian collectors, about 200 texts on the topic of werewolves have been recorded and stored in the EFA. The Munich-born German Jean Baptiste (Johann Baptist) Holzmeyer, who worked in the *Progümnaasium* of Arensburg (now Kuressaare) as the Master of Classics and German Literature, also recorded folklore. In his *Osiliana* (1872–80) he writes of beliefs about werewolves, including a rare court case from the second half of the nineteenth century: a woman was accused in court of running around in the woods in the shape of a wolf for months. In addition, Holzmeyer mentions a man from the neighbouring island of Muhu who would turn into a wolf at night, kill animals and eat his fill, while going out with other men in the daytime to hunt wolves.

The first texts about werewolves on Saaremaa recorded by Estonian collectors can be found in the folklore collection of the Society of Estonian Literati from the 1880s. About a third of the werewolf texts from Saaremaa were recorded between 1929 and 1939. They include material sent in by local correspondents, as well as texts collected by professional folklore scholars. As the region of Saaremaa had remained under-represented in earlier years, the archive team started to arrange collecting expeditions there after the archives had been created. After the Second World War collecting of folklore from Saaremaa was paid even more attention.[10] Taking into consideration that telling werewolf stories must have already been a vanishing tradition at the turn of the nineteenth and twentieth centuries, that it must have been difficult to find people capable of telling the tales, and also the scarcity of folk tales recorded on Saaremaa in comparison with the rest of Estonia,[11] the number of werewolf stories from Saaremaa is by no means small.

In addition to the number of tales, the fact that in the texts from Saaremaa it is often specific individuals who are mentioned as werewolves also suggests that the belief must have survived there longer than in several other regions of Estonia. The people whose names are given include both men and women; the texts also mention male/female couples who go out together 'to run as wolves'. There is a fairly widespread motif concerning calling the werewolf by his or her human name, in which case it has to turn back into a human and stop whatever it has been doing – for instance, killing an animal. However, if a werewolf is called by any of the numerous euphemisms denoting the wolf (for example, 'sheep oldie' or 'forest frog') it gains strength from this and will slaughter the animal.

It is fascinating that some of the old motifs that tend to appear in a more general context in Estonian lore are connected with particular werewolves known by name in the texts from Saaremaa. Thus, motifs such as it taking a silver bullet to kill a werewolf, or beads or a red belt appearing from under the animal hide when a werewolf is being skinned, appear as the driving plot elements in stories about particular werewolves in the lore from Saaremaa. Even plots that can be classified as 'types' of the legends that will be discussed in the next section are connected with particular werewolves on a few occasions. Also the ways of turning oneself into a wolf, the descriptions of which usually accompany fixed-type legends with anonymous characters or else are presented as general observations, are included in tales about particular werewolves in several texts from Saaremaa.

In the texts about people turning into wolves of their own accord, the most ordinary methods involve rolling about on the ground or turning (three) somersaults. Occasionally reciting words of magic is added, but the words themselves are usually not specified. In cases where the words are given, they resemble 'the man into wolf' words recorded in mainland Estonia, listing body parts such as the tail, the ears and the stomach.[12] In some texts, people can become wolves only with the help of magic formulas. In one text, a hole needs to be scraped in the ground with a finger before rolling about there. Putting on a wolf hide can be added to the rolling about, but this can also occur separately.

In addition, the following ways of turning into a wolf can be found in the texts from Saaremaa: crawling (backwards) under the stakes supporting a fence, rolling or crawling under a fence (or a pale) two or three times, turning around oneself three times. The places in which one could turn into a wolf include the following: behind a bush, under a fence, by a stake supporting a fence, on the ground by a stone, upon a stone, and in a smithy under the forge bellows. In one text, the transformation occurs with the help of the *Seventh Book of Moses*, a widespread book of magic in Estonian folklore. The majority of the texts do not mention the modes of transformation back into the human. In several texts that do mention this, the way of regaining human shape appears to be movement similar to that used to become a wolf (e.g. somersaults or crawling under a fence). In one text the werewolf has to butcher a hen in order to be free of the wolf hide. It is interesting that, both in the texts from Saaremaa as well as the rest of Estonia, the pigsty, its back or its corner, are widely suggested as the places to become human again; the pigsty is not known as a place at which to turn into a wolf. The pigsty (which is the animal shed furthest away from the house), as well as several other sites of transformation, are located on the border between the home sphere and the wild zone, or lie close to the border.

In cases where a person is turned into a wolf against her or his will, it is usually simply stated that somebody turned someone else into a wolf. It is only in a couple of cases that the course of activities is specified. In one case, it is reported that the procedure for turning a person into a wolf involved taking earth from the footprints of a wolf and sprinkling it at the feet of the person who was to be transformed. In another text, a godmother who turns her godson into a wolf forces him flat on his back on the ground and jumps over him. In texts from Saaremaa, as well as the rest of Estonia, the most widespread method of restoring those who have been maliciously transformed into wolves consists in offering the wolf some bread from the tip of a knife; in three texts the bread is replaced by a hen that the wolf has to kill, and one text involves a red garter. Bread symbolises civilisation as well as the Host, being thus capable of reintegrating a semi-wild and semi-demonic character into the Christian world. In one text, the werewolf is struck across the back with a rowan stick in order for it to abandon its plan of killing animals and become human again.

What do the werewolf texts from Saaremaa tell us about the differences between ordinary wolves and werewolves, apart from the recognition that a werewolf cannot be killed by an ordinary bullet? It is claimed that werewolves do not get frightened when coming upon people and have more courage to kill than do wolves from the forest. A similar point was made by

Olaus Magnus in his 1555 travel book, which claimed that, although there were many wolves in these parts, the locals believed that they suffered more damage from werewolves than from real wolves.[13]

It also becomes evident from the archival texts that it was believed on Saaremaa that those who have mastered the art of turning into a werewolf will not be able to abandon the habit, but must go on their wolf trips: if they are overcome by their 'wolf need' or 'wolf appetite', they cannot resist it. The appetite often hits them when they are going to church or making bread at home (for instance, when a woman making bread hears the howling of wolves).

Fixed-type werewolf legends recorded on Saaremaa

This section introduces those werewolf legends from Saaremaa whose plots are more widely known and that can be classified according to their plots. I shall begin with the most popular plots. The legend type 'The Other Sleeper Kills an Animal', which is known in both Estonian and Livonian lore and has been given a type number in the catalogue of Livonian folk tales,[14] is represented by the greatest number of versions (thirty). In a less elaborate shape, the same plot also appears in German lore and was published in the collection *Deutsche Sagen* by the Brothers Grimm,[15] but there it involves male characters, not the female ones like in Estonian and Livonian folklore. I am including a version of the legend that was recorded in Kaarma in 1939 and is characteristic of the type, although longer than a text of this type usually would be:

> During the time of serfdom two girls from Hakjala went to do their statutory labour at Pähkla manor. It was a moonlit night in autumn, and there was no sign of sunrise as yet. A mare and a nice plump foal were eating by the road. Seeing this, one girl started to yawn and complain that she was about to fall asleep. She wanted to lie down by the bushes to get a wink of sleep before reaching the manor. The girl who kept her company did not feel like doing that, but finally agreed to the wish of the other. The girls lay down by the bushes to sleep. The one who had lain down against her will feigned heavy sleep at once to see what the other would do. The other one yawned, stood up and went behind another bush. She turned three somersaults and became a wolf. At once, she ran to the foal and killed it. She sucked up its blood and then tore the thickest pieces of flesh out of the thighs of its back legs. She took these in her mouth and put them into the bag she had carried around her neck. Then she loped to the other girl, sniffed at her with her wolf muzzle and threw herself down on her stomach. She rolled onto her back, yawned and became a girl again. She said to her companion, 'Wasn't it a good sleep before sunrise?' They got up together and went on towards the manor. The other did not say anything about having seen her wolf activities.
>
> During the day, when they were eating at the manor, the girl offered the other her fresh meat. The latter told her: 'I don't want your meat; you turned into a

wolf at night and killed the foal and put its thighs into your bag.' Upon hearing this, the girl hit the other's chin with her piece of meat. The chin that had been hit became scorched black at once. When hitting her, the girl said: 'Because you even dared to watch such a thing and talk about it here, half your face will remain black for the rest of your life. Let your black face remind you that you ought not to look at such things nor talk about them.'[16]

Two short studies have been published about this legend type. The first attempts at a deeper understanding of the legend, focusing on the often occurring final motif of the supernatural cooking of the meat;[17] the other discusses it motif by motif.[18] The legend can be interpreted as a story of the girl's temporary flight from the world of everyday social norms and roles. The tellers and listeners of the legend found the story compelling, for it offered brief symbolic defiance of the reigning social order with its rules.

The werewolf legend 'The Farmhand Imitates His Master', with its twenty-seven versions, rates second in popularity on Saaremaa. If the characters of the legend on mainland Estonia are, as a rule, men (the master and the farmhand), in about half of the texts from Saaremaa either one character or both characters are women. The legends with two female characters feature a mother-in-law and daughter-in-law, the old and young mistresses of the farm, old mother and young mother, or the daughter of the family and her brother's wife. In legends with characters of opposite sexes, the opposing main characters are husband and wife, the mistress of the farm and a farmhand, or the mistress and the rest of the household. As an example, I am providing a fairly typical text recorded in Mustjala parish in 1937:

> The old people said that there was a farmhand who went out to the forest to do some logging with his master. Every night the master would say, 'You go home first!' The farmhand would leave. When he reached home, the master was always home before him. The farmhand wondered how it came to be that the master reached home first, as he himself always started off earlier, yet the other man was always already at home. One night he stayed and watched behind some bushes to see how the other man could get home quicker so as to go with him. What he saw: the master went into a hollow under a crooked birch and started to roll around there. Suddenly a wolf stood up there and loped away; there was no man in sight any more. The farmhand made up his mind, went to the same place and started to roll around. He turned into a wolf, went home, but could not go inside to the others, being a wolf. The others were waiting for the farmhand to come home, it was already dark, but there was no man.
>
> Suddenly a wolf with a sad face was seen looking into the room through the window. The master said: 'What a scoundrel, that's what he has been doing! Go and throw a live hen in front of him. Let him eat this, then he can get his wolf hide off him.' The mistress went out and did as the master had ordered. After a while, the farmhand came into the room and was a man again.[19]

While the texts of the type 'The Other Sleeper Kills an Animal' that have been recorded on Saaremaa often mention the names or the dwelling places of the characters, the type 'The Farmhand Imitates His Master' does not indicate the names of characters or their farms. This suggests that the legend type of the master and the farmhand has moved further away from living folk belief than 'The Other Sleeper Kills an Animal'.

The remaining legend types are represented by considerably fewer versions in the archival material collected from Saaremaa. The legend 'The Merchant as Werewolf', which has also been recorded on the neighbouring islands of Hiiumaa and Muhu, is represented by ten versions. In the werewolf material from all over Estonia this type is represented by far the greatest number of versions. As with 'The Farmhand Imitates His Master', this tale lacks named characters and locations and, when retold in the twentieth century, it was regarded as a tale meant for entertainment, not as a true story.

The plot 'The Wife Also Has Wolf Pups', which is virtually unrepresented in the rest of Estonia, ranks fourth in popularity. The only other known recordings of the plot come from Tarvastu in Viljandi County. The plot will be discussed in more detail in the next section. Additionally, the plot 'The Girl as Wolf', which has been recorded all over Estonia, and the type 'Wedding Party into Wolves', typical of Eastern Estonia, are represented by more than one version.

It appears that, in comparison with the material recorded from the rest of Estonia, there is more variation in the texts from Saaremaa, and they are more related to particular persons, thus remaining closer to folk belief. The material from other parts of Estonia, however, includes more versions with well-developed narrative structure that have become removed from folk belief.

Women in werewolf legends from Saaremaa and in Estonian society

The lore from Saaremaa includes plots with female werewolves that are characteristic only of this region, as well as plots in which a woman occupies a role that belongs to men in the rest of Estonia. The female characters in the legend 'The Farmhand Imitates His Master' have already been mentioned. In the legend 'Wedding Party into Wolves', which is rare on Saaremaa and in Western Estonia in general, female characters – a mother and a daughter – replace the male characters known elsewhere.

However, it is only on Saaremaa that the plot is known in which a husband starts to suspect that his wife goes out too often. The man goes outside, discovers wolf pups behind the house and kills them, and the wife becomes either sad or angry. In one version, she tells the husband that he might rather have killed their own son, not the six beautiful wolf pups. In another version she says that had she known he was going to do that, she would have killed him first:

> A man had a wife who would go out as a wolf to kill animals and fetch meat. Once, when their chamber was too cold, the man said: 'The chamber is so cold, the child is cold in here.' The wife answered: 'The child in the chamber has

nothing to complain about. But what are those children to do who are among the straw behind the house?' The man went out to see for himself and found wolf pups among the straw. He picked them up and struck them dead against the fence. On Saturday night, the wife heated the sauna and the man went into the sauna. He was slapping himself with birch twigs, when a wolf opened the door and attacked him with its teeth bared. The only thing the man could do was to take the prongs meant for the coals from the corner and push them into the wolf's throat. The wolf leaped out of the sauna. After that, the wife's throat was wounded for a long time. The wife had gone to punish her husband for having struck the wolf pups dead against the fence, for these were her other children.[20]

In this version of the tale, the usual plot 'The Wife Also Has Wolf Pups' has an added motif, spread throughout Western Estonia, of a spouse attacking his wife (or her husband) in the shape of a wolf. In the texts from Western Estonia, and in the one from Saaremaa in which the story appears as a separate plot, it is the husband who is the attacker. This is also the case in versions of the same folktale that are found in Western Europe.[21] There is another elaboration of the same topic that could be categorised under the same type name. In this tale, the woman wishes to give birth alone and afterwards gives the farmhand a bag in which there supposedly are kittens which she asks him to drown. When the farmhand opens the bag, he sees not kittens, but wolf pups inside it. Some of the texts with both plots occasionally add the explanation that women who go out as wolves can have intercourse with wolves or may be impregnated by wolves in the forest.

In Saaremaa, legends have also been recorded in which wolves give birth to human children. In the rest of Estonia, a story is known in which the people on a farm can see a wolf going into the sauna on Saturday night, and a child is found in the sauna the following morning. The family raises the child, and afterwards a fine lady comes to thank them, explaining that it had been she who was the wolf for someone had turned her into one by magic. On Saaremaa there is a recording from Jämaja of a tale in which a pregnant woman attempts to turn herself into a wolf just for fun and succeeds, but cannot regain her human shape any more. Thus she gives birth to two human children and raises them, while in the shape of a wolf.

In order to understand the reasons for the popularity of female werewolves in Estonia, and particularly on Saaremaa, some knowledge is required of the earlier history of the Estonian family and of women's status in Estonian society. Although the topic has not been researched extensively as yet, it is clear that the status of women worsened considerably after the arrival of Christianisers in Estonia in the thirteenth century. The archaeologists Marika Mägi and Nils Blomkvist have proposed the credible hypothesis that, in ancient times, the communities inhabiting Estonian territory were matrilinear and matrilocal. The regulations concerning inheritance provided in Livonian law from the early thirteenth century determined that both sons and daughters could inherit land on the Estonian and Livonian territories, with the daughters apparently being preferred; additionally, a man's property, including his land, was transferred to his wife after marriage, and to their children after a possible divorce.[22] Such regulations were rare in the context of Western Europe, and even in Northern Europe, and indicate that upon the arrival of Western Europeans radical changes must have occurred in the local society, including the relationships between the sexes. A break is indeed reflected in the legal documents of the thirteenth century: in the later versions of the above-mentioned law, the regulations concerning inheritance have been changed – the law from 1267 declares that, upon marriage, the man's property is transferred to his wife with the exception of fields, pastures and beehives.[23]

That being a woman was no less prestigious than being a man is also proved by archaeological finds from around a thousand years ago. Baltic-Finnish men and women wore similar jewellery, and jewellery associated with women in the neighbouring areas could be worn by men on Estonian territory. At the same time, Baltic-Finnish burials of women reveal objects generally associated with men in neighbouring regions, such as metal belt decorations, horse harnesses and weapons.[24]

If laws can be changed quickly, changing the mentality of a people is a lengthier process. Even a patrilocal, patrilinear and outwardly wholly patriarchal society can retain traces of an earlier, more powerful position of women for centuries. Examples showing that the status of women was fairly different from that of Western European women can be found in trial records, and in descriptions of customs and folklore from the eighteenth, nineteenth and even early twentieth centuries. As late as the eighteenth century it was the custom among the Baltic-Finnish Votic people, who are linguistically closely related to Estonians and inhabit a neighbouring area, that after the birth of a son, a married woman continued to wear a certain type of headdress (the *päästas*-cap) which she would have worn while childless, but after the birth of a daughter the woman could start wearing 'white coifs' that would remain her headcovering for the rest of her life.[25] The fact that Estonian peasant women behaved in a manner that seemed incomprehensible from the point of view of Western European intellectuals is testified by several descriptions by clergymen and chroniclers. Thus, August Wilhelm Hupel, a pastor who lived in Livonia and Estonia from 1757 to the end of his life and could speak Estonian, wrote at the end of the eighteenth century that premarital sex and pregnancy were usual among Estonians. In cases where a young woman became pregnant, she usually married the father of the child, but sometimes another man, or else remained unmarried. In the latter case the parents would gladly let the pregnant daughter stay with them – in cases where the parents did not like the man, they even preferred the latter option to marriage. Should this be the chosen outcome, it was the mother who put a newlywed's cloth cap on her daughter's head, or else the daughter was capped in the presence of the mother.[26] Capping on the grounds of pregnancy was banned in 1792.[27]

The relative freedom of women, at least before marriage (according to Hupel, couples were truly faithful to each other afterwards),[28] had been preserved for centuries, despite the Christian church's fight against it and despite the fact that the society had become patriarchal in its main characteristics long before.[29] Judging by the gender of those accused in witch trials, it can be said that, in these parts, women were not marginalised to the degree that was experienced in Western Europe. The records of witch trials do not tend to accuse women more than men. On the basis of the scant materials of court cases that have been preserved on Saaremaa, it can be claimed that the witches there included quite a few men.[30]

It has been suggested that gender differences were introduced into the belief in witchcraft by demonologists who wished to create a connection between witchcraft and feminine – that is negative – connotations so as to deter men from practising witchcraft.[31] As demonologists had no remarkable influence on the Estonian territory, and women did not have as many negative connotations as they did in Western Europe, the feminisation of witchcraft did not entirely succeed in Estonia. Yet the popularity of the image of the female werewolf shows that it enjoyed at least a partial success.

It is also important to stress the peculiarity of the position of women on Saaremaa. As the men were seafarers and fishermen, the women of Saaremaa had to have a greater power in deciding matters than the women on the mainland. In other seaside locations where the men were away at sea for months, women had a considerable power in decision making, which was not discontinued when the men were home from sea.[32] Thus, the gender differences evident in the werewolf legends from Saaremaa also reflect real-life gender differences in comparison with those appearing in the legends from the mainland.

The wolf in Estonian folk belief and customs

In addition to the social and historical contexts of the periods of the spreading and recording of legends, and to women's position at the time, the image of the wolf among the lower classes has also to be taken into account in interpretations of werewolf legends.

Estonian folklore contains more lore about the wolf than about any other wild animal, and beliefs connected with the wolf deriving from different eras are interwoven. Ivar Paulson has suggested that some aspects of Estonian folk belief that are related to the forest even contain references from the era of hunter-gatherers.[33] The idea of wolves as the pups of St George, to whom God casts down food from above, apparently contains remnants of the pre-Christian notion of the Master of Animals as well as the image of the wolf in the Catholic era. There are several customs related to the positive power of the wolf in Estonian traditions of past centuries. Thus, wolf teeth were worn as a talisman warding off harm, girls who had reached marriageable age were slapped with a wolf's tail, and it was believed that a human hand that had been maimed by a wolf would have healing powers.[34]

Several hundred euphemisms have been used to denote the wolf. That the wolf was attributed a particular significance is testified by a number of additional circumstances. The wolf was held in at least as great an awe as the forest itself. Just like the forest spirit, the wolf – who has been taken for one of the possible appearances of the forest spirit – could punish and hurt people who did not behave correctly in the woods.[35] The reciprocal relationship of wolves and humans is reflected in the reports of sacrifices made to the wolf. There is a description of sacrifices having been made to the pagan gods on the neighbouring island of Hiiumaa at the beginning of the eighteenth century to escape the damage done by wolves. There are nineteenth- and twentieth-century reports from mainland Estonia about sacrifices being due to the wolf (it being left its 'share'), or else it would slaughter the cattle. According to different reports, either the wolf was invited when the cattle were sent out to pasture for the first time in the year, a piece of a slaughtered sheep was sacrificed to the wolf, or it was believed that the wolf had to eat a dog every year. When a wolf was carrying away its prey it was not to be disturbed, and an animal killed by a wolf was not to be touched.[36]

The archival texts from the nineteenth and twentieth centuries reflect the attitude to wolves first and foremost from the point of view of peasants engaged in cattle breeding. Yet it was not just symbolic fear of the alien and unknown forest with which the wolf was identified. The wolf also presented a real danger, and this was no smaller on Saaremaa than it was on the mainland. There were wide pastures and many cattle on the island. According to an account from 1819, there were approximately 6,000 horses, 20,000 cattle and 40,000 sheep on the island.[37] It is not known how many animals were killed by wolves, but it is known that from Martinmas 1822 to Martinmas 1823 more than 30,000 cattle and sheep were taken by wolves in Riga Governorate across the sea.[38] Almanacs encouraged peasants to kill both wolf litters and grown wolves.[39] Although the killer of a wolf received a monetary reward in addition to the skin of the animal, this was not a high enough motivation for the peasants to make them hunt wolves in great numbers. Some hunting was practised, however – for instance, it is known that in 1827 a total of 935 wolves were killed in Riga Governorate.[40]

It seems that the peasants may have had difficulties in attributing only negative qualities to the wolf. Even in the legend of origin that is spread all over Estonia, according to which the wolf was created by the devil, the former becomes a character with partially positive features – an enemy of the devil himself. In this tale, the wolf is created by the devil, who commands it to kill God, but the wolf does not respond. However, when God instructs the wolf to rise and eat the devil, it complies (or, in other versions, it pursues the devil for all eternity).[41] In addition to being able to triumph over the devil, it was believed that the wolf could overcome ghosts and revenants. It is particularly from Saaremaa that many of the recordings of an enmity between revenants and wolves originate.[42] An ambivalent attitude towards wolves also becomes apparent in the belief, recorded on Saaremaa, that if the wolf is called Forest Christ it cannot kill its prey. It is likely, however, that over the centuries Estonians increasingly started to accept the notion of the wolf as a creature with a thoroughly negative meaning, which Christianity had been teaching for a long time.

Some interpretations of the werewolf legends from Saaremaa

It would be too much of a simplification to claim that the Western European stereotype of the woman only became predominant among Estonians during the past couple of centuries, just as the Western European stereotype of the wolf became predominant among Estonians in the same period. It is certainly not possible to make this statement. Yet historical developments in the local mentality and in conceptions about women must be taken into account before applying the feminist theories of Western scholars to the local material. It may easily turn out that the theories prove inapplicable due to differences in cultural and historical developments.

The role of the woman in Estonian society throughout history is a topic that has not been studied as yet and poses numerous unanswered questions. No exhaustive answer has been suggested by any Estonian scholar to the question of why it was predominantly men who were accused in the witch trials of Southern Estonia. The number of questions that have not even been asked is yet larger. Why are female werewolves popular in Estonian folklore? What problems and tensions between family members are reflected in the folklore materials collected in the late nineteenth century? Are regional differences in gender roles reflected in Estonian folklore?

Studying werewolf legends with female characters can make a contribution to the research into some questions related to the field. Looking at such werewolf legends in the context of gender studies, they can be interpreted as resistance to the Western European image of the woman as submissive, pious, humble and passive that reached the awareness of nineteenth-century Estonians mostly via popular literature and pastors' sermons. The active woman protagonist of the tale 'The Other Sleeper Kills an Animal' flees from her daily reality – in which she is bound to fulfil a subordinate role both in the social sense and as concerns her gender – into a world with different rules, into the wild wood where she is the master and can show her power. After having killed an animal and taken the meat, she returns to the everyday world and continues her life as she used to, usually remaining unpunished for her deed.[43]

Is there also a connection between going out as a wolf and fertility magic? A connection does not become explicit in the werewolf legends collected in past centuries, but if the data of the witch trial of Thies from the seventeenth century[44] and wolf-related elements in wedding customs are taken into account its existence seems to have been very likely. Thus, collecting dowry for the bride has been called 'running as the wolf' and 'driving the wolf's tail'; it was said about spinsters that 'even the wolf has never sniffed her'; no wooing was undertaken in February, for it was considered the month when wolves enter oestrus; and there is a report from Saaremaa according to which the bride was fed from the tip of a knife three times when she went to her father's home for the last time – as noted, the most widespread method of returning individuals who have been maliciously transformed into wolves to human form consists in offering the wolf bread from the tip of a knife.[45]

It is possible that fertility was one of the aspects that made it easier to create associations between women and wolves. Another link connecting the two was the conception of both women and wolves as dangerous that apparently was even preserved in the period when the association between wolves and fertility started to become vaguer in the awareness of peasants. It is interesting to note that the components of fertility and danger are connected in lyric *runo* songs recorded in the Karelian region of Finland, that is culturally close to Estonia, in the period from the early nineteenth century to the mid-twentieth century. The songs describe the vagina as the apex of supreme beauty, but also a cruel devourer of the male organ, comparable with a wolf's jaws.[46]

A possible explanation for the importance of maternity in the legends involving female werewolves is that the peasants had sufficient knowledge of the wolves' lifestyle to know that the parental instinct of the she-wolf is so strong that she will express milk in the presence of newborn pups, even if they are not her own.[47] Maternity-related werewolf tales can be interpreted as a protest against the pressure from a Christian mentality that created a total and unnatural divide between maternity and sexuality. Maternity and sexuality have a closer connection than the popular Western psychology of today – which has been deeply influenced by the teachings of Sigmund Freud – would admit.[48]

But gender is not the only topic that the werewolf legends address. What emerges as a more important issue is the theme of social relationships on a more general level. The Estonian werewolf legends would not have evolved into what they are had the top positions in society not been occupied by the Baltic German nobility. The fact is that Estonian peasants were serfs almost until the middle of the nineteenth century and, in early modernity, today's Estonia belonged to the regions in Eastern Europe with the most advanced dependence on serfdom. The Estonian werewolf legends would probably also have been different if the peasants had not been annually threatened by the danger of a famine. Until the middle of the nineteenth century despite the peasants working hard on the manor lands, as well as on their own land, they had to suffer from lack of bread and hunger before the new harvest in seven out of every ten years.[49]

In their discussion of the type 'The Other Sleeper Kills an Animal', Jüri Allik and Aino Laagus write: 'In popular awareness, turning into a wolf was a procedure that made it possible to exit human culture (of one's own) and join the part of nature on which human means of subsistence directly depend.'[50] In the context of werewolf legends from all over Estonia, it is the conflict between social classes that emerges as the primary element – during the lifetime of the tellers, it mostly involved confrontations between farm owners and hired labour, although the theme of the relationship between the peasant and the manor owner also left its traces on the werewolf lore of the late nineteenth and twentieth centuries, while the topic of the relationship between men and women tended to remain in the background. In the legends from Saaremaa, the gender conflict is more foregrounded. This is indirectly proved by a report, recorded on Saaremaa in 1880, of a description of turning into a wolf that claims one should know with certainty whether one wants to become a she-wolf or a he-wolf.

So, in addition to providing a survey of werewolf legends from Saaremaa and some interpretations, I have also attempted to show that, while certainly possible, any gender-specific study of culture should arise from the particular local context, as employing patterns that have been developed elsewhere, and with a different aim in mind, in order to discuss female culture from a different background will leave much unexplained.

Notes

This research was supported by institutional research funding IUT (2-43) of the Estonian Ministry of Education and Research and by the European Union through the European Regional Development Fund (Center of Excellence CECT).

1. Heino Mardiste, 'Loodus: Üldandmed', in *Saaremaa. Loodus, aeg, inimene* 1 (Tallinn: Eesti Entsüklopeediakirjastus, 2002), 13–19 (13–14).
2. Mari Reitalu and Hans Trass, 'Taimkate. Metsad', in *ibid.*, 113–18 (113).
3. Uudo Timm, 'Imetajad', in *ibid.*, 185–7 (186).
4. Oskar Loorits, *Grundzüge des estnischen Volksglaubens 1* (Lund: Carl Bloms Boktrykeri A.-B., 1949), 311.
5. Maia Madar, 'Nõiaprotsessid Eestis XVI sajandist XIX sajandini', in Jüri Kivimäe (compiler), *Religiooni ja ateismi ajaloost Eestis: Artiklite kogumik III* (Tallinn: Eesti Raamat, 1987), 124–45 (138).
6. See Merili Metsvahi, 'Libahunt Thiesi võitlused', in Mall Hiiemäe and Kanni Labi (eds), *Klaasmäel*, Pro Folkloristica 8 (Tartu: Eesti Kirjandusmuuseum, 2001), 101–13; Willem de Blécourt, 'A Journey to Hell: Reconsidering the Livonian "Werewolf"', *Magic, Ritual, and Witchcraft* 2:1 (Summer 2007): 49–67.
7. The 'Girl as Wolf' tale type is included in the Aarne-Thompson tale type index with the classification AT409.
8. Loorits, *Grundzüge des estnischen Volksglaubens 1*, 311.
9. For example, see Estonian Folklore Archives (Tartu, Estonia), MD-0106-04; MD-0106-08.
10. Anu Korb, 'Rahvaluule. Kogumistööst', in *Saaremaa. Loodus, aeg, inimene*, 1, 509–13 (511–13).

11 See Kadri Tamm, 'Statistiline ülevaade kogumisvõistlustest ja folkloristide välitöödest', in Mall Hiiemäe and Kanni Labi (eds), *Kogumisest uurimiseni. Artikleid Eesti Rahvaluule Arhiivi 75. sünnipäevaks* (Tartu: Eesti Kirjandusmuuseum, 2002), 220–39 (225).
12 Estonian Folklore Archives, KKI 10, 142/3 (11) < Mustjala khk, 1949.
13 Olaus Magnus, 'Des Olaus Magnus Bericht über die livländischen Werwölfe. Uebersetzt von Eduard Pabst. Über die Wuth der durch Zauberei in Wölfe verwandelten Menschen', *Archiv für die Geschichte Liv-, Esth- und Curlands* 4 (1845): 101–3.
14 Oskar Loorits, *Livische Märchen- und Sagenvarianten. FFC 66* (Helsinki: Suomalainen tiedeakademia, 1926), Sagen 66.
15 Jacob Grimm, *Deutsche Sagen*, vol. 1, edited by Barbara Kindermann-Bieri and Hans-Jörg Uther (Munich: Dietrichs, 1993), no. 214.
16 Estonian Folklore Archives, ERA II 158, 501/5 (7) < Kaarma khk. – Aadu Toomessalu < Jaan Tänav, b. 1874 (1937).
17 Jüri Allik and Aino Laagus, 'Küps ja toores eesti rahvausundis', in Jaak Põldmäe (ed.), *Studia metrica et poetica II* (Tartu: Tartu Riiklik Ülikool, 1977), 21–39.
18 Merili Metsvahi, 'Neiu hundiks. Libahundimuistendi "Teine puhkajatest murrab looma" analüüs', *Ariadne Lõng: Nais ja meesuuringute ajakiri* 1–2 (2001): 39–51.
19 Estonian Folklore Archives, ERA II 157, 397/8 (1) < Mustjala khk. – Amanda Raadla < Aadu Väärt, b. 1865 (1937).
20 Estonian Folklore Archives, ERA II 157, 398/9 (2) < Mustjala khk. – Amanda Raadla < Aadu Väärt, b. 1865 (1937).
21 See de Blécourt, 'A Journey to Hell'.
22 Nils Blomkvist, *The Discovery of the Baltic: The Reception of a Catholic World-System in the European North (AD 1075–1225)* (Leiden: Brill, 2004): 182–6; Marika Mägi, 'Abielu, kristianiseerimine ja akulturatsioon. Perekondliku korralduse varasemast ajaloost Eestis', *Ariadne Lõng: Nais ja meesuuringute ajakiri* 1–2 (2009): 76–101 (82–3).
23 Marika Mägi, 'Eesti ühiskond keskaja lävel', in Marika Mägi (ed.), *Eesti aastal 1200* (Tallinn: Argo, 2003), 15–42 (24); Mägi, 'Abielu, kristianiseerimine ja akulturatsioon': 84.
24 Mägi, 'Abielu, kristianiseerimine ja akulturatsioon': 68–9.
25 Elina Öpik, *Vadjalastest ja isuritest XVIII saj. lõpul. Etnograafilisi ja lingvistilisi materjale Fjodor Tumanski Peterburi kubermangu kirjelduses* (Reval: Valgus, 1970), 152.
26 August Wilhelm Hupel, *Topographische Nachrichten von Lief- und Ehstland*, vol. 2 (Riga: bey Johann Friedrich Hartknoch, 1777), 136–7.
27 August Wilhelm Hupel, *Neue Nordische Miscellaneen*, vol. 6 (Riga: bey Johann Friedrich Hartknoch, 1795), 564.
28 Hupel, *Topographische Nachrichten*, 138.
29 Even some matrilinear societies are patriarchal; see, for example, Alice Schlegel, *Male Dominance and Female Autonomy: Domestic Authority in Matrilineal Societies* (New Haven, CT: Human Relations Area Files Press, 1972).
30 Piia Pedakmäe, 'Nõiausust Taaniaegsel Saaremaal', *Saaremaa Muuseum. Kaheaastaraamt 1997–98* (1999): 18–25 (23).
31 See Lara S. Apps and Andrew Gow, *Male Witches in Early Modern Europe* (Manchester: Manchester University Press, 2003), 122, 128, 136; Merry E. Wiesner-Hanks, *Women and Gender in Early Modern Europe: New Approaches*

       to European History (Cambridge: Cambridge University Press, 2008), 256, 260; Raisa Maria Toivo, *Witchcraft and Gender in Early Modern Society: Finland and the Wider European Experience* (Burlington: Ashgate, 2008), 85–6.
32 Sandra Cavallo and Silvia Evengelisti (eds), *A Cultural History of Childhood and Family in the Early Modern Age* (Oxford and New York: Berg, 2010), 24.
33 Ivar Paulson, *Vana eesti rahvausk* (Tartu: Ilmamaa, 1997), 51.
34 See Paulson, *Vana eesti rahvausk*, 52; Ilmar Rootsi, 'Hunt kultusloomana eesti rahvatraditsioonis', *Mäetagused*, 40 (2008): 7–24.
35 Paulson, *Vana eesti rahvausk*, 54.
36 Rootsi, 'Hunt kultusloomana eesti rahvatraditsioonis'; Lõuna-Eesti pärimuse portaal ('the portal of South-Estonian Folklore' – a project led by Mare Kõiva from the Estonian Literary Museum; the texts are taken from the manuscripts of the Estonian Folklore Archives), www.folklore.ee/lepp. Accessed 28 May 2011.
37 Evald Blumfledt, *Saaremaa ajaloo põhijoni* (Tartu: Postimees, 1933), 73–4.
38 Otto Wilhelm Masing (ed.), *Marahwa Kalender ehk Täht-ramat 1826 aasta peäle, pärrast Jesuse Kristuse sündimist* (Tartu: J.C. Schünmann, 1826), 23.
39 *Ibid.*; Otto Wilhelm Masing (ed.), *Eesti-ma Rahwa Kalender ehk Täht-Ramat 1829. aasta Peäle* (Tallinn: P.C.G. Dullo, 1829).
40 Masing, *Eesti-ma Rahwa Kalender ehk Täht-Ramat 1829. aasta Peäle*.
41 The map of distribution and a sample text can be found at www.folklore.ee/rl/pubte/ee/eluolu/elu2/167.html. Accessed 21 May 2011.
42 Holzmayer, *Osiliana* I 17, 3, www.folklore.ee/rl/pubte/ee/lru/lru2/lrukax09.pdf. Accessed 21 May 2011.
43 See Allik and Laagus, 'Küps ja toores eesti rahvausundis'.
44 See Merili Metsvahi, 'Werwolfprozesse in Estland und Livland in 17. Jahrhundert. Zusammenstöße zwischen der Realität von Richtern und von Bauern', in Jürgen Beyer and Reet Hiiemäe (eds), *Folklore als Tatsachenbericht* (Tartu: Sektion für Folkloristik des Estnischen Literaturmuseums, 2001), 175–84; de Blécourt, 'A Journey to Hell'.
45 Allik and Laagus, 'Küps ja toores eesti rahvausundis', 28–9.
46 Satu Apo, '"Ex cunno come the folk and force": Concepts of Women's Dynamistic Power in Finnish-Karelian Tradition', in Satu Apo, Aili Nenola and Laura Stark-Arola (eds), *Gender and Folklore: Perspectives on Finnish and Karelian Culture* (Helsinki: Finnish Literature Society, 1998), 63–91.
47 J.K. Badridze, 'Volk. Voprosy ontogeneza povedeniâ, problemy i metod reintrodukcii'/'Wolf. The Ontogeny of Behaviour; Problems and Method of Reintroduction', www.zooproblem.net/povedenie/part3/volk. Accessed 22 January 2011.
48 See, for example, Estela V. Welldon, *Mother, Madonna, Whore: the Idealization and Denigration of Motherhood* (New York and London: Karnac Books, 1992).
49 Marten Seppel, *Näljaabi Liivi-ja Eestimaal 17. sajandist 19. sajandi alguseni*, Dissertationes Historiae Universitatis Tartuensis 15 (Tartu: Tartu University Press, 2008), 61.
50 Allik and Laagus, 'Küps ja toores eesti rahvausundis', 29.

3
'She transformed into a werewolf, devouring and killing two children': trials of she-werewolves in early modern French Burgundy

Rolf Schulte
Translated by Linda Froome-Döring

Late summer, 1598. It is the time of the fruit harvest in the small village of Nezan in the Jura Mountains; fifteen-year-old Benoît Bidel climbs up into a tree to pick the ripe fruit; his younger sister is waiting down below. Suddenly, an animal springs at the girl; she screams, and Benoît realises that a wolf is attacking and about to bite his sister. He quickly climbs down from the tree and pulls out his knife to help his sister. The animal leaves the girl and attacks Benoît himself. In the struggle, the boy sustains serious injuries to his neck from his own knife, and blood pours from the wound. At this moment, a number of villagers who have seen the attack from afar come running and are able to drive the aggressive animal away. They carry Benoît to his parents' house where he is just able to describe the details of the incident. Probably after being asked about the appearance of the animal, he gives a description of it, declaring that it 'had no tail' and 'two front paws shaped like human hands which were covered in fur'.[1] Benoît Bidel dies from his wounds a few days after the attack. The inhabitants of Nezan, an isolated village surrounded by forest on a 1000 metre high plateau in the mountains, do not hesitate long after hearing this news. They interpret the attack as the work of a human being, of a werewolf. Suspicion soon falls on an elderly neighbour, Perrenette Gandillon, who has long been reputed not only to master magic but also to use it aggressively. Gandillon senses the mistrust and flees the village. But this reaction simply confirms the suspicions of the villagers and, as they see it, exposes the woman as the offender guilty of killing a child – a she-werewolf. Gandillon is tracked down, and the lynching which follows is an expression of the people's unbridled rage.[2]

The brutal killing of Perrenette Gandillon as a supposed she-werewolf is indicative of the atmosphere in the mountains of Franche-Comté, a territory in Burgundy, France. The belief that there were people who could turn themselves into wolves and who would savage and kill their fellow humans seems to have been deeply rooted among the inhabitants of this region during the early modern period. Whereas numerous authorities equated such illegal vigilantism with revolt and took severe action against such deeds, there was no such reaction from the local authorities responsible for Nezan. It seems probable that, in such a case of alleged werewolfism, they were not opposed to this poor woman being battered to death.

Cases: from Clauda Jeanprost to Marie Barnagoz and Renoberte Simon[3]

The judiciary was involved in werewolf hunting prior to this incident, but after the lynching of Perrenette Gandillon they pursued this course with greater vigour: Henri Boguet, who had been appointed judge by the abbott of the large monasterial district of Sainte-Claude, instigated intensive searches for alleged werewolves in his district – and found them. At the end of August 1598, he accused two women of death-bringing animal metamorphosis: an old and lame beggarwoman, Clauda Jeanprost, from the village of Orcières, and Françoise Sécretain, who had fled to the region from the neighbouring state of Savoy. At her trial, the latter denied the charge, but died while imprisoned. Jeanprost, however, admitted having attacked people in the shape of a wolf and also of having eaten their flesh. But it was important to her to emphasise that during these attacks she had never touched the inviolable body parts salved by Christ. This defence strategy was clearly intended to convince the judge that, despite the severity of her crimes, Jeanprost still had some remnants of Christian faith. But it was to no avail. The lay court of Sainte-Claude condemned the woman to death by burning; the tribunal was not interested in the fact that a lame old woman who, despite magical metamorphosis, would be equally disabled when in the guise of the beast and was hardly capable of transforming into a fast-running, leaping werewolf.[4] Jeanprost tried three times to escape from the stake, but was caught each time and finally beaten unconscious with a plank by the executioner, who then placed her body in the flames.[5]

In the same year, Judge Boguet had three further women, Clauda Guillaume, Thivienne Paget and Clauda Gaillard, arrested as suspected werewolves in his judicial district. All three were from the bottom stratum of rural society and lived their lives on the edge of hunger and material destitution. In their trials they admitted having rubbed their bodies with an ointment or thrown on a cloak of wolf's fur in order to transform into dangerous beasts, whereupon they had hunted down and consumed children and small domestic animals. Both Gaillard and Paget come across as self-confident women in the trials; they did not initially want to confess to such misdeeds. Eventually, however, and in the face of alleged evidence, confrontation with witnesses or putative accomplices, they were no longer able to keep up their resistance and admitted to having become she-werewolves – and, at the same time, witches – by means of a pact with the devil. The three women, and a man who had been accused at the same time, were condemned by the jury of the lay court and executed in 1598.⁶ In a third wave of trials the following year, and basing their judgment on Boguet's investigation, the judges of Sainte-Claude decided the fate of the rest of the Gandillon family from Nezan. The brother, nephew, and niece, Antonia, of the lynching victim Perrenette Gandillon were brought before the tribunal of Sainte-Claude. While the men were accused of, and admitted to, being werewolves, the woman was accused of witchcraft.⁷

The confessions by the supposed werewolves of Sainte-Claude at the end of the sixteenth century appear to have been made without the use of torture. However, to take this as an indication that the crimes were real or that the statements were made voluntarily would be to fail to recognise the conditions under which such investigations took place at that time. Prison sentences, and thus prisons as such, were not known in early modern Europe; jails were for temporary detention only. A prolonged stay – up to eight months is documented for Sainte-Claude – in such places was intolerable and inhumane. The jails were small, constricted and unheated in winter; vermin were rampant, and the cells stank of excrement. Degraded by the way the bailiffs treated them and by judges who ordered all their hair to be cut off and subjected them to naked body searches, dispirited by the knowledge that they could not pay for any legal counsel, the accused vegetated away. Add to this the fact that they had lost their emotional roots and values – demoralised by the animosity of their once neighbours and without the support of family or friends – and it does not come as a surprise that the violence of the jails or the threat of torture could suffice to make a prisoner aware of, and willing to fulfil, the expectations of the judges.

Both secular and ecclesiastical courts pursued alleged werewolf cases, at least in the sixteenth century. The well-known trial of the two herdsmen Pierre Burgot and Michel Verdun in 1521 fell under the jurisdiction of the Catholic Inquisition, as did the trials of Marie Barnagoz, Perrenette Tornier and Jeanne Guyenot thirty years later. Following the arrest of Tornier's husband, these women were arrested and charged, as a gang of four, of having committed fifteen murders in the guise of wolves.⁸ Unlike the other accused, Perrenette Tornier appealed against her death sentence; the high court, however, dismissed her objections and upheld the verdict.⁹ After the execution, Perrenette Tornier's head was exhibited on a stake to demonstrate to the local population the consequences of such misdeeds.

The 'Parlement' in Dôle criticised the way the trial had been conducted because they felt they had not been duly informed by the Inquisitors. This indicates that the secular authorities were not only stating their claim to the right to prosecute werewolves and witches, but were doing so very pointedly.¹⁰ From this point onwards, werewolves faced persecution by the secular authorities.

At the beginning of the 1570s attacks by wolves in Franche-Comté increased in number. A German-speaking student of Dôle University reported that wolves the size of donkeys had been seen to attack people and livestock in the forests.¹¹ In September 1573, the 'Parlement' of Dôle saw reason to introduce more suitable measures to counteract aggression by wolves. The 'Parlement' was both court and administrative authority in Franche-Comté. In 1573 it issued a regulation permitting the people in certain areas of the county to be armed, not as a defensive strategy against wolves, but as an offensive aimed at the increasing number of humans magically transformed into wolves:

> [T]his court has permitted and permits the residents and inhabitants of the named localities and others, irrespective of the hunting statutes to assemble armed with clubs, halberds, pikes, arquebuses and other cudgels and without fear of punishment to hunt down the named werewolves wherever they might find, catch, shoot or kill them.[12]

In contravention of an otherwise binding statute which laid down the state's monopoly with regard to arms, the court permitted the peasants to carry weapons in a form of organised self-help in the fight against werewolves. The edict was renewed the following year without any fundamental changes to the wording or content.[13]

In 1573, an alleged werewolf fell into the hunters' trap near the town of Dôle. The victim was Gilles Garnier, a hermit, whose case has become well known beyond the borders of Franche-Comté as a classic example of werewolfism. What is not so well known, however, is that his wife Appoline and two other men were also arrested and interrogated by the court as suspects. Garnier eventually confessed to having brought flesh from the bodies of murdered children to his wife in their cave. However, the judges decided that Appoline Garnier was not privy to the crimes of her husband, and she was released from custody.[14]

After the Sainte-Claude trials, the persecution of werewolves in the Jura region was also pursued outside of the monasterial district. Guillama Frayre from St Hymetière was the only person accused of animal metamorphosis during a witchcraft trial involving seven people. The same was true of Guillemette Barnard from Quintigny, who witnesses accused in 1605 of having 'injured a man's buttocks while in the guise of a wolf'.[15] While Frayre was condemned to death,[16] Barnard's case took a surprising turn. The judges rejected the accusation of werewolfism as unfounded, but found her guilty of witchcraft. Then, clearly uncertain of their decision, they condemned her, not to death, but to life-long banishment from the country, coupled with the threat of hanging were she ever to return.[17]

Perrenette Glaon from Pimorin, a village in the plains of Burgundy, was not one of those who were able to profit from such creeping doubts about the reality of werewolves. In 1611 the court found this married woman from the bottom stratum of society clearly guilty, stating that 'she transformed into a werewolf, devouring and killing two children'.[18] However, this accusation was only one among twenty other alleged crimes: the accusations against Glaon ranged from arson and killing of horses to desecration of the Host – crimes which would prove her guilty of witchcraft. Her poverty and behavioural deviance, and here, particularly, the fact that she was known to have had premarital intercourse on a number of occasions, were considered incriminating evidence against her.[19] Glaon was no longer a she-werewolf with witch-like characteristics but a witch with werewolf-like characteristics. Her confession was presumably not made voluntarily but exacted under torture.

Although not always used, torture was the soul of the trials for serious crimes in early modern Europe, and as there was no precise restriction on the duration of torture, when trying cases in which the accused persistently refused to confess, judges in Franche-Comté tended not to rely on the violent nature of the jails alone. Anyone with good knowledge of the witchcraft trials held in France, Germany or Switzerland during this period will know that broken arms, dislocated joints, bloody bodies, fainting fits and premature deaths were characteristic of trials in which the use of instruments of torture, such as thumbscrews and similar vices or the rack, was common practice.[20] Glaon may have had a similar experience. She was burnt in 1611, but the court granted her supposed clemency, allowing her to be strangled prior to burning and thus sparing her the agonies of being burnt alive at the stake.

Another victim of torture, in 1611, was Jeanne Horriel from the heavily forested north-east of Franche-Comté. She, her husband and her father were all tortured, but to the astonishment of the judges she withstood this martyrdom without confessing to animal metamorphosis or witchcraft. The court's official prosecutor accused the three persons of 'having transformed themselves into wolves and other red-coated animals or bulls'. The Horriels had frequently had verbal and physical disputes with a family in the neighbourhood, and it was this family who had ultimately filed charges against them. The unusual fact of a person surviving torture, together with doubts regarding the validity of some of the accusations, made the judges cautious in their decisions. The factual evidence proved the accusations of blasphemy and armed coercion, for which Jeanne Horriel was charged a fine; the court acquitted her, however, of threatening animal metamorphosis.[21]

This trend towards greater leniency continued in the trials of Colette Pinard and Claude Gerard who accused each other of being werewolves and witches in 1612. Both were acquitted.[22] The case of a father and son named Recurdey from Noires in the Jura showed certain similarities. People at the funeral of the men's mother/grandmother saw scratches and wounds on her body and, aware of the dead woman's reputation, identified her as a werewolf. Their vociferous claims impressed the priest, who subsequently refused to give the woman a Christian burial. The court charged the son and grandson with aggressive animal metamorphosis. The older man died while imprisoned, but the charges against his son were dropped and he was sentenced only to a fine for blasphemy.[23]

In 1629, Oudette Champon of Ougney in the valley of the Doubs was also acquitted of the charge of werewolfism. Her trial gives a lively impression of the circumstances under which such accusations arose. In 1620 – nine years before the court trial – a villager by the name of Jean Brun was on his way home at night from festivities involving large amounts of alcohol. While passing the village graveyard he claimed to have seen Oudette Champon turning into a werewolf and rising up into the sky. Brun spread the news of this experience around the whole village. The pressure on Champon grew, although critical voices were heard, doubting the truth of Brun's story. In the end, Champon offered the man money to keep him quiet, agreeing not to take him to court for slander for she was fearful that her mother's reputation as a witch might be to her detriment. Brun, nevertheless, placed charges against her, and the combination of factors – Brun's senses dulled by alcohol and the rumours he spread, as well as Champon's defensive behaviour, motivated by her fear – all finally culminated in an official trial. Champon, however, was able to pay for a lawyer, whose arguments convinced the court; her acquittal was in line with preceding verdicts.[24]

In 1632 the 'Parlement' in Dôle renewed the edict on organised wolf and werewolf hunts for large areas of Franche-Comté after hearing reports of wolf attacks on people and livestock. In fact, the authorities went even further this time and ordered paid hunters to be appointed. When wolves were sighted near a village, the church bells were to be rung and the villagers were to assemble and be counted. This way, claimed the jurists, it would be easier to identify any absentees as werewolves.[25]

A year later, however, the same authorities in Dôle amended the edict and deleted the term 'werewolf'; the human element had now been eliminated. Scepticism towards the concept of werewolves had gained the upper hand amongst the elite of Franche-Comté, and this was reflected in amendments to official regulations.[26]

The concept of the werewolf nevertheless remained particularly alive in the inaccessible regions of the Jura, where several cases of alleged lycanthropy came before the courts. In the mountainous regions where there was little communication with more populated areas, the werewolf paradigm still held strong among both the local peasant population and local jurists.

Pierrette Vichard, a widow and beggarwoman/day labourer lived in the vicinity of Orgelet in the Jura. Of no fixed abode, she slept outside during the summer months, seeking a little shelter close to buildings. When, on a summer's night in 1657, a child was carried off from a farmyard by a wolf, the villagers interpreted this as the deed of a werewolf. As Vichard already had the reputation of a witch, the peasants believed her capable of such a transformation. Suspicions were confirmed when, upon her arrest, she was found to have injuries and grazes, which the peasants interpreted as being the result of the night-time struggle. The 'Parlement' in Dôle took over the case as they considered the werewolf trials a particularly delicate matter which they preferred not to leave to the local authorities. They were unable to obtain a confession from Vichard, and the controversial nature of the debate on the subject characterised the charges brought by the public prosecutor, who was unable to make up his mind whether to accuse her of werewolfism. He argued that the woman had 'in the shape of a human or a wolf carried off and eaten a seven- or eight-year-old child'. The highest court, however, did not follow the prosecutor's line of argument, and in 1658 Vichard was acquitted.[27]

Things did not seem to go as well for Renoberte Simon in the early stages of her trial in 1660. Witnesses had seen a wolf in the fields near her isolated village, Chapelle d'Huin in the foothills of the western Alps. According to their account, Simon had appeared at the precise moment and place where the wolf had disappeared into the forest. They concluded from this that Simon and the wolf must be one and the same creature – a she-werewolf. Simon was arrested on the basis of these assertions. Other witnesses reported that before her arrest Simon had spoken of a master and his mother who made magic ointments to enable metamorphosis into an animal. The authorities even found a pot containing suspicious ingredients in Simon's home, although when asked for the formula, she was unable to give an answer. The public prosecutor then accused her of werewolfism and also charged her with fifty-five further crimes intended to prove her a witch. He made a point of listing her severe deficits with respect to the Catholic faith and accused her of Protestant inclinations. The woman implicated by Simon as having fabricated the werewolf ointment must also have been arrested, but records of a trial can no longer be found. Even this court in the mountain region decided to reject the charges of metamorphosis and possession of a magical transformation cream: in 1660, the same year, she was acquitted of all charges.[28]

It was two men who were charged at the last werewolf trial in Franche-Comté in 1663. However, the court released the two brothers,[29] and with this trial the werewolf finally disappeared into popular culture, where the tradition was long upheld in folklore.[30] Werewolves remained a symbol of a sinister threat representing dark, life-devouring forces, but the official persecution of people as alleged werewolves had come to an end.

She- and he-werewolves

In summary, the werewolf trials began in 1521, with the death sentences for heresy pronounced by the Inquisition courts, and ended in 1663 with acquittals before secular courts. In this period, the legal authorities in Franche-Comté charged a total of forty-four people of werewolfism, twenty-four of them men and twenty of them women. Not only was the number of indictments almost evenly distributed among men and women, but the verdicts also showed considerable similarities. With the exception of a higher proportion of banishments among the male accused and a larger number of acquittals among the women, the courts' verdicts were proportionally almost the same for both sexes; the execution rates were 60 per cent for both men and women. In Franche-Comté, then, the male or female gender was not decisive in determining whether werewolf charges were placed – unlike witchcraft, where charges were generally gender-related.[31]

However, a purely quantitative analysis is deceptive, for it was men who were the first victims of werewolf trials, and it was only because these men accused women of being their accomplices that women were also targeted by the courts.

The stoning of Perrenette Gandillon had already shown that in popular culture werewolves were also a female phenomenon. The judge, Henri Boguet, along with the establishment, now also began to regard women as prime targets in his persecutions. Under Boguet's legal direction an increasing number of women came to be tried for lycanthropy. Of the ten people tried in 1598 for allegedly mutating into aggressive animals, seven were female. However, this development is not clear-cut either, since the central figure of these Sainte-Claude trials was, and remained, 'Gros' Jacques Boquet, one of the local cunning folk who had named numerous other alleged werewolves – and not only when under pressure during court trials. It was not until the seventeenth century that either private individuals or the state prosecuted women independently of men. Guillama Frayre was the first woman to be condemned, in 1604, for her alleged ability to turn into a brutal animal without having any connection with a mixed-gender pack of human wolves. Such individual trials of women as 'primary werewolves' continued to take place, although more women than men were prosecuted in the course of a collective, rather than an individual, trial.

In the course of less than 150 years between 1521 and 1663, the werewolf paradigm had evidently changed. Starting in 1550, but more frequently from 1590 onwards, the courts integrated the werewolf charge into witchcraft trials, defining it as a particularly brutal kind of *maleficium*. In the seventeenth century, this interpretation became an integral part of demonology and was accepted by both the lower and the highest courts. The werewolf degenerated to one of many variants of *maleficium* and thus became a subordinate aspect of the witchcraft trials. The werewolf went, and the witch came. The werewolf hunt had effectively become a witch-hunt. In 1550 there was almost one werewolf trial for every two witchcraft trials, by 1600 this figure had gone down to one in four, and by the middle of the seventeenth century, with the increase in the number of 'classic' witchcraft trials, the proportion further decreased.

Lycanthropy in Franche-Comté proved to be an alleged or supposed means of harming fellow humans in a witchcraft trial which was by no means gender-specific. Certain characteristics were ascribed to all suspected werewolves as to all witches, be they men or women, characteristics which should be abhorred by any Christian person: these persons stood at the end of every scale of moral values.

Some authors who have researched the lycanthropy phenomenon emphasise the sexual deviance of the accused and interpret charges of werewolfism as a contemporary metaphor for accusations of sexually motivated crimes.[32] Statements by witnesses and confessions made by male defendants in Franche-Comté do indeed contain elements of sexual deviance or abuse: in 1521, the two shepherds Burgot and Verdun allegedly slept with animals; a hermit named Garnier was accused in 1573 of having undressed a girl in order to then eat part of her body; it was said of Jacques Verjux in 1599 that he had committed incest with his mother; and the Gandillons allegedly left their victims naked after an attack.[33] Such interpretations are, however, selective and thus do not provide real proof; norm deviations (in the understanding of the times or, in some cases, also in a modern sense) apply only to six of the twenty-two male werewolves in Franche-Comté. Female werewolves, on the other hand, regularly admitted sexual deviance in the form of intercourse with the devil. The accused Sécretain even recounted intercourse with Satan in the form of a drake.[34] The courts, however, rated such crimes as evidence of witchcraft and not of werewolfism. As the perception of witches and werewolves in this region was intermixed, deviation from sexual norms is part of the core image of the crime of witchcraft, but not a distinguishing feature of werewolf accusations in their own right. Women charged with lycanthropy were often also accused of extramarital sexual relations, hypersexuality and occasionally of sodomy, but never of sexual aggression: rape and sexual abuse of children were among the alleged crimes of three men in Franche-Comté, too low a number from which to derive a general theory.

Changes: werewolf images in French culture

All the werewolves of Franche-Comté were called 'loup-garous'. The roots of this French term '[loup]garou' can be discerned in the word 'gerulfus'. This seemingly Romanic term had developed from the concept 'leu warou'. While 'leu' can be traced back to the Latin noun 'lupus', the second part of the word 'warou' is derived from the Franconian word 'wer' meaning man. Through an abrasion of the consonants and a sound shift, 'leu warou' became 'leu garoul'.[35] Gervase of Tilbury then re-Latinised this term and the French 'gerulfus' of the Middle Ages became 'loup-garou', the early modern French word for this phenomenon. The etymology of the word 'loup-garou' then shows that in French-speaking regions the roots of the human wolf are clearly male.

In the French-speaking areas of medieval Central and Western Europe, in contrast to early modern Franche-Comté, only male werewolves are recorded.[36] In the late twelfth-century/early thirteenth-century romance, *Guillaume de Palerne*, a prince who has been turned into a wolf by his stepmother cares like a mother for an abducted child, protects an absconding young couple from their pursuers, and finally becomes a human being again.[37]

A werewolf is also the focal point of one of Marie de France's verse narratives, known as *lais*. Though the exact circumstances of her life are uncertain, it is believed that Marie de France lived in England but was French-born. She seems to have related French folk tales in the Norman and Breton tradition. In *Bisclavret*, she portrays a man as the victim of his wife. For reasons which are not described, the nobleman occasionally, but involuntarily, takes on the likeness of a wolf. The 'bisclavret' is finally able to escape his fate when the king and others are struck by the human-like, genteel behaviour of the beast; thanks to another magic spell he is finally able to resume the form of a man. Similarly, in the contemporaneous *Lai de Melion*, written by an unknown author, a wolf leads his pack to lay waste to the entire land but is eventually also released from the spell which compelled him to this aggressiveness, and he is fully transformed back into a human being. The thus liberated person is also male.[38]

Gervase of Tilbury, Marshall to the Holy Roman Emperor, related folklore and tales from the French-speaking region in which he lived in around 1214. He was also interested in werewolf reports and described two alleged animal metamorphoses in which men became wolves out of sheer despair. Their brutality caused fear and distress in the forests of the Auvergne and Vivarais; nonetheless, they were able, by chance, to cast off the spell by which they had been bound and revert to being non-aggressive human beings. One of the two, who had savaged and eaten children, was released from his fate by having a foot cut off.[39] These tales reflect the basic constellation seen in Marie de France's narrative.

Gervase uses in his tales a term for human wolves which was later used in the sixteenth-century Franche-Comté werewolf trials:

> We have seen in England that humans are often transformed into werewolves when the moon phase changes; the Gauls call this type of people 'gerulfi', and the English 'werewolf', 'were' in English meaning a man.[40]

An involuntarily brutal wolf also appears in a tale by William of Paris (known in France as Guillaume d'Auvergne) written around 1228. The wolf, who turns out to be a human male, is delivered from his fate by a saint. The author, a theologian and Bishop of Paris, presented this as an event which had occurred only in the imagination and not in reality: William of Paris considered the story a means of conveying the message that the belief in human wolves should be renounced and that any alleged transformation took place purely in the imagination. This was fully in accordance with the church doctrine of the time, which considered animal metamorphoses impossible.[41] Werewolves were, doubtless, men but they did not exist in reality, being only figments of folkloristic imagination. Theologically, then, werewolves did not exist in the High Middle Ages.

These werewolf images – even if they had already been distorted and mythicised by the above-mentioned narratives – suggest that the concept of werewolves was probably widespread in French-speaking regions and had not only negative but also ambivalent connotations. The ostracised, the desperate: these were the people who, through betrayal and fate, were forced against their will to become beasts while maintaining their human nature and characteristics, all of which again became predominant when the spell was broken. The view was that werewolves were victims – and men. A collection of folkloristic and popular sayings published in Old French in the fifteenth century makes this quite clear: 'If it is a man's fate to become a werewolf, then it is very likely that his son will also do so. And if he has a daughter and no son, she will become a "mar", a "night mare".'[42] By creating a feeling of suffocation, spirits called 'alp' or 'mar' could, it was thought, cause bad dreams, so-called nightmares.

This lore from the popular culture of the late Middle Ages only links the werewolf paradigm to the male gender under specific circumstances. The ability to metamorphose could be bequeathed patrilineally; this explains why people believed in the existence of werewolf families. The quote from this fifteenth-century source, then, does not indicate that werewolves were always male, but does confirm that this was considered to be the case when the werewolf fate was passed down within a close family group.

There are, however, books and poems which paint a very different picture of these metamorphosing figures – as if gloom and destructivity had not yet reached them. In his sixteenth-century novel, *Gargantua und Pantagruel*, François Rabelais, a man well educated in theology, portrays the werewolf figure as a caricature devoid of any diabolical traits.[43] In 1554, the female writer, Louize Labé, mocked a depressed, somewhat unkempt, and above all, fearful aristocrat as a 'loup-garou'.[44]

By the early modern period, however, werewolves in the area of Franche-Comté were no longer victims or idealised heroes (as some of their counterparts in the Middle Ages had been), but had become real evil-doers; indeed, they were viewed as infinitely aggressive beasts and wicked monsters.[45] There was no longer anything positive to be found in them, all ambivalence had disappeared: the werewolf image had become one of perpetrator rather than victim. Yet these developments were not restricted to changes in the perception of innocence or guilt constellations. The sex-specific profiles were also subject to change: unlike in the Middle Ages, both the ordinary people and the authorities of the sixteenth and seventeenth centuries ascribed women, as well as men, aggressive roles in werewolf form.

Werewolves and wolves

One essential point which she- and he-werewolves had in common was, of course, that there was no such thing as a werewolf – they were a fabrication and a figment of the imagination.

None of the forty-four people accused in early modern Franche-Comté professed *before* the trial to being able to metamorphose into an animal; confessions were extracted in the course of the trials in situations involving mental and physical torture. In two cases, in which the accused actually spoke during the trial of magical means of transformation, the courts were unable to find any evidence. In the case of a peasant arrested in 1573, the alleged magical grease turned out to be a resource to *ward off* potential werewolf attacks.[46] In another case, in 1660, in which an old woman boasted knowledge of werewolf formulas,[47] no record of a trial has been found and it is thus conceivable that the authorities considered her statement to be mere bragging and thus did not press charges. No further material evidence was found in the homes of any of the accused although the law stipulated that house searches be carried out in such cases,[48] and the authorities in Franche-Comté adhered fairly closely to this rule. The only 'wolf's fur' found by the authorities and described by witnesses as suitable for wolf metamorphosis turned out on closer inspection to be a goat-leather coat for the cold winter.[49]

Not one of the accused, whether male or female, was ever detected actually carrying out a crime as a werewolf. Even in the well-known case of Gilles Garnier, the wolf-hunters arrested him, not as a werewolf, but as an alleged murderer who was found close to the body of a dead child.[50] Garnier confessed without being tortured, and one cannot but surmise that there might have been a real murderer concealed behind this wolf-devil. However, one of the scenes of crime was more than 60 kilometres from the hermit's dwelling and in view of his physical weakness, which seems to have been apparent at the trial, it appears very unlikely that he would have been able to cover such distances.

Zoologists characterise the true wolf as a shy animal which sees humans as enemies but not as prey. As a rule, wolves only attack humans under specific conditions, and, if they do so, they normally attack as a pack and only target children. The children most at risk are considered to be those, such as young herders, who have to spend time far from human settlements. Wolves are more likely to leave the forest and venture into land occupied by humans when suffering from rabies and when there is a chance of finding human corpses to devour.[51]

It is evident that real wolves did actually move close in to human settlements in Franche-Comté in the sixteenth and seventeenth centuries, and some of their attacks on human beings were interpreted as the work of humans in the context of a worldview which incorporated magic. Both the populace and the authorities projected real, existential and subconscious fears onto the imagined figure of the werewolf; they combated these fears by attacking and attempting to eliminate from the face of the earth this figure in which they saw the supposed cause of their misery and misfortune. An old and engrained fear and hatred of wolves gave new force to the idea of lycanthropy. This notwithstanding, there was a very real increase in the number of true wolves, and it was this which was at the core of all werewolf trials and must be viewed in the light of the specific ecological and economic conditions in the region.

Franche-Comté: ideal werewolf country

The werewolf panics and the comparatively large numbers of werewolf trials in Franche-Comté represent a relatively unique phenomenon in Europe, with the exception of Latvia and Estonia.[52] In other regions, legal cases against alleged werewolves were rarely anything more than isolated and individual cases, mainly targeting men. This raises the question as to why this particular area saw more persecution than others and why this persecution also involved women.

From 1548 to 1678 Franche-Comté was formally a part of the Holy Roman Empire and formed part of the Burgundian Circle of the Empire. From 1598 onwards, however, the region was ruled by an Archduke from Brussels as part of the Spanish Netherlands. Nonetheless, Franche-Comté remained politically independent and neither were the inhabitants Spanish, under Philip II, nor were they German, under Charles V.[53] Culturally, this land with its 400,000 inhabitants was French; politically, it was classic border country uniting aspects of each of the two states' organisation. The norms of the Carolina, the Imperial Penal Code, influenced jurisdiction in Franche-Comté; however, the judicature, the 'Parlement', resembled French institutions.[54]

Dense forests are still a typical feature of the landscape in Franche-Comté today. In 1590, the chronicler Gollut wrote, in Besançon, that it was possible to 'traverse the entire county under trees'.[55] With the exception of the Doubs valley, the fertility of the soil was so low that only marginal cultivation of the land was possible, and only small and undemanding animals could be kept as livestock; most of the population lived from wood felling, with willow culture playing an important role.[56] In all parts of the county other than the valley of the Doubs, sheep farming was a major source of income, in contrast to most other regions of Central Europe where livestock farming did not play a central role in this period of history.[57] Mountains, forests, low population density in many areas of the territory and a large number of sheep as ideal prey made this a suitable habitat for wild animals, and in particular for wolves. Given these conditions, it is not surprising that werewolf trials also became a part of the witch-hunts in Franche-Comté; due to the large numbers of real wolves and the threat they posed to the local population and their livelihood, people came to identify these animals with the evil of harmful magic. The type of harmful magic conjectured depended on the ecological and economic structure of the respective region. The intensified persecution of werewolves as well as of witches and male witches must be viewed in conjunction with a weakening of the economy from 1590 onwards. Heavy production losses heralded the crisis of the seventeenth century and were the cause of high corn prices in Burgundy and other areas and, to make matters worse, were accompanied in the Alpine regions by long winters and cold summers.[58]

However, these objective factors still do not explain the frequency of werewolf prosecutions in Franche-Comté, since they also applied to other

French-speaking regions such as the Massif Central or the Cevennes, in which the imagined human wolf played a less prominent role. Only by looking into the mentalities, i.e. the subjective factors, can an explanation be proffered. Many bodies of authority viewed Franche-Comté as an outpost of Catholicism which it was necessary to defend, bordering as it did on Protestant territories to the north and east. From the middle of the sixteenth century onwards there was a strong Counter-Reformation movement which fought against all kinds of real or supposed heresies.[59] This grew in strength under Albert of Austria after 1589.

The goal of this new policy was to enhance and strengthen Catholic teachings among laypeople and also among the clergy through the introduction of new orders to the country. At Albert's insistence, Jesuits, Capuchins, Carmelites and Ursulines set up nearly fifty new monasteries in Franche-Comté. These orders supported the rulers' desired programme of new religious and denominational control. This 'renaissance catholique'[60] went hand-in-hand with early modern social disciplining – as expressed by a plaque which the sovereign ordered to be prominently placed in the town hall of Besançon: 'Foelicitatis Obedientia mater' – obedience (or subservience) is the mother of happiness.[61]

The fight against heresy was directed against all kinds of supposedly anti-Catholic deviations, such as those of which the humanist scholar, Gilbert Cousin, who died in prison in 1572, was accused. The political offensive was also aimed at people such as vagabonds and prostitutes whose behaviour the authorities characterised as anti-Christian.[62] This social control is evidenced in the court records in which deficiencies in Catholic faith, premarital sexual relations or material poverty all triggered initial suspicions among the public prosecutors. The authorities perceived anti-Christian groups, as represented by werewolves and witches, to be the centre of organised crime in the early modern era. They believed that the danger of these supposed secret societies lay not only in their capacity to harm humans and animals but also in their involvement in a global conspiracy; werewolves and witches, thus the belief of the time, were not an open force living outside of society but worked secretly and in disguise in the towns and villages, unrecognised and consciously destructive.

Supported by the theories of Catholic authors such as Jean Bodin,[63] and later Henri Boguet, the Franche-Comté authorities truly believed up until the first third of the seventeenth century in the transformation of humans into wolves, and called for the persecution of werewolves and of male and female witches. The edicts and judgments passed by the 'Parlement' right up until the middle of the seventeenth century are living proof of this attitude. The witch image, which viewed witches as primarily female, merged with the werewolf paradigm. This merging of the female witch and the human wolf, conceived in the Middle Ages as two distinct magical figures, brought with it a change in the gender profiles. The one-gender nature of the werewolf in medieval literature and lore became increasingly dual-gender the more rampant the witch persecutions in the region became.

However, werewolf persecution did not ensue from the culture of the elite but had been established in the region for a long time, as Judge Boguet remarked in his demonological work.[64] The concept of *maleficium* in the form of lycanthropy or of witchcraft was widespread amongst the general population. This was reflected in the accusations made by many of the victims and witnesses, as the trials show. The initiative to pursue and prosecute alleged werewolves did not only come from above, as in Sainte-Claude, but also from below.

It is hardly surprising, then, that the biological sex of the accused was no longer of interest in pursuing charges and court cases. The focus was on the harm caused by the werewolves as well as on the injuring party as a person, regardless of this person's sex. In numerous cases, the charge was gender neutral and listed in connection with heresy and norm deviance in the verdicts.[65]

The fight against female and male witches, as against werewolves, can be seen as an integration ideology which united the authorities and populace. Numerous women in Franche-Comté became victims of this view of the world; for them, these were not early modern times, but rather a modern Dark Ages.

Notes

1 Henri Boguet, *Discours execrable des sorciers: ensemble leur proces, faits depuis 2 ans en ça, en divers endroicts de France* (Paris: D. Binet, 1603), 119–20.
2 There are numerous descriptions of this incident on websites on werewolf portals or set up by private users fascinated by the werewolf idea; these frequently contain false information. Even Montague Summers's well-known work contains contradictory and not logically comprehensible details. See Montague Summers, *The Werewolf* (London: K. Paul, 1933), 122, 229. Furthermore, the translations by this self-appointed magic expert are flawed and should no longer be used. See Rolf Schulte, *Man as Witch: Male Witches in Central Europe* (Basingstoke: Palgrave Macmillan, 2009), 94, 277. The above description was penned by the judge in Nezan, Henri Boguet, who, though not present at the trial, had heard witnesses. The basic details Boguet gives of other trials in the region are, by and large, in keeping with some of the information still available in the records of the Sainte-Claude court today. Boguet's presentation of the court cases, the confessions and the verdicts seem on the whole to be credible. See Francis Bavoux, *Les procès inédits de Boguet en matière de sorcellerie dans la grande judicature de Saint-Claude, XVIe–XVIIe siècles* (Dijon: Impr. Bernigaud et Privat, 1958), 16–20. Nonetheless, his interpretations are untenable, unfounded and unacceptable. The records available today for the trial of Perrenette Gandillon's nephew, Georges Gandillon, in which he seriously incriminates his aunt as a she-werewolf and accuses her of being the prime perpetrator, do not contradict Boguet's account of the events in Nezan in 1598. See Sentence des échevins contre Georges Gandillon

vom 24. April 1599, Archives Municipales (henceforth AM) Sainte-Claude, Reg. 26/43 (1599).
3   For the trials, see also Caroline Oates, 'Metamorphosis and Lycanthropy in Franche-Comté, 1521–1643', in M. Feher (ed.), *Fragments for a History of the Human Body: Part One* (New York: Zone, 1989), 305–63. This excellent essay deals with several, but not all of the trials. Another study also deals with some of the trials: Brigitte Rochelandet, *Sorcières, diables et bûchers en Franche-Comté aux XVIe et XVIIe siècles* (Besançon: Cêtre, 1997), 143–51.
4   Wolves are skilled masters of long distances and can run up to 200 km a day; see Erik Zimen, *Der Wolf: Mythos und Verhalten* (Vienna: Meyster, 1978), 196.
5   AM Sainte-Claude Reg. 26/27 (1598); Boguet, *Discours execrable des sorciers*, 25, 109, 123, 127.
6   Boguet, *Discours execrable des sorciers*, 21, 28–30, 71, 111, 121–3, 127, 135. The files for this trial can no longer be traced in the archives of Sainte-Claude.
7   AM Sainte-Claude Reg. 26/43 (1599); Boguet, *Discours execrable des sorciers*, 110–12.
8   Archives Départementales du Doubs (henceforth: ADD), Besançon, France, 2 B 1285 and 10 F 54.
9   Lucien Febvre, *Notes et documents sur la Réforme et l'Inquisition en Franche-Comté* (Paris: Champion, 1912), 25–6.
10 ADD 10 F 54.
11 Testimony of Ludwig Geizkofler (1573), ADD 10 F 42.
12 Edict of the 'Parlement' (1573), ADD 10 F 42.
13 ADD 10 F 42.
14 ADD 2 B 2437; ADD 10 F 42; ADD 10 F 54.
15 ADD 2 B 2465/77.
16 ADD 2 B 2464.
17 ADD 2 B 2465/77.
18 ADD 2 B 2994/90.
19 ADD 10 F 42.
20 Lisa Silverman, *Tortured Subjects: Pain, Truth, and the Body in Early Modern France* (Chicago: University of Chicago Press, 2001); Peter Burschel, Götz Distelrath and Sven Lembke (eds), *Das Quälen des Körpers: eine historische Anthropologie der Folter* (Cologne: Böhlau, 2000).
21 Archives Départementales de Haute Saône, Vesoul, France, B 5049/50.
22 ADD F 10 and F 42.
23 ADD 2 B 3200.
24 ADD F 16, 25, 42.
25 For wording of the Edict, see ADD 10 F 42.
26 Francis Bavoux, 'Les loups-garous en Franche-Comté', *Heures Comtoises* 4 (1952): 3–8.
27 ADD B 3484.
28 ADD 2 B 2515; ADD 2B 1156.
29 Letter of the 'Chambre du parlement', ADD 2 B/2519.
30 Brigitte Rochelandet, *Monstres et merveilles de Franche-Comté: fées, fantômes et dragons* (Yens sur Morges: Cabédita Editions, 2003), 41–51.
31 For Franche-Comté, see Schulte, *Man as Witch*, 31–2, 47, 82–3; Rochelandet, *Sorcières, diables et bûchers*, 75–91.

32 For example, see Charlotte F. Otten, *A Lycanthropy Reader: Werewolves in Western Culture* (Syracuse, NY: Syracuse University Press, 1986), 51.
33 For accusations against Burgot and Verdun, see Jean Bodin (Angevin), *De la démonomanie des sorciers* (Paris: du Puys, 1580), 96; for Garnier, see *Arrest mémorable de la cour de Parlement de Dole, donné à l'encontre de Gilles Garnier* (Lyon: B. Rigaud, 1574); for Verjux, see ADD 2B 2271.
34 Boguet, *Discours execrable des sorciers*, 103.
35 Emmanuelle Baumgartner and Philippe Ménard, *Dictionnaire étymologique de la langue française* (Paris: Lib. Générale Française, 1997), 352, 456; Jean Dubois, *Dictionnaire étymologique et historique* (Paris: Larousse, 1993), 331.
36 With the exception of the 'Werewolves of Ossory' the male werewolf also dominates in the English-language literature of the Middle Ages. See Leslie A. Sconduto, *Metamorphoses of the Werewolf: A Literary Study from Antiquity through the Renaissance* (Jefferson, NC: McFarland and Co., 2008), 26–38.
37 W. Hertz, *Der Werwolf: ein Beitrag zur Sagengeschichte* (Stuttgart: A. Kröner, 1862), 65.
38 Manfred Bambeck, *Wiesel und Werwolf* (Stuttgart: Steiner, 1990), 57–9.
39 Gervasius von Tilbury, *Otia Imperialia*, ed. Felix Liebknecht (Hannover, 1856), liber III, 120; Philippe Ménard, 'Histoires de loups-garous', in Madeleine Bertaud (ed.), *Les Grandes Peurs* (Geneva: Droz, 2003), vol. II, 106, 110–13.
40 *Ibid.*, liber I, 15, 4, my translation (with Linda Froome-Döring).
41 Guillaume d'Auvergne, *De Universo*, quoted in L. Harf-Lancner, 'La métamorphose illusoire: des théories chrétiennes de la métamorphose aux images médiévales du loup-garou', *Annales E.S.P.* 40 (1985): 208–26 (214).
42 'Les evangiles de Quenouilles', quoted in Claude Lecouteux, *Fées, sorcières et loup-garous au Moyen Age* (Paris: Imago, 1992), 118, my translation.
43 François Rabelais, *Gargantua und Pantagruel* (Lyon, 1534), bk. II, ch. 29, s., http://ebooks.adelaide.edu.au/ rabelais/francois/r11g/. Accessed 4 November 2010.
44 Louize Labé, *Débat de Folie et d'Amour* (Lyon, 1554), discours 5, *Bibliotheca Augustana*, http://www.hs-augsburg.de/~harsch/gallica/Chronologie/16siecle/Labe/lab_deb5.html. Accessed 2 November 2010.
45 Sconduto. *Metamorphoses of the Werewolf*, 1, 3–4, 138. In view of the fact that their aggressive acts are ignored, it is arguable whether or not all the medieval werewolves described by Sconduto can be considered heroes.
46 Francis Bavoux, 'Loups-garous de Franche-Comté: identification d'un refuge et observations sur le cas Gilles Garnier', *Nouvelle revue Franc-Comtoise* 1(1954): 48.
47 Trial in 1660 of Renoberte Simon who described a woman as a master in the presence of witnesses: ADD 2B 2515.
48 Carolina: Die peinliche Gerichtsordnung Kaiser Karl V. von 1532 (the Imperial Penal Code) § 52.
49 Trial of Renobert Bardel in 1657, ADD B15940; ADD F 42.
50 *Arrest mémorable … de Gilles Garnier,* 5. See also Oates, 'Metamorphosis and Lycanthropy', 339.
51 Norsk institutt for naturforskning (ed.), 'The Fear of Wolves: a Review of Wolf Attacks on Humans' (Trondheim, 2002), 2, http://skandulv.nina.no/skandulv%20new/Publikasjoner/English%20pdf%20files/NINAOM731.pdf. Accessed 7 July 2010; Erik Zimen, *Der Wolf: Verhalten, Ökologie und Mythos* (Vienna: Meyster, 1997), 400, 411; Alain Molonier and Nicole Molonier-Meyer,

'Environnement et historie: les loups et l'homme en France', *Revue d'histoire moderne et contemporaine* 18 (1981): 225–45 (231).

52 Maia Madar, 'Estonia I: Werewolves and Poisoners', in Bengt Ankarloo and Gustav Henningsen (eds), *Early Modern Witchcraft: Centres and Peripheries* (Oxford: Clarendon Press, 1990), 257–72; Schulte, *Man as Witch*, 32; Robin Briggs, 'Dangerous Spirits: Shapeshifting, Apparitions, and Fantasy in Lorraine Witchcraft Trials', in Katherine A. Edwards (ed.), *Werewolves, Witches and Wandering Spirits: Traditional Belief and Folklore in Early Modern Europe* (Kirksville, MO: Truman State University Press, 2002), 1–24 (6); Peter Dinzelbacher, 'Lycanthropy', in Richard M. Golden (ed.), *Encyclopedia of Witchcraft: The Western Tradition*, vol. III (Santa Barbara, CA: ABC-Clio, 2006), 681; William Monter, *Witchcraft in France and Switzerland: the Borderlands During the Reformation* (Ithaca, NY: Cornell University Press, 1976), 147.

53 Lucien Febvre, *Histoire de Franche-Comté* (Paris: Boivin 1922), 161.

54 Monter, *Witchcraft in France and Switzerland*, 67, 195.

55 F. Gollut (1590), quoted in Febvre, *Histoire de Franche-Comté*, 162.

56 Febvre, *Histoire de Franche-Comté*, 163.

57 Slicher van Bath, 'Agriculture in the Vital Revolution', in E.E. Rich and C.H. Wilson (eds), *The Cambridge Economic History*, vol. V (Cambridge: Cambridge University Press, 1977), 90.

58 Paul Delsalle, *La Franche-Comté au temps des Archeducs Albert et Isabelle 1598–1633* (Besançon: Presses Universitaires Franc-Comtoises, 2002), 16–20; M. Morineau, 'La conjuncture ou les cernes de la croissance', in E. Le Roy Ladurie and M. Morineau (eds), *Historie economique et sociale de la France, tome 1, de 1450–1660* (Paris: Presses Universitaires de France, 1977), 950–5.

59 Lucien Febvre, *Phillippe II. et la Franche-Comté* (Paris: Les Editions Flammarion, 1970), 330–49, 370, 403, 428–36.

60 Febvre, *Histoire de Franche-Comté*, 194; Delsalle, *La Franche-Comté au temps des Archeducs Albert et Isabelle*, 16.

61 Febvre, *Histoire de Franche-Comté*, 194.

62 Paul Delsalle, *La Franche-Comté à la charnière du Moyen Age et de la Renaissance* (Besançon: Presses Universitaires Franc-Comtoises, 2003) 208–24.

63 Bodin, *De la démonomanie des sorciers*, 94–104.

64 Boguet, *Discours execrable des sorciers*, 113.

65 Willem de Blécourt is thus justified in suggesting that werewolves should no longer be viewed in terms of contemporary male and female roles, for the charge was one of bestiality. For de Blécourt, werewolves constitute an 'animal gender'. See Willem de Blécourt, 'The Werewolf, the Witch, the Warlock: Aspects of Gender in the Early Modern Period', in Alison Rowlands (ed.), *Witchcraft and Masculinities in Early Modern Europe* (Basingstoke: Palgrave Macmillan, 2009), 191–213 (208).

4
Participatory lycanthropy: female werewolves in *Werewolf: The Apocalypse*

Jay Cate

Werewolf: The Apocalypse is a table-top role-playing game (RPG), published by White Wolf in 1992. Gameplay is based on a core rulebook (which may be augmented by additional published material), used by a gamemaster or 'storyteller' to devise fictional worlds, scenarios and characters with which player-created characters interact; character creation and interaction is, in part, determined by dice rolls and game rules, and may take the form of combat, acts of magic, social or economic transaction and character development.[1] Play is a group activity and episodic in nature, with individual sessions (involving a coherent and consistent group of players) combining over time to make a game. Daniel Mackay describes the structure of RPGs thus:

> [They are] an *episodic* and *participatory* story-creation *system* that includes a set of quantified *rules* that assist a group of *players* and a *gamemaster* in determining how their fictional *characters'* spontaneous interactions are resolved. These performed interactions between the players' and the gamemasters' characters take place during individual *sessions* that, together, form *episodes* or adventures in the lives of the fictional characters. ... [T]he episodes become part of a single grand story that I call the role-playing game *narrative*.[2]

As Mackay's outline suggests, performance and participation are key factors in the creation of a game's story. While rules are 'quantified', interactions are 'spontaneous'. Moreover, as Dennis Waskul and Matt Lust have argued, this combination of the quantifiable and the spontaneous is complicated by the fact that outcomes within the game 'are always subject to indeterminate probabilities that are also mediated by the roll of dice'.[3]

This chapter will explore the content of an RPG by White Wolf Publishing – one of the games in their World of Darkness series – and examine the role and presentation of the female werewolf within this game. However, as the above overview indicates, this is a problematic undertaking for a number of reasons and requires some introduction.

Narrative in RPGs

When beginning a critical analysis of an RPG, the first – and most pressing – question relates to the object of study itself: what, exactly, is under examination? Studies of RPGs to date have tended to take a sociological or pedagogical approach, with gameplay itself being the primary subject of the analysis, using theorisations of ludic interaction to illuminate the interplay between fantasy, socialisation and social development within the RPG gaming environment.[4] In recent years, the phenomenon of gaming as cultural production has been some critics' concern – an approach which may also consider the maintenance of a particular game's identity, gaming fandoms or the interactions of players with game publishers.[5] What is rarely undertaken, however, is an exploration of a game's narrative, an approach that will be taken in this chapter.

Identifying an RPG's 'narrative', at first glance, seems like an impossible task. As noted by Mackay, an RPG is best understood as a 'story-creation system', which is both 'episodic' and 'participatory'. In Mackay's formulation, a game's 'narrative' exists only through gameplay itself, as performed episodes combine to form a 'single grand story'. Dennis Waskul and Matt Lust similarly point the unpredictability of a game's 'story', describing it as 'an ongoing coauthored narrative' (where the authors are any group of individuals who choose to play the game, at any time and in any setting); for this reason, RPG narrative might be likened to 'discursive impromptu acting'.[6]

Nevertheless, while the 'authors' of a particular game's story are indeterminate – they could comprise anyone who chooses to play the game – and the scenes that move the story forward are the combination of participatory imaginative creation, spontaneous interaction and random chance, there are elements of narrative in RPGs that are easier to define, and which remain (more or less) consistent across gameplay.

The core rulebook for *Werewolf: The Apocalypse* outlines the gaming rules that are to be used for this particular RPG. This includes instructions for character creation and tables of dice scores required to perform particular actions. They also outline the 'world' in which games will take place. 'World', here, should be understood as different to 'setting'; the former is the overarching explanation of existence common to all gameplay, the latter a localised and specific element of an individual game's play (which is determined by an individual gamemaster). This 'world-building' not only explains 'established religious, social and political institutions' that will impact on the creation of setting, but also the 'mood' and 'atmosphere' that will be reflected in story creation.[7] Anecdotal evidence suggests that these 'world' rules are sometimes interpreted rather loosely by players; nevertheless, these rules are a consistent – albeit interpretative – feature of all gameplay. As such, this chapter will focus on narrative elements outlined in the corebook for the game under consideration – particularly the way in which this book constructs ontologies, taxonomies and histories of werewolves.

The second clarification required in this introduction relates to the identification of 'female' werewolves within *Werewolf: The Apocalypse*. As is revealed by the explanations of gameplay above, RPG story creation is a participatory activity, determined by the interaction of players. Character creation is inseparable from this. There are, as yet, no definitive studies of RPG demographics; work that has been done in this area has tended to be localised (either in terms of particular gaming groups or particular game systems) and testimonial.[8]

If one compares RPGs to other contemporary gaming activities, this reliance on player testimony is understandable. For example, recent studies suggest that women make up around 45 per cent of computer game players.[9] However, if one considers the way in which a player engages with a computer game – even a massively multiplayer online role-playing game (MMORG) like *World of Warcraft* – an important difference is revealed. Game piracy notwithstanding, playing a computer game requires a purchase or registration on the part of an individual. Participation in a table-top RPG does not require a player to identify themselves as an individual within an economic transaction prior to playing, and so it is far harder to determine who, exactly, is playing these games.[10] Thus, at the time of writing, understandings of the gender of RPG players rely heavily on anecdotal evidence and a group's community visibility (particularly in internet communities and gaming conventions). Such evidence suggests that RPGs are primarily played by male players, and that most choose to play as male characters.[11]

How, then, can we speak of 'female werewolves' in stories that may well have no female characters? This chapter suggests that the corebook for *Werewolf: The Apocalypse* not only allows such discussion to be possible, but also integrates tropes of femininity and femaleness into a construction of lycanthropy in a uniquely sustained and complex way. Regardless of individual story and character creation, the narratives of this particular RPG posit an undeniable relationship between werewolves and femininity that both draws on and subverts the tropes of each category.

The World of Darkness

The World of Darkness games were introduced in 1991 with the publication of *Vampire: The Masquerade*. The games make use of the 'storyteller system' of gameplay, and take place in the eponymous 'world' of the series title.[12] The games are divided into two sub-series: 'classic' World of Darkness (to which *Werewolf: The Apocalypse* belongs) and 'new' World of Darkness (a later sub-series). As noted above, the corebook for *Apocalypse* offers guidance for players on the mechanics of the gameplay system, but also introduces the idiosyncratic 'classic World of Darkness' in which games are expected to take place:

> *Werewolf* is set in a Gothic-Punk world – a World of Darkness. Externally, little differs between our world and this World of Darkness – the established religious, social and political institutions are much like those of our own planet. The World of Darkness, however, is a *film noir* environment – the cities are labyrinthine and gloomy, the bureaucrats are corrupt, and the important people have skeletons in their closets. ... The counterculture of the cities, sick of the oppressive physical and social tableau, rebel with words, dress, music and often violence.[13]

The 'Gothic-Punk' aesthetic of the classic World of Darkness can be recognised as a significant departure from earlier RPG worlds. It differs greatly, for instance, from the faux-medieval setting of the Dungeons and Dragons system, which has been described as 'a fantasy world ... that chaos that comes when civilization has collapsed, a parenthesis open to the rule of violence (and to the imperative of using it first); an outlet for the release of irrationality'.[14] In contrast, Rachel Mizsei Ward (referring specifically to *Vampire: The Masquerade*) suggests that White Wolf's 'Gothic themes of vampires, romance and politicking are ... of more interest to female players, with *World of Darkness* games often having more female players than other settings'.[15]

While the problem of verifying the numbers of female players remains, Ward's claim that the 'Gothic themes' of the World of Darkness might be 'of more interest to female players' is an interesting one. The Gothic mode is one that has been frequently associated with female audiences since its inception. In aligning the world of their games with the Gothic, it is not unreasonable to suggest that White Wolf are implying a more 'feminine' setting than the conventional medieval RPG worlds with their 'rule of violence'.

Nevertheless, this distinction between World of Darkness's 'feminine' Gothic and Dungeons and Dragons' 'masculine' medieval is, arguably, a superficial one, which relies upon (and reinforces) gender stereotypes and generalisations. In order to refine the argument for World of Darkness's difference, it is important to consider the nuances and specifics of the 'Gothic-Punk' world. And, for the purposes of our argument here, it is important to consider the inhabitants of the world.

While the World of Darkness as a series contains many different types of being, *Apocalypse* focuses specifically on werewolves, and players are encouraged to select from different types of werewolves when creating their characters (though it is possible to play as races from other World of Darkness games). Of course, a werewolf can (and does) mean different things to different people; thus, the *Apocalypse* corebook begins by introducing and outlining what a 'werewolf' is in this particular context.

Beyond the wolf man

Significantly, the corebook does not begin with either an ontology or a taxonomy, but rather a narrative, which gives a clear indication, not only of how werewolves are to be understood in the game, but also how layers of gendering will intersect with this. In the comic that opens the book, and which sets out some of the game's backstory, the combination of 'masculine' and 'feminine' stories is clear, as is the way the game will merge tropes from different genres and narratives of the werewolf.

The first of Tony Diterlizzi's illustrations is of an older (presumably male) figure, whose long hair – dressed with a feather – and necklaces code him as a Native American tribal leader (i). However, this is immediately contrasted with the appearance of the narrative's protagonist, Evan, which references tropes of twentieth-century horror cinema, particularly films including male werewolves. Evan wakes up at night in a strange place, with torn clothes and a feeling of dread. 'Not again ...' he states, before offering more information: 'The dreams ... the wolves ... and these scratches – what's going on?' (ii) If this scenario is not familiar enough to reader-players, when Evan returns home he finds his father reading a newspaper with headline: 'Wolf Man Spotted!' (ii)

The 'Wolf Man' paradigm of lycanthropy is, perhaps, the most 'masculine' a werewolf story can be. Early examples of this paradigm can be found in medieval literature, in texts such as *Bisclavret* and *Guillaume de Palerne*; it appears as the dominant form of lycanthropy in twentieth-century cinema, in films such as *The Wolf Man* and *An American Werewolf in London*. In such narratives a man – singular – is forced to undergo involuntary transformation, becoming a feral beast at odds with his civilised, human self. He prowls as a solitary animal, separated from the homosocial bonds that would otherwise have confirmed his identity, but retains some redeeming 'human' quality (nobility in earlier texts, guilt or remorse in later ones) that allows him to eventually reintegrate with his former community. As other chapters in this collection reveal, it is rare for this paradigm of lycanthropy to be used in texts concerned with female werewolves.

However, while the opening of Evan's narrative in the *Apocalypse* corebook relies on a familiarity with the Wolf Man paradigm, this is undermined by the large illustration that precedes the introduction of the protagonist. The image of the Native American tribal leader hints at a different model of lycanthropy, with different gendered expectations. As noted, the figure in the first illustration appears to be male, but the racial coding employed serves to differentiate this figure's masculinity (and, one assumes, lycanthropy) from that of Evan, his father and the 'Wolf Man' of the newspaper headline.

As has been argued by numerous scholars, in Anglo-American cultural productions, juxtaposition of white and Native masculinities often serve to validate 'virulent Anglo manhood while in turn rendering Indians "feminine" through their submission'.[16] Moreover, associations of Native Americans with werewolves, reasonably common since the nineteenth century, have tended to present Native lycanthropes as pack-based (rather than solitary), aligned with nature (rather than representative of an involuntary split with civilisation) and spiritually potent (rather than guilt-ridden). From a Euro-

American perspective, these associations point to the 'feminine': a connection to family, nature and interiority being common tropes of femininity, in distinction to the traits of individuality, civilisation and violence characteristic of masculinity.

It may be something of a stretch to argue that this cultural history is conveyed in any real depth through the juxtaposition of the images on the first two pages of the book; however, this contrast is fundamental to the overall development of werewolf ontology in the *Apocalypse* corebook, and also has implications for character development and gameplay. However, it is important to note that this is not a simple differentiation of models of lycanthropy based on racial contrast: the World of Darkness is constructed through more complex layers of tradition, narrative and implication. This can be demonstrated by further analysis of the corebook's initial 'backstory'.

As the short graphic narrative progresses, Evan is confronted by monstrous werewolves who kill his parents and encourage him towards violence. However, he is rescued from these monsters by a man who describes himself as 'Lord Albrecht, Silver Fang Scion of the House of Wyrmfoe, Grandchild of King Morningkill' (vii). At this point, the narrative changes from a Wolf Man story of a single man afflicted by a terrible curse, to one that incorporates a history, a genealogy, a mythology and – most significantly – tribal identities, all of which are highlighted by Albrecht's somewhat verbose nomenclature. On the following page, the word 'Garou' is introduced as an alternative to 'werewolf' – taking the reader-player further away from the cinematic productions of the twentieth century, and hinting at an older history for these beings – and this is followed by a strip of four panels drawn in a pseudo-woodcut style (contrasting with the contemporary graphic art of the rest of the comic) offering a succinct history of the Garou (viii). The first of these panels states: 'We were Gaia's chosen, gifted with the power to defend the earth from her foes.' Following this, Albrecht introduces the main 'foe' that the Garou face: the Wyrm. The Wyrm is a primordial force of destruction, which highlights the consistent environmental message behind the in-game mythology; for instance, Albrecht explains to Evan: 'That oil spill on TV, that was no coincidence. It was the Wyrm's doing.' (viii)[17] While Albrecht's European name and epithets superficially distance him from the image of the tribal elder that opened the narrative, his alignment with the natural world, spirituality and group-based (rather than individual) identity connect the two men, and further distance the reader-player from the Wolf Man paradigm of lycanthropy.

The next werewolf Evan is introduced to is female. Mari is first depicted wearing boxing gloves and hitting a punchbag. She is angry, has a short, punky haircut, multiple earrings and a spiked collar. The illustration of Mari is the first of several verbal and visual illustrations of female werewolves in the corebook, all of which make use of a similar blending of undeniable 'femaleness' with defensive aggression, confrontation and brute strength. For instance, one image depicts a huge humanoid wolf with snarling face and vicious claws, next to a large-breasted woman wearing a barely-there leather bikini, long hair and knee-high boots and holding a bow and arrow (20). At first glance, this appears to be a rather conventional piece of fantasy art, juxtaposing an implausibly dressed and anatomically suspect female with a vast and threatening monster. However, more careful attention reveals that the wolf and the woman are wearing the same headband and bracelets; the implication, therefore, is that they are two forms of the same person.

Mari's first response to meeting Evan and Albrecht is aggression towards the latter, but she immediately softens when she hears that Evan is 'a lost cub' (x). They are then attacked, and Evan is told to 'step sideways ... into the spirit world' (x). Evan loses his male companion when he enters the spirit world, but is accompanied by Mari. Her appearance is now subtly different – most notably, her eyes are rounder and her hair has softened into a short bob (xii). She introduces Evan to the 'Weaver, who wants to trap the world in her pattern web' and 'the Wyld', a kind of embodiment of nature at its most primordial (xiii). She explains that the 'Wyrm' was once a force of balance, but was caught in the 'Weaver's insane web' and now seeks to destroy Gaia (xii). Thus, the comic sets up the opposing deific forces – the Weaver and Gaia – as female, with the concomitant feminine tropes of maternity and madness being stressed. Evan questions Mari about Gaia, asking if she is the 'Earth Mother', and Mari replies that she 'is more than that, child. She is your mother. She is mother to us all.' (xii) Mari also encourages Evan to change into a wolf, telling him that his human form 'is but one of many' (xii), echoing shamanistic depictions of shape-shifting and lycanthropy.

This narrative is a reader-player's first introduction to the world of *Apocalypse*. This 'world' is continually reaffirmed throughout the corebook; it is elaborated on in further short narrative passages, and reflected through the rules for gameplay. For example, the comic is followed by another narrative, in which a Garou named Brian is introduced to the history of his kind by 'an old Native American man crouched over a woodstove' (4), and a short piece entitled 'The Prophecy of the Phoenix' explains that 'the endless disasters of the humans ... are destroying the Mother's every organ; now she shakes in agony and rage, vomiting ashes into the sky' (17). The werewolves of *Apocalypse* exist in a world predicated on feminised narrative tropes of spirituality and pseudo-Native shamanism, deification of female creation, and rejection of a masculinised anthropocentrism.

The Garou in gameplay

Players are encouraged to be familiar with this world-building backstory. However, in practice, this familiarity may be mediated through the gamemaster, who has the creative freedom to utilise or ignore aspects of the corebook's 'history' as befits the particular game being played. A game player may not have read the corebook in its entirety, but this would not prevent full participation in story-creation if salient points of history and ontology are presented by the gamemaster prior to play. Therefore, in order to determine the extent to which the werewolves in *Apocalypse* are feminised, it is also important to consider how this narrative introduction to the World of Darkness is continued through the gaming rules, and the specific narrative constraints that are put on story and character creation.

Once a gamemaster has designed a setting and loose narrative for a game, players must 'create' the characters they will role-play during sessions. There are ten tribes from which a player can choose when creating a character. Each of these tribes echoes a 'type' of being from folkloric, literary or mythological traditions, though these traditions may have little to do with werewolves. For example, the 'Fianna' tribe draw inspiration from the Celtic *daoine sidhe* (and are described in the corebook as '[l]ong-time allies and friends' of the 'faeries' (259); the 'Get of Fenris' are modelled on the Norse berserker tradition, though this is combined with modern European history in that some 'have embraced the racist Aryan-supremacy ideal' (95).

The *Apocalypse* corebook is at pains to avoid gendering the imagined player. Throughout the book third-person singular pronouns switch between feminine and masculine for the presumed player (and, by extension, character). Nevertheless, there are subtle points that reveal gender assumptions. For instance, the table of dice-rolls to determine 'battle scars' explains that a score of eleven results in an injury named 'Ahem …': 'Because of … er, extensive injuries, you are, if male, unable to sire children, and both your Charisma and Manipulation are reduced by one when you speak aloud.' (199) The book offers no equivalent 'battle scar' for a female player-character who rolls a score of eleven. Similarly, the description of the Get of Fenris tribe indicates that they 'are consummate chauvinists, however, and sneer at "civil rights" and "empowerment"' (95), closing down the possibility of playing a Get character as female or non-white.

Interestingly, though, *Apocalypse* offers a counterpoint to the assumption of male identity in the form of the Black Furies, a tribe 'composed almost entirely of female Garou' (92). Naturally, of all the tribes in the game, the Black Furies represent the most sustained blending of tropes of lycanthropy with tropes of femininity and draw on classical traditions in order to do this. Firstly, the tribe's name references the Erinyes or Furies of myth; secondly, they claim an affiliation with 'Luna, in her aspect as Artemis the Huntress' and a descent from 'she-wolves' (92); finally, the Black Furies 'give away or kill their male children' (92), in an echo of various narratives of the Amazons. The Black Furies are also associated with a particular form of female violence found in classical traditions – they are the protectors and avengers of the Wyld, dwell in 'the deepest wilderness' and fight 'against any insult to women, nature or the Goddess' (92). What is apparent in the presentation of the Black Furies is the way in which *Apocalypse* constructs werewolves, not only through various traditions and narratives of lycanthropy, but also by combining this with various other types and archetypes from across (mainly European) history and culture.

The Get of Fenris and Black Fury tribes are the only two choices a player can make that (implicitly or explicitly) determine the gender of the character they are playing. Similarly, though certain auspices (castes, which are also selected by players during character creation) may imply a conventionally 'masculine' or 'feminine' role within the tribe – for instance, the 'Ahroun' caste is that of a warrior, whereas the 'Theurge' is the spiritual intercessor – there are no limitations placed on the gender of characters within them. The initial implication of this lack of gendered constraint is that, despite the emphasis on the feminine (and the feminised) in the world's backstory, there is nothing to prevent a player purely drawing on tropes, ideals and stereotypes of masculinity: a lupine member of the Get of Fenris with Ahroun auspice, for instance, would potentially combine an animalistic nature with chauvinistic beliefs and a berserker-esque warrior role. However, while such combinations can be (and are) played with satisfaction in *Apocalypse*, the overarching game rules mediate the extremities of such masculinisation, and, I argue, offer an insistent, though implicit, feminisation of *all* werewolf characters, regardless of breed, tribe or auspice.

While few constraints are placed on player choice in character creation (aside from the predetermined categories from which such choice can be made), overall gameplay *does* place implicit limitations on behaviour and interaction. These limitations are fundamentally related to the narrative of the game, and reflect the concerns of the corebook's backstories.

The first limitation that is placed on character development and behaviour is that an individual must – except in unusual circumstances, which are possible (but discouraged) according to the core rules of the game – belong to a pack, a group of werewolves (usually of different tribes) who have joined together to travel, work and fight as a coherent social unit. Moreover, they must be a functioning member of that pack. The corebook's chapter on 'setting' makes it clear that this is an inescapable facet of werewolf identity within the World of Darkness: 'Garou tend to think of themselves in communal terms, and they thus realise that most creatures have some sort of contribution to make toward the whole' (34). This is confirmed in the practical instructions for character creation in the following chapter:

> It is your responsibility to create a character who fits into the group. If you fail to cooperate with the others and disrupt the story because of it, you will have to create a new character. Life as a werewolf is far too difficult for animosity to exist within a pack; sometimes survival itself depends on pack members' ability to work together. (74)

This instruction is, of course, necessarily linked to the nature of RPG play. As a participatory and cooperative group activity, an RPG relies on a degree of group cohesion. Most stories – in any game system – will be disrupted by 'animosity' within the group, and most will require cooperation of some sort to ensure 'survival'.

However, *Apocalypse* further insists on this pack mentality. Though there is a designation of 'ronin' for a solitary werewolf, players are encouraged to avoid developing characters of this type: 'Some ronin go insane or become Wyrm-tainted. These lonely night-stalkers are responsible for many legends of "man-eating werewolves" and the like' (40). The use of the term 'ronin' itself, a word that is taken from the Japanese term for a lone Samurai warrior, links 'lone wolves' to an exclusively male, exclusively martial identity. As the corebook insists, such a 'pure' masculine warrior identity is inconsistent with the overall aims of gameplay.

The significance of 'pack' within the game prevents characters from relying solely on masculine or hypermasculine tropes in character creation and behaviour. Conversely, however, it insists upon the integration of feminine tropes – and, specifically, tropes of female lycanthropy – into any and all characters. The concept of the werewolf pack itself has a particular connection to the cultural history of female werewolves, rather than traditions of presenting male werewolves. One of the earliest literary mentions of a female werewolf – in Gerald of Wales's *The History and Topography of Ireland* – has the she-wolf living alongside the he-wolf.[18] Aside from a brief fashion for presenting female werewolves as 'lonely night-stalkers' in Victorian literature,[19] the dominant presentation of female werewolves from the Middle Ages onwards has been as part of a social unit comprising other werewolves or other humans.[20] As already argued, the dominant fictional presentation of male werewolves during the same period was the Wolf Man paradigm, and, where male werewolves have been presented as members of a pack, this social unit has (almost) always included females.[21]

I posit two possible (related) reasons for this association of the 'pack' with female werewolves. The first is the implied association of a pack with a family, thus connecting it to the feminised domestic sphere.[22] The second is the necessary foregrounding of social interaction and social (as opposed to societal) politics in the maintenance of pack dynamics. This can function to privilege normative feminine behaviours of communication and negotiation over normative masculine ascendancy and aggression. While the creation of a pack does not negate the possibility of violence and hierarchy, these behaviours are usually inward-facing and ritualised, with challenges for supremacy and autonomy often being figured in familial terms. Where violence is outward-facing, it is most commonly employed in the maintenance and protection of the social unit. In *Apocalypse*, the importance of pack socialisation and communication is stated explicitly in the corebook:

> While a pack exists, its members are bound by very deep ties. Human friendship combines with lupine instinct to forge nearly unbreakable bonds. In most situations, the pack is very nearly of one mind; other creatures who observe a werewolf pack in action often wonder if its members share a telepathic link. Individual members of a pack may feel rivalry or even animosity toward other members, but rare indeed is the werewolf who will not defend her packmate to the death. (37)

Significantly, here, bonding and communication are presented as the primary attributes of a pack. Violent behaviour is mentioned, but it is figured in terms reminiscent of the image of the 'she-wolf' – protective, territorial and fiercely loyal.[23]

In its feminisation of the werewolf, however, *Apocalypse* goes further than a superficial privileging of the social over the solitary in character creation. The rules of gameplay related to story development similarly discourage the adoption of typically (hyper)masculine traits. Unusually for an RPG, *Apocalypse* clearly suggests possible storylines that do not take combat or violent campaign as their starting point. One aspect of the world of *Apocalypse* is an abiding prohibition on Garou mating with their own kind, and the offspring of such unions are born deformed and sterile. One of the potential plots listed under 'Common Stories and Chronicles' takes this as its underlying conceit:

> Garou are emotional beings, and the passions evoked by love can be felt as strongly among them as among humankind. Because their numbers are dwindling, some Garou feel that it is their duty to find a mate and produce offspring. Others can't help but heed these emotions. Stories can built around the active search for a mate or even the happenstance of meeting someone who can return your love. But what if your love is another Garou? (57–8)

The possibility of playing a game entirely devoted to the quest for love (or copulation) is mirrored by the *im*possibility of playing a game entirely devoted to wanton and brutal violence. In order to inflict the most damage on an opponent (either a gamemaster-performed non-player character or, less commonly, the character of another player), a werewolf must assume its 'Crinos' (half-human, half-wolf) or 'war' form, which is described as resembling the werewolves of horror films. However, game rules limit the length and number of times such a form can be assumed, and penalise players who remain in 'war form' for too long. This is done, in part, through the use of 'Rage' points, which must be consistently balanced with 'Willpower' and 'Gnosis' (wisdom) points in order to successfully survive and function within the game. When 'Rage' exceeds 'Willpower', for instance, a player's performance in other aspects of the game (specifically those involving social interaction) is hampered by limitations placed on the number of dice that can be rolled in attempts to perform tasks (performance being determined by the combined score of several rolled decahedral dice in this system). Thus, a practical impediment is placed on a character's ability to complete actions, outside of character or story creation. Put simply: if a player chooses to have their character too frequently overcome with rage or aggravated violence, the odds are stacked against them.

This idiosyncratic discouraging of a game's focus on combat and 'war' campaigns, and the concomitant emphasis on harmony as a principle of character development is something that *Apocalypse* shares with other classic World of Darkness games, particularly *Vampire: The Masquerade*. *Apocalypse* seeks to rationalise this idiosyncrasy by specifically linking it to aspects of lycanthropy and lycanthropic identity – a rationalisation with more basis in narrative tradition and tropes than the earlier attempt to do so with vampires. Most significantly, and unsurprisingly for a twentieth-century narrative, *Apocalypse* associates werewolves with the moon, which underlies much of the corebook's advice about balanced character development.

Lunar determinism and femininity

The trope of lycanthropic transformation being determined by lunar influence is, largely, a creation of twentieth-century cinema, with few earlier literary narratives making this specific connection. While there is evidence of an earlier folkloric association of werewolves with the lunar cycle, this is often figured in terms of tidal patterns rather than the moon itself and reflects a folk tradition linking werewolves to water.[24] The more recent cinematic tradition makes little (if any) reference to tides, and instead concentrates attention on the monthly cycle of lunar phases and its cultural connotations. Specifically, it connects lunar-defined werewolf transformation to insanity, mutability and menstruation. As some critics have suggested, the lunar connection serves to feminise both female *and* male werewolves.[25]

Apocalypse echoes some of the traditions of werewolf cinema, but also rejects others. Again, this is a combination of narrative constraints relating to gameplay and the integration of non-lycanthropic tropes into this particular incarnation of the werewolf. Werewolf transformation, in this narrative, is not dictated by lunar phase; a character might shift forms regardless of whether or not it is a full moon. However, the moon (personified as Luna) plays an important role in character creation and development.

The castes ('auspices') from which a player must choose when creating a character are said to reflect the phase of the moon under which the Garou is born. The corebook explains this in characteristically portentous terms: 'Luna, sister to Gaia, is mentor to all Garou. It is Gaia who nurtures, but it is Luna, the Garou's wise and crazy aunt, who provides the children with paths to follow' (87). This explanation of the lunar 'auspices' relies on traditions of the mutable and insane moon (it is both 'wise and crazy'), while also figuring this in terms of the wholly female pantheon. The moon is related to the earth in a familial – specifically sororal – relationship, and to the Garou as an aunt, stressing matrilineality and female creation as an underlying principle of werewolf ontology.

Apocalypse discourages gameplay that is dominated by combat and campaigns of violence. Nevertheless, the Garou are presented as being violent creatures – reflecting the (anecdotal) evidence that most RPGs do use conflict and confrontation as a central narrative concern. It is telling that the corebook's charts of required dice scores are overwhelming devoted to outlining the outcomes of combative interactions; they list dice-rolls required for inflicting and sustaining wounds, explain how these are altered through the use of particular weapons, and outline the lasting effects of combat on physical and mental health. The game's backstory seeks to mitigate this violent ontology through its situation within a feminised system of righteousness, justice and environmental/familial protection.

In the second narrative of the corebook, the need for violent behaviour is explained to Brian, a newly turned Garou. This explanation is given as coming directly from Luna: 'These are Gaia's Garou. They shall protect Her from the Wyrm, who hungers for Her. All pay respect to them, for they are our Mother's warriors' (6). Rather than originating from a self-serving desire for autonomy, ascendency or material gain, the violence of the Garou is thus determined by a desire to maintain a relationship with the 'Mother' and preserve her purity. 'Mother' is silent in this, but it is significant that desire for the maternal is vocalised by a deified female, rather than male, figure.

The role of Luna as mediator and director of violence is insisted upon throughout the corebook, making it hard to separate combat and war from the feminine. Even the 'Ahroun' auspice – the warrior caste which I earlier referred to as the most stereotypically masculine social class – is understood through this integration of the feminine. Descriptions of the Ahroun call him 'the slayer, the mad man-wolf, Rage incarnate', but qualify this with an insistence on his identity as 'the vessel of Luna's Rage, the talons of Gaia's fury' (91). This reference to 'Luna's Rage' implies a connection between the Ahroun and the insane moon, as well as a subtle association with the putative monthly rage and fickleness of the menstruating woman prevalent in popular culture.[26] Despite the fact that a Garou of any tribe might have the Ahroun auspice, the reference here to this caste being 'the talons of Gaia's fury' verbally aligns them with the only exclusively female tribe of the game, the Black Furies, who see Luna as 'Artemis the Huntress', reminding the player of a Classical connection between the (female) moon and a particular mode of physical violence.

Feminised and masculinised RPG worlds

As already shown, *Apocalypse* consistently feminises its werewolves through the combined effects of feminised narrative tropes (including environmental/familial protection, spirituality, pack identity and lunar determinism), the elevation and deification of the feminine and the non-normative (specifically Native) masculine, and rule-based constraints to discourage the adoption of (hyper)masculine behaviours. This sustained combination allows us to read the female (or, more accurately, the feminine) in *all* of *Apocalypse*'s werewolves, regardless of the particularities of any one 'ongoing, coauthored narrative'.

This strategy of feminisation is thrown into sharp relief when compared to a more recent RPG by White Wolf. The 'new World of Darkness' games were introduced in 2004, with *Vampire: The Requiem* and *Werewolf: The*

Forsaken among the new titles. With the launch of this new series of games, the 'storytelling system' was revised and streamlined, with fewer choices offered during the character creation process being a notable alteration.[27]

The werewolves of *Forsaken* are not Garou, as in *Apocalypse*, but rather 'Uratha', which distances them from the literary traditions evoked by the earlier title. They are no longer warriors who battle a forthcoming environmental apocalypse, but rather an 'ancient race, part wolf, part human' who, 'were once lords among man and beast in a hunter's paradise at the dawn of the world – but they destroyed that paradise with their own claws'.[28] This introduces concepts that had largely been absent from *Apocalypse*, with the dominion and hierarchical social classification of 'lords' in opposition to the shamanistic spirituality of the earlier game. The predatory violence inherent in the 'hunter's paradise' and the Uratha that '[c]ull their prey' is at odds with the protective and tribal fierceness of the Garou. The loss of the former paradisiacal home as a punishment for transgression signals a Christian framework, with particular reference to the doctrine of Original Sin.

This Christianisation of the world of werewolves is continued throughout *Forsaken*'s corebook, with the deific female figures of *Apocalypse*'s cosmos replaced by a single, patriarchal figure: Father Wolf (though this figure has been destroyed by the Uratha's 'original sin' prior to the world of the game being established). There is a reflection of one of *Apocalypse*'s primal females, the Weaver, in the later game's 'Spinner-Hag', who 'scuttled through primeval forests and under great mountains'; however, before the narrative of the game begins, players are told that 'Father Wolf caught her and tore her to bits' (38).

Forsaken offers some counterpoint to the potential monotheistic, Abrahamic inflection of its world in the figure of Mother Luna, who 'descended to earth' in 'the form of a woman of flesh' and gave the Uratha's ancestors 'the power to change shape' (22); however, Luna's role in this RPG is continually weakened by the masculine figure to which she is aligned and by her characterisation as 'fickle and moody' (29). Father Wolf is the 'greatest and most valiant' lover of Luna, and it is he who offers the werewolves 'senses, strength and speed' (22).

This use of religious iconography, long after all the deific figures (with the possible exception of Mother Luna) are dead, to maintain and enforce codified social roles and behaviours can be seen throughout the corebook. For instance, while the Garou of *Apocalypse* are prevented from mating with one another due to the possibility of deformed offspring, female werewolves in *Forsaken* are given a more explicit warning:

> When a mating between Uratha conceives, the results are horrific and painful. An Uratha female who has been impregnated by another werewolf finds herself going through the expected symptoms of pregnancy: a nine-month gestation, morning sickness and the rest. She cannot conceive during this time, and does not menstruate. At the end of this false pregnancy, the Uratha mother

experiences a relatively brief, extraordinarily painful labor that produces only a rush of blood. (44)

Given that there is no concomitant bodily punishment for the male Uratha involved in such a conception, this warning is strikingly reminiscent of the punishment of Eve in Genesis 3:16.

Elsewhere, aspects of narrative that are feminised in *Apocalypse* are reconfigured and reimagined through a masculinised Christian lens. The Uratha have a primordial relationship to a deity figure, but as 'loyal servants' to a 'mighty spirit that … meted out punishment to those who broke the ancient bans' (22). They 'form packs', but often 'don't mean to' and 'avidly take advantage of the perks of leadership once they achieve them' (41). Unlike the packs in *Apocalypse*, the werewolf packs in *Forsaken* have an alpha.

One of the most distinct differences between the werewolves of *Apocalypse* and those of *Forsaken* is the continual emphasis on inherent violence and predation in the werewolves. There is little suggestion that a game could be run that centred on a quest for love or companionship, and attention is explicitly drawn away from communication, negotiation and non-combative interaction. Uratha are 'the predator, the destroyer, the beast' (14); they are 'instinctively destructive creatures' (27). Moreover, they are characterised predominantly through a discourse of sin, culpability and shame in a way that the protective and spiritually potent Garou were not.[29]

This brief comparison with the narrative of *Forsaken* reveals how the mechanisms of gender identity might be considered in a narrative that does not need to feature female player-characters for its development.

If one considers the 'narrative' of an RPG as the overarching features of world-building, ontology and mechanics common to all participatory and episodic 'stories', *Apocalypse* and *Forsaken* are two substantively different texts, despite the similarities found in the practical aspects of gameplay. The gendering of the respective werewolves is a vital feature of this difference. In the later game, werewolves are figured through a discourse of sin, shame, hierarchy and predation, and emphasis is placed on the horror and guilt of individual identity. Significantly, while this has some common ground with the Wolf Man paradigm of male werewolf fiction, it perhaps speaks more clearly to twentieth- and twenty-first century depictions of (male) vampires, particularly in its use of isolation, depravity and the struggle for ascendancy as a principle of identity formation.

Conversely, the matristic and matrilineal world of *Apocalypse* consciously tries to distance its werewolves from an Abrahamic interpretation of existence, by eschewing patriarchal monotheism in favour of a patchwork of pagan traditions and belief systems. Like the later RPG, *Apocalypse* often integrates elements into its werewolf ontology that are not drawn from earlier lycanthropic traditions: the Celtic mythology of fairies, the Classical legends of the Erinyes and the Amazons, Native American shamanism, New Age Gaia worship. Nevertheless, multiple strands of the werewolf's long cultural history, such as involuntary and voluntary transformation, lunar determinism and a pseudo-lupine pack formation and protection, are also found within the backstory of the corebook.

The narrative tropes of lycanthropy used in *Apocalypse* are drawn more from traditions of presenting female, rather than male, werewolves in Euro-American culture. Moreover, the non-lycanthropic tropes with which these are mixed often come from traditions of presenting the feminine, or, in some cases, the non-normative masculine. This idiosyncratic mixture of literary, folkloric and mythological history results in a species of werewolf that is always, in some way, female.

If the anecdotal and localised statistics are to be believed, less than a third of *Apocalypse*'s players (and, by extension, characters) are female. RPGs remain, in both the popular imagination and the testimony of players, a predominantly male leisure activity. Thus *Apocalypse* is, perhaps, a unique cultural production: it is a narrative that repeatedly produces female werewolves even where no females are present.

Notes

1. 'Gamemaster' is the generic term used by RPG players to denote the individual responsible for the creation of a particular series of episodic adventures and non-player characters, and for the overall control of the scenarios therein. Different game systems use different names for this role; the White Wolf World of Darkness series uses 'storyteller'.
2. Daniel Mackay, *The Fantasy Role-Playing Game: A New Performing Art* (Jefferson, NC: McFarland, 2001), 4–5, original emphasis.
3. Dennis Waskul and Matt Lust, 'Role-Playing and Playing Roles: The Person, Player, and Persona in Fantasy Role-Playing', *Symbolic Interaction* 27:3 (Summer 2004): 333–56 (335).
4. See, for example, Waskul and Lust, 'Role-Playing and Playing Roles'; Gary Alan Fine, *Shared Fantasy: Role Playing Games as Social Worlds* (Chicago: University of Chicago Press, 1983).
5. See, for example, Rachel Mizsei Ward, 'Copyright, Association and Gothic Sensibilities: *Underworld* and *World of Darkness*', in Brigid Cherry, Peter Howell and Caroline Ruddell (eds), *Twenty-First-Century Gothic* (Newcastle-Upon-Tyne: Cambridge Scholars Publishing, 2010), 149–66.
6. Waskul and Lust, 'Role-Playing and Playing Roles', 343, 341.
7. Mark Rein-Hagen, Robert Hatch and Bill Bridges, *Werewolf: The Apocalypse*, 2nd edition (Stone Mountain, CA: White Wolf, Inc., 1994), 29. This work is quoted extensively in this chapter, referenced by page numbers in brackets.
8. See, for example, various articles in *RPG=Role Playing Girl Zine* (August 2009). Waskul and Lust's 2004 study also uses player testimony, and this is drawn from a specific gaming group playing the Dungeons and Dragons system.
9. See the Entertainment Software Association's 2013 report 'Essential Facts about the Computer and Video Game Industry', http://theesa.com/facts/pdfs/ESA_EF_2013.pdf. Accessed 10 October 2013.
10. I do not dispute that individual economic transactions are a significant part of the RPG 'industry': books, particularly, are commercially produced and

sold. However, an individual player has no requirement to own these books to participate in a game; all that is needed is for the books to be available to the group as a whole. Moreover, with the introduction of open-source gaming licences and game system wikis (collaboratively edited websites), the status of the core rulebook (and other 'canonical' publications) as required purchase has been weakened. Some game systems, particularly Dungeons and Dragons, encourage the purchase of other game paraphernalia, such as character figurines, but this is not the case with the World of Darkness games.

11 See, for example, Meghan McGinley, 'You Play Like a Girl', *RPGirl Zine* (August 2010): 30–3. McGinley claims that women 'comprise less than 20% of the hobby' (30).
12 The idiosyncratic mechanics of this game system, and the ways in which it differs from other systems of RPG play, are not the concern of this chapter and are, perhaps, of interest and relevance only to readers familiar with multiple RPG systems of play. Of importance for this chapter, however, is the storyteller system's utilisation of a 'D10' (decahedral die) rather than a 'D6' (cubic die) to determine outcomes of character creation and interaction. The increase in possible dice-determined outcomes necessarily entails a wider scope for potential story and character creation.
13 Rein-Hagen, Hatch and Bridges, *Werewolf: The Apocalypse*, 29.
14 Daniel Dayan, 'Copyrighted Subcultures: Review of *Shared Fantasy: Role Playing Games as Social Worlds* by Gary Alan Fine', *American Journal of Sociology* 91:5 (March 1986): 1219–28 (1226).
15 Ward, 'Copyright, Association and Gothic Sensibilities', 152.
16 Peter L. Bayers, 'William Apess's Manhood and Native Resistance in Jacksonian America', *MELUS* 31:1 (Spring 2006): 123–46 (126–7). See also, Anthony E. Rotundo, *American Manhood: Transformations in Masculinity from the Revolution to the Modern Era* (New York: Basic Books, 1993); Timothy Sweet, 'Masculinity and Self-Performance in the Life of Black Hawk', *American Literature* 65:3 (1993): 475–99.
17 The environmental message of *Apocalypse* is neither subtle nor denied by the game designers. The corebook contains a statement to this effect on its final page: 'Our commitment to the environment remains unchanged. White Wolf pledges to put 3% of the profits from this book toward helping environmental issues. That means you are helping by buying this book. One of the causes the EAC [Environmental Action Committee] has been instrumental in aiding since its creation is the fight against the proposed "wolf kill" in Alaska.' (Rein-Hagen, Hatch and Bridges, *Werewolf: The Apocalypse*, 294).
18 Gerald of Wales, *The History and Topography of Ireland*, John J. O'Meara (trans) (1951; London: Penguin, 1982), 70.
19 See Carys Crossen's Chapter 7 for discussion of two such texts.
20 One exception could be the film *Ginger Snaps* (2000, dir. John Fawcett); however, I would argue that Ginger's close and complex relationship to her sister Brigitte (who becomes a werewolf herself in the sequel) keeps Ginger as a member of a social unit throughout the film. See also, Alan Moore's graphic story 'The Curse' (*Swamp Thing* 40 (September 1985)), in which Phoebe, though a predatory and lonely lycanthrope, is constructed through her role as part of a (dysfunctional) social unit. Like Ginger, Phoebe's acts of violence are focused inwards on the domestic sphere, rather than outwards on random prey.

21 There has been a trend in fiction, of late, towards the association of the werewolf pack with military units and other exclusively male social structures and groups. See, for example, D.L. Snell and Thom Brannan, *Pavlov's Dogs* (New York: Permuted Press, 2012); Jason Starr, *The Pack* (London: Penguin, 2011). Nevertheless, at the time of writing, this trend is too recent to determine the extent to which it will challenge or overtake the popularity of the Wolf Man paradigm.

22 See Hannah Priest, 'Pack versus Coven: Guardianship of Tribal Memory in Vampire versus Werewolf Narratives', in Simon Bacon and Katarzyna Bronk (eds), *Undead Memory: Vampires and Human Memory in Popular Culture* (New York: Peter Lang, 2014). As Priest argues, however, this familial structure often revolves around the patriarchal figure of the father or 'sire', particularly in the late twentieth and early twenty-first centuries.

23 For examples of the complex and contradictory historical construction of the she-wolf as protective, territorial and fiercely loyal, see Cristina Mazzoni, *She-Wolf: The Story of a Roman Icon* (Cambridge: Cambridge University Press, 2010); Helen Castor, *She-Wolves: The Women Who Ruled England Before Elizabeth* (London: Faber and Faber, 2011).

24 See, for example, Francisco Vaz da Silva, 'Extraordinary Children, Werewolves, and Witches in Portuguese Folk Tradition', in Éva Pócs and Gábor Klaniczay (eds), *Witchcraft Mythologies and Persecutions* (Budapest: Central European University Press, 2008), 255–68.

25 See, for example, Aviva Briefel, 'Monster Pains: Masochism, Menstruation, and Identification in the Horror Film', *Film Quarterly*, 28:3 (2005): 16–27

26 See, for instance, Moore, 'The Curse' for an explicit association of pre-menstrual syndrome, female anger and violent lycanthropy. A widely-circulated internet meme succinctly sums up this popular association; a picture of a snarling and salivating werewolf is captioned: 'Ever wondered why there are no female werewolves? Because it would be unfair if they turned into crazed man-eating creatures of the night twice a month.' See http://weknowmemes.com/2013/09/ever-wonder-why-there-are-no-female-werewolves/. Accessed 10 September 2013.

27 See 'Points of Difference', *White Wolf Wiki*, http://whitewolf.wikia.com/wiki/World_of_Darkness. Accessed on 20 September 2012.

28 Carl Bowen, Rick Jones, James Kiley, Matthew McFarland and Adam Tinworth, *Werewolf: The Forsaken* (Stone Mountain, CA: White Wolf Publishing, Inc., 2005), 14. Subsequent quotations from this work are referenced by page numbers in brackets.

29 See, for example, the explanation of how Uratha 'commit sins' and the subsequent 'degeneration [dice] rolls' taken to penalise this (*Ibid.*, 181–3).

5
Fur girls and wolf women: fur, hair and subversive female lycanthropy

Jazmina Cininas

Introduction

In the opening lines of Justine Larbalestier's novel *Liar*, the protagonist, Micah Wilkins, introduces herself as having been 'born with a light covering of fur. After three days it had fallen off, but the damage was done.'[1] Right from the beginning, Larbalestier sets the reader up to view hirsutism as shorthand for compromised humanity, and especially femininity. The tomboyish Micah – who describes herself as 'not black, not white; not a girl, not a boy; not human, not a wolf. Not dangerous, but not exactly safe. Not crazy, but not exactly sane ... a non-person who belonged nowhere'[2] – gradually reveals herself to be a pathological liar suffering homicidal delusions of lycanthropy. Throughout the novel, sprouting hair consistently operates as the primary signifier of Micah's deviancy from cultural norms, as well as offering the first physical manifestation of her psychotic episodes.

Larbalestier's hirsute (anti)heroine reflects Western society's long, complicated relationship with fur, a relationship which becomes further complicated when the fur is not worn, but rather 'grown' by the human body, especially the female body. Notwithstanding three waves of feminism, John Bulwer's 1654 declaration that 'woman is by nature smooth and delicate; and if she have many hairs she is a monster'[3] still holds true almost four centuries later. The glut of depilatory products on the market (never mind the proliferation of Brazilian waxing salons) advertises that female body hair – in any form – remains disturbing to social sensibilities and conventions. Anxieties reach their zenith when female hair growth exceeds not only the social parameters set for her gender, but also those for her *species*.

From sixteenth-century hirsute celebrities, the Gonsalus sisters, through popular Victorian 'missing links', to contemporary wolf girls and female lycanthropes, the hairy woman is regularly portrayed as a violator of social and biological boundaries. This chapter provides an overview of the relationship between the hairy woman and the female werewolf figure and the ongoing complexities of the social attitudes towards fur/body hair and the feminine.

Hairy Marys and well-heeled furry femmes

The hirsute femme has not universally been depicted in a negative light. Pre-dating Bulwer's seventeenth-century condemnation of female body hair, the wild or hairy woman might signify a rejection of worldly conceits and was a familiar – and sympathetically treated – motif for the visual artists of early modern Europe. Hairy saints such as Mary Magdalene, for example, were viewed as symbolising a New Eve, a return to Eden before the Fall. Sculptor Tilman Riemenschneider's *Maria Magdalena* from the end of the fifteenth century (1490–92) employs the serene countenance, sloping shoulders, elegant limbs and long flowing hair that conform to Renaissance ideals of beauty, despite her hairy pelt. Unlike the female werewolf's fur that has most frequently pointed to transgressive – and aggressive – sexuality, the Magdalene's body suit of tight curls protects her modesty after she is stripped naked and banished to the wilderness by rendering her less sexually attractive to men, even if the artist leaves her breasts bare. Bess Bradfield argues that the hirsute Magdalene's 'voluntary embrace of a life like an animal in the wild' becomes the very attribute 'which elevates her out of her true bestiality ... into the company of heavenly angels'.[4] Magdalene's hairy nakedness, or *nuditas naturalis*, redeems her 'from her earlier nudity (or *nuditas criminalis*) which [served as] a sign of vice in the sinner'.[5]

The shaggy coat also signifies the Magdalene's penitential renunciation of worldly vanities by linking her to existing iconographies of wild folk who lived supposedly innocent lives free from the vices of civilisation. The same model might have posed for the Nuremberg Chronicle's woodblock illustration of a member of the Gorgades tribe,[6] a race of wild, hairy women described by Pliny the Elder in his *Natural History* of first century CE, and said to have lived near the blissful islands of the Hesperides.[7] Travelogues by the fifth century BCE Carthaginian navigator, Hanno, surfaced in Basel, Switzerland, in the sixteenth century for example, with stories of North African islands populated by hairy women finding their way into Greek, French and Italian translations.[8]

Such images suggested that a benevolent romanticism surrounded hirsute female races and enabled 'wolf girls' Antonietta, Maddalena and Francesca Gonsalus, renowned for their unusual hairiness, to find favour as 'marvels' in the French royal court of sixteenth-century Europe.[9] While it is easy to transpose contemporary political correctness onto the employment of hirsute individuals for 'diversion', the Gonsalus sisters' position in the courts needs to be understood in the context of the sixteenth century, during which time a resident hirsute family could be rationalised as demonstrating erudition, even if the practice were no less exploitative than the freak shows of subsequent centuries.

Life-size portraits of the Gonsalus family in courtly attire were commissioned in 1582 for Archduke Ferdinand II's *wunderkammer* at Ambras Castle in Innsbruck (where they are still on display), giving their name to Ambras syndrome: a form of congenital hypertrichosis. Precursors to the museum, *wunderkammern* were encyclopaedic cabinets of curiosities showcasing the acquisition and expansion of knowledge, as well as the conquest of new territory. Housing the spoils of early European exploration and colonisation, *wunderkammern* featured eclectic displays of biological and geological specimens alongside examples of the monstrous or the novel as well as religious and cultural artefacts, their relative categories, boundaries and hierarchies still to be defined. Certainly, an element of colonial exploitation and self-aggrandisement is present in the *wunderkammern* of the time, but inclusion in such a collection was not determined by freakishness or deviation from the norm (at least not the way it is presently understood), but rather by the capacity to evoke wonder and curiosity, as a conduit to new knowledge.

Ambras syndrome has come to be known informally as 'werewolf syndrome', nevertheless it is clear that the artists of the day viewed the Gonsalus sisters' hairiness as belonging within the sympathetic iconography of the hairy female saints, rather than the demonised iconography of the lycanthropic witch, despite the werewolf trials that were taking place throughout Europe at the time.[10] The regal dress in the portraits suggest that the Gonsalus sisters came to enjoy a measure of privilege and regard; Duke Ranuccio Farnese, for example, is believed by Merry Wiesner-Hanks – author of the sisters' biography, *The Marvelous Hairy Girls* – to have bought a house in Parma for Maddalena's dowry when she married in 1593.[11] Influential scholars such as Ulysee Aldrovandi were also drawn to the hirsute family, producing several texts and woodcut illustrations of the sisters in a demonstration of highbrow erudition. Where twenty-first-century popular sensibilities relegate the display of hirsute individuals to the 'lowest common denominator' realm of the freak show and tabloid exploitation, the sixteenth-century Gonsalus family was seen as properly belonging among the privileged and educated audience of Europe's courts.

The sisters' exact situation remains uncertain, however, particularly given that it is unlikely the Gonsalus family ever owned or commissioned their own portraits. Despite her courtly finery, the letter that Antonietta displays in Lavinia Fontana's 1590s portrait of her reads more as a history of 'provenance' rather than personal biography, tracing her 'tenure' from King Henry to the Duke of Parma to Lady Isabella Pallavicina,[12] for whom she 'seems to have been kept as some sort of pet'.[13] Nor do the Gonsalus family portraits that hang in Ambras Castle necessarily confer courtly privilege. Christiane Hertel argues that while the 'formal, courtly, full-length portrait'[14] of Maddalena conforms to 'a format usually reserved for members of the nobility',[15] this is incongruous with the cave setting and sitter's hirsute condition. According to Hertel, Maddalena's composure in the portrait implies that the cave is a natural and 'proper attribute' for the characterisation of a hirsute individual; as a consequence Maddalena appears 'polarized, belonging at once to court culture and to primitive nature, to the space of utmost public importance and to the most hidden place in nature'.[16]

The family also appear in two zoological compendiums produced around 1600, one by Dutch artist Joris Hoefnagel (folios 1 and 2 of his *Animalia Rationala et Insecta (Ignis)*)[17] and the second probably by Hapsburg court painter Dirck (de Quade) van Revestyn (c. 1570–1650).[18] In both instances, members of the Gonsalus family are dressed in their courtly finery and afforded the 'privileged' position at the very beginning of their respective volumes, albeit as members of the animal kingdom. The inscriptions accompanying Hoefnagel's folios present the Gonsalus family's hirsutism as both a blessing and a curse, describing the condition as 'at once a natural marvel and as a divine trial, thus as a visible sign of the invisible God's providence'.[19] It might be argued that human/animal hierarchies are a human conceit, and as such permeable boundaries between humanity and the other primates, and the inclusion of humans in an encyclopaedia of the animal kingdom demonstrates refreshingly non-speciesist thinking. The fact that the Gonsalus family are the only *homo sapiens* represented in these compendiums, however, suggests that the authors nevertheless considered mankind as properly separate from their fellow animals, with hirsute individuals raising fundamental anxieties as to what it was to be human, and at what point one stopped being so.

Women who lie with the wolves

Demonstrating this ambivalence towards hirsute individuals, the hairy female body has also been viewed as a manifestation of animalistic lust since at least the Renaissance. In the sixteenth century, physiognomists believed that wantonness corresponded with thickness of hair,[20] and the perception that hirsuteness indicates primitive, 'unbridled, perverse, and pathological sexuality' has proven especially stubborn.[21] Merran Toerien and Sue Wilkinson, in their exploration of body hair and constructions of the feminine, list various examples of hairiness in women being associated with lasciviousness, prostitution and sexual deviancy from throughout the ages.[22]

The hirsute individual's perceived undermining of the integrity to human boundaries was underscored by beliefs that extreme hairiness may be the result of cross-species coupling between humans – or more specifically women – and animals, a belief that persisted until relatively recently. For example, the midwifery handbook, *Aristotle's Masterpiece*, which was first published in 1684 continued to be popular into the nineteenth century. The author, believed to be William Salmon, states that '[s]ome monsters are begotten by a woman's unnatural lying with beasts'[23] and cites the example of a child born in 1603 with canine features from the navel down, the apparent offspring of a woman 'generating with a dog'.[24]

Mary E. Fissell provides an analysis of the frontispiece featuring a hirsute woman with a black child, variations of which adorned multiple editions of *Aristotle's Masterpiece*. She writes:

> A woman's animal nature and insatiable appetite could lead her to engage in sexual relations with animals. Worse, the treachery of the maternal imagination is such that a woman might only imagine such relations in order to produce such a [hirsute] being. Animality is thus invoked by the story or image of the hairy woman in at least three ways: women are like animals, women might have sex with animals, and women might imagine sex with animals.[25]

While Wiesner-Hanks might be overstating the case in her summation: 'When people looked at the Gonzales [sic] sisters ... they saw beasts or monsters as well as young women, but this was also true when they looked at most women',[26] her assessment that the hirsute sisters' lives 'highlight this complex relationship between beastliness, monstrosity, and sex' cannot be dismissed out of hand.[27]

Anxiety over *homo sapien* purity was once again re-ignited, if not amplified, in the nineteenth century in the wake of Darwin's *The Descent of Man* and the concurrent and widespread interest in taxonomy. Rosemarie Garland-Thomson explains:

> As the narrative of the natural world shifted from one of divine determination to secular explanations, early science viewed exceptional bodies as indices to the order of things ...[28]

Freak shows were also at the height of their popularity at this time, marketing themselves as pseudo-intellectual forums in which those who conformed to statistically verifiable norms could observe, discuss and feel superior to, quantifiably 'deviant' bodies, in effect operating as 'a stage upon which all sorts of cultural anxieties [could be] played out and managed'.[29] Social hierarchies were sanctioned by arguments of a natural order, 'one which [could] be discerned through careful observation of "facts"'.[30] Hirsute celebrities such as Julia Pastrana (1834–60), who toured throughout Europe and North America in the mid-nineteenth century, simultaneously reinforced and disrupted such hierarchies; her advertising monikers 'non descript' (meaning 'unclassifiable') and 'Bear Woman' fuelling uncertainty as to whether Pastrana was properly – or fully – human.

Even without the excess hair and accusations of bestiality, the 'science of women',[31] that flourished amidst the Victorian preoccupation with classification has been accused of objectifying women as a 'separate species from man',[32] with hirsute women serving as the most visible 'proofs'. Indeed, nineteenth-century commentator George C.D. O'Dell describes Pastrana as a 'semi-human' blend of woman and orang-utan, referring to her throughout his chronicle as 'it'; the strictly grammatically correct (if no longer strictly enforced) pronoun for animals.[33] O'Dell highlights the incongruity of Pastrana's 'docile' nature, intelligent eyes and command of the Spanish language with her 'terrifically hideous ... jaws, jagged fangs and ears'.[34] Mercilessly promoted as 'The Ugliest Woman on Earth',[35] the bearded and hairy Pastrana presented 'a walking metaphor for disorder: standing at the crossroads of male and female, animal and human, savage and civilised … refus[ing] to keep *this* separate from *that*'.[36]

The currency and popularity of debates surrounding hirsute women as manifesting boundary violation and species deviance was such that after Pastrana's premature death in 1860, her manager-husband, Theodore Lent, had her embalmed and continued to exhibit her profitably for a further twenty years. In fact, Pastrana's career continued for over a century, concluding only in 1972 when her body was toured throughout the United States with the *Million Dollar Midways* amusement park, prior to being retired to the Oslo Forensic Institute.[37]

Two decades after Pastrana's death, Krao Farini[38] (1876–1926), whose body was 'also overgrown with a … coating of soft, black hair'[39] enjoyed similar press coverage to, and provoked similar anxieties as, Pastrana, throughout her career as a 'missing link'. During her London exhibition in 1883, American showman Guillermo Antonio Farini promoted Krao as a 'perfect specimen of the step between man and monkey',[40] as living proof of Darwin's theory of evolution. A decade later the Zoological Gardens in Frankfurt continued to promote Krao as 'The Missing Link' in advertising for their 1894 exhibition of the hirsute celebrity. Handbills depicting a naked, overtly hairy Krao in a jungle setting underscored her simian characteristics as well as her 'essential primitiveness'.[41] Populist scientific accounts in the 1880s argued whether Krao should be properly classified as human or monkey, 'as part of a separate race or [as] a member of a transitional species, or merely [as] a true "freak of nature"'.[42]

Nadja Durbach argues that the colour of Krao's skin had as much to do with her 'missing link' advertising spin as did its furriness. She suggests that Krao's exoticism was exploited to bolster Imperialist British conceits of inherent superiority, and sanction the colonisation of 'primitive' others, while Garland-Thomson makes parallel observations about Pastrana.[43] It should be remembered that women's suffrage and the abolition of slavery were hotly contested issues in late nineteenth-century Britain and America, and that much science at the time was directed towards 'policing the category of the human by questioning the full humanity of women and people of colour in order to justify exclusionary practices'.[44] Cindy La Com argues:

> Such displays [of 'missing links'] referenced Darwinian theories of evolution to shore up racist and imperialist biases by assuring white viewers that England and America had not just the right but the duty to colonize the 'backward' lands which were the home of these human savages. As [Garland-]Thomson puts it, 'if science justifies dominant power relations, it also legitimates the dominant body, which is both the marker of cultural power and the ticket of admission into that power.'[45]

Edward Long's infamous study of Jamaican society a century earlier illustrates the porosity of the lines separating racism, misogyny and speciesism. The anthropologist argued that black races were incapable of developing beyond a certain 'measure', going on to discriminate them 'from the rest of men not in *kind* but in *species*' (original emphasis).⁴⁶ Long furthermore identified the orang-utan and some black races as having 'the most intimate connexion [*sic*] and consanguinity', proposing that frequent 'amorous intercourse [took place] between them'.⁴⁷ He even goes so far as to state: 'I do not think that an orang-utan husband would be any dishonour to an Hottentot female.'⁴⁸ (Note that Long fails to make a similar declaration for the inverse, i.e. that an orangutan wife would not dishonour an Hottentot man.) There is little doubt that Krao's 'half-woman, half-monkey' advertising spin, in conjunction with her 'exotic' status, resurrected earlier suspicions and superstitions that hirsutism was born of zoophilia; Krao's 1899 appearance at London's Westminster Aquarium caused one indignant member of the public to demand that the act be withdrawn on the grounds of indecency, condemning the show's 'revolting' invitation to 'behold the result of copulation between a woman and one of the most filthy beasts'.⁴⁹

Retrograde freaks and the werewolf gene

While the hairy woman's subversive sexual behaviour might be viewed as an assault upon conventional Western gender divisions by confusing 'in several ways a number of the orthodox categories of being upon which the social structure was hung',⁵⁰ greater anxieties surround her apparent transgression of species borders. Late nineteenth-century popular 'scientific' evaluations of Krao as a throwback to an earlier step on the evolutionary ladder were contingent upon her coming from a hirsute family. A.H. Keane, who was granted an audience with the seven-year-old Krao, wrote at the time that the 'exceptional scientific importance' of this otherwise 'distinctly human child' was due to her family history (which, as it turns out, was fabricated). This not only reportedly contained other hirsute members, but also supposedly hailed from central Laos, birthplace of a second celebrity hirsute family – the Sacred Hairy Family of Burma – making Krao 'living proof of the presence of a hairy race in Further India'.⁵¹ If Krao were no more than a freak, an anomaly, she would no longer qualify as a missing link as the latter was contingent upon her being a member of a transitional species;⁵² a hairy heritage gave credence to the arguments that Krao was 'a regular production in the regular order of Nature'.⁵³ Similarly, the fraudulent promotion of Pastrana as a member of the (non-existent) 'Root-Digger Indian' tribe, notable for their brutish appearance and manners, also cast her as a missing link prototype.⁵⁴

Hairy individuals continue to feature in evolutionary debates. Some biologists propose that congenital generalised hypertrichosis (CGH) 'is a manifestation of a genetic atavism' – the residue of an earlier evolutionary stage that, like supernumerary nipples or caudal appendages, is no longer expressed in the general population, but which nevertheless remain dormant in our genetic makeup.⁵⁵ Such theories cause especial anxiety amongst creationists, who insist on humanity's genetic independence from – and moral superiority to – all other species. For example, Thomas H. Awtry, taking pains to point out his PhD credentials and his long-standing study and teaching of creationism, rejects that CGH is a genetic atavism, summing up: 'Evolution, like werewolves, is a myth.'[56]

Those born to excessive body hair, especially those for whom hirsutism is a genetic inheritance, generate ongoing fears about the corruption, pollution and regression of the human gene pool. However, unlike previous centuries, hirsute individuals are being distanced from their simian heritage as 'missing links' and increasingly attributed lupine lineages through conflation with the werewolf, particularly on screen. In Thom Fitzgerald's 2001 film, *Wolf Girl* (aka *Blood Moon*), the star of a Canadian travelling freak show is a young woman covered from head to toe with a thick pelt of hair – the signature symptom of congenital hypertrichosis or werewolf syndrome. The Romanian-born Tara is promoted on carnival banners as 'The Terrifying Wolf Woman' while her surname, Talbot, makes her the cinematic descendant of the iconic Hollywood werewolf Larry Talbot, aka *The Wolf Man*, both her name and her provenance reinforcing the allusions to a lycanthropic inheritance.

In the beginning of *Wolf Girl* the fully hirsute Tara conforms to Victorian representations of hairy women who, despite transgressing countless social and biological boundaries, were nevertheless promoted as paragons of femininity and civility. While Pastrana and Krao may have been promoted as 'missing links', promotional material and newspaper reports took pains to emphasise their ladylike manners and accomplishments. Pastrana was reportedly a polished dancer, singer and linguist, 'possessed [of] a womanly figure and disposition [and taking] much care with her toilet and dress'.[57] One of her biographers, Saltarino, emphasised Pastrana's intelligence, gentleness and warm-heartedness in the face of her painful awareness that her grotesque appearance would always deny her 'the warmth and affection she craved for'.[58] Francis T. Buckland described her as 'charitable' and possessed of 'great taste in music and dancing'.[59] And as Krao entered her teens, her publicity material saw jungle settings replaced by feminine dresses, and a shift in emphasis on her being a 'cultured, intelligent lady who spoke five languages'.[60] Krao was further celebrated for her sweet disposition and popularity amongst her fellow performers – traits that reappear in the Tara Talbot characterisation – as well as her 'truly feminine delight' in the fashions of the day.[61]

The incongruously feminine dresses, accomplishments and manners may well have been a strategy to heighten, rather than compensate for, the 'brutishness' of the hirsute women's appearance; however, the inverse might also be true: superficial beastliness can serve to exaggerate inherent innocence and virtue, a notion that persists into the twenty-first century. The 'Werewolves' episode of US television show *CSI: Crime Scene Investigation* (6:11, 2006) sees a man murder his sister's hirsute fiancé, Hayden Bradford, unable to bear the thought of his own familial DNA being degenerated by the 'human werewolf gene'; a secret witness to the crime is Hayden's even hairier sister, Allison. Allison lives in a secret room in her brother's house and orders everything she needs to survive from the internet, her self-imposed exile from society serving to keep her girlhood innocence intact – to the point of still playing with dolls despite being well into her teens – in stark contrast to the brutal prejudices of society that saw her brother murdered.

Although he does not name them, *CSI* lead Gil Grissom clearly makes reference to the Mexican Aceves family, five generations of whom have been born with Ambras/werewolf syndrome or CGH, which some have proposed as a medical foundation for belief in lycanthropy.[62] The family's credentials as the world's hairiest people have attracted Fox Television's *Guinness World Records* and *Ripley's Believe It Or Not* among other sensationalist documentary makers, and have earned Luisa Lilia de Lira (Lilia) Aceves and her family careers in the circus as 'The Wolf Girl' and 'wolf children'.[63]

Given that hirsute females trigger 'our inchoate and deep-seated anxieties about violations to the integrity of our bodies',[64] it is perhaps unsurprising that real-life hairy girl Lilia Aceves and her family have sought refuge in the circus at various stages of their lives to escape discrimination by their fellow Mexicans. Grissom's reference to the Aceves family in *CSI* is intended to highlight the limited opportunities available to hirsute individuals for a public life free from discrimination or exploitation, and it is clear that Allison's self-exile is largely driven by her desire to avoid such a fate herself. The references to werewolves reinforce societal attitudes that continue to locate hirsute individuals amongst monsters and the monstrous in the Western popular imagination.

Like the Aceves family members, the fictional Tara is cruelly tormented and discriminated against by local teenagers and would have been killed at birth by superstitious villagers had her mother not abandoned her to the travelling sideshow in desperation. Maternal abandonment itself forms a recurring theme in hirsute wolf-girl narratives: Allison Bradford's mother fakes her own death so that she may escape the humiliation of bearing a hirsute daughter in the *CSI* episode, while Micah's parents abandon her to the family farm or the asylum when her lycanthropy manifests itself in Larbalestier's *Liar*. Admittedly the latter's lycanthropic turns correspond with homicidal episodes: first Micah kills her younger brother, Jordan, then her secret boyfriend, Zachary, but this is only revealed to the reader in the latter part of the novel.[65] Even so, it is almost as though the fundamental maternal instincts of these women are over-ridden by a deeper biological allegiance to their species, driving them to abandon their daughters rather than violate societal norms and expectations.

Away from the spotlight, *Wolf Girl*'s Tara is compassionate and considerate towards the fellow members of the freak show, in stark contrast to the wild wolf woman persona she is compelled to adopt for her performances. In a telling early scene, Tara applies lipstick and pins back her hair while admiring herself coquettishly in the mirror. The viewer is led to believe that she is preparing for her show, only to discover that this is the version of herself that Tara *wishes* could be put on public display – Tara the lovely young woman, rather than Tara the wolf-girl abomination. The lipstick and pretty hair clips are removed and substituted with false fangs and claws – her actual stage make-up – as Tara resigns herself to her culturally prescribed roles of 'savage' and sexual non-entity, and relinquishes her fantasy of acceptance and desirability. In effect, Tara is depicted as having fewer options available in terms of her public presentation and reception than her precursors in the nineteenth and sixteenth centuries, who were, at least, permitted to promote their feminine, cultural and social virtues.

Tara Talbot dutifully acts out the howling brute in a cage, pandering to stereotypes of the furred primitive for the sake of her troupe, despite her private longings. The ringmaster introduces Tara as 'one of nature's cruellest mistakes: a savage combination of woman and animal', implying a trans-species violation made possible by the porosity of human/animal boundaries, as indeed does the film's title. We see in the audience the exaggerated forms of staring that Garland-Thomson describes as being engendered by freak shows and sustained by 'the very entanglements and contradictions of the identities it works at creating', simultaneously enforcing and challenging 'the lines between self and the other, the human and nonhuman, the ordinary and the extraordinary'.[66] When the ringmaster goes on to ask the audience to 'take pity' on Tara, and to empathetically identify with the hirsute teen by imagining 'what it must be like to be so deformed ... so revolting and disgusting to others', he underlines the permeability, and vulnerability, of the audience's own biology.

So desperate is Tara for acceptance beyond the cloistered environment of the freak show that she is willing to risk the unknown side-effects of an experimental depilatory serum in order to rid herself of her offending follicles. Ironically, the serum that increasingly delivers Tara from her bestial pelt also causes an inverse deterioration in the self-control and the 'humanity' that were such marked features of her persona while she was hirsute. Her increasingly antisocial behaviour and impulses descend ultimately into violent cannibalism of a former female tormentor – with lesbian overtones thrown in for good measure. Tara finally achieves her idealised external human form at the cost of her internal humanity.

A real wolf appears in the woods at this time, and – significantly – is depicted as being less dangerous than the depilated Tara, driving home the young woman's fall from grace. While taking the reverse route, Tara's 'fur' nevertheless operates in much the same way as Mary Magdalene's penitential pelt, symbolising the hirsute teen at her most humane, most innocent and, ironically, most obedient to social ideals for feminine behaviour, if not appearance. The 'beastly' hirsutism that identifies Tara as less than human to the freak-show audience, nevertheless encapsulates Tara at her most human: an inverse werewolf, in effect.

Larbestier's characterisation of Micah in *Liar* conflates the tropes of the werewolf and the hirsute individual to not only exploit deep-seated anxieties of species and racial integrity, but also as a vehicle for exploring an extended range of contested boundary transgressions, including gender, sexuality, morality and the grey zone between delusion and deception. Micah, the 'half-breed' child of a French mother and black father – himself of mixed, though uncertain, race – blames her paternal lineage for her 'tainted hairy genes'.[67] The exact nature of the taint shifts throughout the course of the novel in a series of reveals, each, in turn, exposed as a lie and replaced by a new 'truth'.

Initially, Micah's 'family illness' is confined to the realm of aberrant human biology: an excess of body hair that appears periodically throughout her life, including, most significantly, with the onset of puberty. Although the hair grows back within a day or two of waxing, electrolysis or laser removal, Micah is able to keep her hirsutism at bay through strict daily medication. This is introduced to the reader as a contraceptive pill for the management of severe acne and crippling period pain, only to have this explanation repeatedly superseded by a series of 'true' purposes for the pill. Almost halfway through the novel, Micah confesses:

> I'm a werewolf.
> There, I've said it.
> The heart of all my lies.
> Of the family's lies.
> You guessed it already, didn't you? What with the fur I was born in, the wolf in my throat, my weird family. That explains everything … Micah the werewolf.[68]

Micah's grandmother and great aunt offer a range of theories for the origin of the family's werewolf gene, including a separate branch of humanity evolved from wolves, or cross-species sexual relations between a woman and a wolf. Recalling the CGH (Congenital Generalised Hypertrichosis) acronym, Micah herself proposes Horizontal Gene Transfer (HGT) between human and wolf DNA,[69] although she attributes her own hereditary condition to generations of inbreeding amongst her father's survivalist relatives. As such, Micah's hirsutism includes transgression of sexual taboos amongst its many signifiers, serving as visible punishment for the Wilkins family's incest.

Clues scattered throughout the novel, however, point to the Wilkins gene as actually being responsible for hereditary mental illness. Micah's self-confessed pathological lying is, in fact, a decoy for her psychotic delusions, enabling her to remove herself from her most horrifying self-truths. Micah narrates:

> You think my being a werewolf is the biggest lie of all … You think I killed him too. Trapped in my delusional state, believing I am a werewolf, I killed Zach. Believing I'm a werewolf is the only way I can live with what I did.[70]

Micah's hairiness/lycanthropy may serve as the index of her polluted identity – whereby her compromised humanity signals equal corruptions of species, race, sanity and morality – but by placing her outside the parameters of polite society, Micah is also freed from the obligations of conforming to society's rules. Furthermore, it becomes clear that the seventeen-year-old prefers the alternative reality offered by her lupine identity to the truth of her compromised sanity and homicidal tendencies. Above all else, however, she prefers the hirsute wolf to the truth of her gender.

The first lie to which the athletic, tomboyish Micah confesses is pretending to be a boy and throughout the novel there are clues that this is the lie she most wishes were true. Micah states this explicitly when she muses: 'I would be a better boy than I'd ever been a girl'[71] and even more bluntly: 'I wish I was a man.'[72] After the death of Zachary – her secret boyfriend – Micah has recurring fantasies (initially presented as 'truths') of becoming physically intimate with Zachary's public girlfriend, Sarah: fantasies which might also be read as a desire to identify as male. Nevertheless, for all of the boundary transgressions that Micah's hirsutism signifies, and however much a hirsute woman may represent 'a symbolic threat to the gendered social order,' Larbalestier does not present Micah's over-active follicles as transgressing her sex.[73] Instead, they are the marker *of* her sex.

While admitting the possibility of male werewolves, Micah nevertheless sees their lycanthropy as resulting from female influence, explaining: 'A boy wolf can stay human forever – all he has to do is never go near a girl wolf.'[74] By the end of the novel, it is revealed that the pill which Micah takes to suppress her period pain, then her hirsutism, then her lycanthropy and finally her psychotic episodes, is a contraceptive pill after all, surreptitiously taken daily by Micah to ensure that she never menstruates, that she never conforms to this exclusively feminine signifier of womanhood. All of Micah's lies and transgressions stem from her desire to be a boy, to be the son she believes her parents preferred to her, to be the brother she killed the year her gender was confirmed beyond doubt when she began menstruating. It is Micah's aberrant, unwanted womanhood that manifests in the fur and the wolf, and that she attempts to keep at bay with synthetic hormones.

The latest virtues of lupine ladies

The hirsute woman throughout history has been viewed as closer to the animal world than her non-hirsute counterpart, whether her family were the only human representatives in a zoological compendium in the sixteenth century; whether she was promoted as the missing link between human and simian ancestors in the Victorian era, or whether she is imagined as a wolf-girl/werewolf hybrid in twenty-first-century narratives. Lupine body hair visibly manifests the 'mobile, elastic fictions or borders' between humans and animals;[75] however, this perceived proximity to the animal is not necessarily indicative of compromised humanity or a sub-human status. In some instances the hirsute femme may offer an opportunity to redress earlier histories plagued by 'highly problematic ideological tropes' such as racist or speciesist hierarchies.[76]

In a radio lecture first broadcast on BBC Radio 4 in 1994, Marina Warner explores the symbolic value of wild animals and the porosity of human/animal boundaries in texts beginning with the medieval romance, *Valentine and Orson*, Orson being a bearlike, wild, hairy man. Warner eventually arrives at the 1990s video game, *Altered Beast*, the goal of which is to progress through multiple animal guises until one reaches the ultimate incarnation, the Golden Werewolf. Warner identifies a 'pronounced change of sympathy' in texts exploring human–animal allegiances since the eighteenth century, suggesting:

> The threat of entropy in nature, brought about by human achievements ... has never been so seriously nor perhaps ... so acutely felt. Nature, newly understood to be somehow uncontaminated, innocent, nurturing and spontaneous, beckons as a remedy to the distortions and excesses of progress.[77]

Warner also explores various retellings of *Beauty and the Beast*, drawing especial attention to Angela Carter's 'The Tiger's Bride', first published in her anthology, *The Bloody Chamber*, in 1979. In particular, Warner highlights Carter's inversion of the traditional ending; the author has Beauty, not the Beast, undergo metamorphosis. Warner quotes the passage:

> And each stroke of his tongue ripped off skin after successive skin, all the skins of a life in the world, and left behind a nascent patina of shining hairs. My ear-rings turned back to water and trickled down my shoulders; I shrugged the drops off my beautiful fur.[78]

The removal of Beauty's human skin and the dissolution of her earrings free her from the conceits of human society and return her to a state of innocence, embodied by her newly revealed hirsutism. Warner observes: 'In modern myth, it's not that the boundary has been eroded between human and animal – rather, the value given to each side in the contrast has changed', and concludes: 'The new myth of the wild calls into question the privilege of being human at all.'[79]

Just as the 'bestial' appearance of the hairy Magdalenes and blissful Gorgades signified the renunciation of the vanities of civilisation, contemporary artists are revisiting the figure of the hirsute woman, as a vehicle not for exploring corruption within the afflicted individual, but rather of the society in which she finds herself. Rebecca Stern attributes the resurrection of Julia Pastrana in works by poet Wendy Rose and artists Holley Bakich and Kathleen Anderson Culebro (among others) to a backlash against the 'freakish rituals [such as] Brazilian waxing, fad dieting, Botox injections [and] liposuction' that Western women are increasingly compelled to undergo in order to conform to standards of beauty, with Pastrana re-emerging as a 'figure of resistance and empowerment'.[80]

Similarly, Los Angeles painter and sculptor, Erik Mark Sandberg, creates deliberately gauche portraits of hairy children that speak of the ostentation and exploitation inherent in contemporary consumer culture, and for which his home town is particularly famous. Sandberg captures the hairy 'underbelly of glamour'[81] in a culture of materialism, idolatry and entertainment coupled with the paranoia surrounding promiscuity, addiction and genetic modification. Inverting the notion of hirsutism as a rejection of worldly vanities, Sandberg's portraits and busts visibly manifest the wholesale absorption of rampant consumer culture by those most susceptible to the relentless bombardment of mass marketing – the young. The rampant hair follicles signify corruption not only of individuals, but also the society in which the young teens find themselves.

In an age of social networking, YouTube and reality television, the promise of instant celebrity comes with the fine print of equally instant – and merciless – scrutiny and criticism, as well as the pressure to conform to superficial ideals of appearance. Sandberg's hairy girls carry the poignancy and self-consciousness of lives lived in the public domain by those most vulnerable to exploitation. Yet the shameless grotesqueness of Sandberg's subjects allows them to transcend conventional notions of attractiveness to create a self-possessed, defiant beauty. Emerging from a culture that preaches tolerance of difference yet sets impossible ideals of youth and beauty, and routinely witnesses anorexics starve themselves in the midst of an obesity epidemic while addictions to steroids, Botox and cosmetic surgery give rise to grotesque parodies of former selves, Sandberg's contemporary Pastranas offer a perversely appealing, and liberating, alternative.

In a similar vein, the hirsutism of *CSI*'s Allison Bradford and *Wolf Girl*'s Tara Talbot may mark them as outside the parameters of the norm, but is not necessarily emblematic of their own monstrosity. Rather, the young women's hirsutism marks their selfless virtue and innocence, serving to highlight the vanities and prejudices of contemporary Western society. It is not until Tara conforms to social expectations for female appearance that she, too, becomes a monster, capable of murder and cannibalism. The true monsters in these narratives are intolerance, exploitation and vanity.

Donna Haraway's contention that we have entered a 'mythic time', in which 'we are all chimeras', and her argument for '*pleasure* in the confusion of boundaries and for *responsibility* in their construction',[82] allows for the possibility of imagining the hirsute woman/wolf-girl/female werewolf as a hybrid that exceeds the categories of male or female, woman or wolf, human or animal. Haraway's notion of the chimera permeates even the conflicted character of Micah, who explains in the final pages of her narrative:

> I used to think I was nothing ... I thought that half of everything added up to nothing ... I don't think that now: half of everything is something, not nothing.
> *Lots* of somethings.[83]

However problematic and fraught her hirsute or lupine selves may be, they allow Micah to escape the socially and biologically pre-determined confines of her gender and the horrific consequences of her mental illness. While I am not proposing that Haraway's 'pleasure in the confusion of boundaries' extends to condoning homicide, these alternative realities nevertheless offer Micah the freedom of an alternative moral compass, at times intoxicatingly liberating, that enable her to live with what she has done and who she is. Her self-alignment with the animal is not the key source of her polluted humanity, but rather her only hope of redemption, as well as a chance to believe herself to be *more* than she is as human.

Conclusion

In the early 2000s, an advertisement for the depilatory cream 'Hair No More' appeared in women's magazines throughout Australia and Europe, featuring a female werewolf on the left – the 'before' position – and a svelte, depilated model on the right – the 'after' position. The advertising slogan promised 'From werewolf to goddess overnight'. The ad is reflective of recent narratives in which the hirsute femme shift is less likely to be aligned with a simian 'missing link', and more likely to be imagined as lupine. It would also appear to confirm that the many-haired woman is still, quite literally, imagined as a monster, despite the centuries that have passed since John Bulwer made his pronouncement in 1654. However, the fluid boundaries that are exemplified by figurations of hirsute individuals are matched by the shifting perceptions of the hairy woman herself.

The hirsute heroine has been a complex and contradictory figure throughout history, her perceived intimacy with the animal world casting her as either less or more than her non-hirsute counterparts, sometimes both simultaneously. While this new breed of multi-dimensional she-wolf continues to signify aberration and corruption of species, gender and moral boundaries, she is equally likely to draw attention to the vanities and prejudices of the society in which she lives, in a call for adaptability and tolerance, multiple viewpoints and multiple possibilities. Lupine body hair may continue to be perceived as a curse, although it need not necessarily condemn the hirsute heroine to sub-human status, and in some instances even signifies her moral or biological advantage. The hairy woman's visible animal biology continues to offer a narrative device for explorations of the monstrous, even if her manifold, contradictory manifestations ultimately challenge us to re-consider where true monstrosity lies.

Notes

1. Justine Larbalestier, *Liar* (Crows Nest, MA: Allen & Unwin, 2009), 3.
2. *Ibid.*, 320.
3. John Bulwer, 'Anthropometamorphosis' (1654), quoted in Merry Wiesner-Hanks, *The Marvelous Hairy Girls: The Gonzales Sisters and Their Worlds* (New Haven, CT: Yale University Press, 2009), 46.

4   Bess Bradfield, 'The Hair of the Desert Magdalen: Its Use and Meaning in Donatello's *Mary Magdalen* and Tuscan Art of the Late Fifteenth Century' (1–15) 11, MA essay published online at *York Medieval Yearbook: MA Essays from the Centre for Medieval Studies* I (2002), www.york.ac.uk/teaching/history/pjpg/Magdalen.pdf. Accessed on 7 June 2009.
5   *Ibid.*, 11.
6   Bayerische Staatsbibliothek has created a digitised copy of the *Nuremberg Chronicles*, or *Liber Chronicarum*. For the illustration of the Gorgades see http://daten.digitale-sammlungen.de/bsb00034024/image_95. Accessed on 6 March 2013.
7   Pliny the Elder, *Natural History 6. 200* (trans. Jonathan Couch) (London: George Barclay, 1847–48), 163–4, found at University of California Digital Library, http://archive.org/details/plinysnaturalhis00plinrich. Accessed on 3 May 2013.
8   According to Wiesner-Hanks, these hairy women were really apes; while the latter began appearing in art and stories in the twelfth century, chimpanzees, monkeys, gorillas and baboons could still be mistaken as the exotic human races told of in ancient texts, the confusion reinforced by equally fantastic tales of discovery and wonder brought back from the New World and the Far East. See Wiesner-Hanks, *Marvelous Hairy Girls*, 57. Wiesner-Hanks speaks elsewhere about confusion of humans with other primate species. See especially 29 and 55–9.
9   Alternative spellings include Gonzales and Gonsalvus. The hirsute family travelled throughout Europe; their first names are likewise subject to national variations.
10 Two of the best-known werewolf trials of the late sixteenth century include those of Gilles Garnier, who was executed in the Parlement of Dôle, France, in 1574, and Stubbe Peeter, who was executed in the German town of Bedbur in 1589. Demonstrating that women were also subject to suspicions of demonic lycanthropic, a sensational broadsheet produced by woodblock artist Georg Kress (active 1591–1632) in Augsburg Germany in 1591 reports an astonishing incidence of mass female transformation into wolves. Currently known by the title *Of 300 Witches and Their Pact with the Devil to Turn Themselves into She-Wolves at Jülich, 6 May 1591*, the broadsheet depicts the destruction of men, boys and cattle by a horde of ravening she-wolves and comes complete with graphic rhyming descriptions of brains being sucked and hearts being eaten. The broadsheet is reproduced in Walter L. Strauss, *The German Single-Leaf Woodcut 1550–1600, Volume II* (New York: Abaris Books, 1976), 548.
11 Wiesner-Hanks, *Marvelous Hairy Girls*, 127.
12 Wiesner-Hanks offers the following translation of the letter: 'Don Pietro, a wild man discovered in the Canary Islands, was conveyed to his most serene highness Henry the king of France, and from there came to his excellency the Duke of Parma. From whom [came] I, Antoniette, and now I can be found nearby at the court of the Lady Isabella Pallavicina, the honourable marchese of Soragna.' *Ibid.*, 4–5.
13 *Ibid.*, 29.
14 Christiane Hertel, 'Hairy Issues: Portraits of Petrus Gonsalus and his family in Archduke Ferdinand II's *Kunsthammer* and their contexts', *Journal of the History of Collections*, 13:1 (2001), 1–22 (5).
15 *Ibid.*

16 *Ibid.*, 4–5. Hertel also offers an alternative explanation: that caves are particularly significant to Canary Island culture and as such might operate as a reference to the Gonsalus's ethnicity. See *Ibid.*, 12.
17 One of the four-volume set on animals that Hoefnagel painted *c.* 1575–82 currently in the National Gallery of Art, Washington.
18 There is some confusion as to the miniature's authorship: Wiesner-Hanks lists both van Ravesteyn and Joris's son, Jacob Hoefnagel, as possible contenders. See Wiesner-Hanks, *Marvelous Hairy Girls*, 112.
19 Hertel, 'Hairy Issues', 8.
20 For example, physiognomist Giovanni Battista della Porta. See Merran Toerien and Sue Wilkinson, 'Gender and Body Hair: Constructing the Feminine Woman', *Women's Studies International Forum*, 26:4 (2003), 333–44 (337).
21 Nadja Durbach, 'The Missing Link and the Hairy Belle: Krao and the Victorian Discourses of Evolution, Imperialism, and Primitive Sexuality', in Marlene Tromp (ed.), *Victorian Freaks: The Social Contexts of Freakery in Britain* (Columbus, OH: Ohio State University Press, 2008), 134–54 (147–8).
22 See Toerien and Wilkinson, 'Gender and Body Hair', 337.
23 Aristotle, pseudonym of William Salmon, 'The Midwife's Guide: Illustrated,' *Aristotle's Master-Piece*, Part 1, Chapter 5 (New York: Published for the Trade, 1846), 30.
24 *Ibid.*
25 Mary E. Fissell, 'Hairy Women and Naked Truths: Gender and Politics of Knowledge in *Aristotle's Masterpiece*', *William and Mary Quarterly*, 3rd Series, LX:1 (2003), 43–74 (54).
26 Wiesner-Hanks, *Marvelous Hairy Girls*, 10.
27 *Ibid.*
28 Rosemarie Garland-Thomson, 'Narratives of Deviance and Delight: Staring at Julia Pastrana, the "Extraordinary Lady"', in Timothy B. Powell (ed.), *Beyond the Binary: Reconstructing Cultural Identity* (New Brunswick, NJ: Rutgers University Press, 1999), 81–104 (86).
29 Cindy La Com, 'Ideological Aporia: When Victorian England's Hairy Woman Met God and Darwin', *Nineteenth-Century Gender Studies*, 4:2 (2008), www.ncgsjournal.com/issue42/lacom.htm. Accessed 7 June 2009.
30 *Ibid.*
31 Anne E. Walker, *The Menstrual Cycle* (London: Routledge, 1997), 7.
32 Walker makes this criticism of *Das Weib*, the most influential (and chiefly anthropological) work of the time on the 'science of women'. *Ibid.*, 7.
33 George C.D. O'Dell, *Annals of the New York Stage*, vol. 6 (1850–57), quoted in Garland-Thomson, 'Narratives of Deviance and Delight', 83.
34 *Ibid.*
35 Rebecca Stern, 'Our Bear Women, Ourselves', in Marlene Tromp (ed.), *Victorian Freaks: The Social Contexts of Freakery in Britain* (Columbus, OH: Ohio State University Press, 2008), 200–33 (218).
36 *Ibid.*, 206, original emphasis.
37 Garland-Thomson, 'Narratives of Deviance and Delight', 85. After having been stored at the Anatomy department of Oslo University, Pastrana's embalmed remains were returned to Mexico for burial in February 2013.

38 Showman and freak show manager Guillermo Antonio Farini (birth name William Leonard Hunt) gave his stage name to the young Krao when he launched her career as a 'missing link'.
39 A.H. Keane, 'Krao, the "Human Monkey"', *Nature*, 27:689 (1883), 245.
40 Pamphlet promoting Farini's 1883 exhibition of Krao at the Royal Aquarium, Westminster, cited in Durbach, 'Missing Link and the Hairy Belle', 137.
41 *Ibid.*, 144.
42 *Ibid.*, 136.
43 See *Ibid.*, 150. Durbach directly credits Garland-Thomson's 'Narratives of Deviance and Delight'.
44 Garland-Thomson, 'Narratives of Deviance and Delight', 91.
45 La Com, 'Ideological Aporia'.
46 Edward Long, 'The History of Jamaica. Reflections on its Situation, Settlements, Inhabitants, Climate, Products, Commerce, Laws and Government' (1774), quoted in Sara Salih, 'Filling Up the Space Between Mankind and Ape: Racism, Speciesism and the Androphilic Ape', *Ariel*, 38:1 (2007), 95–111 (108).
47 *Ibid.*, 107.
48 *Ibid.*
49 Durbach, 'Missing Link and the Hairy Belle', 150.
50 Garland-Thomson, 'Narratives of Deviance and Delight', 90.
51 Keane, 'Krao, the "Human Monkey"'. Both claims were later proven to be fabrications.
52 Durbach, 'Missing Link and the Hairy Belle', 139.
53 'The Missing Link', *The Evening Herald*, Tuesday 13 March 1883, 2, National Library of New Zealand, *Papers Past*, http://paperspast.natlib.govt.nz/cgi-bin/paperspast?a=d&d=PBH18830313.2.21. Accessed 3 May 2013.
54 Garland-Thomson, 'Narratives of Deviance and Delight', 92.
55 S. Henahan, 'Atavistic "Werewolf" Gene Localized', *Access Excellence: National Health Museum*, June 1995, www.accessexcellence.org/WN/SUA05/wolfman.html. Accessed on 3 May 2013.
56 Thomas Awtry, 'The "Werewolf" Gene: A Reawakening Gene of Human Evolution, or a Harmful Mutation?', *Creation*, 18:51 (1995), found at www.answersingenesis.org/creation/v18/i1/werewolf.asp. Accessed on 8 May 2009.
57 A.E.W. Miles, 'Julia Pastrana: The Bearded Lady', *Proceedings of the Royal Society of Medicine*, 67 (1973), 160–4 (10).
58 Signor Saltarino (pseudonym) wrote *Fahrend Volk*, a book on circus and freak-show people in 1895, which has been the primary source of much information on Pastrana. See Miles, 'Julia Pastrana'.
59 Francis Trevelyn Buckland, *Curiosities of Natural History* (1860), quoted in Garland-Thomson, 'Narratives of Deviance and Delight', 98.
60 Robert Bogdan, 'The Social Construction of Freaks', in Rosemarie Garland-Thompson (ed.), *Freakery: Cultural Spectacles of the Extraordinary Body* (New York: New York University Press, 1996), 23–37 (33).
61 Durbach, 'Missing Link and the Hairy Belle', 149.
62 See, for example: L. Illis, 'On Porphyria and the Ætiology of Werwolves', *Proceedings of the Royal Society of Medicine* (Meeting 2 October 1963), 57 (January 1964): 23–6, www.ncbi.nlm.nih.gov/pmc/articles/PMC1897308/pdf/procrsmed00212-0043.pdf. Accessed on 3 May 2013.

63 A video of this broadcast is available online. See 'Guinness World Records – Werewolf Syndrome', YouTube, www.youtube.com/watch?v=uf5Rs9EM6oM. Accessed on 5 March 2013.
64 David A. Gerber, 'The "Careers" of People Exhibited in Freak Shows: The Problem of Volition and Valorisation', in *Disability & Society*, 7:1 (1992): 53–69, quoted in La Com, 'Ideological Aporia'.
65 The cause of Zachary's death remains ambiguous in the novel. Micah may simply believe herself responsible when in fact Zachary was killed by wild dogs.
66 Garland-Thomson, 'Narratives of Deviance and Delight', 82, 83.
67 Larbalestier, *Liar*, 80.
68 *Ibid.*, 155.
69 Also known as Lateral Gene Transfer. Outside genetic engineering, it is generally restricted to single cell organisms that are able to incorporate DNA from other organisms without having inherited it.
70 Larbalestier, *Liar*, 155.
71 *Ibid.*, 8.
72 *Ibid.*, 59.
73 Toerien and Wilkinson, 'Gender and Body Hair', 341.
74 Larbalestier, *Liar*, 164.
75 Salih, 'Filling Up the Space Between Mankind and Ape', 109.
76 *Ibid.*, 109.
77 Marina Warner, 'Beautiful Beasts: The Call of the Wild', the fourth lecture of the Managing Monsters' series, *Reith Lectures*, broadcast 16 February 1994 on BBC Radio 4, http://downloads.bbc.co.uk/rmhttp/radio4/transcripts/1994_reith4.pdf. Accessed 10 May 2013. Also published in Marina Warner, *Six Myths of Our Time: Little Angels, Little Monsters, Beautiful Beasts and More* (New York: Vintage Books, 1995), 80.
78 Angela Carter, 'The Tiger's Bride', *The Bloody Chamber* (Croydon: Vintage, 2006), 56–75 (75).
79 Warner, 'Beautiful Beasts', 71, 75.
80 *Ibid.*, 224.
81 Artist statement sent in email correspondence with the author, August 2010.
82 Donna J. Haraway, *Simians, Cyborgs, and Women: The Reinvention of Nature* (New York: Routledge, 1991), 150.
83 Larbalestier, *Liar*, 320.

6

Female werewolf as monstrous other in Honoré Beaugrand's 'The Werewolves'

Shannon Scott

In American and Canadian literature of the nineteenth century, indigenous peoples of North America were frequently equated with wild animals, particularly wolves. The parallel between wolves and Native Americans first emerged during America's colonial period in the seventeenth century, when Northeastern tribes and wolves came to represent the colonists' fight for survival in the wilderness of a new and 'untamed' country. Indigenous peoples were equated with wolves as 'game' and considered fair sport for British colonists. For example, in 1638, a Massachusetts law declared: 'Whoever shall shoot off a gun on any unnecessary occasion, or at any game except an Indian or a wolf, shall forfeit 5 shillings for every shot.'[1] In addition, Native Americans in the north-east and south-east were required to produce 'without compensation' one or two wolf pelts for each tribal hunter as an annual tribute to British colonists.[2]

By the nineteenth century, wolves had been hunted to extinction in the north-east and their loss has often been linked in literature with the forced removal of North American tribes from their land. In a journal entry from 23 March 1856, Henry David Thoreau associates the loss of indigenous animals in Massachusetts with the absence of indigenous peoples:

> But when I consider that the nobler animals have been exterminated here – the cougar, panther, lynx, wolverine, wolf ... I cannot but feel as if I lived in a tamed, and, as it were, emasculated country. ... As if I were to study a tribe that had lost all its warriors. ... Many of those animal migrations and other phenomena by which the Indians marked the season are no longer to be observed.'[3]

Other nineteenth-century authors such as Catharine Maria Sedgwick, Lydia Maria Child, James Fenimore Cooper and Honoré Beaugrand chose to set their narratives during America's colonial period when Native Americans and wolves were still mainly in possession of their land and considered a threat to European colonists.[4] By repeatedly depicting First Nations peoples as predatory, savage and wolf-like, nineteenth-century writers suggested that Native Americans and white colonists were ultimately incompatible, and that Native Americans, like wolves, were a threat that must be eradicated in order to create a peaceful nation. Consequently, this depiction also justified nineteenth-century efforts to dispossess indigenous people from their land. Susan Scheckel contends that the forced removal of Native American tribes from their lands in the nineteenth century became something that had to be 'forgotten' from the national consciousness as the country attempted to build a positive national identity through literature.[5] One method of rewriting history and avoiding the ethical dilemma of 'Indian removal campaigns' was for white authors to set their texts in a period of history when indigenous peoples were more in control of their land and thus could be portrayed as purely predatory.

In 'The Werewolves', published in 1898 in *Century Illustrated Magazine*, Canadian author Honoré Beaugrand takes the motif of 'Indians' as wolf-like one step further by transforming them completely into *loup-garous* or werewolves. Set during Queen Anne's War in 1706, Beaugrand's text emphasises the strained relations between French soldiers, fur traders and members of the Iroquois Confederacy, particularly the Mohawk or Kanien'kehá:ka nation residing in the Kahnawá:ke community near Montreal. La-Linotte-Qui-Chante (the finch who sings) is a Mohawk woman who lives on the Kahnawá:ke reserve and marries a French corporal named Baptiste Tranchemontagne (cut mountain). The marriage soon deteriorates due to Baptiste's infidelity, and La-Linotte-Qui-Chante takes revenge by supernatural means. Although Beaugrand's story depicts tribes in the Iroquois Confederacy (Oneidas, Cayugas, Onondagas, Mohawks and Senecas) as 'loup-garous', the animalism is eventually distilled down to a single figure – Linotte – whose ability to transform into a wolf proves fatal to the hero. As a werewolf, Linotte is the ultimate symbol of otherness in nineteenth-century fiction – female, indigenous and monstrous.

Linotte's name translates as 'linnet' or 'finch' in French, a songbird more commonly associated with fragility (or 'traditional' feminine virtues), as opposed to ferocity or savageness. Her deceptively sweet name highlights Beaugrand's theme of enchanting exteriors that disguise beastly intentions so that beauty becomes a quality not to be trusted. The name 'Linotte' may also imply that the female antagonist is of lower intelligence, because it can mean a 'hare-brained person, a scatterbrain'.[6] Although Linotte's name is misleading in its connection with songbirds, her 'wolfish' traits appear well before readers are aware of her ability to physically transform into a wolf. When she is first introduced, and until nearly the end of the tale, Linotte refuses to speak, and her silence is significant not only because it illustrates a failure to communicate in 'human' terms, but it also perpetuates a common racist myth found in nineteenth-century texts. In Beaugrand's story, the languages of the Iroquois are either completely absent or utterly unintelligible, comprising 'outlandish chants', 'infernal laughter' and 'howling and yelling'.[7] The Iroquois appear to communicate entirely by means of animalistic and deafening cries as opposed to words. Lawrence Rosenwald argues that some white authors (namely Cooper) intentionally depict Native American languages as deficient and simplistic as a way to further justify removal.[8] If Native Americans possess no significant language or culture to be preserved, then their eradication is not such a great loss.[9] It is only recently, in the 1970s, that schools on Kahnawà:ke and Akwesasne began formal instruction in the Mohawk language and culture.[10]

In addition to her silence, Linotte travels at speeds and distances much greater than the French troops, reaching Fort St Frédéric well before the rest of the soldiers to catch up with her unfaithful husband. Her speed is comparable to wolves, notable for their ability to travel long distances, as well as their capacity to cover ground quickly. Linotte's speed and endurance allude to her werewolf identity and make her even more of an antithesis to conventional European notions of domesticity, further suggesting the impossibility of acculturation or assimilation. If women, who are of the fairer and gentler sex, act as wild and barbaric as the men, what hope is there for peaceful cohabitation?

However, Iroquois women, unlike European women in the seventeenth and eighteenth centuries (particularly in literary representations), were not relegated exclusively to the domestic sphere. Many tribes in the Iroquois Confederacy, including the Mohawk nation featured in Beaugrand's narrative, were matrilineal and occasionally matrifocal, so that Native women held significant power and authority within the tribes. Nancy Bonvillain notes that Mohawk women 'controlled distribution of both the food that they produced and the resources and goods contributed by their husbands and sons'.[11] Doug George-Kanentiio adds that political positions were nominated by Mohawk women while traditional governments featured an equal number of men and women.[12] Declarations of war had to be approved by women, especially clanmothers, as did decisions regarding capital punishment and where refugees would be placed once adopted into the tribe.[13]

Karen L. Kilcup writes that 'Indian women were often more valued' due to their participation in tribal economic and political life.[14] The respected position of women in many tribes arguably led Andrew Jackson to recommend specifically targeting Native women during the US campaign against the Seminoles in 1837. When Jackson suggested troops go into Seminole villages and kill women, he claimed their mission would not be successful unless they harmed Native women in particular; he wrote that their mission would be 'like a combined operation to encompass a wolf in hammocks without knowing first where her den and whelps were'. Jackson utilised wolf imagery to dehumanise and demonise the Seminole tribe and justify his own military ruthlessness.[15]

There are also similarities in strategy in terms of literary representations. In Sedgwick's *Hope Leslie* (1827), William Fletcher describes Magawisca as a 'captive' from a 'wolfish tribe [who] were killed or dislodged from their dens'; however, Sedgwick troubles the parallel between wolves and Native Americans by providing tribes with a motive for their 'wolfish' behaviour.[16] In fact, William's son, Everell, attempts to rationalise their wolfishness to his mother, claiming 'hunted, as the Indians are, to their own dens ... they need the fierceness of the wolf'.[17] Beaugrand offers no such rationalisation for the wolf-like qualities of the Mohawk or Linotte. In his tale, the Mohawk have no justification for their transformation into wolves. They are simply bloodthirsty and ruthless by nature, while the French are portrayed more often than not as clueless and superstitious.

Riddled with historical and cultural inaccuracies, 'The Werewolves' unfolds through dual narratives recounted by two narrators, a fur-trapper and a sergeant, both of whom claim first-hand knowledge of their respective stories. Recounted to an audience of drunk and raucous Frenchmen gathered at Fort Richelieu for Christmas, the tales mainly centre on the Iroquois who are 'burning farm-houses, stealing cattle and horses, and killing every man, woman, and child whom they could not carry away to their own villages to torture at the stake' (814). In Beaugrand's text, the Iroquois represent a direct threat to European settlers attempting to cultivate land, 'burning farms-houses' and 'stealing' domestic livestock. Increasingly in the nineteenth century, indigenous people were viewed by the United States government, as well as by the Canadian government, as a barrier to 'progress', since both countries desired tribal land for agricultural and industrial expansion. In the nineteenth century, the tribes living at Kahnawá:ke were also fighting government appropriation of their lands. According to Gerald F. Reid, '[d]uring the middle decades of the nineteenth century the Canadian economy was undergoing an important transition' where 'reserve land was expropriated for the construction of part of the Lake St. Louis and Province Railway'.[18] Land along the St Lawrence River was taken from the Kahnawá:ke reserve to build wharves and other transportation facilities, despite tribal protestations.

Susanne Opfermann adds, 'the traditional justification for expropriation' was that Native Americans did not make 'proper use of and improve the land, whereas white Christians did'.[19] The 'proper use' of land often meant clear-cutting forests for large scale crop cultivation and raising domestic animals for consumption. Throughout the nineteenth century, crop cultivation became a necessity due to continued population growth, and more land was needed for railroad expansion and immigrants settling communities in western territories. However, this expansion had a devastating affect on indigenous peoples, leading to their removal, starvation and genocide. In 1831, Lewis Cass, the Secretary of War under Andrew Jackson, composed 'Removal of the Indians', where he claimed: 'Like the bear, and deer, and buffalo of his own forests, an Indian lives as his father lives. ... He never attempts to imitate the arts of his civilized neighbours.'[20] Cass, contrasting Native Americans with animals, considers not only the forests, but the tribes who live and hunt in forests, as obstacles to agricultural and national growth.

In addition to accusations of 'burning farms', Beaugrand's tale-tellers also claim that the Iroquois attack settlers and refuse to spare women and children from their apparently motiveless destruction. The settlers who survive the attacks only live long enough to be tortured and burned alive. While it is historically accurate that the Iroquois took captives in war to make up for losses sustained during illness or warfare, the captives were often adopted into the tribe, especially if they were women or children. In 1704, one such captive taken by the Mohawk tribe was Eunice Williams who later chose to stay with her Mohawk husband at the Kahnawá:ke settlement despite repeated pleas from her brothers and father, the Reverend John Williams.[21] In *Hope Leslie*, Catherine Maria Sedgwick essentially fictionalises this event when Hope's sister, Mary, decides not only to stay with her husband, Oneco, a member of the Mohawk tribe, but to adopt the Catholic faith preached by Jesuit missionaries at Kahnawá:ke. In Beaugrand's narrative, since both the tale-tellers and the audience of listeners are intoxicated, the accusations of the Mohawk killing women and children are somewhat ironic, somewhat cast in doubt; however, they still perpetuate a damaging and inaccurate stereotype of the Iroquois as pitiless and cruel to their captives.

Of course, the Iroquois in Beaugrand's text do not simply *behave* as wolves that attack innocent farmers and their livestock, they actually *transform* into werewolves. In a scene reminiscent of the frenzied bloodlust displayed by the Huron after capturing the Uncas in *The Last of the Mohicans*, a French fur trapper describes a scene of cannibalistic savagery as the Iroquois gather around a bonfire to devour their white victims:

> [H]alf human and half beasts, with heads and tails like wolves, arms, legs, and bodies like men, and eyes glaring like burning coals, were dancing around a fire, and barking an outlandish chant that was now and then changed to peals of infernal laughter ... [and] unearthly howling and yelling. (817)

The ritualistic dancing and cannibalistic practices of the 'red devils' is directly linked to their religious status as 'heathens' (815). Beaugrand's narrator makes it explicit that the Iroquois transform into werewolves because they are 'renegades' or First Nations peoples who have 'accepted the sacrament only in mockery' (817). This could display the ignorance of the fur-trappers regarding the Midwinter Ceremony where all nations in the Iroquois Confederacy gather for six to eight days of ceremonies and festivities – the final event being 'sacred dancing and a communal feast'.[22] Yet the conflict appears mainly about religious practices since Cooper also focuses on the 'renegade' or 'heathen' quality of the Huron tribe (who were also connected to French Catholicism), depicting their ceremonies as 'unhallowed' and linking them to stereotypical conceptions of European witchcraft.

Cooper's character, Duncan, a soldier recently arrived from Britain, witnesses a scene that 'resemble[s] some unhallowed and supernatural arena, in which malicious demons had assembled to act their bloody and lawless rites'.[23] The Native Americans or 'malicious demons' are endowed with 'supernatural' powers, which stem from an unholy source, creating a tableau suggestive of Hell. The rights they perform are 'lawless' because they violate a Christian doctrine. In particular, one 'withered squaw' or 'hag' acts as a sort of sorceress-ringmaster to the demonic scene, lighting the bonfire that exposes the 'inflamed visages' of the Huron and conducting a ritual that will ultimately lead to the sacrificial-style killing of Reed-that-bends: the 'withered squaw ... moved into the circle, in a slow, sidelong sort of dance, holding the torch, and muttering the indistinct words of what might have been a species of incantation'.[24] The Native woman behaves as a 'witch', incanting and dancing in a hypnotic manner as if she is casting a spell. A similar scene appears in Sedgwick's *Hope Leslie* when Nelema mimes the movements of a snake during a healing ceremony: 'She writhed her body into the most horrible contortions, and tossed her withered arms wildly about her as if she might assume the living form of the reptile whose image she bore.'[25]

The 'true' Christianity of the Iroquois, particularly Mohawk, converts who were the largest presence on the Kahnawà:ke reserve, was in doubt in the early eighteenth century. Jesuit priests at Kahnawá:ke were never entirely certain which Iroquois had 'devoutly' converted to Catholicism and which had conveniently converted only to maintain their traditional rituals and beliefs.[26] Members of the Mohawk nation were the predominant inhabitants of the Kahnawá:ke settlement. In 1667, Jesuit missionaries funded by Louis XIV founded the first settlement that became known as Kahentá:ke or 'at the meadow' and 'La Prairie de la Magdelaine' in French. Members of the Mohawk tribe joined the settlement in larger numbers than other tribes in the Iroquois Confederacy due to its strategic trade location, rich hunting grounds and relative safety from attack by other tribes. In addition, Jesuit missionaries offered economic incentives, including food, land and housing, to indigenous peoples who agreed to settle at Kahentá:ke.[27] In 1669, the French and Native Canadian settlements separated and the First Nations peoples relocated to Lachine Rapids, renaming the settlement Kahnawá:ke or 'at the rapids'.[28] Due to their ties with the French, the Mohawk at the Kahnawá:ke settlement became politically and economically aligned with France. In 1684, the Native settlers at Kahnawá:ke broke away from the Iroquois Confederacy, who were frequently siding with the British in battles against the French.[29] The Native Canadian community at Kahnawá:ke stood with the French during Queen Anne's War (1702–13) when Beaugrand's narrative takes place.

Susan Sleeper-Smith argues that French Catholicism in the seventeenth and eighteenth centuries was used as a means to avoid relocation westward as well as a way to 'network' and 'gain social prominence', particularly for Native women married to French fur traders.[30] As the number of Jesuit priests on tribal settlements such as Kahnawá:ke began to decline in the eighteenth century, Native women often 'assumed the role of lay practitioners', maintaining 'matrifocal households' as well as their tribe's spiritual practices.[31] In Beaugrand's text, the French soldiers and fur trappers fear the 'renegade Indians' and condemn their form of Catholicism. Beaugrand no doubt meant this condemnation ironically, since his portrayal of Catholicism is rife with mocked superstitions, including the protective use of four-leaf clovers and rosary beads.

In the late 1890s, when Beaugrand's text was first published, the suspicion that Native Canadians had ostensibly converted to Catholicism only to 'lapse' back into their traditional beliefs was aroused again when tribal leaders of the Kahnawá:ke community attempted to keep the Sisters of St Anne from establishing their order on tribal land and teaching their brand of Catholicism in all Native schools. The Kahnawá:ke community had to continually fight government interference in their school system as the Sisters of St Anne took charge of community schools.[32] As mayor of Montreal in 1885 and 1886,[33] Honoré Beaugrand may have been aware of these controversies or others involving land appropriation, yet the Iroquois he depicts in his text are not nineteenth-century community leaders fighting to keep the government from clear-cutting their land or forcing dogmatic and repressive education on their children, instead they are the 'wolfish' and unintelligible 'renegades' of the early eighteenth century fighting French settlers and soldiers.

Linotte is similarly viewed as a 'renegade' for her lapsed Catholicism; she is not granted the full agency or transgressive power of a female werewolf who shape-shifts to exact revenge on a cruel and fickle husband. Although Linotte 'had been baptized and duly received in our holy religion, having afterward relapsed into idolatry, [she] had been turned into a loup-garou, condemned to roam by night, while keeping her usual appearance during the day' (821–2). Linotte's animal transformation is a Christian punishment – a divine condemnation, something that happens to her as opposed to a power she utilises at her will for her own purposes. Thus the ability to transform is not a gift or even a choice since, as a shape-shifter, she lacks the authority to time and control her metamorphosis.

This is a very Western view of animal transformation. As Christians attempted to spread their religion to the indigenous peoples in the 'New World', animal transformation was increasingly viewed as demonic and associated with witchcraft. Joslyn Cassady notes that Inuit cultures in Arctic Alaska whose tribal members adopted Christianity were more likely to view animal transformation as 'heathenish' and 'retribution from Satan'.[34] However, before Christianity spread, there was an 'unproblematic fluidity between human and nonhuman persons' in Inuit culture that was 'seminal to transspecies communication'.[35] This 'fluidity', at least in the Inuit culture, was broken by European religious superstitions stemming from medieval and early modern notions of witchcraft.

As a shape-shifter, Linotte's transformations are due not only to her lapsed Catholicism but also her identity as a scorned woman. If the relationship between the 'young Indian maiden' and Baptiste Tranchemontagne, a corporal in the French army, is not exactly promising, it is at least cemented in the bond of marriage (818). After a brief courtship, Baptiste and Linotte are married 'Indian fashion, without much ceremony' (819). Contrary to Beaugrand's depiction of marriage on the Kahnawá:ke reserve, Native Canadian marriage ceremonies were often as elaborate, sacred and binding as French ceremonies. If they were wed 'Indian fashion', there would have been a ceremony where clan leaders congratulated the couple, followed by a communal feast and dancing.[36] There are three principal clans in the Mohawk nation: the Bear Clan, the Turtle Clan and the Wolf Clan. It is possible Linotte is part of the Wolf Clan since her nature is 'aggressive', and she is closely associated with wolves; however, the attributes of Wolf Clan people need not fit generalisations.[37]

Yet, there seems to be nothing authentically Mohawk about their union, since Baptiste gives Linotte's father 'an old musket' in exchange for her hand in marriage (819). Again, if they had been married according to Mohawk tradition, they both would have needed the consent of their mothers, not Linotte's father.[38] Furthermore, Linotte would not have left her household to resettle near Baptiste (819). In Mohawk culture, the property is held by the bride and it is the husband who joins her home and lives on her land.[39] This can be true even in the case of intermarriage. Gerald Reid writes that 'French men who married women from Kahnawá:ke were adopted into families and clans. ... Men still joined the wives in their households.'[40] In fact, 'marriage ceremonies' at Kahnawá:ke often 'took place in the Catholic Church'.[41] Thus Baptiste and Linotte were possibly married by a Catholic priest; however, after their nuptials, Baptiste treats Linotte little better than a mistress.

As a result of his disloyalty, the marriage soon sours and Linotte becomes 'fearfully jealous of Baptiste' – a quality that is considered to be particularly 'Indian' (819). When Baptiste leaves for Fort St Frédéric, Linotte follows him, even though he does not invite her. Shortly afterwards, the Governor-general of Quebec offers 'a grant of land' and 'a dowry of eighty pistols in money' to any soldier who gets 'marrie[d] and settled in the country' (819). Baptiste jumps at the opportunity, abandoning his union to Linotte, and hurriedly finding himself a French girl residing at the white settlement of La Prairie. After he makes 'up his mind to leave the service and to profit by the liberal offers of the government' (819), Baptiste asks the girl to become his wife. Yet, from a historical perspective, his marriage to Linotte would have been more advantageous than his marriage to the girl at La Prairie. If Baptiste desired to settle at Kahnawá:ke and go into the fur-trade, like several characters in 'The Werewolves', he likely could not have found a wife with more 'business' connections than Linotte. Sleeper-Smith notes that French and Native Canadian marriages were valuable for both parties if they were involved in the fur trade.[42] In the seventeenth and eighteenth centuries, French fur trappers gained powerful connections by marrying Native women whose families were already established in the trade, and Native wives often acted as business surrogates for their husbands.[43] Instead, Baptiste spurns Linotte in his hasty desire to marry a white woman who will secure him a temporary supply of government funds.

In the illustrations provided by Henry Sandham, which accompany Beaugrand's story in *Century Illustrated Magazine*, the French girl from La Prairie is depicted from the neck up as if she were posing in a cameo. She is

"A PRETTY GIRL WHO LIVED AT LAPRAIRIE."

blonde and wears her hair drawn back into a bun; the expression on her face is prim and remote, signifying refinement; no smiles or come hither glances.

The neckline of her dress is fairly high and she wears no ornamentation – no necklaces or earrings. In contrast, the illustration of Linotte features her entire body as she leans leisurely backward against a rock. The pose accentuates the feminine aspects of her body – namely her hips and breasts. Her long hair hangs loose down her back and her arms are bare. In the illustrations, as in the text, Linotte is the object of white male desire, but she is treated without respect compared to her peevish-looking European counterpart, and her body is on display in a manner that would not be considered appropriate for a French-Canadian woman. The position and exposure of her physical form suggest licentiousness not domesticity. Chantal

LA-LINOTTE-QUI-CHANTE.

Bourgault Du Coudray claims that 'Beaugrand combines anxiety about female sexuality with fears of racial degeneracy'.[44] Thus Linotte may be a sexualised object of the male gaze, but she still signifies 'degeneracy' due to her racial identity. As the late nineteenth-century discourse on racial regression and eugenics became more contentious, Beaugrand creates a Mohawk character denied an identity as a wife and mother, possibly because her children would carry on a 'degenerate' lineage.

Despite Baptiste's negligent behaviour as a husband, Linotte still considers herself to be his legal wife. As a result, Baptiste becomes increasingly 'embarrassed' and 'annoyed' by her presence (820). He eventually explains his new situation to her and takes 'it for granted that she had become reconciled to the idea of a final separation between them' (820). Baptiste foolishly accepts her silence as acquiescence and fails to foresee Linotte's rage or the revenge that she begins to plot.

The rivalry between the two women leads to further historical inaccuracies. After Linotte learns that Baptiste intends to marry another woman, Baptiste's French fiancée mysteriously contracts smallpox. In a bizarre reversal of facts, the Iroquois in Beaugrand's text actually infect the Europeans with smallpox. Although smallpox 'was then raging among our Indian allies' (820), Beaugrand has the French fiancée become infected through contact with indigenous tribes. In the seventeenth and eighteenth centuries, smallpox repeatedly devastated the Mohawk population in and near Kahnawá:ke. In 1634, smallpox wiped out more than half of the total Mohawk population in just a few months.[45] However, in Beaugrand's story, it is the French girl at La Prairie who perishes from the disease, which is allegedly given to her by Linotte who 'bring[s] to her the germ of that disease' (822). As a strong believer in the prevention of smallpox through compulsory vaccinations, Beaugrand must have been aware of this contradiction.[46] Yet, in this text, Linotte is not only the carrier of sexual degeneracy, but also the carrier of disease.

Devastated by the impending death of the French girl for whom he seems to have little if any genuine feeling, Baptiste goes into a 'large family living room' (most likely a Longhouse) and finds his current wife sitting quietly by the fire 'as the Indians are wont to do' (820). Linotte offers to help Baptiste's sickened fiancée in an oddly stiff and European-sounding speech:

> 'The white maiden whom you love so much will be dead before morning, if I do not come to the rescue. I will go back to Caughnawaga, and ask for a potion that will cure her from our medicine-man. Meet me tonight at twelve o'clock, at the first turn of the road, among the pine trees on the riverside.' (820)

Baptiste, without suspicion of her motives, agrees to meet her at the crossroads at midnight. He fails to recognise the significance of such a traditionally ominous, liminal space, although readers familiar with European folklore would easily identify the crossroads in a darkened forest as a dangerous location. Marina Warner claims that the 'cultural filters' by which colonisers, such as the French in Canada, would attempt to understand the colonised culture were often 'classical myths' or folklore.[47] Douglas Freake and Carole Henderson Carpenter further link Canadian literature and European folklore as a way for Canadians to define 'self' when interacting with indigenous cultures.[48] Freake and Carpenter specifically write that 'French Canadians (such as ... Henri Beaugrand) wanted to preserve the memory of folk culture' and have 'used it in nostalgic remembrance of their past virtually as the childhood of their people'.[49] In this way, Beaugrand uses European folklore as a way to form a new identity for French Canadians outside of France and also as a way, inaccurate and westernised as it may be, to perceive and attempt to comprehend Native culture. Throughout 'The Werewolves', Beaugrand repeatedly approaches Iroquois mythology through the lens or filter of French folklore while simultaneously polluting, or at best ignoring, Native folklore, particularly regarding animal transformation.

Once Baptiste arrives at the crossroads, he 'perceive[s] a pair of eyes glaring at him from the underbrush', which belong to 'a wolf' (820). He fires his gun, but misses a 'wolf of enormous size' (820). Although the distinguishing characteristics are never made quite clear, Baptiste recognises the creature to be a 'loup-garou', and he cuts 'a cross into its forehead' to deter it with a Christian symbol (821). When this tactic fails, he 'completely cuts off one of the fore paws of the animal, who uttered a terrible yell resembling the scream of a woman' (821). The 'growl' that so distinctly belonged to a wolf now transforms into the 'scream' of a woman in pain. Although Linotte's bestial state justifies his violence, the 'womanliness' of her scream indicates that she is victimised while not completely transformed into a wolf. However, her identity as a werewolf and her motivation as a jealous wife clear Baptiste of any wrongdoing. The trick (and this is true in all Victorian stories that feature a female werewolf) is to kill the beast, which is acceptable, but not the woman, which is taboo.

Beaugrand utilises the European motif of the 'tell-tale injury' to reveal Linotte's bestial transformation. The severing of a forepaw belonging to a she-wolf is a trope found in French folktale. In 'The Werewolves', the 'tell-tale injury' similarly reveals Linotte's intention to murder Baptiste, as well as exposing her identity as a shape-shifter and a witch. Because Beaugrand utilises werewolf motifs culled from European folklore (the tell-tale injury, the idea that the 'hide is turned inside out, with their hair growing inward' (817), and the use of Christian symbols to ward off perceived evil), Linotte's ability to transform into a wolf is referred to as 'witchcraft', which either ignorantly or deliberately overlooks the significance of animal transformation in Native American and Canadian mythologies. Whereas in early modern witchcraft tracts and treatises, the werewolf often transforms as the result of a curse or a deal with the devil, animal transformation in indigenous cultures is not typically associated with devilry, or the loss of self, and instead signifies skill and power. The wolf, which was hunted to extinction or near extinction throughout Western Europe, was not hunted with the same abandon by

Native American and Canadian tribes, nor was the transformation into a wolf associated with the demonic. However, in Beaugrand's story, the 'tell-tale injury' reveals Linotte to be a witch in the Western European (Christian) tradition. When a 'human arm, evidently that of an Indian woman' is discovered by Frenchmen, they immediately suspect it to be 'the arm of the renegade squaw' (822).

Henri Boguet, a judge who presided over the most infamous witch trials of the early modern period, wrote of this phenomenon in his treatise on witchcraft, *Discours des Sorciers* (1509). Boguet described a real-life case in Auvergne where a 'huntsman went his way along a valley' when 'he was attacked by a large wolf'.[50] The huntsman was 'compelled to grapple with the wolf' and 'took his big hunting knife, and with it cut off one of the wolf's paws'.[51] Later, the huntsman 'removed the paw from his sack' only to discover that it had turned into a hand wearing 'a gold ring' that he 'recognized as belonging to his wife'.[52] As a result, the huntsman:

> entertained an evil suspicion of her; and going into the kitchen, he found his wife nursing her arm in her apron, which he took away, and found that her hand had been cut off. Thereupon the gentlemen seized hold of her; but immediately, and as soon as she had been confronted with her hand, she confessed that is was no other than she who, in the form of a wolf, attacked ... she was afterwards burned at Ryon.[53]

The severing of her hand/paw reveals Linotte's intention to murder Baptiste, but it does not lead to a confession or even to her death. Beaugrand may utilise a European motif, but he has placed it in a 'New World' context where the consequences have changed.

Although this trope was often deployed in witch trials to excuse executing women for witchcraft, Linotte faces no 'burning stake' for her transgression; instead, she survives, albeit scarred and maimed. In contrast, Baptiste is 'burned at the stake by Mohawks' while a 'one-armed squaw' takes 'special pleasure in inventing the most abominable devices to add to [his] suffering' (823). Linotte metamorphoses into the inquisitor, the torturer, the witch-burner. Her revenge for being scorned and maimed is swift and painful, and there is no comeuppance for the murder of her husband. In fact, Linotte, who has remained silent throughout the tale (with the exception of her single speech), effectively silences her French husband by 'pull[ing] out his tongue by the root' before she 'crushe[s] his skull with a tomahawk' (823). Underneath all the blood and gore that saturate Beaugrand's ending is a view of the frightening 'New World' through the lens of an old European one. As a result, what manifests from the interaction between two cultures becomes a warning that European traditions no longer win out in a landscape where a huntsman who is foolish enough to marry a werewolf can and will lose everything.

Notes

1. Barry Lopez, *Of Wolves and Men* (New York: Scribner, 1978), 170.
2. *Ibid.*, 172.
3. Henry David Thoreau, *I to Myself: An Annotated Selection From the Journal of Henry D. Thoreau*, ed. Jeffrey S. Cramer (New Haven, CT: Yale University Press, 2007), 261–2.
4. Author and politician, Honoré Beaugrand, is also occasionally referred to as Henri or Henry Beaugrand.
5. Susan Scheckel, *The Insistence of the Indian: Race and Nationalism in Nineteenth-Century American Culture* (Princeton, NJ: Princeton University Press, 1998), 3.
6. Denis, Gerard, *The New Cassell's French Dictionary* (New York: Funk & Wagnalls, 1962), 454.
7. Honoré Beaugrand, 'The Werewolves', *Century Illustrated Magazine*, 56.6 (1898): 814–23 (817). Further references are given in brackets.
8. Lawrence Alan Rosenwald, *Multilingual America: Language and the Making of American Literature* (Cambridge: Cambridge University Press, 2008), 24.
9. *Ibid.*, 24. Although Cooper used John Heckewelder as a primary source for his text, he ignored Heckewelder's contention that Native American languages were extremely complex. See *ibid.*, 23–4.
10. Doug George-Kanentiio, *Iroquois Culture and Commentary* (Santa Fe: Clear Light Publishers, 2000), 14.
11. Nancy Bonvillain, *Native Nations: Cultures and Histories of Native North America* (New Jersey: Prentice-Hall, Inc., 2001), 69.
12. George-Kanentiio, *Iroquois Culture and Commentary*, 54–5.
13. *Ibid.*, 56.
14. Karen L. Kilcup, 'Writing "The Red Woman's America": An Introduction to Writing by Earlier Native American Women', in Karen Kilcup (ed.), *Native American Women's Writing 1800–1924: An Anthology* (Oxford: Blackwell Publishers, 2000), 1–12 (2).
15. Ronald Takaki, *Iron Cages: Race and Culture in 19th-Century America* (Oxford: Oxford University Press, 1990), 102.
16. Catharine Maria Sedgwick, *Hope Leslie*, ed. Mary Kelley (New Jersey: Rutgers University Press, 1999), 21.
17. *Ibid.*, 24.
18. Gerald F. Reid, *Kahnawá:ke: Factionalism, Traditionalism, and Nationalism in a Mohawk Community* (Lincoln, NE: University of Nebraska Press, 2004), 18, 19.
19. Susanne Opfermann, 'Lydia Maria Child, James Fenimore Cooper, and Catherine Maria Sedgwick: A Dialogue on Race, Culture, and Gender', in Karen L. Kilcup (ed.), *Soft Canons: American Women Writers and Masculine Tradition* (Iowa City: University of Iowa Press, 1999), 27–47 (36).
20. Takaki, *Iron Cages*, 83.
21. John Demos, *The Unredeemed Captive: A Family Story from Early America* (New York: Vintage Books, 1994), 178.
22. George-Kanentiio, *Iroquois Culture and Commentary*, 43.
23. James Cooper, *The Last of the Mohicans* (New York: Penguin Books, 1986), 237.
24. *Ibid.*, 237, 242.
25. Sedgwick, *Hope Leslie*, 104–5.
26. Reid, *Kahnawá:ke*, 5.

27 *Ibid.*, 6.
28 *Ibid.*, 7.
29 *Ibid.*, 10.
30 Susan Sleeper-Smith, 'Women, Kin, and Catholicism: New Perspectives on the Fur Trade', in Rebecca Kugel and Lucy Eldersveld Murphy (eds), *Native Women's History in Eastern North American Before 1900: A Guide to Research and Writing* (Lincoln: University of Nebraska Press, 2007), 234–74 (237–8).
31 *Ibid.*, 238, 244.
32 Reid, *Kahnawá:ke*, xvii.
33 André Sénécal, 'The Economic and Political Ideas of Honoré Beaugrand in *Jeanne la Fileause*', *Quebec Studies*, 1:1 (1883): 200–7 (201) .
34 Josslyn Cassady, '"Strange things happen to non-Christian people": Human–Animal Transformation Among the Inupiat of Artic Alaska', *American Indian Culture and Research Journal*, 32:1 (2008): 83–101 (84).
35 *Ibid.*, 85.
36 George-Kanentiio, *Iroquois Culture and Commentary*, 64.
37 Tom Porter, *And Grandmother Said … Iroquois Teachings as Passed Down Through the Oral Tradition* (Bloomington, IN: Xlibris, 2008), 102; 105–6.
38 *Ibid.*, 227.
39 George-Kanentiio, *Iroquois Culture and Commentary*, 64.
40 Reid, *Kahnawá:ke*, 14.
41 *Ibid.*, 14.
42 Sleeper-Smith, 'Women, Kin, and Catholicism', 235.
43 *Ibid.*, 237.
44 Chantal Bourgault du Coudray, *The Curse of the Werewolf: Fantasy, Horror and the Beast Within* (London and New York: I.B. Tauris, 2006), 47–8.
45 Reid, *Kahnawá:ke*, 2.
46 John Stockdale, 'Honoré Beaugrand (24 March 1848–7 October 1906)', *Dictionary of Literary Biography: Canadian Writers Before 1890*, vol. 99 (New York: Gale Research, Inc., 1990), 20–2 (21).
47 Marina Warner, *Fantastic Metamorphoses, Other Worlds* (Oxford: Oxford University Press, 2002), 62.
48 Douglas Freake and Carole Henderson Carpenter, 'Folklore and Literature: Canadian Contexts', *Ethnologies*, 21 (1999): 97–114 (98).
49 *Ibid.*, 102.
50 Henri Boguet, *Discours des Sorciers* (1590), trans. by E. Allen Ashwin, in Charlotte Otten (ed.), *A Lycanthropy Reader: Werewolves in Western Culture* (Syracuse: Syracuse University Press, 1986), 77–90 (80).
51 *Ibid.*
52 *Ibid.*
53 *Ibid.*

7

'The complex and antagonistic forces that constitute one soul': conflict between societal expectations and individual desires in Clemence Housman's *The Werewolf* and Rosamund Marriott Watson's 'A Ballad of the Were-wolf'

Carys Crossen

Introduction

The nineteenth century was a significant one in terms of the figure of the female werewolf. The history of the werewolf in fiction was by this point nearly 5,000 years old,[1] and although the female werewolf had appeared in chronicles and treatises on witchcraft prior to 1800, such as Henri Boguet's *Discours execrable des sorciers*, she had not yet appeared in works of fiction that were wholly imagined and created by a single author. Montague Summers remarks in his Preface to Boguet's text that there is 'scarcely a paragraph that is not indicative of the most scrupulous inquiry' and 'most jealous loyalty to the truth'.[2] Boguet's *Discours des sorciers* and other witchcraft tracts are supposedly researched and based on actual incidents, and the female werewolf only made her debut in written fiction in 1839, in Frederick Marryat's *The Phantom Ship*.[3] Moreover, although there was precedent for female authors writing about the werewolf, in Marie de France's *Bisclavret*, earlier stories were focused on the ancient figure of the male werewolf.

But in the nineteenth century, at the *fin de siècle,* female authors at last began to produce fiction about the female werewolf. Two of the most interesting examples of this, which have been curiously neglected by critics, are Clemence Housman's novella *The Werewolf* (1896) and Rosamund Marriott Watson's poem 'A Ballad of the Were-wolf', which was written under the pseudonym Graham R. Tomson and published in 1891. Both these works are of significance because the figure of the female werewolf is utilised to great effect in order express concerns and anxieties about issues facing the Victorian woman. The female werewolf's potential for subversion of societal norms and expectations in any era is considerable, and the female lycanthrope was put to excellent use in this regard by these Victorian authors. Susan Brown notes, 'in their poems, lives and poetry, women poets were expected to represent the domesticity, refinement and purity associated with specifically British or English women'.[4] The werewolf, however, by tradition representative of wildness, violence and unnatural forces such as magic and superstition, was the antithesis of these expectations. As Sandra Gilbert and Susan Gubar suggest in *The Madwoman in the Attic*, the 'dark double' appeared regularly in Victorian women's fiction, representative of the rebellious, supressed urges of both the female characters and possibly also their authors.[5] Gilbert and Gubar elucidate what they mean by the 'dark double':

> Confined within uncomfortable selves as well as within uncomfortable spaces, [the] heroines cannot escape the displaced or disguised representatives of their own feared impulses. Therefore they are destined to endure the repetition of what Freud called 'the return of the repressed.[6]

The werewolf, famously characterised by Freud as the 'beast within',[7] often embodying the unconscious suppression of socially unacceptable urges towards sexuality, violence, and death – particularly where women are concerned – is uniquely suited to this representation. Both Housman and Marriott Watson utilise the figure of the werewolf to give expression to specific conflicts and 'feared impulses' encountered by both their authors and more generally by middle-class, educated women in the late Victorian era. In order to illustrate what I mean by this, I shall first provide a brief overview of the authors and their lives before moving on to an analysis and comparison of their respective texts.

The authors: Clemence Housman and Rosamund Marriott Watson

Clemence Housman was the younger and less well-known sister of A.E. Housman, but was also an author and illustrator. However, in the years since her death both her work and the woman herself have fallen into almost complete obscurity. Biographical details about her are scarce, but some details of her life can be gleaned from books about her brothers, Alfred and Laurence. Though a dutiful daughter, she was 'freed from the Victorian bonds of home' and permitted to attend art school with Laurence Housman in London.[8] She was deeply religious and devoted to High Church Anglicanism. However, Housman was also an ardent suffragette and spent time in prison for tax evasion. She was photographed standing with Laurence outside the prison; A.E. Housman wryly termed it 'a lovely portrait of my disreputable relatives'.[9] Clemence never married, but remained devoted to her brother and they served as lifelong companions for each other. Laurence himself never married either and it has been suggested that he may have been gay: Sandra S. Holton makes this assertion in her history of the suffrage movement.[10] Clemence's own sexual preferences are unknown. Their two-person household was an eccentric one that allowed for fluidity and mixing of gender roles. Laurence Housman's biographer Rodney Engen offers a gem of an anecdote when writing 'she was "Uncle Clem" to her nephews and nieces due to her low-pitched voice; he, with his high-pitched voice, was "Aunt Laurence"'.[11] Housman was not a prolific author, writing only three novellas in her lifetime, but her story *The Werewolf* occupies a pre-eminent position in nineteenth-century werewolf fiction, with critics labelling it 'the classic werewolf story of the late nineteenth-century'[12] and noting that it met with critical acclaim when first published.[13]

The life of Rosamund Marriott Watson is a complete contrast to that of Housman. She was twice divorced, and lived with her last partner out of wedlock. Moreover, these relationships produced four children, three of whom she was forced to relinquish to the custody of their respective fathers when divorcing them.[14] Whereas Housman was principally an artist and wrote in prose, Marriott Watson was predominantly a poet, making much use of the ballad, which is often regarded as a particularly feminine medium.[15] She was lauded and accepted in literary circles under the pen name Graham R. Tomson, derived from the name of her second husband, and she became acquainted with writers such as J.M. Barrie and Oscar Wilde, winning much admiration. She nevertheless relinquished her literary fame and many of her friends upon her second divorce, choosing instead to write as Rosamund Marriott Watson. She was a celebrated poet during her lifetime, devoted to aestheticism, but like Housman fell into obscurity after her death. 'This marital and poetic history indicates a principal reason for Graham Tomson's nearly entire erasure from literary history', states Linda K. Hughes, though she goes on to assert Watson's 'cultural significance'.[16] Hughes attributes this significance to Marriott Watson's unconventional lifestyle, the merits of her poetry, and particularly her choice of poetic subject matter: marriage and the problems it engendered for women, a subject few other women poets approached.[17]

'So hideous and terrible a thing': Housman's *The Werewolf*, masculine love and feminine rebellion

A summary of Housman's *The Werewolf* runs thus: it focuses on twin brothers, Sweyn and Christian, who live in a snowy, remote land which, arguably, is a version of medieval Denmark.[18] Both brothers are renowned hunters and trackers, although Sweyn is considered the superior in most athletic pursuits. It is emphasised that he is the more handsome and dashing of the two, as well as the more self-absorbed and selfish, while his morally superior brother is often slighted by him. One night, a knock and a voice are heard at the door, but when it is opened no one is present. The voices of an old person, a child and a man are heard before Sweyn opens the door to a beautiful young woman, who gives her name as White Fell. Sweyn is instantly infatuated; Christian alone perceives that she is a werewolf, after he sees wolf tracks leading up to the doors of their homestead, but none going away from it. Christian's attempts to warn people of White Fell's menace are dismissed as jealousy and later insanity and his effort to kill her by dousing her with holy water fails. However, after two people go missing after being kissed by White Fell (a child and an old woman, in an echo of the unseen people at the door) everyone grows suspicious with the exception of Sweyn, who refuses to acknowledge any slander against the woman he so admires. Matters come to a head when Christian realises that his twin is marked as the next victim. He chases White Fell across the tundra, knowing that if he glimpses her turning into a wolf at midnight she will be trapped in animal form for eternity. He chases her down, despite being severely injured by her, and White Fell tears out his throat – only to be killed by his blood, for 'no holy water could be more holy, more potent to destroy an evil thing than the life-blood of a pure heart poured out for another in free willing devotion'.[19] The next day Sweyn tracks them; he finds Christian's body lying alongside a huge white wolf, and realises Christian has re-enacted the Crucifixion story and has suffered and died for his sins.

The story is termed a religious allegory by Charlotte Otten,[20] and indeed there are several allegorical features such as the significant naming of Christian, the temptation of the fallible Sweyn by a woman in a reference to the story of Adam and Eve, Christian's death pose, arms flung out to the side mimicking Christ on the cross, and of course, White Fell's status as a werewolf. Although the immediate connection – perhaps opposition would be a more accurate term – of the werewolf with Christianity may not be immediately apparent, Adam Douglas identifies parallels between the wolf and the Devil in medieval theology, suggesting that 'the eternal enemy of the lamb is of course the wolf, and the shift toward Christ the Lamb led to the growing use of lupine imagery in Satanic iconography'.[21] Douglas admittedly is referring to wolves rather than werewolves in this passage, and there are also numerous examples of good Christian werewolves in literature, particularly during the late medieval period: Joyce E. Salisbury comments on the 'many fine qualities' of literary werewolves from this era.[22] However, I believe Douglas's observation to be a useful one in analysing *The Werewolf*. The parallel between Christian and Christ, the emphasis on Christian's meekness and other gentle qualities suggest Christ the Lamb, all of which conspires to cast White Fell as the Satanic werewolf suggested by Douglas's analysis. And if we probe a little further into the nature of Sweyn's sin and Christian's sacrifice, Housman's ardent Christian beliefs, as well as the moral convictions of Victorian society appear to strengthen this reading of the story. Sweyn's sin, for all his admiration of White Fell's beauty and physical strength in the story, is not the sin of sexual experience – his only physical contact with the werewolf appears to be a single kiss, which White Fell herself uses to mark her victims rather than to seduce them. Sweyn's sin is not his admiration – or his love – for White Fell, but his contempt for Christian.

In middle-class Victorian society of the late nineteenth century – the society inhabited by the Housman family – love between men, the deep abiding love between male friends, particularly brothers, was considered to be the highest, most spiritual form of affection that existed, and men were encouraged to develop such relationships. The male-dominated institutions of the nineteenth century – the church, parliament, the armed forces, and most importantly the public schools – sidelined women and emphasised relations between men. Such homosocial bonds are not uniquely Victorian: Jeffrey Richards states that such friendship in Victorian society was 'steeped in the past' and founded upon 'the medieval chivalric ethic',[23] thus making it a particularly appropriate topic for Housman's story with its medieval setting. Such love was composed of:

> [firstly] a brotherhood, of a spiritual rather than a physical kind. Secondly, it involved notions of service and sacrifice, frequently death on behalf of the beloved. Thirdly, it [was] higher than, and different from, rather than a substitute for, the love of women.[24]

Sweyn's sin in the context of the story is his rejection of this bond; he turns away from his twin and from the high, spiritual love offered to him by Christian. His fall is not a fall into sexual sin, as one might expect, but a fall from brotherhood. His redemption at the end of the story is signalled by his realisation of all Christian has suffered and sacrificed for him, and by his realisation of White Fell's dual nature – not difficult now that she has turned back into a huge white wolf in death. Housman further emphasises the parallels with the Crucifixion story by describing how Sweyn carries Christian's body back to their homestead in rather biblical-sounding language: 'he knew surely that that night he entered hell, and trod hell-fire along the homeward road, and endured it only because Christian was with him'.[25] Despite Christian's death, Sweyn comes to recognise the purity and devotion of his love and reciprocates at last, realising the Victorian ideal of manly love.

This exaltation of brotherly love and condemnation of female wickedness and temptation is in keeping with what we know of Housman as a devoutly religious woman, a lover of stories about selflessness and self-sacrifice. Housman's High Church beliefs would have brought her into regular contact with what was, at the time, an overwhelmingly patriarchal institution. Carol Engelhardt Herringer asserts that 'in neither church nor chapel … could women preach or hold positions of authority; their role in religious assemblies as in the home was to support male authority'.[26] It seems unlikely that such an ardent suffragette would have accepted this exclusion and submission to male authority, but Housman openly expresses her faith in her writings, which in the case of *The Werewolf* and her later work *The Unknown Sea*

(1898) centre on devout young men, in the first book eliminating, in the second saving the soul of a beautiful, sinful young woman. True wickedness and sinfulness is the province of women in her stories, which would suggest that Housman internalised social beliefs of her day concerning woman's innate moral weakness. Victorian girls, in order to preserve their purity were usually left 'morally untested' under the watchful eyes of their mother, as Martha Vicinus notes wryly.[27] But Lynda Palazzo, in her study of Christina Rossetti's *Goblin Market* (1862) – another text that has sometimes been interpreted as Christian allegory – has commented that 'if women's suffering has its source in gender oppression by men, there is real difficulty in accepting the efficacy of a male saviour who would thus seem to be participating in such oppression'.[28] Admittedly there is little outright female suffering in *The Werewolf*, unless we count White Fell's one female victim whose death is not described, or White Fell herself, who does die but whose death is apparently a swift one. But what is evident in the text is Christian's complete and utter determination to destroy White Fell; no other resolution to the story is considered for a moment. Christian may be cast as the saviour in the story but it is undeniable that he is the main proponent of White Fell's eventual demise.

Clemence Housman herself was no stranger to the demands of home and family; after losing her mother at an early age she cared for her younger siblings, and in later years virtually supported her family by taking over the role of clerk to her father's ailing business.[29] Her brother Laurence later recalled that she was often awake until two o'clock in the morning working through their father's neglected paperwork. Laurence's biographer Rodney Engen speculates that this sacrifice was not without its painful aspects; he notes some lines from a poem written when Housman was nine: 'her brows were knit in everlasting pain/ Hers were the lips that never smiled again'.[30] Engen goes on to say that 'there was also, especially now, a poignancy about those lines. They seemed to summarise the self-sacrificing Clemence as she pored over her father's neglected tax work.'[31] It seems that Clemence Housman, while debarred from having a professional life akin to her father's, was expected to facilitate her father's own career, in addition to nursing her mother and taking care of her younger brother, in the self-sacrificing tradition of Victorian women. One wonders at the noticeable absence of fathers and father-figures in *The Werewolf* and whether it was a reflection on Clemence's own family experience.[32] So why would a woman accustomed to painful repression of herself and who fought against the same collude with the oppression of a woman, even if only in fictional form?

Guessing at authorial intent is always dangerous, particularly when we know so little about an author, but it is possible that Housman's religious beliefs and her family obligations may have played a role in her killing off her female werewolf – subconsciously if not mindfully. As noted, she had a passionate belief in the High Church, with its patriarchal hierarchy and its central story of supreme male sacrifice. It is not so surprising then, that she kills off her female wolf, the sworn enemy of the lamb and of Christ, the Lamb of God. To have her triumph would be unthinkable. But in trying to adhere to this interpretation we encounter a problem: Christian, representative of church, home and patriarchal authority, does not triumph either. Housman's religious beliefs were clearly an influence on her work – but there were other passionately held convictions in her life, and foremost amongst these was her belief in women's suffrage. An ardent supporter of the suffragette movement and a militant suffragette herself, Housman has never been described as a feminist or a supporter of women's rights beyond the vote. But her life offers some clues as to her stance on women's rights. Despite Housman's devotion to her family, she was able to study art and eventually became an author and artist. Moreover, she remained unmarried throughout her life; in *Sexual Anarchy*, Elaine Showalter observes that 'by the turn of the century, there were feminists and suffragists who saw celibacy as a "silent strike" against oppressive relations with men'.[33] Indeed, it is unlikely that Housman could have proceeded with an artistic career and study had she been tied to a husband and children. She chose independence and some measure of freedom, in an era when according to the social mores of the day 'the perfect lady's sole function was marriage and procreation'.[34] Housman's beliefs in women's rights and her own desire for autonomy appear to have found expression, in concert with – or in opposition to – her religious conviction, by appearing in her lycanthropic novella.

The first indication of this comes in the story's depiction of its ostensible villainess, the werewolf White Fell, and it is in this portrayal that the religious allegory described earlier begins to falter. Housman's story is written from the point of view of her hero Christian, so it is difficult to obtain a rounded view of White Fell's character, biased as Christian is against her. Christian's own belief in White Fell's evil is unshakeable: adjectives and descriptions such as 'dreadful, so hideous and terrible a thing', are continually employed to describe her.[35] But Housman herself appears to have had far more ambiguous feelings towards her lycanthropic creation. Although Christian finds White Fell abhorrent, there is a sense of a sneaking admiration for White Fell's fearlessness and independence within the text (certainly her choice of life as a huntress is never criticised). It would also be tempting to read homosexual desire into Housman's lingering descriptions of White Fell's physical beauty: 'wonderful and beautiful was that wrist, slender and steel strong'.[36] The appearance of her male characters in contrast, is mentioned briefly at the start and seldom remarked upon afterwards. Unfortunately, given that we know so little of Housman herself, this must remain conjecture, although it is entirely possible that it was not simply sibling loyalty to Laurence that led Clemence to avoid marriage throughout her life. Moreover, although Christian determinedly depicts White Fell as monstrous, Housman's text appears a little uncertain as to where the monstrosity lies, in White Fell or in Christian's imagination. White Fell is a werewolf indeed, but precisely *why* this ensures her wickedness is never quite established; certainly her actions are not as horrendous as Christian's disgusted loathing of her suggests. Christian is described as 'curdling with horror' as he watches her in one scene, yet White Fell is only playing with a toddler and is not hostile or violent towards anyone.[37] Certainly, it is strongly implied that she is responsible for two deaths in the tale, those of the child, Rol, and an old woman, Trella. We do not actually witness these deaths – they occur 'offstage' as it were, which has the effect of distancing the audience from White Fell's brutality. Also, White Fell herself is not conventionally monstrous in appearance; she does not actually turn into a wolf except when she dies. That White Fell brings death is a reasonable assumption, but then death will be a frequent occurrence in such a harsh, remote land, and not necessarily an evil thing. White Fell's monstrosity is at best understated, at worst a projection of Christian's own fears and jealousies, as Sweyn certainly seems to believe.

Is White Fell, at first glance the representative of evil in the tale, therefore an avatar for the female author, embracing the liberty Housman herself struggled to obtain? White Fell quite literally breaks out of her own skin into the shape of a wolf, shedding all constraints of a womanly form. She dresses like a man: 'the fashion of her dress was strange, half masculine and yet not unwomanly'.[38] She roams and hunts like a man, and it is emphasised that she can match Sweyn, the peak of manly physical perfection, in all athletic pursuits save those requiring brute strength – and then only because she is smaller and lighter. Her unparalleled freedom must have been enticing, however guiltily, to a woman who was forced to sacrifice herself for the good of her family for several years at least. Housman's divided loyalties – her religion and family obligations on one hand, freedom, suffrage and independence on the other – appear divided between White Fell and Christian, between the werewolf and her most implacable foe. And there is no compromise, no resolution between them; both die at the climax of the tale. It is one or the other, or none, but never both. White Fell is too rebellious, too unfeminine by the standards of the day to be allowed to survive, while Christian is too devoted to his belief in her evil. But even White Fell's rebellion has a fatalistic quality to it; she cannot fight, only flee.

White Fell, with her beauty, her rebelliousness, her efforts to escape, is an inheritor of a long literary tradition of feminine monstrousness, one that Gilbert and Gubar argue has its origins in 'the first woman and the first monster'.[39] In their examination of the monstrous female in literary history, Gilbert and Gubar focus closely on a figure from Jewish apocrypha, one that closely resembles White Fell: Lilith, Adam's first wife. Referring to 'apocryphal Jewish lore' as well as Lilith's appearances in more recent literature – such as George McDonald's *Lilith*, published the year before Housman's *The Werewolf* – Gilbert and Gubar assert that 'the problem Lilith represents has been associated with the problems of female authorship and female authority'.[40] For them, Lilith is emblematic of the difficulties surrounding female authorship, despite the fact that her story does not centre around writing or penmanship. According to Gilbert and Gubar, Lilith's attempts at authorship come when she tries to define herself: an act for which she pays a terrible price.[41] There is no middle ground: either women are doomed to a life of silence and passivity, or else their 'monstrous pen tells a terrible story' and must also be silenced.[42] At first it seems a stretch to apply this version of Lilith to Housman's story; after all, White Fell is no author. The figure of Lilith does correspond to that of Housman herself, however, who did use her pen to tell 'terrible stories', full of pain, suffering and sacrifice. And Lilith's rebelliousness against the authority of her husband (as Gilbert and Gubar tell it) does have some parallels with White Fell's flight across the tundra:

> [W]hen he [Adam] tried to force her submission, she became enraged and, speaking the ineffable name, flew away to the edge of the Red Sea ... Lilith preferred punishment to patriarchal marriage, and she took her revenge against God and Adam by injuring babies – especially male babies.[43]

It is impossible to say if Housman had Lilith's story in mind when writing, but White Fell does follow this pattern of rebellion, albeit in reverse order; she is presumably the one responsible for a little boy's vanishing, and later she flees and is punished by death for refusing to submit to Christian('s) authority. But like Lilith, her ancestor, White Fell's 'one woman revolution emphasises her helplessness and her isolation, for her protest takes the form of a refusal and a departure, a flight of escape rather than an active rebellion like, say, Satan's'.[44] Housman too emulated the escapes of White Fell and Lilith, running from the confines of marriage and family to life as an artist in London. But with no resolution offered between patriarchal repression and female/wolfish rebellion within the story, we must be left to wonder if Housman herself achieved any form of resolution between her religion and her ambitions.

'The tane of us shall fa'': Marriott Watson's 'A Ballad of the Were-wolf' and the problem of marriage

Conflict of a different nature soon becomes apparent when reading Rosamund Marriott Watson's poem 'A Ballad of the Were-wolf'. Marriott Watson's poem, written in Scottish vernacular, opens on a dark, stormy night in a remote farmhouse, a setting not unlike that of Housman's *The Werewolf*. A farmer's wife sits brooding by the fire: her husband enters and immediately upbraids her, asking why she looks so angry when 'I have scotched yon great grey wolf/ That took our bairnies twa'.[45] The farmer goes on to boast that he slashed at the wolf with his knife, slicing off one of its front paws. He tosses the pouch containing the wolf's paw into his wife's lap, promising that 'an' the next time that we meet, gudewife/ The tane of us shall fa'', meaning that one or both of them will perish in the ensuing conflict.[46] The wife opens the pouch: it does not contain a wolf's paw, but a woman's hand. The wife rises, still silent, and slowly unwinds the cloths wrapped around her right arm, revealing a bloody stump where her hand ought to be. The poem ends with this revelation – its audience can only guess at the eventual outcome of the struggle that will presumably result. Although at first glance Watson's poem differs considerably from Housman's work, making use of the medium of poetry instead of prose and writing in Scottish dialect rather than Housman's polished, formal style of language, there are more than a few similarities present if we examine the poem closely. Marriott Watson's choice of the ballad style in composing this poem is particularly notable; as mentioned, the ballad was considered to be a particularly feminine medium. K.K. Ruthven asserts that:

> The denial of a classical education to women was bound to have the effect of making them feel somehow unqualified to write the 'learned' poetry preserved in a high-brow print culture which dissociated itself from such 'vulgar' manifestations of oral culture such as the ballad. It is therefore no mere coincidence that women were custodians of the ballad tradition in the crucial period when ballads were first collected and printed.[47]

Marriott Watson's choice of the ballad form also unexpectedly aligns her work with that of Housman. Although Housman did not make use of the ballad tradition when writing her novella, she does refer to it in a scene where White Fell sings a mournful dirge to an assembled audience, Sweyn and Christian among them. White Fell's song attracts the attention of Trella, an old woman who is a repository of old ballads, stories and folklore. Trella states that White Fell reminds her of her dead daughter, and that White Fell sings with the same voice. Trella's efforts to align White Fell with her daughter suggest an attempt by the older woman to claim a literary heir, to find another daughter to pass her store of knowledge on to. This attempt at passing on 'vulgar' oral culture is of course thwarted by the efforts of Christian, exponent of the written word of God. Despite the fact that this oral tradition does not survive the old woman who embodies it, Trella's knowledge proves accurate and useful when used against White Fell, suggesting that she holds power via her storytelling. Marina Warner has explored the etymology of the phrase 'old wives' tale' in her study of fairy tales, claiming that the label authenticated 'the folk wisdom of the stories by stressing the old woman who had carried on the tradition'.[48]

Marriott Watson's poem is also an attempt to transmit, to pass on this 'vulgar manifestation'. Her choice of the feminine form of the ballad was quite possibly deliberate, a conscious decision *not* to use more masculine forms of poetic expression. Gilbert and Gubar suggest, when reviewing the startlingly high number of orphaned and homeless women in nineteenth-century literature by women, that 'what all these characters and their authors really fear they have forgotten is precisely that aspect of their lives which has been kept from them by patriarchal politics: their matrilineal heritage of literary strength, their female power'.[49] This female power is thwarted in Housman's story by Christian's destruction of White Fell – but also, it must be admitted, by White Fell herself, who is implied to have killed Trella and so rejected her position of literary heir to a feminine tradition. However, this could also represent another element of the feminine struggle for self-assertion and subjectivity. Marianne Hirsch asserts that:

> The heroine who wants to write, or who wants in any way to be productive and creative, then, must break from her mother, so as not to be identified with maternal silence. Like Electra and Antigone, she must find a male substitute for maternal nurturance, one that will aid her in gaining access to a more conventional definition of heroism.[50]

Although Hirsch perhaps did not mean her theory to be applied quite so literally, there are many echoes of Housman's own experience in this passage; 'the maternal silence' could be interpreted as her mother's death or her family's expectations of her, and Housman did indeed 'break' from her family (and presumably her mother's memory) in order to become a writer and artist. Moreover, it also suggests that White Fell's killing of Trella represents an attempt to find her own voice, rather than being continually associated with that of her 'mother'. With Trella gone, White Fell is free to sing her own songs, to be productive and creative.

Marriott Watson, in choosing the ballad form for her poetry, sidesteps the issue of her heroine's mortality and need for a literary heir, by incorporating her matrilineal literary heritage into her text's form rather than its content. Hilary Fraser, when examining the figure of the Victorian poetess, states that:

> Women poets were frequently obliged to develop strategies to negotiate or subvert the masculine literary history that was their only inheritance in order to intervene as speaking subjects in a literary tradition that had them typecast as silent objects of desire and inspirational muses.[51]

Watson's efforts to subvert this masculine literary history come not only in this ballad form, but also in her choice of poetic subject: the conflict between husband and wife. Her 'gudewife' is eventually revealed to be, like White Fell, a werewolf, which as shown at the start of this chapter, was often encoded as a distinctly male monster. This choice of the werewolf in itself could be interpreted as an effort to subvert masculine literary history, given that for thousands of years the female werewolf was non-existent in written fiction. However, it is notable that throughout the poem, the wife remains totally silent: she never speaks for herself, only holding out her maimed arm in response to her husband's vows of vengeance. Again, she bears more than a passing resemblance to White Fell, who, despite her aforementioned singing, is a remarkably silent character, seldom speaking throughout Housman's story. But surely in rendering her female character mute, Marriott Watson is in fact colluding with, rather than subverting, the literary tradition that rendered female characters silent in the first place. This, however, turns out not to be the case. As a wife sitting by the hearthside, awaiting the return of her husband, the wife of the poem is at first glance the typical 'angel in the house', the angelic figure of domesticity first eulogised by Marriot Watson's near-contemporary Coventry Patmore. But Marriot Watson's 'gudewife' is no angel: her silence, by the end of the poem, has become distinctly ominous, suggesting that no further words are needed and that violence will be the only resolution to the rift between the spouses. When analysing the poem, Linda K. Hughes states that '[t]he "Werewolf" ... represents woman's wildness that can underlie a tame exterior', and it is to the husband's detriment that he realises this too late.[52] The 'gudewife' may be a typical Victorian hearth angel in that she is silent, but she is silent only because she has no need of words: she has a maimed arm to display in order to reveal the truth, and presumably she will also have claws and teeth to defend herself with. Her silence aligns her with the wolf that she turns into, which is also presumably mute, again suggesting the wildness and animalistic impulses that may lurk behind an angelic appearance.

Moreover, Marriott Watson's choice of the werewolf as the central figure for her poem actually suggests a link to and a subversion of the angel in the house. Hughes, in an analysis of the work of a Victorian author named John Fiske, suggests that:

> Fiske linked these amalgams of human and beast [werewolves and swan maidens] to the figure of the angel; because, as Fiske argues, the figure of the werewolf originated in the howling night wind, the werewolf is a 'leader of departed souls' ... Graham Tomson likewise links the bird-bride and the female werewolf to the angel – the angel of the house.[53]

Again, the figure of the silent wife waiting by the hearth suggests the figure of the angel. But the suggestion of the werewolf as a 'leader of departed souls' is particularly interesting in the context of Marriot Watson's poem. I have already quoted the line which describes the werewolf 'that took our bairnies twa'. Although not dwelt upon in this poem, this single line contains the disturbing suggestion of maternal infanticide, of the wife and mother killing her children. The children's exact fate is not revealed within the poem, which says only that they were taken away by the werewolf, but the implication is that they were killed. This is the complete antithesis of the Victorian conception of womanhood as destined for matrimony and motherhood: the wife of the poem is an unnatural mother, either slaughtering or abandoning her children in defiance of social prohibitions. Again, it is possible to see parallels between Marriott Watson and her lycanthropic creation, given that in order to pursue her love affairs Marriott Watson was forced to relinquish custody of her own children, an action that could be interpreted as abandonment.[54] This also aligns Watson's werewolf with other 'unnatural' women in myth and legend, most obviously the aforementioned figure of Lilith, who according to apocryphal tradition took revenge on God and Adam by killing children.

The disappearance of the couple's children mentioned in the poem, as well as the discord between husband and wife, suggests the dissatisfaction Victorian women, Marriott Watson among them, may have experienced with domestic life. Marriott Watson's solution to this frustration was apparently, like Lilith, to flee it, but the 'gudewife' of the poem confronts it head on. The wife's repressed frustration, of course, finds shocking expression in the form of the werewolf. Hughes suggests something very similar when speculating upon the 'wildness' that may lie behind a woman's 'tame' façade. It would not be too much of an exaggeration to suggest that, by the standards of her day, Marriott Watson may also have been considered 'wild'. She was divorced not once, but twice in an era when divorce was difficult to obtain and carried a great deal of social stigma, and when custody of any children passed automatically to the husband. Marriott Watson, as noted, lost custody of three children in this manner. Moreover, she remained unmarried throughout her last great love affair, which, coupled with the fame (later transformed into notoriety after her second divorce) she had achieved as the poet Graham R. Tomson, ensured that she and her lover were left social pariahs.[55] In this regard, Marriott Watson herself can be aligned with the figure of the werewolf, a creature that lived beyond the realms and borders of human society in nineteenth-century fiction. Of course Marriott Watson's situation was not quite this extreme, but the parallel remains.

Notably, in 'A Ballad of the Were-wolf' Marriott Watson approaches a subject few other Victorian poets attempted: that of marriage and conflict within marriage. To return to the idea of the frustration with domesticity, perhaps the 'wildness' in Marriott Watson's 'gudewife' could be read as stemming from a resentment and anger towards her husband and possibly also towards her children. Marriott Watson's presentation of the fracas that may result between a married couple is a bleak one: as noted, it presumably ends with the death of one or both spouses. But the poem is notable in that it offers a subversion of and argument against the Victorian notion that marriage and motherhood were the only suitable occupations for a woman. Hughes has observed that Marriott Watson's problems in her first marriage started, perhaps not coincidentally, in the year that saw the first publication of her work,[56] and so presumably Marriott Watson was well aware of the difficulties and hardships awaiting a woman who tried, as Clemence Housman also tried (and eventually succeeded), to escape 'the Victorian bonds of home'. But the wife in 'A Ballad of the Were-wolf', despite her womanly silence and dutiful waiting by the hearth, cannot reconcile herself to the role of wife and mother. She is presumably responsible for the deaths of her 'bairnies', and it becomes impossible for her to reconcile her lycanthropy with her marriage – her husband will not accept it. He will not even accept her anger: when the wife dares to glower at him, he admonishes her, saying that she should welcome him home and criticising her for 'the red licht in [her] e'e!'[57] The wife is not permitted to express unfeminine emotions such as rage and bitterness, and she must suppress all such feelings in order to please her husband. The result, when the repressed feelings eventually return in the form of the wolf, is bloody and vicious.

Marriott Watson's choice of a wife and mother figure for her werewolf, rather than a presumably unmarried woman such as White Fell, is significant in this regard. The expectation of middle-class women of the Victorian era was that they would find fulfilment through marriage and procreation. Shirley Foster comments on this supposition:

> One of the most pervasive ideologies of the age rested on the assumption that the ideal womanly virtues – sacrifice, self-effacement, moral purity, service – were best expressed in the vocations of wife and mother. To be truly feminine, a woman must fulfil the beneficent functions which nature has assigned her.[58]

Although Marriott Watson's 'gudewife' has apparently fulfilled these vocations – she is both a wife and a mother – by Victorian standards, it is highly doubtful that she could be considered 'truly feminine'. Yes, she is married and has had children, has fulfilled the functions assigned to her by nature, but at the same time she has resisted and subverted them. Like White Fell, she is in rebellion against her subordinate role to her husband, evidenced by her anger, and she completely goes against the nurturing role expected of the Victorian mother by killing or at the very least abandoning her children. It is worth noting that none of the four women examined in this chapter – the two fictional lycanthropes and their respective authors – actually fulfil the prescribed roles necessary for 'true' femininity. Housman and her lycanthropic creation both remained unmarried and childless, preferring freedom and independence over having to submit to the demands of a husband and family. By contrast, both Marriott Watson and her 'gudewife' married and bore children, but failed to embody the ideal womanly virtues such as sacrifice and service, with Marriott Watson placing her desire for love and personal success ahead of duties to her already-existing husband and children, and doing this twice. Her lycanthropic wife also fails to embody the womanly virtues listed by Foster, and ultimately fails to fulfil the functions of wife and mother. The potential of the werewolf for subversion is exploited to dramatic effect in Marriott Watson's poem, with the poet combining the antithetical figures of the good wife and the werewolf to emphasise the problems that could arise in marriage, as well as expressing feminine dissatisfaction in the restrictive role assigned by society. Was any of Marriott Watson's own dissatisfaction with her marriage expressed in this poem? As with Housman, this must remain speculation.

Conclusion

So what conclusions can be drawn from the works of Housman and Marriott Watson, which are among the earliest examples of female authors utilising the figure of the female werewolf in their writing? First of all, the female werewolf's potential for feminine empowerment is evident in both texts. Both White Fell and the 'gudewife' display strength, resolution and wildness, despite some of the darker aspects of their natures. Neither is particularly violent or overtly sexualised, but their refusal to conform to social pressures by other methods is evident. Both the 'gudewife' and White Fell participate in what Showalter has termed a 'silent strike' against the repressive role of the perfect Victorian woman, the angel in the house, and both do it by refusing to submit to a man, whether a husband or an opponent. However, for the most part, the potential for female power and subversion remains precisely that – potential.

Yet another similarity between the works is that neither can offer any kind of true resolution between the conflicting forces present. No resolution can be achieved between Christian and White Fell, between Housman's faith and her suffragette convictions; no resolution seems possible between Marriott Watson's character of the husband, demanding wifely obedience, and his wife, refusing to submit and in fact attacking her husband in wolf form. Marriott Watson too, though she defied societal expectations of her as wife and mother, paid an exceedingly high price for doing so, losing as she did her children, friends and literary reputation. The lesson offered by these texts appears to be that, at the time, there was no compromise to be found between these opposing factions – except in death. A grim solution, but it appears to be the only method by which these rebellious women can find some measure of escape from the constraints imposed upon them, both by men and by society. Chantal Bourgault du Coudray has noted that while the male werewolf could often be redeemed from his lycanthropic status, very often the only fate for a female werewolf was what she rather poetically terms a return 'to the earth from whence she came'.[59] Du Coudray admittedly does not affirm that she is referring to Victorian literature when making this statement, but the examples she offers to support this statement are all drawn from nineteenth-century literature (and include Victorian authors such as George Reynolds and Rudyard Kipling). Moreover, as du Coudray observes, in the context of Victorian literature redemption would be problematic at best for the female werewolf. To be a woman who defied convention meant isolation and alienation, as the example of Lilith shows us, or in extreme (literary) cases, exile or death, as in the case of White Fell and the gudewife.

But the legacy of nineteenth-century female writers who featured the female lycanthrope, such as Housman and Marriott Watson, is not devoid of optimism. Although White Fell met her eventual death (the fate of Marriott Watson's 'gudewife' remains a mystery), many of the female werewolves who followed them in the twentieth and twenty-first centuries would discover ways to survive the dictates of society, and even reconcile the demands made on them as women with the demands of being a werewolf. These later werewolves also realise some of the potential only ever hinted at in the work of Housman and Marriott Watson: the potential for female empowerment through sexuality and violence. Angela Carter was the forerunner of this particular trend in stories such as 'Wolf-Alice' and 'The Company of Wolves', but a recent explosion in popularity of the fictional werewolf ensures that many more female werewolves are appearing in written fiction. Whereas White Fell and the 'gudewife' are seldom (if ever) permitted to engage in violence, or express themselves sexually, many of the female werewolves who follow them are sexual, independent and not afraid to fight should the need arise. The female werewolf could not be reconciled with society, or vice versa, when Housman and Marriott Watson were writing, but their female werewolves offered examples of feminine independence and strength, characteristics that have been passed down to their literary descendants. And although their authors may have fallen into obscurity in the years following their deaths, the increasing popularity of the werewolf, particularly in literature, suggests that White Fell and the 'gudewife' may be revived to inspire a new generation of female werewolves with their resistance to and subversion of patriarchal society, and a new vision of what Clemence Housman herself termed 'the complex and antagonistic forces that constitute one soul', whether the subject is the soul of a woman, the soul of a werewolf or both combined.[60]

Notes

1 Brian J. Frost, *The Essential Guide to Werewolf Literature* (Madison, WI: The University of Wisconsin Press 2003), 81.
2 Montague Summers, 'Editor's Preface', in Henri Boguet, *An Examen of Witches*, trans. E. Allen Ashwin (Mineola, NY: Dover Publications, 2009), v–xxv (vi).
3 Frost, *Essential Guide to Werewolf Literature*, 81.
4 Susan Brown, 'The Victorian Poetess', in Joseph Bristow (ed.), *The Cambridge Companion to Victorian Poetry* (Cambridge: Cambridge University Press, 2000), 180–202 (189).
5 Sandra Gilbert and Susan Gubar, *The Madwoman in the Attic: the Woman Writer and the Nineteenth-Century Imagination* (London: Yale Nota Bene, 2000), 360.
6 Ibid., 443–4.
7 Chantal Bourgault du Coudray, *The Curse of the Werewolf: Fantasy, Horror, and the Beast Within* (New York: I.B. Tauris, 2006), 66. Freud, to my knowledge, never actually termed mankind's unconscious desires as 'the beast within', but as du Coudray observes, he used the word 'wolfish' to describe the unconscious and du Coudray refers to his characterisation of the unconscious as 'the beast within' repeatedly.
8 Richard Perceval Graves, *A.E. Housman: The Scholar-Poet* (London: Routledge and Kegan Paul, 1979), 64.
9 Ibid., 138.
10 Sandra S. Holton, *Suffrage Days: Stories From the Women's Suffrage Movement* (London: Routledge, 1996), 140.
11 Rodney Engen, *Laurence Housman* (Stroud: Catalpa Press Ltd, 1983), 28.
12 Charlotte F. Otten, *A Lycanthropy Reader: Werewolves in Western Culture* (Syracuse, NY: Syracuse University Press, 1986), 283.
13 Frost, *Essential Guide to Werewolf Literature*, 81.
14 Linda K. Hughes, '"Fair Hymen Holdeth Hid a World of Woes": Myth and Marriage in Poems by "Graham R. Tomson" (Rosamund Marriott Watson)', *Victorian Poetry* 32:2 (Summer 1994): 97–120 (97).
15 K.K. Ruthven, *Feminist Literary Studies: An Introduction* (Cambridge: Cambridge University Press, 1984), 117.

16 Hughes, 'Myth and Marriage', 99.
17 *Ibid.*, 99.
18 The clues lie in an illustration by Laurence Housman of Christian approaching a church; the carving to the right appears to be St Michael slaying the dragon. St Michael was a popular saint in Scandinavia, and his cult developed early in Denmark in particular. See Clemence Housman, *The Werewolf* (London: Bodley Head, 1896), frontispiece.
19 Clemence Housman, 'The Were-Wolf', in Otten, *Lycanthropy Reader*, 286–320 (316).
20 Otten, *Lycanthropy Reader*, 283.
21 Adam Douglas, *The Beast Within: A History of the Werewolf* (New York: Avon Books, 1992), 115. Douglas states that the connection of the wolf with the Devil first became popular in the thirteenth century; however, Housman apparently uses the same connection for this story.
22 Joyce E. Salisbury, *The Beast Within: Animals in the Middle Ages* (London: Routledge, 1994), 166.
23 Jeffrey Richards, '"Passing the Love of Women": Manly Love and Victorian Society', in J.A. Mangan and James Walvin (eds), *Manliness and Morality: Middle-Class Masculinity in Britain and America, 1800–1940* (Manchester: Manchester University Press, 1987), 92–122 (93).
24 *Ibid.*, 93.
25 Housman, 'The Were-Wolf', 320.
26 Carol Engelhardt Herringer, *Victorians and the Virgin Mary: Religion and Gender in England, 1830–85* (Manchester: Manchester University Press, 2008), 144.
27 Martha Vicinus, *Suffer and be Still: Women in the Victorian Age* (London: Indiana University Press, 1972), ix.
28 Lynda Palazzo, *Christina Rossetti's Feminist Theology* (Basingstoke: Palgrave, 2002), 27.
29 Engen, *Laurence Housman*, 18.
30 *Ibid.*, 17
31 *Ibid.*
32 Sweyn and Christian's father is never mentioned in the story, nor are any other fathers, although it is suggested that Sweyn and Christian's mother is a person of some influence. Aside from the brothers, adult male figures are curiously absent from the entire work.
33 Elaine Showalter, *Sexual Anarchy: Gender and Culture at the Fin de Siècle* (London: Virago, 1992), 2.
34 Vicinus, *Suffer and be Still*, x.
35 Housman, 'The Were-Wolf', 304.
36 *Ibid.*, 303.
37 *Ibid.*, 294.
38 *Ibid.*, 291.
39 Gilbert and Gubar, *Madwoman in the Attic*, 35.
40 *Ibid.*, 35–6.
41 *Ibid.*, 35.
42 *Ibid.*, 36.
43 *Ibid.*, 35.
44 *Ibid.*

45 Rosamund Marriott Watson, 'A Ballad of the Were-wolf', in Montague Summers, *Werewolf* (Whitefish, MT: Kessinger Publishing Co., 2003), 266–7 (266), ll.11–12.
46 Marriott Watson, 'Ballad of the Were-wolf', l.24.
47 Ruthven, *Feminist Literary Studies*, 117.
48 Marina Warner, *From the Beast to the Blonde: On Fairy Tales and Their Tellers* (London: Vintage, 1995), 19.
49 Gilbert and Gubar, *Madwoman in the Attic*, 59.
50 Marianne Hirsch, *The Mother/Daughter Plot: Narrative, Psychoanalysis, Feminism* (Bloomington, IN: Indiana University Press, 1989), 45.
51 Hilary Fraser, 'Victorian Poetry and Historicism', in Joseph Bristow (ed.), *The Cambridge Companion to Victorian Poetry* (Cambridge: Cambridge University Press, 2000), 114–36 (123).
52 Hughes, 'Myth and Marriage', 104.
53 *Ibid.*, 105.
54 Linda K. Hughes, *Graham R: Rosamund Marriott Watson, Woman of Letters* (Athens, OH: Ohio University Press, 2005), 230.
55 *Ibid.*, 218–30.
56 Hughes, 'Myth and Marriage'.
57 Marriot Watson, 'Ballad of the Were-wolf', l.8.
58 Shirley Foster, *Victorian Women's Fiction: Marriage, Freedom and the Individual* (London: Croom Helm, 1985), 5.
59 Du Coudray, *Curse of the Werewolf*, 56.
60 Housman, 'The Werewolf', 302.

8
I was a teenage she-wolf: boobs, blood and sacrifice

Hannah Priest

In 1984, Neil Jordan's film *The Company of Wolves* was released. Based on the short fiction of Angela Carter, the film used a portmanteau storytelling format and vivid, visual symbolism to draw a clear and unequivocal parallel between female adolescence, menarche and lycanthropy. Jordan's film was not the first piece of cinema to connect the teenage body to the transformation into werewolf; Gene Fowler Jr.'s *I Was a Teenage Werewolf* was released in 1957, and presented lycanthropy as related to the hormonally driven male adolescent body in a way that would be revisited by Rod Daniels in his 1985 comedy horror film, *Teen Wolf*.

However, unlike *I Was a Teenage Werewolf* and *Teen Wolf*, *The Company of Wolves* specifically focused on female adolescence, and drew parallels between the pubertal female body and the lupine that reconsider femininity, femaleness and corporeality in a number of ways. Catherine Orenstein suggests, in Jordan's film, that the 'heroine's bestial side is an acknowledgement not only of her natural sex drive but also of her sexual complexity'.[1] This reading of the text – which is not an unusual one – situates the relationship between lycanthropy and the female sex as a 'natural' one, and one that is first revealed and explored at the onset of puberty. Again, *The Company of Wolves* is not the first narrative to have made this explicit connection, and much of the symbolism presented by Jordan has its basis or inspiration in Carter's texts.[2] Nevertheless, the film is one of the earliest texts to take lycanthropy-inflected female adolescence as its primary narrative focus: the film offers a relationship between hormonally-driven bodily change, developing sexual identity and a 'heroine's bestial side' that is both naturalised and universalised in such a way as to make it *the* metaphor for teenage female lycanthropy – at least in some examinations of the female werewolf.

This chapter considers presentations of adolescent female lycanthropes in fantasy fiction written after Jordan's 1984 film, focusing specifically on texts in which a teenage female is both the central character and the intended reader. As I will argue, while some sense of the connection between lycanthropy and menarche (or, more generally, menstruation) remains, recent fiction has moved away from presenting this as a primary metaphor for adolescence. Nevertheless, tropes emerge in the 1980s that are developed in the fiction of the early twenty-first century, which seek to situate the negotiation of lycanthropy alongside the development of a young woman's identity. This is, in many respects, grounded in a concept of corporeality, and of 'hegemonic ideas about acceptable and unacceptable female bodies'.[3] However, it is equally bound up in discussion of social identity, interaction and sacrifice. In addition to this, while earlier texts (and, indeed, some later horror narratives) present the lycanthropic menarche as a 'natural' part of female development, fantasy fiction written in the decades following Jordan's film instead presents change as a negotiable and voluntary process, which can be reconfigured and repurposed where necessary (or desired).

The curse

First published in 1989, Suzy McKee Charnas's short story 'Boobs' tells the story of Kelsey, an eighth-grade girl (age 13–14 years) who has developed 'boobs' and started her periods before anyone else in her class. Kelsey finds herself transformed (almost overnight) from a lean tomboy who could wrestle and race with the boys, to a full-chested and hormonal woman. She does not embrace these changes, and they are accompanied by mockery and physical violence from her male classmates – in particular, from Billy Linden. Not only does Billy break Kelsey's nose when she stands up for herself, but he also boasts about other assaults, including the rape of a seventh-grade girl.[4]

Thus, the story suggests, as Kelsey begins puberty, she enters a world of sexual violence and vulnerability, quite distinct from her pre-pubescent existence. Elsewhere, references to the dangers and consequences of sexual behaviour surround Kelsey's transformation. Her classmate Rita is shunned by others because her brother has AIDS. One night, Kelsey overhears her father and stepmother 'messing around right through the walls'; shortly afterwards, her stepmother falls pregnant and encourages Kelsey to see a new sibling as 'good preparation for being a mother [her]self later on'.[5] Kelsey responds to this with disgust:

> Sure. Great preparation. Like Mary O'Hare in my class, who gets to change her youngest baby sister's diapers all the time, yick. She jokes about it, but you can tell she really hates it.[6]

Kelsey's interjection of 'yick' here highlights the liminality of her adolescent state. While the onset of menstruation and the development of breasts supposedly signals the state of womanhood (with maternity 'naturally' following soon after), Kelsey's reaction is in a childlike idiom. The early part of Charnas's short story associates Kelsey's first period with an (unwanted) entry into an 'adult' reality of rape, disease and motherhood. Her stepmother tries to frame this as a positive event – claiming menarche as a tribal rite of womanhood – but Kelsey only sees menstruation in terms of awkwardness, odour and 'gross' discharges.

However, the night that Kelsey starts menstruating is the night she first becomes a werewolf. In this respect, 'Boobs' has some parallels with the horror film *Ginger Snaps* (2000, dir. John Fawcett), in which the connection between female lycanthropy and adolescence is also explored. Nevertheless, there are some marked differences between Charnas's story and *Ginger Snaps*, and these have much to do with genre – as well as having implications for the development of the female werewolf in young adult (YA) fiction in the early twenty-first century.[7]

While Ginger's transformation into a werewolf in the 2000 film is presented as *paralleling* (in a grotesquely exaggerated fashion) a girl's pubescent metamorphosis, Kelsey's lycanthropy represents an *escape* from adolescence. Ginger's first period (which coincides with her being bitten by a savage creature in the woods) marks the beginning of a decline into uncontrollable sexuality, rejection of sibling loyalty, drug use and violence; the film can be read as a 'metaphor not just for the horrors of puberty, but also for the limits placed on female sexual subjectivity'.[8] However, as Chantal Bourgault du Coudray argues, '[i]n horror, nature is an alien presence (the beast within)' and, although du Coudray's argument here relates to the male werewolf, we can read Ginger as being a victim of a 'nature' that is 'forcing [her] to behave like an animal against [her] conscious will'.[9] 'Boobs', on the other hand, is a work of fantasy, and, therefore, is intended to offer its readers 'far more positive and accepting relationship with the inner wolf, a stance that promotes survival'.[10]

Kelsey's disgust at both puberty and the adult world it entails is a rejection of the loss of control such changes require. Though Kelsey's lycanthropy only occurs during a full moon, it is presented throughout 'Boobs' as a willed transformation – one that is in opposition to the involuntary metamorphosis of the pubescent body:

> I mean it felt – interesting. Like something I was doing, instead of just another dumb body-mess happening to me because some brainless hormones said so.[11]

There is no moment of 'infection' or 'infliction' of werewolfism for Kelsey. Unlike Ginger, she is not bitten by a werewolf. Indeed, there is no indication in 'Boobs' that any other werewolves exist. The change into werewolf is something that Kelsey deeply desires, and it comes about as a result of her attempts to gain control over her unruly body. That this is a desire common to many teenage girls is made clear when Kelsey remembers Edie Siler, a girl who starved herself to death in the tenth grade:

> I understood her perfectly. She was trying to keep her body down, keep it normal-looking, thin and strong, like I was too, back when I looked like a person, not a cartoon that somebody would call 'Boobs'.[12]

Kelsey's lycanthropy is thus presented as an avoidance of puberty – likened more to anorexia than adolescence – and the body she inhabits as a wolf is closer to that of her 'normal-looking, thin and strong' child-body than her 'cartoon' woman-body. As a wolf, she is lean and can run fast without 'boobs bouncing and yanking in front'.[13] Her eventual encounter with Billy Linden in the woods is one of violence – she rips his throat out – not of sexuality, as Billy believes it to be. Kelsey has regained the physical dominance over boys that she had as a tomboy child, although, whereas once she would get the upper hand in wrestling, she now tears out their guts. Significantly, this physical domination is presented as a specifically female behaviour. Kelsey's dislike of 'boobs' does not masculinise her, but rather aligns her with a non-normative teenage femininity. As Judith Halberstam states, tomboyism is often 'associated with a "natural" desire for the greater freedoms and mobilities enjoyed by boys', but it 'remains comfortably linked to a stable sense of a girl identity'.[14] Kelsey wishes to retain her tomboyism beyond its appropriate existence as a 'childhood' identification, and so is subject to 'severe efforts to reorient' her gender identity towards the 'conformity' of womanhood.[15] What lycanthropy offers is a way of resisting these efforts.

However, 'Boobs' is not simply a story about rejecting womanhood and remaining a girl/she-wolf forever. It is a story about self, transformation and control, which connects it to the later narratives of teen female werewolves, which tend not to rely on menstrual and pubertal metaphors in their construction of lycanthropy. Kelsey's narrative ends with her more successfully integrated into teenage (rather than adult) life. She rekindles her friendship with a girl named Gerry-Anne and is asked out on a date by a male classmate. Her transformations into a werewolf have allowed her to slow down the dangerous descent into adulthood and sexuality taken by some of her peers, and have given her the confidence to take things at her own pace. Unlike the seventh-grader raped in Billy's garage or the anorexic Edie Siler, Kelsey is able to choose her own rate of metamorphosis and ensure her own survival.

Although Kelsey's lupine transformation is governed by a monthly cycle, Charnas also suggests that lycanthropic transformation must be desired in order to occur. Conversely, Kelsey reveals anxiety about its possible permanence:

> I mean, suppose that was it, suppose having killed and eaten in my wolf shape, I was stuck in this shape forever? Like, if you wander into a fairy castle and eat or drink anything, that's it, you can't ever leave. Suppose when the morning came I didn't change back?[16]

Charnas's narrator draws a distinction between the world of the werewolf and the world of the 'fairy castle'. Fairies here can be understood as representing the allure (and the threat) of permanence and the denial of change.[17] Werewolves, in Charnas's narrative, *should* be the polar opposite of this, as they promise continual change and flux. The fear of the young protagonist is not that she will transform from human to wolf, but rather that she will be forced into one unchanging identity position.[18]

The bone-popping, sinew-stretching transformation scene remains a staple of werewolf cinema, and indeed much werewolf fiction. Nevertheless, young adult female werewolf stories often offer something different – rejecting terrifying *moments* of transformation in favour of sustained *narratives* of transformation. It should be remembered that it takes the entirety of *Ginger Snaps* for Ginger to fully transform into a werewolf, despite being 'infected' early in the film; similarly, in *Ginger Snaps 2: Unleashed* (2004, dir. Brett Sullivan), Ginger's sister Brigitte is transforming gradually throughout the film. When Ginger and Brigitte are werewolves – when they reach the end of their transformation – the narrative ends. While Charnas's Kelsey adopts wolf form regularly, we can read an underlying anxiety about the possibility of transformation – and, by extension, narrative – coming to an end.

Going through some changes

In the female werewolf YA fiction of the early twenty-first century, it is rare to find lycanthropy explicitly associated with menarche, as it is in 'Boobs' and *Ginger Snaps*. In part, this is reflective of the different age of the heroines and the exploration of post-adolescent (rather than adolescent) femininity. The YA novels under consideration in the remainder of this chapter have heroines aged between sixteen and nineteen, thus the onset of menstruation is unlikely to be an integral part of their narrative.[19] However, the menstrual cycle more generally is also rarely presented as 'a key lycanthropic trigger' in contemporary YA she-wolf fiction.[20] Nevertheless, transformative bodily identities remain a significant feature of these narratives.

In Maggie Stiefvater's *Shiver*, the first novel in her Wolves of Mercy Falls series, the teenage heroine Grace Brisbane meets an attractive young man named Sam Roth who, it transpires, is a werewolf. This follows the common generic pattern of an 'ordinary' high school girl meeting a mysterious, brooding young man, who is later revealed to be some type of supernatural creature – often a vampire, werewolf, fairy or fallen angel. This chapter will refer to novels that use this opening premise as paranormal romance, as this is a common classification in publishing and marketing. Moreover, this categorisation encourages a focus on both the 'paranormal' and 'romance' aspects of the texts, which perhaps further explains the move away from the association of menstrual narratives and lycanthropy. The menstruating werewolf – and the menstruating woman more broadly – is often read as (potentially) evoking the image of the *vagina dentata*, and, thus, the *castatrix*.[21] While this continues to be a significant association within horror, the paranormal romance genre rarely posits such a relationship between the young woman, her own body and the bodies of men around her.[22]

As is standard in paranormal romance, Stiefvater's werewolf trilogy begins with an ostensibly human girl meeting a nonhuman male. However, like much of the female werewolf fiction under consideration here, this paradigm is undermined by an early acknowledgement of the heroine's own 'monstrous' identity. Grace herself was attacked by werewolves as a child, causing her to become somewhat obsessive about wolves and isolating her from her peers. Although she has been bitten, Grace is *not* a werewolf, but she *should* be – she has been 'infected', but has never undergone the transformation. This is explained by the fact that, in Stiefvater's novels, werewolf metamorphosis is controlled by changes in temperature: werewolves are wolves in the winter and humans in the summer. Shortly after her attack, Grace's inattentive father accidentally locked her in a car during a heat wave. The subsequent fever after being 'cooked' prevented Grace from ever 'shifting'.

Not only is Grace 'supposed' to be a werewolf, she also strongly desires to be one. At the beginning of *Shiver*, we see this desire clearly:

> During those long months, I had imagined great adventures where I became a wolf by night and ran away with my wolf to a golden wood where it never snowed.[23]

Importantly, Grace desires temporary transformation: she wishes to be a wolf 'by night', but to return to human form during the day.

As Grace gets to know Sam, she discovers that lycanthropy is, in fact, a dangerous thing. It results in a gradual loss of the human self, and death after ten or fifteen years. Much of *Shiver*, therefore, is concerned with Grace's search for a 'cure' for Sam; she is ultimately successful in this search.

At the beginning of *Linger*, Sam is now a 'cured' human, but Grace still longs for transformation. Despite knowing that Sam hated his lycanthropy and is happier as a human, Grace is still obsessed with the idea of being a werewolf. The first words of the second novel are: 'This is a story of a boy who used to be a wolf and a girl who was becoming one.'[24] Grace is not a werewolf but rather a *becoming-werewolf*.

Eventually, Grace's lack of physical transformation begins to make her ill. With the help of his friends Cole and Isabel, Sam realises that, though 'wolf toxin' is dangerous, it is the shift between forms that helps the body cope with the 'infection'. Thus, it is not healthy to be either immutably wolf or immutably human – one needs to switch between the two regularly in order to survive. The protagonists find a dead wolf in the forest who has not 'shifted' for over a decade; shortly afterwards, Grace becomes seriously ill, having also resisted 'shifting' for a number of years. The only thing that can save her is forcing her to transform.

So, at the very end of *Linger*, Grace becomes a werewolf. The metamorphosis is narrated by Sam, but there is no visual moment of change because he averts his eyes. Instead, Grace's change is described thus: 'And then she cried out, and the girl I knew was gone, and there was only a wolf with brown eyes.'[25] While this may seem somewhat anti-climactic compared with scenes of tearing muscles and elongating bones, it has taken two full novels to get Grace to this point.

Transformation as a process, rather than an instance, is also posited in Bree Despain's Dark Divine series. In the first novel, *The Dark Divine*, the heroine – also called Grace – begins her narrative as an 'ordinary' human, though it is soon revealed that the young man she has feelings for is a werewolf. Like Stiefvater's Grace, Despain's protagonist has an undeniable connection to lycanthropy and is eventually bitten and infected. Throughout the novel, Despain's Grace contends with her developing relationship with Daniel (the lycanthropic love interest of the series) as well as her relationships with her parents, siblings and peers.

Despain's Grace must balance a negotiation of her role within the social world with a recognition of her role within the paranormal world. Werewolves, in *The Dark Divine*, are primarily figured as monstrous; they began as 'Hounds of Heaven', divinely ordained demon-slayers, but have long since degenerated into ferocious and dangerous creatures.[26] Grace must determine whether Daniel is redeemable, or whether he will fall victim to a prophesised descent into uncontrolled bestial rage. More importantly, she must decide how much of the 'monster' she is willing to accept into her own life, and how much of a transformation she should endure.

Ultimately, Grace accepts transformation as necessary and important in her life and her relationship with Daniel. She has been bitten by a werewolf, and so she submits to her metamorphosis. However, it is significant that Grace does not assume lupine form in *The Dark Divine*. As with Stiefvater's novels, the transformation of the female werewolf is a lengthy process and lacks a visual and visceral moment of change. The first novel in Despain's series ends with Grace explaining her fear and frustration at her lack of change:

> 'But the wolf *is* in me. My wounds healed so fast … and I feel stronger. I feel like all I want to do is run. … It will take me over someday.'[27]

Grace's transformation has begun – she has the accelerated healing and increased strength of the werewolf – but it is not yet complete. A full bodily change will not occur until the second book of the series.

Amazing Grace

The coincidence of the heroines' names in the Dark Divine and Wolves of Mercy Falls series has interesting implications for a consideration of female werewolves in YA fiction. The concept of 'grace' is an important aspect of characterisation in these novels. In both Despain and Stiefvater's novels, to become a werewolf is not simply to indulge in a selfish desire or as 'a release for sexual hunger';[28] it is part of a reciprocal 'gift' that is shared between the heroines and their lovers.

Stiefvater's *Shiver* narrates the heroine's journey through lycanthropic desire, from her first infection towards her eventual transformation. However, this plot is intertwined with the concomitant narrative of her lycanthropic lover, Sam, with chapters alternately narrated by Grace and Sam. Sam's relationship to lycanthropy is different; he has more experience of it, understands its dangers and wishes to reject this aspect of his identity. Grace, therefore, must balance her own desire to transform with her boyfriend's contradictory desire to end metamorphosis and become 'fixed' as a human.

It is not Grace herself who eventually devises a possible cure for lycanthropy, but rather her friend Isabel (the human sister of another werewolf, Jack). Isabel decides to infect Jack, Sam and new werewolf Olivia with bacterial meningitis, believing that the subsequent fever will 'cook' and eradicate their wolf sides. Nevertheless, while the 'plan' belongs to Isabel, the 'gift' of the cure falls to Grace. It is Grace who administers the vial of infected blood to Sam, and it is she who will bear the burden and weight of responsibility for the outcome. When it comes to the reality of injecting family and friends with potentially fatal infected blood, Isabel is unable to act.[29] Grace must assume the lead role in carrying out the procedure, despite knowing that she may be contributing to the death of the young man she loves.

The cure Grace offers does not work as intended. Jack dies of meningitis within a few days, and – significantly – the female werewolf Olivia rejects the cure in favour of succumbing to inevitable seasonal metamorphosis. However, the werewolf that Grace loves, the one for whom the cure was intended as a 'gift', does survive. Sam recovers from meningitis, finds his lupine side has been destroyed, and is eventually reunited with Grace in the final pages of the novel. This reunion represents an inversion of the book's opening scenes, in which a human Grace yearns to run in the winter forest with the lupine Sam: now Grace is further along in her own transformation to wolf form and Sam approaches her as a human. To save her lover, the heroine has accepted guilt and responsibility, but also lycanthropy.

This notion of lycanthropic 'grace' – the self-sacrificing gift that the heroine can bestow on her troubled and imperilled lover – is arguably developed further in Despain's Dark Divine series. Despain's werewolves are presented within a more overtly Christian framework than those in any of the other novels under consideration here.[30] As noted, werewolves themselves are divinely created, though are presented as 'fallen' in the present of the novel. The heroine, whose full name is Grace Divine, is also the product of religion – not only in a general sense, as a person constructed through a Christian worldview, but in a specific and personal sense, as the daughter of a Christian pastor. Like Stiefvater's heroine, Despain's Grace is determined throughout the first book of the series to find a cure or resolution for lycanthropy, especially when she realises it not only affects her lover but also her brother.

Daniel, the werewolf love interest of the series, explains to Grace that he fears a descent into the bestial madness and immorality that inevitably follows lycanthropy. He makes her promise that she will kill him as soon as she sees any sign of this. Towards the end of *The Dark Divine*, Daniel is faced with a confrontation that will, it seems, entail such a loss of control; however, things are complicated by the fact that Grace is now infected with lycanthropy herself and, as soon as she kills for the first time, her own soul will be in jeopardy. Grace is faced with a choice: save herself or save Daniel.[31] Grace chooses to risk her own immortal soul in order to save Daniel's. Tellingly, it takes only one short paragraph before her decision is made:

> I could not break this promise.
> *I am grace.* …
> *I will be the monster for you.*[32]

In the novel's final pages, it is revealed that the heroine's choice was a piece of misdirection. She was able to save Daniel's soul without endangering her own. The lovers are reunited, with Daniel explaining that, because she killed him as 'an act of love', he was able to be cured without Grace forfeiting her own identity.[33] This explanation reinforces the idea of the heroine's acceptance of lycanthropy being an act of grace, as Daniel says 'only the ultimate gift of love could have freed [his] soul'.[34]

While Grace's choice itself is free of the ominous consequences she imagines, her act of choosing is still a fundamentally important one. It is her willingness to make that choice that is 'the ultimate gift'. Moreover, Grace's gift has not only saved her lover, but has also allowed her a further level of control over her own life. Daniel tells her that her 'grace' in saving him means that she herself may not be at risk from 'the curse' of the werewolves:

> 'You don't have to become one of the dark ones. You can fight it. You can turn this curse into a blessing. You can become the hero. You can become truly divine.'[35]

By accepting her role as 'grace divine', the heroine is able to be the werewolf she wants to be, finally integrating her lycanthropic desire with her Christian sense of purpose and self.

Grace Divine's acceptance of lycanthropy is a 'gift', but it is also a sacrifice – just as Grace Brisbane (in Stiefvater's novels) sacrifices her own peace of mind and well-being in order to save Sam. Significantly, in both books, this leads to a reunion with a (presumed lost) lover and a heightened sense of self-integration and awareness. These narratives suggest that, while regular transformation is an important and necessary facet of lycanthropic identity, this must be combined with a willingness to act for the 'greater good' when it is appropriate.[36]

Call of duty

Andrea Cremer's Nightshade series offers a different 'type' of werewolves to those found in Stiefvater and Despain's fiction; nonetheless, an emphasis on integrating personal desire with the 'greater good' is, once again, presented and explored. Cremer's werewolves are a different species to humans – though the possibility of 'turning' a human or 'removing' a werewolf's 'wolf' is revealed as the trilogy progresses – and live in a pack-based, hierarchical and ritualised society. The werewolf pack is rigidly patriarchal in structure, with an 'alpha' and his mate dictating behavioural roles to the werewolves under their rule. This is made more complicated in Cremer's novels, as the werewolves (called 'Guardians') are ruled by a race of ostensibly supernatural beings called 'Keepers'.

The heroine of Cremer's trilogy, Calla, is the daughter of the alphas of the Nightshade pack. In the second chapter of the first novel, *Nightshade*, an arranged marriage is made between Calla and Ren, the son of another pack's alpha. This union has been arranged by the Keepers to form a new pack, and to ensure the authorised breeding of new Guardians. Calla knows her place in werewolf society and accepts the forthcoming union as part of her duty. However, she has some doubts: she dislikes the new emphasis placed on her 'finesse' as a 'mate' over her prowess as a 'warrior'.[37] Additionally, a further question has been raised about the proposed union by Calla's unexpected interaction with a boy with 'eyes the color of winter moss' (later named as Shay) in the previous chapter.[38] Generic expectations lead the reader to assume that this emphasis on the boy's eyes signals his future role as love interest.[39]

Thus, Calla finds herself attracted to two potential lovers – Ren and Shay – and some of the novel's conflict results from this. The choice is between the young man she desires and the young man she is expected to marry. Calla's loyalty to her pack – presented throughout the series as a visceral and inherent bond – dictates that it is her duty to choose Ren. She accepts this, aware that she has a role to play in the maintenance of a society larger than herself and her own desires. On the day of her union to Ren, however, Calla finds that Shay is to be offered as a sacrifice; she and Ren are expected to perform a ritual killing as part of the ceremony.[40] Thus, the heroine's dilemma becomes not a choice between duty and desire, but a choice between two different sacrifices: if she kills Shay, she sacrifices an innocent life to a brutal ritual; if she saves Shay, she sacrifices the well-being and stability of her pack. The narrative's continual intensification of Calla's dilemma highlights the importance of sacrifice in the construction of the teen werewolf.

Calla chooses to give Shay the 'gift' of life (and freedom), accepting her own ostracism and physical jeopardy as a consequence. However, *Nightshade* does not end with the optimistic promise of *Shiver* and *The Dark Divine*. After Shay is freed and Calla flees from the retribution of her pack, the pair are ambushed by the 'Searchers', mysterious and murderous enemies against whom the Guardians are sworn to fight. The novel ends with Calla reflecting on her fate:

> I'd risked everything to save Shay. Letting stillness ease my trembling limbs, I closed my eyes and saw his face, remembering the freedom I'd felt in his arms, the possibility of a life unlike any I'd imagined. I wondered if my capture had

snuffed out that dream ... Despair threatened to drag me down, but I fought back, clinging to a single, flickering thought. *Shay loves me.*[41]

Calla's narration here moves between despair and hope about her own future, but it represents an affirmation of the correctness of her choice. The risk she has taken to save Shay remains the 'single, flickering thought' that she has done the right thing, even though she lies in an enemy prison (apparently permanently) separated from her packmates and her lover.

Nevertheless, the ending of *Nightshade* is not a final resolution, but rather a cliff-hanger. This is the first instalment of a trilogy, not a standalone narrative, and the large number of unresolved plot points in *Nightshade* indicates a potential sequel.[42] The second book in the series, *Wolfsbane*, begins where *Nightshade* ends, and develops the narrative of Calla's duty and sacrifice even further.

Wolfsbane begins with the revelation that Calla's reality is based on systematic deception. The Searchers explain that the relationship between the Guardians and the Keepers is not a 'natural' one, but rather one of subservience and oppression. The stories of Searcher attacks have been fabricated by the Keepers to quell rebellion among the Guardians. Calla is invited to join with the Searchers to reveal the truth to her packmates, and to save the other werewolves from the totalitarian and violent regime of their Keepers. Thus, while the first novel framed the female werewolf's decision as a personal choice between duty and desire, the second book presents a choice between self-preservation and the preservation of the pack. This decision is far easier for Calla to make:

> I already knew the answer. I'd risked everything to save Shay. And I'd do it again in a heartbeat if it meant I could get back to my packmates. If I could save them.[43]

From this point in the series narrative, Calla's focus is consistently on what is 'right' for her pack. Although the third book returns to the 'love triangle' plot of *Nightshade*, with Calla revisiting her choice between Ren and Shay, the main narratives of the second and third books revolve around Calla's role as warrior, leader and saviour of her pack.

The series ends with a strong validation of Calla's awareness of duty and sacrifice, as these are shown to serendipitously coincide with her personal desires. She leads her werewolf pack into a war against the Keepers and saves her brother from being punished as a traitor. The (arguably) fortuitous death of Ren in battle allows for a neat resolution of the love triangle, and Calla is able to end the trilogy in her 'correct' role with her lover and her packmates:

> Calla's golden eyes surveyed her pack. A golden brown wolf bounded out of the forest, coming to greet her. Shay circled Calla, nipping at her until she barked a protest ... it sounded like laughter.[44]

In this ending, the conflicting aspects of Calla's identity are integrated. Her role as alpha no longer precludes a relationship with Shay, as he is able to be an alpha wolf alongside her. Her success in battle has allowed her to reconcile with her pack. In addition to this, the series ends with an implicit comment on Calla's existence as a shape-shifter – the noise that is both a 'bark' and 'laughter' reveals the harmonious co-existence of wolf and human within the heroine. Calla becomes an example of what Elizabeth Clark terms the 'hopeful werewolf': she is an '[i]ntegrated and cyclic female' who has 'power but [does] not abuse it', 'use[s] appropriate but not excessive violence' and 'show[s] solidarity with other women'. Importantly, these traits go hand-in-hand with Calla 'benefit[ting] from an integration of [her] human and wolf-y nature'.[45]

This 'happy ending' notwithstanding, Cremer's novels offer a more sustained and complex presentation of sacrifice than the 'gifts' and 'grace' presented in Stiefvater and Despain's novels. These texts share common ground, however, in their insistence on the female werewolf's need to deny selfish desire and work towards the 'common good'. Arguably, this mode of presenting the teenage female werewolf finds its epitome (and its inverse) in Stephenie Meyer's Twilight series, in the figure of Leah Clearwater. Unlike the other werewolves discussed in this chapter, Leah is a peripheral, rather than central, character, and this results in a different narrative trajectory and resolution. Nonetheless, it is possible to read similar tropes of characterisation in Meyer's work, though these exist in a less sustained and more implicit form.

Sacrifice – in particular female sacrifice – is a narrative motif that runs throughout the entire Twilight series. It is most explicit in the explanation for the existence of the Quileute werewolf pack. When the (human) heroine Bella discovers that vampires and werewolves exist, she is presented with a series of oral and tribal histories from the Quileutes.[46] One of the most important foundational narratives of the tribe is 'the story of the third wife's sacrifice'.[47] This story explains the first 'invasion' by vampires, and the actions of Taha Aki (the first of the Quileute werewolves) and his third wife. In retaliation for the death of his sons, Taha Aki attacks a vampire; when he appears to be about to lose, his wife stabs a knife into her own chest, ensuring the vampire is distracted by 'the lure of the fresh blood'.[48]

Given that the existence of werewolves in the Twilight series is predicated on such narratives of sacrifice, it is hardly surprising that the series' only female lycanthrope is expected to deny self-preservation in favour of tribal duty. Like that of the male werewolves, Leah's transformation is involuntary – in these novels, werewolves are 'made' when there are too many vampires in the tribe's territory, and their transformation is purely to facilitate the ferocious protection of a marginalised and vulnerable community.

However, unlike the male werewolves, Leah's sacrifice is presented as peculiarly personal and, to an extent, gendered. Before her involuntary change, Leah is introduced as a character whose own desires have been thwarted by the 'reality' of lycanthropy. In Meyer's novels, werewolves are subject to an experience called 'imprinting', in which they develop an unbreakable and 'absolute' bond to a 'soul mate' without being able to exercise any control over it.[49] When he becomes a werewolf, Leah's 'high school sweetheart' Sam imprints on her cousin, Emily, regardless of any prior feelings he had for Leah. Both Emily and Leah are forced to accept this situation, with Emily entering into a relationship with Sam and Leah reconciling herself to heartbreak. Jacob Black, Bella's closest friend amongst the werewolves, states simply that: 'Leah got the worst end of the stick ... She puts on a brave face. She's going to be a bridesmaid.'[50]

Leah's 'brave face' is destroyed when she is transformed into a werewolf. Given that Meyer's werewolves' thoughts are transmitted telepathically to other pack members, and that individual members of the group have no control over this, Leah's metamorphosis forces her to share the details of her heartbreak with the entire Quileute pack – including her former lover Sam. Moreover, she receives no sympathy from her packmates or the other characters in the novel; the vampire hero Edward Cullen says that '[s]he's making life exceedingly unpleasant for the rest of them', before advising Bella that he is 'not sure she deserves your sympathy'.[51] That Edward speaks for the overall narrative focus of *Eclipse* is evidenced by the fact that his revelation about Leah represents a very brief interlude; Bella's response to Edward's short explanation of Leah's lycanthropy is that '[t]he pack is fascinating', entirely subsuming Leah's individual identity into an otherwise exclusively male group identity.

Though Edward insists that she is using her telepathic connection to the male werewolves to cause trouble, Leah performs her role as tribal werewolf correctly. She observes the commands of her alpha, despite the fact that he is her former lover, and takes part in a battle against vampires. In the final book of the series, however, Leah's loyalty and sense of duty become conflicted, and she is faced with a dilemma.

When Bella becomes pregnant with Edward's child in *Breaking Dawn*, the final book of the series, the Quileute werewolf pack is divided. Some of the pack believe that the child should be killed and that, if she allows Edward to transform her into a vampire, Bella should also be killed. Jacob defies this decision, and leaves to form his own pack – one that has an uneasy alliance with the vampiric Cullen family. Leah's younger brother Seth follows Jacob, and – unexpectedly for the male werewolves – the vampire-hating Leah joins them.[52] She claims her split from the Quileute pack is to stop her little brother becoming 'a vampire chew toy', but Jacob suspects (and Leah confirms) this is an excuse for her ending telepathic communication with Sam.[53]

However, as Leah's involvement with Jacob's new pack necessitates her spending more time with the Cullens and with the pregnant Bella, her allegiances shift. Throughout this section of *Breaking Dawn*, Jacob's loyalty is entirely to Bella. He wishes to protect the Cullens only because to hurt them would be to place Bella in danger. He views the vampiric baby growing inside the heroine as an 'abomination' and believes that Bella's safety would be best secured by forcibly terminating the pregnancy. Many members of the

Cullen family agree, but Jacob is confronted by Edward's sister, Rosalie, who is determined that the pregnancy will go ahead. Rosalie has already indicated to Bella that she regrets her own vampirism, particularly the fact that, as a result, she is unable to bear children.[54] She is determined that Bella will become a mother, and that she will become one as a human.

And, in this, Rosalie finds an ally in Leah. In a telepathic communication, Leah tells Jacob: 'That blonde vampire you hate so much – I totally get her perspective.'[55] When Jacob grows angry at this, Leah continues: 'I'm talking about being a genetic dead end, Jacob'.[56] Leah has stopped menstruating on her metamorphosis into a werewolf, and she no longer believes she can bear children. Jacob confirms this in his own narration when he remembers that 'she'd realized that her body wasn't following the normal patterns anymore'; Leah describes this as being 'menopausal'.[57] This presentation of Leah as a prematurely menopausal woman does not deny her femininity, but rather aligns her with the tomboy Kelsey in 'Boobs', as both have adopted a non-normative, but exclusively female, identity position. The important difference, however, is that Kelsey chooses to prolong her tomboyism through lycanthropy, whereas Leah's menopause is the unwanted consequence of an involuntary transformation.

Furthermore, this supernatural menopause links her explicitly with the similarly sterile Rosalie, and encourages Leah to vehemently protect Bella's right to choose:

> I just want the options I don't have, Jacob. ... And ... if Bella asked *me* to help her with this ... I'd probably do the same as the bloodsucker. ... Because, if it was turned around, I'd want Bella to do that for me. And so would Rosalie. We'd both do it her way.[58]

Significantly this is the first time Leah has referred to a vampire by their first name in the entirety of the series.

Leah's narrative throughout the Twilight novels, though it is a minor subplot often abandoned in favour of the central protagonists' self-examination, reveals a consistent and intense focus on the woman's loss of autonomy. Leah has no bodily autonomy – she is betrayed by her menopausal human body as much as her unwanted lycanthropy. She has no mental autonomy – she must share her most intimate thoughts with the unsympathetic and, occasionally, cruel males around her. Her life was predetermined from the moment Taha Aki's third wife took her own life to save her tribe.[59]

A time for change

At the end of Maggie Stiefvater's Wolves of Mercy Falls trilogy, Grace Brisbane is offered a resolution denied to Leah Clearwater. She realises that her long-desired life as a werewolf is not sustainable. In the long term, it will cause her isolation from her family, friends and lover, and a gradual decline into permanent lupine form (with the associated curtailed life span).

She accepts that she, like Sam before her, must submit to the cure and allow herself to be infected with bacterial meningitis. In many ways, the book ends on a surprisingly muted note for a YA paranormal romance. Grace is unsure about the efficacy of the cure, and the narrative ends before the readers are reassured that Grace will survive the infection.[60]

However, Grace's explanation as to why she has made this potentially life-threatening decision reaffirms the importance of choice that has been apparent throughout the series:

> Part of me felt a prickle of loss, because some days, I loved being a wolf. I loved this feeling of *knowing* the woods, of being a part of them. The utter freedom of it. But more of me hated the oblivion, the confusion, the ache of wanting to know more but being unable to. For all that I loved being a wolf, I loved being Grace.[61]

Once again, there is a sense of sacrifice in the female werewolf's narrative. Grace must give up 'this feeling of *knowing* the woods' in order to avoid 'the oblivion, the confusion'. This is, in part, a relinquishing of 'freedom', but it is also a way of reconnecting with the self. At this stage in her story, Grace sees 'being Grace' as distinct from 'being a wolf'. She chooses to prioritise the former.

By becoming werewolf, Grace has allowed her identity and relationships with others to develop. Her relationship with Sam, as well as the maturation of her relationship with her parents, is enabled entirely through Grace's gradual transformation into a werewolf. However, she realises that if she remains that way for too long, these relationships will descend into stasis and eventually disintegration.

Grace's association with lycanthropy is a complex one. In the first two novels, she is becoming a werewolf; in the third, she *is* werewolf. At the end of the final chapter, she is preparing to be a former werewolf. This suggests that we might read the heroine's relationship to lycanthropy as constantly in need of reconfiguration and negotiation.

This is affirmed through comparison with other YA texts. Cremer's Calla, for instance, whose identity is so carefully fixed and defined in the series' opening, is forced to reconsider her own nature and the natures of those around her, as the 'reality' of her existence is undermined and reshaped. And Despain's Grace, after spending all of *The Dark Divine* terrified of the 'curse' of the werewolf, discovers a freedom in the subsequent novels to reinvent the werewolf according to her own sense of morality and identification. Lycanthropy is the means through which these young women's identities can be understood, rejected and transformed.

YA female werewolf fiction of the early twenty-first century contains a wealth of 'types' of werewolves – from the divinely created to the naturally evolved, from spirit warriors to supernatural abominations – but the presentation of the *experience* of lycanthropy reveals important consistencies and a relationship to earlier teenage she-wolf fiction. While there has been a move away from metaphors of menarche and hormonal transformation, the idea of bodily (and social) autonomy remains central.

However, autonomy, while encouraging some degree of self-determination, is understood and mediated through a wider framework of grace, duty and sacrifice, as well as a sense of a 'greater good' that extends beyond personal choice and desire. Teenage lycanthropy, for females, is presented as a constant process of negotiation and reconfiguration, as a result of both internal development and external moderation. To paraphrase Simone de Beauvoir: one is not born (or made), but rather becomes, a she-wolf.

Notes

1. Catherine Orenstein, *Little Red Riding Hood Uncloaked: Sex, Morality, and the Evolution of a Fairy Tale* (New York: Basic Books, 2002), 168.
2. See Jazmina Cininas, 'Beware the Full Moon: Female Werewolves and That Time of the Month', in Maria Barrett (ed.), *Grotesque Femininities* (Oxford: Inter-Disciplinary Press, 2010), 3–36.
3. Elizabeth M. Clark, '"Hairy Thuggish Women": Female Werewolves, Gender, and the Hoped-For Monster', MA dissertation (Georgetown University, 2008), 22.
4. Suzy McKee Charnas, 'Boobs', in Pam Keesey (ed.), *Women Who Run With the Werewolves: Tales of Blood, Lust and Metamorphosis* (Pittsburgh: Cleis Press, 1996), 25–42 (36).
5. *Ibid.*, 31, 36.
6. *Ibid.*, 36.
7. I use 'YA' to refer only to texts written after 2005, when the term was developed as a publishing category. It is to be understood as a 'classificatory device' relating to the marketing of these novels, and not a reflection on content or characterisation. See Chris Richards, *Forever Young: Essays on Young Adult Fictions* (New York: Peter Lang, 2008), 13.
8. April Miller, 'The Hair that Wasn't There Before: Demystifying Monstrosity and Menstruation in *Ginger Snaps* and *Ginger Snaps Unleashed*', *Western Folklore* 64:3–4 (2005): 281–303 (281).
9. Chantal Bourgault du Coudray, *The Curse of the Werewolf: Fantasy, Horror and the Beast Within* (London: I.B. Tauris, 2006), 140.
10. *Ibid.*, 140.
11. Charnas, 'Boobs', 31.
12. *Ibid.*, 27.
13. *Ibid.*, 33.
14. Judith Halberstam, *Female Masculinity* (Durham, NC and London: Duke University Press, 1998), 6.
15. *Ibid.*, 6.
16. Charnas, 'Boobs', 35.
17. On the trope of permanence in YA fairy fiction, see Hannah Priest, 'Fairy Lovers and the Threat of Permanence', in Elizabeth Nelson, Hannah Priest and Jillian Burcar (eds), *Creating Humanity, Discovering Monstrosity* (Oxford: Inter-Disciplinary Press, 2010), 241–50.

18 Kelsey's fears are reminiscent of a plot device used in another late twentieth-century female werewolf fantasy text. In Annette Curtis Klause's 1997 novel, *Blood and Chocolate*, the teen protagonist is accidentally trapped mid-transformation and forced to assume an unchanging half-human, half-wolf form. This permanence is presented as horrific in a way that her regular transformation is not. See Annette Curtis Klause, *Blood and Chocolate* (New York: Delacorte Press, 1997), 253.
19 While the heroine of *Ginger Snaps* is of a similar age, it is made clear in the film that she is 'unnaturally' late in starting her periods.
20 Cininas, 'Beware the Full Moon', 5.
21 See Cininas, 'Beware the Full Moon', 13; Barbara Creed, *The Monstrous-Feminine: Film, Feminism, Psychoanalysis* (London: Routledge, 1993), 105–21.
22 A notable exception in teenage she-wolf fiction can be found in Klause's *Blood and Chocolate*, 168. Here, the teen heroine's lunar-determined lycanthropic transformation is linked to a voracious and (to some) threatening sexual identity, and these combine to emasculate the protagonist's human boyfriend. In many respects, the presentation of sexuality in *Blood and Chocolate* fulfil the generic expectations of horror werewolf fiction, though it has the 'positive and accepting' resolution of fantasy. On the association of animal transformation and sexual desire in horror, see Tanya Krzywinska, *Sex and the Cinema* (London and New York: Wallflower Press, 2006), 155.
23 Maggie Stiefvater, *Shiver* (London: Scholastic, 2009), 16.
24 Maggie Stiefvater, *Linger* (London: Scholastic, 2010), 1.
25 Ibid., 413.
26 I have written elsewhere about the role of the werewolf as demon-slayer in Despain's series. See Hannah Priest, 'Pack versus Coven: Guardianship of Tribal Memory in Vampire versus Werewolf Narratives', in Simon Bacon and Katarzyna Bronk (eds), *Undead Memory: Vampires and Human Memory in Popular Culture* (New York: Peter Lang, 2014).
27 Bree Despain, *The Dark Divine* (London: Egmont, 2010), 370.
28 Du Coudray, *The Curse of the Werewolf*, 114.
29 Stiefvater, *Shiver*, 407.
30 While current popular opinion reads Stephenie Meyer's Twilight series as grounded in religious ideology, references to Mormonism in these novels (if, indeed, they exist at all) are implicit, in distinction to the explicit Christian ideology and culture presented in Despain's fiction. See Margaret M. Toscano, 'Mormon Morality and Immortality in Stephenie Meyer's Twilight Series', in Melissa A. Click, Jennifer Stevens Aubrey and Elizabeth Behm-Morawitz (eds), *Bitten by Twilight: Youth Culture, Media and the Vampire Franchise* (New York: Peter Lang, 2010), 21–36.
31 Despain, *The Dark Divine*, 356–7.
32 Ibid., 357, original emphasis.
33 Ibid., 370.
34 Ibid., 370.
35 Ibid., 372.
36 I use 'greater good' here to mean a (somewhat) undefined sense of a broader sphere of interest than the heroine's own desires. This is constructed differently in Stiefvater and Despain's novels. In the former, it is figured in terms of social

37 Andrea Cremer, *Nightshade* (London: Atom Books, 2010), 18–19.
38 *Ibid.*, 5.
39 Descriptions of eye colour are used throughout YA paranormal romance as a primary indicator of both potential attraction and supernatural status. See, for example, the introduction of the love interest in Despain, *The Dark Divine*, 42; Stiefvater, *Shiver*, 1; Jennifer Lynn Barnes, *Raised by Wolves* (London: Quercus, 2010), 57; Stephenie Meyer, *Twilight* (London: Atom Books, 2006), 20.
40 Cremer, *Nightshade*, 365.
41 *Ibid.*, 452, original emphasis.
42 In the UK paperback edition, the final chapter of Cremer, *Nightshade* is followed by an 'exciting preview' chapter from its sequel, *Wolfsbane*.
43 Andrea Cremer, *Wolfsbane* (London: Atom Books, 2011), 13.
44 Andrea Cremer, *Bloodrose* (London: Atom Books, 2012), 405.
45 Clark, 'Hairy Thuggish Women', 89. Although I have not discussed Calla's relationships with other women specifically, Clark's notion of 'solidarity' is an apt one through which to understand Calla's empathetic interactions with other female characters, both lycanthropic and Searcher.
46 The werewolves in the Twilight series are all Native Americans, contrasted with the Euro-American vampiric invaders. There is not scope in this chapter to discuss the full implications of this specific racial coding, though it raises significant issues of gender, narrative and identity. See Priest, 'Pack versus Coven'; Natalie Wilson, 'Civilized Vampires Versus Savage Werewolves: Race and Ethnicity in the Twilight Series', in Click, Stevens Aubrey and Behm-Morawitz (eds), *Bitten by Twilight*, 55–70.
47 Stephenie Meyer, *Eclipse* (London: Atom Books, 2007), 223.
48 *Ibid.*, 228–9.
49 *Ibid.*, 109–10.
50 *Ibid.*, 111.
51 *Ibid.*, 370.
52 On the initial revelation of Bella's pregnancy, Leah had unequivocally advocated killing Bella and her baby. See Stephenie Meyer, *Breaking Dawn* (London: Atom Books, 2010), 185.
53 Meyer, *Eclipse*, 209, 212.
54 *Ibid.*, 148–9.
55 Meyer, *Breaking Dawn*, 290. Italics are used in the text to distinguish between telepathic and verbal communications, but I have chosen not to preserve that element of formatting here.
56 *Ibid.*, 290.
57 *Ibid.*, 291, 292.
58 *Ibid.*, 293.
59 Arguably, the mirror image of Meyer's Leah can be found in Jennifer Lynn Barnes's *Raised by Wolves*. In this text, the human heroine, who has been raised by werewolves, adopts the identity position of 'two-legged, furless, wolf-less werewolf' (129). This character's desire to be a werewolf, despite the fact that she is not, leads her to adopt lupine behaviour, assume the role of alpha, protect her pack and mechanically augment her body to mimic lycanthropic physicality. As a result, she ends her narrative (almost) as lycanthropic as her companions. This

forms a clear contract to Meyer's female werewolf, who is powerless to change her identity.
60 Maggie Stiefvater, *Forever* (London: Scholastic, 2011), 488.
61 *Ibid.*, 489.

9

The case of the cut-off hand: Angela Carter's werewolves in historical perspective

Willem de Blécourt

In the 1984 film *The Company of Wolves*, a scene occurs in which the father of the heroine Rosaleen returns home from a wolf hunt, carrying a small bundle. He is upset.

> Father: When I cut it off the carcass for a trophy, it was a forepaw. The forepaw of the biggest wolf I ever saw.
> Mother: The wolf that killed our Alice?
> Father: Aye, maybe. [*He puts the bundle on the table.*] When I cut it with my knife, it was a forepaw. I swear. A grizzled, giant wolf. And then, before my very eyes.
> [*He unfolds the bundle. Mother gasps.*]
> Rosaleen: Whose is it, Daddy? Is it someone you knew?
> Father: What do I know whose hand it is? All I know is what I see.
> Mother: Get it out.
> Rosaleen: Was it a wolf or a man you killed?
> Father: When I killed it, it was a wolf. It turned into a man. Seeing is believing.
> Rosaleen: Is it? What about touching?
> [*She goes to the table where the hand is now clearly visible, a ring on the ring finger. Her hand moves towards it, almost touches it.*]
> Mother: Get it out!
> Father: Whatever it is … now it's dead meat.
> Rosaleen: Do we bury it or burn it, Daddy?
> [*Her father looks at her, stands up, grasps the hand and throws it into the fire. Rosaleen steps near, looks at it while it burns.*]

The film was directed by Neil Jordan from a script he co-wrote with Angela Carter. The version of the scene in the (penultimate) film script is similar. There, the hand is identified as 'a man's hand, severed at the wrist'.[1] The film was preceded by a radio play, also called *The Company of Wolves*, broadcast on BBC Radio 3 on 1 May 1980. This play was solely written by Carter and also contained the hand scene. In the radio play, it is also a man's hand and, when Granny and the hunter have concluded their tale (without much dialogue, but with an interruption by the werewolf emphasising that his human skin is now the same as the girl's), Red Riding Hood (as the girl is called in this version), expresses her thoughts:

> But I would be sorry for the poor thing, whatever it was, man or beast or some benighted 'twixt and 'tween thing, trapped by a mean trick and finished off without its supper[.][2]

In its turn, most of the radio play derived from the short story 'The Company of Wolves'. Only the passage with the hand is based on Carter's 'The Werewolf', the preceding short story in *The Bloody Chamber*. In the latter story, it is the unnamed girl herself who meets a wolf on the way to her grandmother, 'but she made a great swipe at it with her father's knife and slashed off its right forepaw'. She finds her grandmother in bed, feverish, and discovers that her hand is missing and that the paw she carries in her basket has become a human hand:

> But it was no longer a wolf's paw. It was a hand, chopped off at the wrist, a hand toughened with work and freckled with old age. There was a wedding ring on the third finger and a wart on the index finger. By the wart, she knew it for her grandmother's hand.[3]

Though a ring is seen in the film, but not commented upon, the link to the grandmother disappeared when the gender of the wolf was changed from female to male.

Carter's stories have frequently drawn interpretations. Cristina Bacchilega presumes that Carter 'tells tales that reactivate lost traditions, trace violently contradictory genealogies, and flesh out the complex and vital workings of desire and narrative'.[4] According to Andrea Gutenberg, Carter, who in 'The Werewolf' had the granny witch stoned to death, paid 'tribute to a historical dimension which mostly affected (old) women'.[5] Kimberly Lau argues that because she made a werewolf of the grandmother, Carter produced 'a phallic mother', 'in transgendering her by aligning her with the predatory male of the Little Red Riding Hood tradition'.[6] 'The Werewolf' is almost exclusively seen as a feminist rewriting of Little Red Riding Hood.[7] While there certainly is a presence of Little Red Riding Hood in Carter's tale, and explicitly so in the radio play, an alternatively informed reading is still possible.

Moreover, the relation of Carter's 'The Werewolf' to both a presumed oral tradition and a reconstructed history can be redrawn, which will put the 'extra' layer attributed to Carter's work into perspective. This chapter will not attempt to offer a new interpretation of her werewolf stories, nor of Jordan's *The Company of Wolves* which derived from them and has been typified as 'a heterotopia woven out of overlapping discourses on metamorphosis'.[8] To flesh out meaning can be tricky and, especially in the case of Carter, it has been observed 'that there is no one meaning she gave to change, no single tone in which she sings of it'.[9] The aim of this chapter, rather, is to discuss how, over the course of time, a single motif such as that of the severed limb acquires different connotations. Because of the opening chosen, it is necessary to frame the discussion by engaging with the discourse surrounding Neil Jordan's and, especially, Angela Carter's work.

Angela Carter's wolves

Carter's original story 'The Werewolf' is a collage. Its opening, which sets the scene in the cold north, reveals it as a comment on Clemence Housman's late nineteenth-century novella *The Werewolf*, a Christian allegory about brotherly love, which is discussed in detail by Carys Crossen in Chapter 7 of this volume. In a snowy Nordic landscape a beautiful woman clad in a white pelt first removes the 'idle' members of the household, one very young and one old; in this way, the contrast between the flock and the predator is introduced. Then White Fell, as the woman is known, comes between twin brothers, Sweyn and Christian. When one of them succumbs to her lure, the other finds him dead, next to the body of a great white wolf, and takes him in his arms:

> The dead man stood upright within his arm, frozen rigid. The eyes were not quite closed, the head had stiffened, bowed slightly to one side, the arms stayed straight and wide. It was the figure of one crucified, the blood-stained hands also conforming.[10]

In 'The Werewolf' Carter demonised the image:

> To these upland woodsmen, the Devil is as real as you or I. ... At midnight, especially on Walpurgisnacht, the Devil holds picnics in the graveyard and invites the witches; then they dig up fresh corpses, and eat them. Anyone will tell you that.[11]

When the people in this place find a witch, 'they stone her to death', and they later do the same to the grandmother. They also hang garlic on doors as a protection against vampires. The lynching, relatively rare in the history of witch persecution, probably refers to the historical case of Perrenette Gandillon in 1598 in Franche-Comté, but the vampires do not belong there. It provides an example of the story's fragmented character.

The allusion to Housman may clarify the initial female gender of Carter's wolf. In this, she paid tribute to a British nineteenth-century Gothic literary tradition which featured the female werewolf as a Venus in furs, a *femme fatale*. This tradition also comprises stories by Frederick Marryat and Gilbert Campbell.[12] In reaction, Carter clads her heroine in 'a scabby coat of sheepskin to keep out the cold'.[13] The reverse identification of the wolf from Little Red Riding Hood with the grandmother also harks back to Carter's experiences as a child, when her grandmother used to read the story to her and play the wolf:

> She liked, especially, to pounce on me, roaring in personation of the wolf's pounce in Red Riding Hood at the end of the story.[14]

> When my grandmother read 'Little Red Riding Hood' to me, she had no truck with that sentimental nonsense about a friendly woodcutter carefully slitting open the wolf's belly and letting out the grandmother; when she came to the part about the wolf jumping on Little Red Riding Hood and eating her up, she used to jump on me and pretend to eat me.[15]

The severed paw theme is likewise incorporated in Gothic werewolf stories where it concerns a male werewolf.[16] In turn, these drew on an existing French case which entered the literature in the late sixteenth century. In the *Discours exécrable des sorciers* by the judge Henri Boguet, a huntsman meets a wolf, fails to shoot the beast, but manages to cut off a paw:

> As he told his friend the tale he drew the paw from his pouch, and found therein no paw but a woman's hand with a gold ring upon one of the fingers, a jewel the gentle man immediately recognized as belonging to his wife.[17]

It is the only historical instance of a 'demanated' she-wolf.[18] Because he gave place and date (Auvergne 1588), it is reasonable to assume that Boguet saw the story in a pamphlet or some other print. There is conspicuously little of a 'folk' tradition here. The ostensibly corresponding witchcraft motif of the wound transferred from cat to woman is different, as the cat is not killed and it is usually not the paw that changes back into a hand, but rather the woman who is found the next day with a similar wound.[19] In the context of historical werewolves, the motif of the severed paw turns up once more in one of the pamphlets on the 1589 trial of Peter Stump, the first German werewolf trial, which still contained a number of French elements.[20] Soon afterwards, the theme becomes obsolete. It is absent in the many nineteenth- and twentieth-century werewolf legends collected by folklorists.

The conclusion that Carter's werewolf story 'exposes the original by weaving it, not with literary intertexts, but with the folkloric traditions about wolves and werewolves', and thus with an 'oral voice', has to be reassessed.[21] There is cutting and pasting and rearranging and if there was ever, in an undetermined past, something oral, it has long since acquired the physicality of paper and ink. On her own admission, Carter was 'a rather booksy person'. In 'The Werewolf' she mostly agitated against her paternalistic British literary predecessors.

'Wolf-Alice' is the last story in *The Bloody Chamber* and the most developed of the werewolf trilogy. Partly written in dialogue with the seventeenth-century play *The Duchess of Malfi*, it places two different werewolf interpretations in confrontation with one another: the feral child versus the ghoul. The first is female, suckled and raised by wolves; the second is male, eating the flesh of the deceased. Both are outcasts. Although it has been claimed otherwise, they are a long way removed from either werewolves or Little Red Riding Hood.

Little Red Riding Hood and the werewolves

When Carter published her werewolf stories in 1979, folklorists were still debating how to categorise 'Little Red Riding Hood'.[22] The main issue was not Perrault's story; he had obviously written it himself and, because of the popularity of his booklet, most nineteenth- and twentieth-century recorded versions were clearly retellings, rather than examples of an independent 'oral' tradition. Many a folklorist left the story alone when an informant mentioned it, as it contradicted the orality premise. Its few recordings do not reflect either the distribution of *Mother Goose* (as it became known in English) or that of the separate illustrated broadsheets which carried its stories further.[23] The question was much more whether Perrault had been original or had adjusted already available story elements to his own educative purpose. The answer is a matter of opinion which, in turn, depends on the validity of the supporting arguments. To unreservedly consider Little Red Riding Hood as a 'folktale' is careless.

Notwithstanding its different ending, which was derived from the fable 'The Wolf and the Seven Kids', the story 'Rötkappchen', published by the Brothers Grimm in their *Fairy Tales* (no. 26), is not another oral variant. Jacob and Wilhelm Grimm obtained their text from Jeannette Hassenplug, at the time a teenager who particularly liked fairy-tale plays and had likely seen a performance of *Leben und Tod des kleinen Rothkäppchens* by Ludwig Tieck (1800), or otherwise have read the book version. She was also familiar with French fairy tales by Perrault and Madame d'Aulnoy, not through any oral tradition carried by nursemaids but because she had read their books and, unlike her sister Marie, retold some of their stories without contributing many of her own ideas. Wilhelm Grimm deleted most of her contributions when compiling the second, revised edition.[24]

The French 'Story of Grandmother', recorded in Nièvre in about 1885, is often taken as being similar to the one that would have inspired Perrault two hundred years earlier.[25] A girl on her way to bring bread and milk to her granny meets a *bzou* at a crossroads. The creature takes the road of the pins, whereas the girl goes along the road of the needles. By the time the girl arrives at her granny's house, the *bzou* has already arrived and taken the opportunity to process Granny into meat and blood, in which the girl partakes. She is then told to throw her clothes into the fire, one by one, because she does not need them any more. After an exchange with the *bzou* about his appearance, she tells him she needs to go outside to relieve herself. She then runs back home. It has been argued that the elements in this story that were not incorporated into Little Red Riding Hood would have been left out by Perrault because of the cruelty, puerility and impropriety.[26] Historically this is a very strange construction, for one reason because it would imply that these extra elements remained unaltered through a long series of retellings. A good story-teller adds *coleur locale*, and this would also have happened in late nineteenth-century France; other than wishful thinking, there is no indication that this particular story can be projected two hundred years back in time.[27] During most of the nineteenth century Little Red Riding Hood was performed on stage, as a comedy, a melodrama and a comical opera, and these versions have to be taken into account when dealing with the 'oral' texts.

There is, however, one werewolf story rarely mentioned by Little Red Riding Hood commentators, which fulfils the historical requirements much better. It is known as 'The Werewolf Husband' and tells of a man attacking his wife, or a boy his girlfriend, in the form of a wolf. Afterwards, when he has turned into a human once more, he is recognised by the threads of her clothing between his teeth. Unlike Little Red Riding Hood, versions of 'The Werewolf Husband' have been found which date from before the publication of *Mother Goose*.[28] However, it remains questionable whether Perrault utilised it, because none of its specific traits found their way into Little Red Riding Hood. It is much more likely that Perrault wanted to tell his own specific *conte du loup* (wolf tale), which he filled with a number of veiled references to much younger contemporary aristocratic women narrators of *contes des fees* (fairy tales), just as he confronted them with his own *contes de ma mère l'oye* (Mother Goose tales) and his own *conte de peau d'âne* (tales of the donkey skin), all designations for particular groups of stories. The then current *contes des loups* were fables, which Perrault modernised by elaborating on the saying 'avoir vu un loup' (to have seen a wolf), which, when applied to a girl, meant that she had lost her innocence. It indicated a sexual assault and not by an animal.

One of the main other reasons for hypothesising a historical connection between Little Red Riding Hood and werewolves, is that the oral versions 'were primarily discovered in those regions where werewolf trials were most common in the 15th, 16th and 17th centuries'.[29] This only makes sense where it concerns indigenous werewolf stories; in the case of Little Red Riding Hood, the printed distribution went far beyond the areas of the werewolf trials and its oral reception was not documented systematically enough to allow for any conclusion. On the other side of the equation, history is misrepresented too. There were certainly not 'thousands if not hundreds of thousands of those cases';[30] werewolf trials were hardly 'common' in the fifteenth century – overall counts of werewolf trials do not exceed several hundred – and a precise mapping of the Little Red Riding Hood stories shows some discrepancy with the distribution of persecuted 'werewolves'. For instance, a substantial number of people (though 300 at the most) were prosecuted as werewolves in what is now Germany, where very few versions of Little Red Riding Hood have been collected. Nevertheless, the hypothesis *is* supported by the suggestion of a direct connection between Perrault and a werewolf trial:

> The oldest version of the fairy tale, incorporated by Perrault in his collection of the late seventeenth century, might have links to Touraine, as the mother of the author originated from there. In 1598 a certain Jacques Raollet was

sentenced to death in Angers in the Touraine, because he would have attacked children in the shape of a werewolf and killed them. After a revision of his verdict by the Parliament of Paris [the French equivalent of the Supreme Court], Raollet [Roulet] was acknowledged as a neglected madman and delivered to the Hospital Saint Germain des Prez in Paris. This trial thus took place at a time when the parents of Perrault or a nursemaid could participate in the events.[31]

Perrault could indeed have heard about it. As a 'modern' man of letters, he could also have read the literature on werewolves and learned that they were considered to be deluded by the Devil (as indeed Roulet was considered to be), that the whole matter belonged to the superstitions which he had left far behind, and have decided not to write about them.[32] Sexually dangerous, transvestite 'wolves' who, like in the fables, talk but keep their own shape, would have been more than enough to use.[33] On the other hand, the possibility cannot be excluded that the brothers Briffault, who in 1885 told the 'Grandmother' story, had come across one of the then current publications of the Roulet case and decided to spice up their version of Little Red Riding Hood with some cannibalistic details (or that their source had done so). Their story was only one variant among many, and a proper study needs to consider them all in detail, the stage versions and broadsheets included.[34] Angela Carter certainly knew 'The Story of the Grandmother' from its publication by Paul Delarue and used it in her short story 'The Company of Wolves', substituting, among other details, the needle of a compass for knitting needles.

Skins of shame

The story commonly known as 'Peau d'âne' ('Donkeyskin', or 'All Fur' in the translated Grimm version) resembles werewolf stories because of the shared animal skin. The late seventeenth-century text by Perrault deals with a princess who is wanted by her father as his new queen. Her mother died and made the king promise to remarry only if he could find someone more beautiful than she was. With the help of a fairy, the princess manages to keep her father at bay, but finally has to flee the court, clad in the skin of the king's prized, money-producing donkey. If this story has any relation to everyday concepts, if only everyday concepts of the past, this needs to be sought in earlier examples. One of the main characteristics of fairy tales, as they were developed at the late seventeenth-century French court, is that they were distanced from daily life. Perrault, apart from dressing the tale in mockery, did not undertake any fieldwork, but used existing – primarily printed – narrative material.[35] An earlier version of his story can be found in Basile's *Lo cunto de li cunti*, 'L'orsa' (II.6), where the girl changes into a she-bear with the help of an old woman:

> Now, listen to me: tonight when your father tries to play the part of a stallion, although he is more like an ass, put this little stick into your mouth. You will then immediately become a bear and can run away, for he will be so frightened

that he will let you escape. Head straight into the woods, where heaven is guarding your future.[36]

The bear image clearly belongs to Basile's experimentation, and may also have references to the earlier comedy *La chiappinaria* (1609) in which a man who has fallen in love disguises himself with a bear skin.[37] The name of the kingdom in 'L'orsa', 'Rocc'Aspra' (Barren Rock), seems to point at the king's inability to sire sons;[38] the wood where the heroine finds refuge is situated outside civilisation. When Perrault replaced the bear with the donkey, he may have taken his cue from Basile's 'ass'. There are also earlier, sixteenth-century French examples where the donkey skin occurs in the context of love affairs, which in their turn may have been related to the Italian comedy.[39]

In the seventeenth-century skin stories the princess's honour remains intact. However, the fact that she is wearing an animal skin should indicate that at one point in the story's development she was understood to have been animalised, that the deed had taken place and she was, as Marina Warner expresses it, wearing 'a skin of shame':

> [I]n this early fairy tale, he [the jackass] marks the daughter with her father's sin: the sign of the donkey conveys his lust. She becomes a beast, after her father has behaved like one. ... The wronged and runaway daughters wear the pelts of beasts, coats of rushes, and other 'natural' disguises because they have been violated, by their father's assault or by another's, and it has contaminated them, exiled them.[40]

Significantly, there is a similar transgression in the other main incest story cluster: the Maiden Without Hands, where the father–daughter union is first consummated and later avoided.

Medieval literary werewolves, often interpreted as 'sympathetic',[41] are probably more appropriately termed apologetic, their involuntary transformation yet another sign of shifting guilt. If there was any underlying 'folk' werewolf, it was the outlaw, the perpetrator of a sexual transgression who was marked with the skin of the beast. Among other things, medieval werewolves were associated with incest, as is shown in the *Volsunga Saga* where Siegmund commits incest with his sister. He and their son later come upon wolf skins and change into wolves, which marks them as outsiders and outlaws.[42] In the Welsh *Mabinogion* branch 'Math, Son of Mathonwy', the issue is slightly more complicated, but points in the same direction of the transgression of sexual boundaries and the animalisation of incest. Two brothers are punished for the rape they have committed; over three consecutive years they become alternately a male and a female animal and have offspring: a stag and a doe, a wild boar and a sow, and a wolf and a bitch. As the magician who transforms them says: 'Let your nature be the same as that of the animals in whose shape you are.'[43] The Welsh and Icelandic examples may be marginal in relation to Italy and can hardly be seen as 'explicitly Christian',[44] but they still point to the medieval presence of the association and thereby to its potential communication.

In early modern werewolf persecutions, people were accused of obtaining the wolf-skin from the Devil; the motif also occurs in the first French trial of 1521.[45] In Renaissance Italy, the metaphorical story circulated that such a skin was only visible underneath the human skin: werewolves were 'hairy on the inside'.[46]

The maiden without hands

Father–daughter incest was a theme in a number of medieval narratives and its history reaches back into the thirteenth century, to the French poem *La Manekine*, itself based on even earlier texts.[47] The poem tells of the king of Hungary's daughter, who is desired by her father. She cuts off her left hand (without bleeding to death) and flees to Scotland, where she marries the king. While he is away at a tournament in France, she gives birth to a son, but her mother-in-law intercepts the correspondence and Manekine (so called because she is *mancus*, mutilated) is barely able to save herself. After seven years, the central characters all find each other back in Rome, including the woman's father and even the lost hand, which is reattached by prayer.

Alan Dundes has interpreted this sort of story as an articulation of the girl's point of view; she wanted to marry her father but was prevented by the prevailing taboo. The hand is removed, Dundes argues, because it was guilty of 'sexual sinning', that is to say, masturbation.[48] However, a more adult approach may be more relevant here, since the notion that women are punished for the sins of their fathers does not have to be so far-fetched. The early modern Italian versions of Straparola (in his *Le piacevoli notti* of 1550) and Basile, where the maiden's hand is simply admired, are in all likelihood later rationalisations; the earlier *Manekine* sounds more plausible as the daughter tells her father that he cannot have a handicapped queen. As Nancy Black argues:

> On a metaphoric level, her sacrifice demonstrates her obedience to a higher law than that of her father; in fact, her action may be understood as an acceptance of the sin of the father, paying penance for it with the loss of her hand.[49]

It may also be possible to read the hand, or more specifically what is on it, as a betrayal of the incident and as a token of the infringement of the girl's honour. One of the stories in the *Gesta Romanorum* (c. 1300) describes how a Roman empress's guilt over incest with her son and infanticide is written in blood on the palm of her hand.[50] Then again, perhaps the father in *Manekine* has literally 'taken' the girl's hand, as 'in marriage'. That this would all have been the girl's fantasy needs to be qualified.[51]

The medieval incest theme is characterised by attempts to exonerate the father. This is in line with the Biblical story of Lot, whose daughters seduced him when he was asleep. Aristocratic literature was often apologetic, and in this case the father's infatuation is manipulated until it becomes the wish of his dying queen, a decision of the royal council, and even a dispensation from the pope.⁵² If the story articulates family relations, it opposes a victimised, suffering young woman with a white-washed father.

The medieval incest stories seem to stand apart from the werewolf stories. Nevertheless, traces of animalisation are present in the description of the princess's offspring,⁵³ and these also appear in stories in which she merely escapes. In the 'Woman from St. Gilles' from the *Scala Celi* (c. 1300), the mother of the king (to whom the heroine is later married) pretends that her daughter-in-law has given birth to a boy with the head of a dog.⁵⁴ An Italian text of 1385 mentions 'two little monkeys, who were the most nasty and deformed creatures one had ever seen'.⁵⁵ In the thirteenth-century *Hélène de Constantinople*, the protagonist is accused of giving birth to two dogs.⁵⁶ In *La Manekine* the child is described as hairy; he (allegedly) has four feet and eyes deep in his big head. This seems to suggest that the children were born of incest, but that the connection was slowly disappearing. In Straparola's later rendering, the children are normal but killed by the ever-lusting father who then accuses his daughter Doralice of killing them. Normally such a scheme is devised by the mother-in-law, but this author applies frequent gender shifts. These are simply variants, consciously written by authors who wanted to put a different accent on the story than their predecessors.

On the basis of adjacent, contemporary and earlier stories, it can be concluded that Boguet's late sixteenth-century account of the dismembered female werewolf referred to above contains a double incest metaphor as it features both the animalisation and the demanation. Even the ring on the werewolf's hand, which eventually found its way into the twentieth-century film *The Company of Wolves*, echoes Straparola's *Tebaldo*. Here, the girl's mother is on her death bed and 'as she was dying, she asked her husband, whom she loved dearly, never to wed another woman unless that lady's finger fit the ring which she herself wore'. In this instance, the girl escapes in a chest.⁵⁷ The double metaphor in the 1588 French story may perhaps be explained as a compensation for the lack of the incest theme at the text's surface, and future researchers will have to find out whether or not the veiled references have a political connotation.⁵⁸

The folklore of the film

The process of assemblage that characterises Angela Carter's 'The Werewolf', 'A Company of Wolves' and, to a lesser extent, 'Wolf-Alice', continued with the writing of the screenplay. For example, the tale of the two sisters, the eldest of whom, also called Alice, is killed by the wolves, bears a remarkable resemblance to the dominant late eighteenth-century account of the Beast of Gévaudan.⁵⁹ Granny's remark 'they say the priest's bastards often turn into wolves as they grow older'⁶⁰ refers to Guy Endore's *The Werewolf of Paris* of 1934 (or was taken directly from a French folklore publication). The story

Rosaleen tells the wolf in Granny's house in the published screenplay[61] is one of the very few about Irish werewolves.[62] When it was revised in the final version of the film as the story of the she-wolf 'who came from the world below to the world above', it was not because of its original Irishness, but to bring it more in line with its narrator. All the fragments of different origin were now placed within the 'structure of story within a story within a story', defined by a sleeping Rosaleen.[63] But when two people collaborate on the basis of stories written by one of them that are already in the public domain, differences are bound to ensue.

A number of commentators have vented their anger when confronted by the divergence between Carter's short werewolf stories and the feature-length film *A Company of Wolves*. In the opinion of Maggie Anwell, Carter's challenge of 'patriarchal views of femininity' was lost in the transition to the screen. Anwell objects to the metamorphosis of Rosaleen, because it reduces her to 'the symbol for repressed desire'.[64] Fairy tale specialist Jack Zipes expresses himself even more strongly: Jordan 'made numerous infuriating changes'. He continues: 'In Jordan's hands, the frame of the film is wooden, symbolically blunt, offensive, and, in the end, a pathetically flawed strategy to encase a series of related tales'.[65] Counter opinions point to the contextualisation and situating of these tales within the film's structure, which actually allows the girl more agency than in the preceding story.[66] Zipes fails to penetrate the different layers of the film, and his indignation hides behind Carter's unease with the last scene.[67] His critique also relates to his (arguably untenable) views on the prehistory of the Perrault story, which he interprets as being about a 'helpless girl, who subconsciously contributed to her own rape'.[68] Without qualification, he posits the last scene of *The Company of Wolves*, in which Rosaleen wakes up and is reunited with her animal self, as pointing to her defencelessness.

Carter, who was of course very well capable of defending herself, conceded that it was Jordan's film:

> We wrote the script together at the kitchen table, and there didn't seem to be any point in writing things he didn't want to film. In the final analysis any film is the director's movie. ... On the whole I am very happy with it. Its purpose and meaning are not intended to be clear. I'm not sure of its meaning; it is supposed to be an open-ended film, with a plentiful amount of material for interpretation.[69]

Jordan found that in writing with Carter the script 'became gothic and sensual, acquiring a special kind of horror. Images began to come from nowhere, lurid and illogical, but somehow perfect.'[70] The ending, which should have echoed Rosaleen's last story, concerned him too. They had wanted the girl to wake up and dive into the floor, back to her forest, thus fusing dream and reality. This could not be realised; however, it still became an ambiguous finale. As Jordan stated: 'I didn't want the film to end with the girl under threat; it's a liberation in a way.'[71] Later he admitted: 'I think the ending now blunts the film as a whole because she actually mastered these wolves. She'd made them do her bidding and she ends up embracing this wolf.'[72] It was Jordan who turned the Red Riding Hood from the radio play into the dark-haired Rosaleen, in homage to the female personification of Ireland.[73] He was also responsible for a number of other Irish references.[74]

On a different level, Carter's stories purport to show that women can be as powerful as wolves, too, and that little girls lost in the woods may very well be able to take a stand against predators. The film partly carries this same message; it is also far more structured than the constituting stories and differentiates more clearly between Rosaleen and her grandmother. While the latter's stories abound with warnings, Rosaleen's show compassion. The hand scene belongs to Rosaleen's experience, visually translated as touch. The scene displays a crucial transition in the storyline, as it shows her first actual confrontation with shapeshifting. As has been remarked, it is also 'the thematic centre of the film, which seeks to question the validity of seeing'.[75] Together with the stress on telling, hearing and commenting,[76] the film offers plenty of material to rethink male-dominated narrative space. But while *The Company of Wolves*, a 'menstrual movie' which depicts a girl's 'passage to sexual maturity',[77] is saturated with (heterosexual) female sexuality, there is never the deviance of incest.

The art of subversion

Angela Carter wanted to 'extract the latent content from the traditional stories'. At the same time, she admitted that it was hard to talk about a 'latent content of stories which are explicitly about cannibalism, incest, bestiality and infanticide'. Her comment on interpreting the Little Red Riding Hood wolf as a sexual assailant was:

> You can of course read the story of its symbolism as it appears to us now, but three or four hundred years ago it would have been a rough nursery game with a real moral: you shouldn't lurk around the forest, and not because of seducers.[78]

Yet as a novelist, Carter represented primarily a contemporary, late twentieth-century opinion, albeit one informed by folklorists and historians, about werewolves and the original orality of Little Red Riding Hood. Unfortunately, much of the academic output she relied on was marred by muddled methodology and uninspired copying. In their turn, the critics were hardly critical enough to see through the unsupported assumptions and their criticism primarily contributed to upholding concepts, such as a lower-class orality or a regulation of sexuality through 'witch-hunts', that derived from male nationalist romantic ideology.[79] What exactly is 'extracted' then, becomes questionable.

As a result, Carter did not explore Perrault's text or its reception,[80] but a nineteenth-century fabrication. She neglected elaborating on the wolf's acting as grandmother, although she was 'deeply fascinated with female impersonation, as a literary device, as a social instrument of disruption, as an erotic provocation'.[81] Why should a warning of a genuine wolf have been expressed in a story about a little girl and her granny? But perhaps she was only offering her interviewer one side of the story on that point. In another interview in the same year, she said: 'the latent content is violently sexual. And because I am a woman, I read it that way.'[82] As she saw it, in the movie, 'the wolves represent a lot of things, though basically they are still libido'.[83] One wonders what she would have made of a woman who gave birth to animals.

The 'multiple voices' Carter reinserted into the tales were not the 'lost voices' of the presumed 'peasants' by whom, according to the theories of folklorists, the stories would have been told, but at most those of the disparate authors and editors of the folklore collections. These voices were also cited out of context. Writers can get away with that and create their own contexts, but critics should be wary and do their homework. Whether an author will still appear convincing when she presents a story made out of notes taken from a variety of sources (without revealing them, as the historian is compelled to do), depends on how familiar her readers are with the subject of her 'research'. Ignorance can be an advantage.

Instead of teasing out the 'latent content', Carter altered the existing stories and subverted them. Red Riding Hood undresses in front of the werewolf to 'sleep' next to him in the initially only handwritten version of one of the Nièvre stories; mostly she is just eaten, which may amount to the same. However, she nowhere turns into a wolf herself. The young women in the animal skins were anything but proud of wearing them. Then again, in Perrault's cynical rendering of the skin tale, they hid their beautiful dresses underneath, found their Prince Charming and became quite respectable. Carter made them defiant, shameless and self-conscious and, while doing so, reassigned the traditional gender of the werewolf. She connected, in fact, to the then current cinematic image of the werewolf as the menstruating man.[84] Female werewolves were very hard to find in Western European folklore texts, with their overwhelming majority of male werewolves. Thus they were invented. That the paw underwent a gender change in the other direction resulted from narrative demands when the theme was incorporated into the radio play.

This chapter could have followed a somewhat different line of enquiry by taking another scene from *The Company of Wolves* as its point of departure. I could have selected the nest scene, which leads deeper into Neil Jordan's fictional work, his Irish background and the Catholic discourse on reproduction. It would also have been possible to concentrate on the wedding scene, where all the people at the party are turned into wolves, which directs the researcher to the male Gothic authors fantasising about white female werewolves and the sensitivities of the historical ethnography of the Baltic, for the story is Livonian and Finnish.[85] However, the question as to why the she-wolf's paw was severed needed an answer first.

Notes

1 Angela Carter, *The Curious Room: Plays, Film Scripts and an Opera* (London: Chatto and Windus, 1996), 224.
2 Carter, *Curious Room*, 67.
3 Angela Carter, *The Bloody Chamber and Other Stories* (London: Gollanz, 1979), 109.
4 Cristina Bacchilega, *Postmodern Fairy Tales: Gender and Narrative Strategies* (Philadelphia: University of Pennsylvania Press, 1997), 59.
5 Andrea Gutenberg, 'Shape-shifters from the Wilderness: Werewolves Roaming the Twentieth Century', in Monika Mueller (ed.), *The Abject of Desire: the Aestheticization of the Unaesthetic in Contemporary Literature and Culture* (Amsterdam and New York: Rodopi, 2007), 162–80, esp. 163.
6 Kimberly J. Lau, 'Erotic Infidelities: Angela Carter's Wolf Trilogy', *Marvels and Tales* 22 (2008): 77–94, esp. 82.
7 See, for example, Catherine Orenstein, *Little Red Riding Hood Uncloaked: Sex, Morality, and the Evolution of a Fairy Tale* (New York: Basic Books, 2002), 165; David Gurnham, *Memory, Imagination, Justice: Intersections of Law and Literature* (Farnham: Ashgate, 2009), 144–5.
8 Eliza Filimon, 'Cinematic landscapes: Angela Carter's Movie Adaptations', *Romanian Journal of English Studies* 6 (2009): 47–59, esp. 53.
9 Caroline Walker Bynum, *Metamorphosis and Identity* (New York: Zone, 2001), 173.
10 Clemence Housman, *The Were-Wolf* (London: Lane, 1896), 122.
11 Carter, *Bloody Chamber*, 108.
12 Brian J. Frost, *The Essential Guide to Werewolf Literature* (Madison, WI: University of Wisconsin Press, 2003), 59–61, 76–9.
13 Carter, *Bloody Chamber*, 109.
14 Angela Carter, 'Foreword' to *The Fairy Tales of Charles Perrault* (London: Gollancz, 1977), 13.
15 John Haffenden, *Novelists in Interview* (London and New York: Methuen, 1985), 83. Carter's grandmother preferred the Perrault version over the one published by the Grimms.
16 Frost, *Essential Guide to Werewolf Literature*, 57–9.
17 Montague Summers, *The Werewolf* (London: Kegan Paul, 1933), 228.
18 The word 'demanated' is used throughout this chapter to refer to the act of having one's hand removed. As there is no neat equivalent of 'decapitated' to refer to hands, the term has been supplied.
19 Among other places: Wilhelm Hertz, *Der Werwolf: ein Beitrag zur Sagengeschichte* (Stuttgart: Kröner, 1862), 71–3. Summers, *The Werewolf*, 240, mentions that the cat story appeared in seventeenth-century English plays. See also Bacchilega, *Postmodern Fairy Tales*, 160 n.22; if the werewolf story was 'well-known', it was through the publication of the 1588 account, also referred to by Chauvin de Beauvincourt and De Lancre.
20 Willem de Blécourt, 'The Werewolf, the Witch, and the Warlock: Aspects of Gender in the Early Modern Period', in Alison Rowlands (ed.), *Witchcraft and Masculinities* (Basingstoke: Palgrave 2009), 191–213, esp. 196–9.
21 Jessica Tiffin, *Marvelous Geometry: Narrative and Metafiction in Modern Fairy Tale* (Detroit: Wayne State University Press, 2009), 86.

22 See Christine Shojaei Kawan, 'Rotkäppchen (AaTh 333)', *Enzyklopädie des Märchens* 11 (2004): 854–68.
23 See the paucity of variants in Johannes Bolte and Georg Polívka, *Anmerkungen zu den Kinder- und Hausmärchen der Brüder Grimm*, I (Leipzig: Dieterich, 1913), 234–5; see also Aarne-Thompson-Uther Index (ATU) 333.
24 See Willem de Blécourt, *Tales of Magic, Tales in Print: On the Genealogy of Fairy Tales and the Brothers Grimm* (Manchester: Manchester University Press, 2012), 98.
25 Achille Millien, 'Le petit chaperon rouge, V. Nouvelle version de la Nièvre', *Mélusine*, 3 (1886–1887): 428–9. Orenstein, *Little Red Riding Hood Uncloaked*, 93, calls it a 'premodern antecedent'.
26 Jack Zipes, *The Trials and Tribulations of Little Red Riding Hood* (New York and London: Routledge, 1993), 25, 346–8; Alan Dundes (ed.), *Little Red Riding Hood: A Casebook* (Madison, WI: University of Wisconsin Press, 1989), 13–20, based on a study by Paul Delarue published in 1951.
27 Marina Warner, *From the Beast to the Blonde: On Fairy Tales and their Tellers* (London: Vintage, 1995), 181, made the same mistake by writing that Perrault 'adapted a traditional story', whereupon she summarises the one of 1885.
28 On the story in the *Évangiles des quenouilles*, see Claude Lecouteux, *Elle courait le garoux: lycanthropes, hommes-ours, hommes-tigres: une anthologie* (Paris: Corti, 2008), 189–90.
29 Zipes, *Trials and Tribulations*, 20; Marianne Rumpf, *Ursprung und Entstehung von Warn- und Schreckmärchen* (Helsinki: Suomalainen Tiedeakatemia, 1955), 8.
30 Zipes, *Trials and Tribulations*, 19.
31 Rumpf, *Ursprung und Entstehung*, 8, my translation; see also Zipes, *Trials and Tribulations*, 20. The spelling of the name is, according to her source, Chauvincourt.
32 See Gérard Gélinas, *Enquête sur les contes de Perrault* (Paris: Imago, 2004).
33 On Perrault and transvestism, see Orenstein, *Little Red Riding Hood Uncloaked*, 198–200.
34 See Walter Scherf, *Das Märchenlexikon* (Munich: Beck, 1995), 687–689; Bacchilega, *Postmodern Fairy Tales*, 158, n.11. Between 1887 and 1900 the journal *Mélusine* published ten different versions of the story, among them another one from Nièvre.
35 Maren Clausen-Stolzenburg, *Märchen und mittelalterliche Literaturtradition* (Heidelberg: Winter, 1995), 357–361; Suzanne Magnanini, 'Postulated Routes from Naples to Paris: the Printer Antonio Bulifon and Giambattista Basile's Fairy Tales in Seventeenth-Century France', *Marvels and Tales* 21 (2007): 78–92.
36 English translation in Jack Zipes, *The Great Fairy Tale Tradition: From Straparola and Basile to the Brothers Grimm* (New York and London: Norton, 2001), 35.
37 Rudolf Schenda, 'Kommentare', in Giambattista Basile, *Das Märchen der Märchen: das Pentamerone* (Munich: Beck, 2000), 590.
38 Nancy L. Canepa, *From Court to Forest: Giambattista Basile's* Lo cunto de li cunti *and the Birth of the Literary Fairy Tale* (Detroit: Wayne State University Press, 1999), 123, 126.
39 Bolte and Polívka, *Anmerkungen*, II (1915), 50–1, 1547, 1570.
40 Warner, *From the Beast to the Blonde*, 325, 358.
41 Bynum, *Metamorphosis and Identity*, 94, 238.

42 Kaaren Grimstad (ed.), *Volsunga Saga: the Saga of the Volsungs* (Saarbrücken: AQ, 2000), 97, and Grimstad's comments, 33.
43 Patrick K. Ford (ed. and trans.), *The Mabinogi and Other Medieval Welsh Tales* (Berkeley, CA: University of California Press, 1977), 97.
44 Elizabeth Archibald, *Incest and the Medieval Imagination* (Oxford: Clarendon, 2001), 220.
45 See, amongst others, Rolf Schulte, *Man as Witch: Male Witches in Central Europe* (Basingstoke: Palgrave, 2009), 23–4.
46 First published in Job Fincel, *Wunderzeichen* (1556); see Rainer Alsheimer, 'Katalog protestantischer Teufelserzählungen', in Wolfgang Brückner (ed.), *Volkserzählung und Reformation* (Berlin: Smith, 1974), 417–519.
47 Ingrid Bennewitz, 'Mädchen ohne Hände: der Vater-Tochter-Inzest in der mittelhochdeutschen und frühneuhochdeutschen Erzählliteratur', in Kurt Gärtner, Ingrid Kasten and Frank Shaw (eds), *Spannungen und Konflikte des menschlichen zusammenlebens in der deutschen Literatur des Mittelalters* (Tübingen: Niemeyer, 1996), 157–72.
48 Alan Dundes, 'The Psychoanalytic Study of the Grimms' Tales: "The Maiden Without Hands" (AT 706)', in *Folklore Matters* (Knoxville: University of Tennessee Press, 1989), 112–50; see also Alan Dundes, '"To Love my Father All": a Psychoanalytic Study of the Folktale Source of *King Lear*', in Dundes (ed.), *Cinderella: a Casebook* (Madison, WI: University of Wisconsin Press, 1988), 229–44.
49 Nancy B. Black, *Medieval Narratives of Accused Queens* (Gainesville, FL: University Press of Florida, 2003), 38.
50 Wilhelm Dick (ed.), *Die Gesta Romanorum* (Erlangen and Leipzig: Deichert, 1890), 12–14, cap. 13: 'De regina, que de filio concepit et partum iuguluit'.
51 See Archibald, *Incest and the Medieval Imagination*, who briefly discusses and discards the Freudian interpretations (170), but also draws attention to several texts in which the daughter is portrayed as dominant (188, 233–4), representing 'the worst fears of male writers' (191).
52 Scherf, *Märchenlexikon*, 830; see also Albert Wesselski, *Versuch einer Theorie des Märchens* (Reichenberg: Kraus, 1931), 140.
53 Noted in passing by Dundes, 'The Psychoanalytic Study', 142. Archibald glosses over the theme, only referring to the children's portrayal as 'monsters': *Incest and the Medieval Imagination*, 153, 160.
54 Albert Wesselski, *Märchen des Mittelalters* (Berlin: Stubenrauch, 1925), 29–31, no. 10, after the 1480 edition of the *Scala Celi* (c. 1300).
55 Giovanni Fiorentino, 'Dionigia' (1385), quoted in Zipes, *Great Fairy Tale Tradition*, 507–11; Hans-Jörg Uther, *Märchen vor Grimm* (Munich: Diederichs, 1990), 84–92, n.16
56 Catherine Velay-Vallantin, *L'histoire des contes* (Paris: Fayard, 1992), 101.
57 Zipes, *Great Fairy Tale Tradition*, 27; Scherf, *Märchenlexikon*, 1178.
58 Also mentioned in Archibald, *Incest and the Medieval Imagination*, 145–6.
59 Catherine Velay-Vallantin, 'Little Red Riding Hood as Fairy Tale, Fait-divers, and Children's Literature: the Invention of a Traditional Heritage', in Nancy L. Canepa (ed.), *Out of the Woods: the Origins of the Literary Fairy Tale in Italy and France* (Detroit: Wayne State University Press, 1997), 306–51.
60 Carter, *Curious Room*, 206.
61 *Ibid.*, 241–3.

62 John Carey, 'Werewolves in Medieval Ireland', *Cambrian Medieval Celtic Studies* 44 (2002): 37–72.
63 Remark by Neil Jordan, quoted in Mario Falsetto, *Personal Visions: Conversations with Independent Film-Makers* (London: Constable, 1999), 164.
64 Maggie Anwell, 'Lolita Meets the Werewolf: *The Company of Wolves*', in Lorraine Gamman and Margaret Marshment (eds), *The Female Gaze: Women as Viewers of Popular Culture* (London: Women's Press, 1988), 76–85, 195–6. See also Bacchilega, *Postmodern Fairy Tales*, 50–2.
65 Jack Zipes, *The Enchanted Screen: the Unknown History of Fairy-Tale Films* (New York: Routledge, 2011), 148.
66 Charlotte Crofts, 'Curiously Downbeat Hybrid or Radical Retelling?: Neil Jordan's and Angela Carter's *The Company of Wolves*', in Deborah Cartmell, I.Q. Hunter, Heidi Kaye and Imelda Whelehan (eds), *Sisterhoods: Across the Literature/Media Divide* (London: Pluto Press, 1998), 48–63.
67 Bacchilega, *Postmodern Fairy Tales*, 164, n.42 reports a personal communication by Zipes.
68 Zipes, *Trials and Tribulations*, 27.
69 John Harpenden, *Novelists in Interview* (London and New York: Methuen, 1985), 85.
70 In Angus Finney, *The Egos Have Landed: The Rise and Fall of Palace Pictures* (London: Mandarin, 1997), 68.
71 Paul Taylor and Steve Jenkins, 'Wolf at the Door … Down in the Woods', *Monthly Film Bulletin* 51:608 (1984): 265–6.
72 In Falsetto, *Personal Visions*, 166.
73 Keith Hopper, 'Hairy on the Inside: Revisiting Neil Jordan's *The Company of Wolves*', *Canadian Journal of Irish Studies* 29:2 (2003): 17–26.
74 Sharon McCann, '"With Redundance of Blood": Reading Ireland in Neil Jordan's *Company of Wolves*', *Marvels and Tales* 14 (2010): 68–85. That the hand scene 'has an additional relevance in relation to Irish cultural history' (73), is diluting the rest of her presentation; not every chopped-off hand can be considered within the same category.
75 Emer Rockett and Keith Rockett, *Neil Jordan: Exploring Boundaries* (Dublin: Liffey Press, 2003), 40.
76 Aptly articulated by Crofts in 'Radical Retelling', 55–7.
77 Chantal Bourgault du Coudray, *The Curse of the Werewolf: Fantasy, Horror and the Beast Within* (London and New York: I.B. Taurus, 2006), 124.
78 Haffenden, *Novelists in Interview*, 84.
79 See Laura Mulvey, 'Cinema Magic and the Old Monsters', in Lorna Sage (ed.), *Flesh and the Mirror: Essays on the Art of Angela Carter* (London: Virago, 1994), 230–42.
80 She recognised Perrault's craftmanship in her article: 'The Better to Eat You With', *New Society* (1976); see Angela Carter, *Shaking a Leg: Collected Journalism and Writings* (London and New York: Penguin, 1997), 451–5.
81 Warner, *From the Beast to the Blonde*, 194.
82 Quoted in Bacchilega, *Postmodern Fairy Tales*, 69.
83 Haffenden, *Novelists in Interview*, 84.
84 Walter Evans, 'Monster Movies: a Sexual Theory', *Journal of Popular Film* 2 (1973): 353–65.

85 Marjatta Jauhiainen, *The Type and Motif Index of Finnish Belief Legends and Memorates* (Helsinki: Suomalainen Tiedeakatemia, 1998), 165–6; Merili Metsvahi, 'Die Frau als Werwölfin (AT 409) in der estnischen Volkstradition', in Willem de Blécourt and Christa Agnes Tuczay (eds), *Tierverwandlungen. Codierungen und Diskurse* (Tübingen: Francke, 2011), 193–219.

10

The she-wolves of horror cinema

Peter Hutchings

Beyond the curse

Does it always have to come down to the curse, the curse of blood, the curse of biology? Certainly there is something to be said for the idea that being a werewolf entails inevitable surrender to the natural, primal or beastly. Indeed this way of thinking might seem especially apt for the figure of the female werewolf. As Chantal Bourgault du Coudray notes, 'the pervasive cultural association of femininity with nature, embodiment and biology has animated most accounts of female lycanthropy'.[1] From such a perspective, the fact that the modern werewolf – at least since the influential 1941 film *The Wolf Man* (dir. George Waggner) – has frequently been presented as subject to the monthly lunar cycle can with a degree of ease be connected to the menstrual cycle, even when the afflicted lycanthrope is male and where the unwanted transformation into beast thus acquires the added humiliation of being rendered, in certain respects at least, feminine.[2] Du Coudray again: 'horror narratives of anguished men who suddenly find themselves governed by "the curse" of lycanthropy have demonized the monthly cycle'.[3]

The concept of the werewolf as 'menstrual monster' is not just something that has been conjured up by critics and cultural historians. A number of contemporary female werewolf fictions explicitly invoke an association between lycanthropy and menstruation, sometimes in a manner that has the potential to disrupt and challenge conventional definitions of what it means to be female. Notable in this respect is the Canadian horror film *Ginger Snaps* (2000, dir. John Fawcett), which is possibly the best-known of all contemporary female werewolf stories. Its pointed association of female sexual maturation with lycanthropic transformation has generated a great deal of discussion about the extent to which this, and other representations of its kind, supports a progressive feminist critique of oppressive patriarchal understandings of female sexuality.[4] More generally, Barbara Creed has argued that the monstrous-feminine in horror cinema invokes notions of the biological – not least menstrual and other processes associated with female reproductivity – in a manner that invites both fascination and disgust.[5]

Approaches of this kind align broadly with an ideological-analytical method that is prevalent in horror criticism. Put baldly, from such a perspective horror monsters are seen to represent, in coded or tacit form, socially specific forms of 'otherness', which tend to be contained both by narrative process and by the fact of their being marked as 'other'. The extent to which a film renders the monster in terms of this otherness or presents it with some sympathy determines the film's ideological status as potentially reactionary or progressive, although whether horror can do away with the notion of otherness entirely and still remain what we think of as horror is moot; as Robin Wood, a key exponent of this approach has noted: 'The genre carries within itself the capability of reactionary inflection, and perhaps no horror film is entirely immune from its operations.'[6] To give an obvious instance, the figure of the female werewolf articulates anxieties around female independence and female sexuality. Demonising and killing off the monster is potentially a means of managing and containing the threat thereby posed to a patriarchal normality, while presenting the monster with a degree of sympathy – as is the case in *Ginger Snaps* – opens up possibilities for a critical interrogation of social structures and beliefs that create and promote particular categories of otherness. However, in both cases, the reactionary and the progressive, the female werewolf generally remains a monster throughout and is thereby bound into generic conventions requiring that something be denoted in terms of otherness.

This approach to the horror genre has proved very productive in a range of contexts. However, at the same time, the tendency evident within it to probe beyond the surface detail of horror films in order to discover significance, or to render that detail symptomatic of something other than what it ostensibly appears, does mean that other features of the films concerned can be unjustly marginalised or marked as unimportant, while potentially less important elements are rendered prominent in the analysis in question. For example, the absence of an explicit menstrual theme from *Ginger Snaps*'s sequel and prequel, *Ginger Snap 2: Unleashed* (2004, dir. Brett Sullivan) and *Ginger Snaps Back: The Beginning* (2004, dir. Grant Harvey) has proved something of a problem for those critics who want to bind them closely to the original as disquisitions on female biological otherness, with the result being that some readings of the later films seem rather forced in their attempts to find menstrual or associated events buried within narratives that, ostensibly at least, are preoccupied with other things. By contrast, Sunnie Rothenburger has provided a fascinating account of all three *Ginger Snaps* films in terms of Canadian national identity that picks up on elements of setting and landscape not widely explored in earlier writings on the films, but which only mentions menstruation in passing.[7] That even *Ginger Snaps*, the *locus classicus* of contemporary cinematic female lycanthropy, can credibly be interpreted in a manner that does not centre on female biology should at the very least alert us to the possibility of there being other ways of thinking about the subject.

This chapter sets out to explore some of these other ways. It does not do this to displace or dispel menstruation-centred or abjection-based readings; in some instances such readings are clearly effective and insightful. Yet a survey of horror cinema's female werewolves suggests that there is often more to this figure than just biology, and in specific cases a film's preoccupations can lead us away from the idea of the female werewolf as 'cursed' or inevitably doomed to biological subjection into new areas. In particular, the chapter will identify some of the cinematic strategies for the visual presentation of the female werewolf. It also considers the issue of female violence as it relates to this particular horror monster in terms both of agency and of representation. In doing this, it focuses on some basic, even mundane, questions that often get overlooked in more straightforwardly ideological analysis – namely 'what does a female werewolf look like?' and 'what does it do?' It is the chapter's contention that a film's posing of, and attempts to answer, such questions informs and shapes both narration and style, and an appreciation of such elements can feed back into and ultimately bring nuance to more ideology-based readings. Horror cinema's female werewolf emerges from this as both more complex and more variegated in her various manifestations than has sometimes been allowed by horror criticism.

Who or what is the She-Wolf of London?

There are not many female werewolves in horror cinema. Clearly there are some, however – and more so in recent horror productions than in classic horror cinema of the 1930s, 1940s and 1950s – but there are far fewer than there are male werewolves. Having noted this, there is nothing necessarily significant in this paucity of female lycanthropy; all sorts of other non-cinematic monsters have only a marginal place in horror cinema, or no place at all. It might not reflect the situation in folkloric and literary sources where female werewolves are not uncommon, but throughout its history horror cinema has tended to be very selective in what it takes from non-cinematic sources and has been driven instead primarily by what is commercially popular either within cinema itself or in other media. At the same time, however, there is something intriguing about horror cinema's treatment of the female werewolf. This might possibly derive from the female werewolf's status as an unusual monster, but, nevertheless, it helps to separate it out from some of the conventional ways of representing the altogether more common male werewolf.

As a way of engaging initially with the figure, this chapter now turns to the Universal horror film *She-Wolf of London* (1946, dir. Jean Yarbrough).[8] This might seem a perverse choice with which to begin, partly because it does not actually feature a female werewolf and partly because it is far from being a horror classic. To put it mildly, *She-Wolf of London* was not especially well-received on its initial release and has not fared well since so far as its critical reputation is concerned. The dismissive 1946 review in the *New York Times* went so far as to give away the entire plot in its first sentence, such was its contempt for any audience that wanted to see the film: 'To report, as we are about to do, that the heroine of the new horror picture at the Rialto is the victim of a diabolical old crone, who is working overtime to convince the fair young thing that she is a maniacal killer, is to summarise the plot of *She-Wolf of London*.'[9] More recently, *Halliwell's Film, Video and DVD Guide* summed it up as a 'risibly inept semi-horror melodrama with a highly implausible solution and poor production', while the authoritative *Aurum Film Encyclopedia: Horror* has dismissed it as a 'feeble potboiler ... there is no werewolf, just a crazed killer, no atmosphere and an unbelievably bogus London setting'.[10] In order to clarify the meaning of the film's title, one has to add to the *New York Times*'s plot summary the fact that the 'old crone' – to whom we will return shortly – plays on the heroine's fears that she might be physically transforming into a wolf, while a credulous police officer also believes that a werewolf might be responsible for a series of brutal murders.

It seems fairly obvious that the makers of *She-Wolf of London* were inspired by the commercial success of RKO's *Cat People* (1942, dir. Jacques Tourneur), in which a young woman is similarly troubled by the fear that she can transform into a wild animal, although in that case the animal is a panther – with *The Aurum Film Encyclopedia* also suggesting a connection with the more obscure 'family haunted by a curse' project *Undying Monster* (1942, dir. John Brahm).[11] From this perspective, the idea of the female werewolf becomes a rather outré plot innovation, with a wolf standing in for a panther. At the same time, however, *She-Wolf of London* also offers a kind of whodunit in which we are encouraged to guess who the killer (and potentially the werewolf) is, with most of its characters going out of their way to act suspiciously in the course of the narrative in order to promote their status as suspects. This format recurs later in werewolf cinema – for example in *The Beast Must Die* (1974, dir. Paul Annett) and *Cursed* (2005, dir. Wes Craven) – and it tends to involve both male and female suspects, with the possibility of female lycanthropy thereby absorbed into a more general sense that anyone, regardless of gender, and indeed class, race or age, could turn out to be the monster.[12]

What is arguably more interesting than the way in which *She-Wolf of London* deploys the idea of the female werewolf as a narrative lure is the film's engagement with the prospect of a female-generated violence. This prospect was inherent in a title that, one suspects, was, in true exploitative fashion, concocted by the studio's marketing department. It referred back, of course, to the Universal production *Werewolf of London* (1935, dir. Stuart Walker) (in which both of the werewolves involved were male), just as an earlier Universal horror *Dracula's Daughter* (1936, dir. Lambert Hillyer) referred back to *Dracula* (1931, dir. Tod Browning), with the reference to women in both adding a new twist to an original male-centred horror story. In the case of *Dracula's Daughter*, which was a direct sequel to *Dracula*, this involved the introduction of some thinly disguised lesbian elements. In the case of *She-Wolf of London*, which was not a sequel and operated in an entirely different register from the supernatural *Werewolf of London*, the translation of the werewolf's violence into potentially female form posed more problems for the filmmakers.

As one might expect from a film featuring a possible werewolf, the violence in *She-Wolf of London* turns out to be decidedly grisly. This being a 1940s film, we are actually shown very little gore but what happens off-screen is described in surprisingly graphic detail. The film's main violent event in this regard involves the slaughter of a ten-year-old boy. Characters describe this unfortunate victim as 'torn to pieces' and 'horribly mangled', while someone comments to the increasingly nervous heroine: 'The idea that a frail girl like you could literally tear a boy of ten to pieces is utterly ridiculous.' Indeed the idea that the heroine Phyllis Allenby might be capable of any violent acts is absurd, for, as played by June Lockhart, she remains unremittingly passive and physically frail throughout the entire narrative. Of course, if she were a werewolf, things might be different, but that kind of transformation is never offered up by a film that eventually rejects the possibility of a supernatural solution to its murder mystery. But equally, the prospect of the film's villainess, the she-wolf of the title, meting out such extraordinary violence is also ridiculous and impossible. It is worth looking in more detail at, to borrow the *New York Times*'s phrase, the 'diabolical old crone' from this perspective. As played by character actor Sara Haden, Martha Winthrop is undoubtedly diabolical in intent, but the 'old crone' designation seems harsh. Haden was forty-seven years old at the time of the film's production, and the character she plays, who is the mother of an adult daughter, is of a comparable age. One wonders if the 'old crone' label reveals some inadvertent critical hyperbole on the part of a 1940s critic struggling to bring together this symbol of domesticated and genteel femininity with an off-screen scene of visceral and gory violence, although one could also argue that this turns out to be a problem for the filmmakers as well.

It is interesting in this regard how enervated *She-Wolf of London*'s narrative turns out to be. Although it has some of the qualities of the 1940s 'female gothic' cycle of films discussed by Helen Hanson in both its predominantly domestic settings and its focus on female characters, it is entirely lacking in the investigative drive associated with that cycle.[13] As already noted, the heroine Phyllis is passive throughout, showing minimal curiosity about what is going on around her, while the film's ostensible hero does little more than wander around aimlessly and make a few accusations, all of them incorrect. Although Phyllis survives a murder attempt at the film's conclusion, she does not save herself and neither is she rescued by someone else. Instead Martha Winthrop, the she-wolf, dies in an accident; while chasing away a curious maid, she stumbles, falls down some stairs and ends up stabbing herself with a knife that she was planning to use on the heroine. The hero arrives too late to do anything other than look on in surprise.

Clearly *She-Wolf of London* requires this particular violent woman to be a threatening and destructive presence, to the extent that she cannot readily be stopped by a series of ineffectual male characters (alongside the hero, the police authorities are particularly useless in the film), but at the same time it struggles to present her as actually dangerous, hence the film's anti-climactic trajectory. This is not just to do with what can and cannot be presented on the screen during the 1940s – obviously we cannot be shown a small child being torn to pieces – but it also has to do with the representational impossibility of this kind of violence. In other words, how is Martha Winthrop/Sara Haden capable of such an act, not just culturally (women don't do things like that according to dominant cultural norms) but also, and more importantly, physically; how can this particular body do that to another body? In this, she stands at some distance from that other violent woman of 1940s American cinema, film noir's femme fatale who, with considerably more credibility, either wields a gun or arranges for an associate or fall guy to commit violence on her behalf. Arguably, Winthrop/Haden also exists apart from more contemporary action heroines with their gun-wielding and finely honed martial arts skills, for her violence is a violence of the body, emanating from the body and always proximate to it, a violence that entails the physical destruction, a literal rending apart, of another body. Not a female werewolf as such but certainly a she-wolf, an exceptionally violent woman, and in all her contradictoriness a figure that resonates throughout later werewolf cinema.

Transformations and possibilities

What is interesting about *She-Wolf of London* is its simultaneous posing of and ultimate failure to answer a simple if perhaps perverse question, which might be phrased as 'how can you be a woman and rip someone apart with your bare hands?' Of course one way of dealing with this conundrum that was not available to the non-supernatural *She-Wolf of London* is to transform the woman into something other than a woman, something that is physically capable of ripping someone apart – for example a wolf or equivalent beast. Films such as *Cry of the Werewolf* (1944, dir. Henry Levin) or the more recent *An American Werewolf in Paris* (1997, dir. Anthony Waller); *Ginger Snaps*; *Dog Soldiers* (2002, dir. Neil Marshall); *Cursed*, *Wild Country* (2005, dir. Craig Strachan); and *Blood and Chocolate* (2007, dir. Katja von Garnier) depict women transforming completely into wolves or wolf-like creatures so that they end up visually indistinguishable from male beasts.

In other examples of bodily transformation, the woman is turned into something resembling the hirsute male werewolf associated with the Universal horror tradition of the 1930s and 1940s, and most of all Lon Chaney Jr.'s rendition of the role in *The Wolf Man* and its numerous sequels: in other words, transformed into something less feminine, more masculine. This version of the female werewolf first appears in the Mexican production *La Loba* (1965, dir. Rafael Baledón) and is also a prominent feature in another Mexican horror *Santo versus the She-Wolves* (1972, dir. Rubén Galindo and Jaime Jiménez Pons) as well as showing up in more comedic form at the end of the American horror *The Howling* (1981, dir. Joe Dante). However, it has not proved popular as a strategy for depicting female werewolves, possibly because female hirsuteness still remains something of a social taboo (although, as the recent production *The Wolfman* (2010, dir. Joe Johnston) demonstrates, it remains viable in the context of male werewolves). In addition, this way of showing the monster still keeps it in recognisable female form, again leaving the issue of physical strength unresolved. It is worth noting in this respect that the female werewolf in *Santo versus the She-Wolves* is, for all her hairiness, still filmed voyeuristically and remains visibly female beneath her hair (clad as she is in a kind of furry bikini), and, perhaps connected with this, is easily defeated halfway through the film and is subsequently replaced by a far more formidable male werewolf.

So while the female werewolf offers the prospect of extreme visceral violence, the location of that violence is often placed at some distance from the woman herself, either in animal or animalistic form. An interesting and arguably distinctive feature of some female werewolf films in this regard is their fascination with the moment of transition from woman to beast. This does not refer to the fetishistic fascinations exerted by certain kinds of body-centred special effects (although these are sometimes also involved in these moments, especially in more contemporary horror films). Instead it involves a certain way of showing the woman caught up in a process of becoming that, perhaps paradoxically given that it entails leaving behind an identity, registers in terms of elegance, poise and self-control, and lacks the focus on pain evident in the now classic special effects-led human-to-beast transformations that feature in *An American Werewolf in London* (1981, dir. John Landis) and *The Howling*, in both of which the bodies being agonisingly and messily transformed are male.

Let us consider a few examples in this regard, beginning with the British horror film *Dr Terror's House of Horrors* (1965, dir. Freddie Francis), a horror anthology project that contains a Scottish-set werewolf story. Here there turn out to be two werewolves; a male one, whom we see briefly as a wolf but never in human form, and its female partner. In human form, she is played by Ursula Howells as a sophisticated and attractive blonde forty-something widow. By the end of the story, however, it is clear that she is about to become a beast and slaughter the unfortunate male protagonist. But we are not shown her in beast form. Instead there is a shot of her hairy hand elegantly playing with some silver bullets which she had earlier stolen from the soon-to-be-dead hero, followed by a close-up of her face as her change into something else progresses. The darkening of her hair, and also the skin via make-up and lighting, gives definition and strength to the face, with this further accentuated via the character's intent gaze into the camera. This clearly registers for her as a moment of empowerment and self-possession; in terms of the story, it is the moment of her triumph. However, as is the case with other cinematic female werewolves, the actual exercise of that power through violence involves becoming something other than this, something other than female, with that final transformation not shown to us.

Similar pre-transformation moments of poise occur, albeit within different contexts, in *The Beast Must Die* and *An American Werewolf in Paris*. In the first of these, the wife of the film's hero is shown in the seconds leading up to her transformation into a ferocious wolf holding – as does the *Dr Terror* she-wolf – a silver bullet as a lone tear runs from her right eye. Unlike *Dr Terror's House of Horrors*, there is a distinct impression here of the character's sadness at leaving behind the human form, but again the pose is elegant, and everything else about this moment – from the woman's refined appearance to the genteel drawing-room setting – speaks of a domestic decorum against which the woman's state of being in transformation registers as disruptive. At the same time, however, there is also a sense in which this moment is one of beauty, indeed of a kind of maximal beauty with the female body caught in the last instance before it becomes something else. Interestingly, the fact that in this case the woman is black, and that the film in which she appears was marketed in some territories under the title *Black Werewolf*, suggests an alignment with 1970s 'blaxploitation horror' and in so doing complicates any sense of the monstrous residing solely in gender.[14] The multiple werewolves of *The Beast Must Die* involve combinations of gender and race distinctions – a black male werewolf, a white male werewolf, and a black female werewolf – that undermine any sense of the female werewolf as an entirely self-contained category of monster.

In *An American Werewolf in Paris* too, in the moment just before the female werewolf played by Julie Delpy turns into a CGI-generated wolf-beast, she contemplates the moon above. Her face is made-up to signify a transformation in process, with this resulting, as with *Dr Terror's House of Horrors*, in a more pronounced definition of her facial features – the nose, the jaw, the eyes – that accords with an enhanced physicality and strength but which at the same time is offered in terms of a pose of self-possession, with the head turned slightly to one side, as if the character is offering herself up to be photographed.

In both *The Beast Must Die* and *An American Werewolf in Paris*, the female beasts that eventually appear out of these transformations are indistinguishable from male beasts in the films. So it is in such transitional moments, as short-lived as they are, rather than in later representations of bestial slobber and gore, that these films seek to show the female werewolf in a way that differentiates it from its male counterpart, caught in a process of becoming that yields a kind of transient beauty and which denotes empowerment, poise and elegance in a manner that stands in tension with the more usual association of the lycanthropic state with unwanted subjection and wildness. In effect, moments like this return us to the impossibility of a body-centred female violence that was first made evident in the earlier *She-Wolf of London*. Through casting the woman as a liminal figure immediately before a de-gendering physical transformation, these moments posit a violence that cannot itself be represented in terms of the human female body. They do this by aestheticising the body, rendering its surfaces harder and more clearly delineated, but at the same time accentuating its femininity, emphasising that which will be lost in the transformation to come. Indeed, *She-Wolf of London* also features, in its own modest way, such a moment of becoming. When the 'she-wolf' reveals to the heroine her diabolical plan, her expression and posture change, become more extreme and stylised. This does not last long, and a few seconds later the villainess is lying dead at the bottom of a flight of stairs. Nevertheless, there is a comparable sense here of a woman beginning to transform beyond herself, where that change is articulated in terms both of femininity and of a non-feminine future violence.

Horror's new she-wolves

It is worth remembering that the term 'she-wolf' is used in *She-Wolf of London* to denote both female werewolves and violent women. In fact, it can be argued that the showing of women as violent agents who are in some way or other dissociated from the actual practice of violence is also evident in a group of contemporary horror films that do not feature female werewolves but which do feature violent woman, or she-wolves, as main protagonists. Looking at these films from a shape-shifting or lycanthropic perspective can cast an interesting new light on them, as well as indicating that some of the issues raised by what is admittedly a small corpus of female werewolf films might be of broader significance.

The violent women to be discussed here are characters who are threatened and attacked and respond with an extraordinary level of visceral, close-up physical violence, with this associated visually with a transformation in their appearance – from conventional prettiness to something dirtier but also stylised and aestheticised to the extent that in its own perverse way it becomes a site of visual pleasure. To a certain extent, this representation of the female protagonist falls into the familiar category of 'the final girl', the heroine – or female hero – of the slasher film who ends up defeating the killer and surviving while everyone else around her dies.[15] Indeed the final girl does offer a model of female violence, albeit one that has undergone a series of changes over the years, from the primarily defensive violence evident in the original slashers of the late 1970s and early 1980s to a more stylised and proactive violence in the supernatural-themed 1980s cycles such as the *Nightmare on Elm Street* films on to the more realistic, but also collaborative, violence in the *Scream* films of the 1990s and their many imitators. However, the more recent manifestations of this figure from the early 2000s onwards take the violence and gore to a new level of intensity and extremity, and the physical transformations wrought on the final girl – if that is what one still wants to call her – go way beyond what occurred in earlier horrors.

A fairly straightforward illustration of this is provided by comparing the character of final girl Laurie Strode in John Carpenter's original and highly influential slasher film *Halloween* (1978) and Rob Zombie's recent remake, also entitled *Halloween* (2007). In both, Laurie (played by Jamie Lee Curtis in the original and Scout Taylor-Compton in the remake) starts out as a pleasant, eminently normal American teenager. Each Laurie then undergoes a series of traumatising experiences, although, in the case of Jamie Lee Curtis, the character does not change visually to any great extent in the course of the film, bar some minor wounds and dishevelment to accompany her upset and tears. By contrast, the remake's Laurie becomes noticeably darker, literally and figuratively, begrimed and with her face covered in her own blood. She is also much more violent than the original Laurie, screaming in rage in the final scene as she shoots the killer point-blank in the face.

Other examples of this befouling of the contemporary horror film's female protagonist, with extreme dirtiness associated with the exercise of extreme violence, can be found in *The Descent* (2005, dir. Neil Marshall) and its sequel *The Descent Part 2* (2009, dir. Jon Harris), in which Sarah (played by Shauna Macdonald), initially an equable, eminently ordinary woman, becomes in the course of both films a veritable killing machine, whose actions include gorily killing various cannibalistic troglodytes with her bare hands or with rudimentary stabbing or bludgeoning instruments. Or in *Eden Lake* (2008, dir. James Watkins), in which Jenny, a dedicated teacher (played by Kelly Reilly), having become suitably begrimed while on a journey gone bad into the countryside, stabs a young boy to death. Or in the French film *Switchblade Romance* (2003, dir. Alexandre Aja), in which Marie (Cecile de France), nice enough when clean, is capable when covered in dirt and blood of striking a man repeatedly in the head with a pole wrapped in barbed wire and tearing apart another man with a chain saw. Or in *P2* (2007, dir. Franck Khalfoun), in which businesswoman Angela (Rachel Nichols), once dirtied by her own blood, deals with her tormentor by stabbing him in the eye and then, as he lies helpless before her, setting him on fire. And others, to the extent that one might reasonably argue that, quietly and unobtrusively, the filthy and extremely violent woman has become something of a conventional figure on the contemporary horror scene.

One possible, and indeed rather obvious, interpretation of these representations involves seeing them in terms of the abject, with an accompanying sense of their projection of female biological Otherness. However, such an approach is arguably of limited use when it comes to explaining the association of the begrimed woman with acts of extreme violence perpetrated by that woman. As was the case with the female werewolves, there is an artfulness to these bodily transformations, with the blood, dirt and other noxious substances deployed and choreographed so that they contour the face and body, bestowing new visual definition and interest to surfaces and their textures. When combined with the patterns of stylised movement associated with the practice of violence, a surprising elegance and beauty yet again emerges.

What separates these images from those of the female werewolves discussed above is that in the contemporary horror films they represent an endpoint for the characters concerned. These women do not transform into something beyond this, something non-human; instead they unleash extraordinary violence on their tormentors while still in visibly feminine shape, albeit a transformed one. So on a very straightforward literal level, one might say that the kind of female violence unthinkable in the likes of *She-Wolf of London* has now become thinkable, capable of being represented. At the same time, however, and in female werewolf fashion, this female violence still retains an aura of impossibility. This is all too evident in the ways in which the women caught up in these transformations are shown to become lost, and dissociated from themselves, in their violence. So Laurie ends up deeply traumatised in the remake of *Halloween* (far more so than the Jamie Lee Curtis version of the character); Sarah is isolated and possibly mad in *The Descent* (at least in the European release version – the American release version offers a more positive conclusion), and suffers a violent death in *The Descent Part 2*; Jenny is about to be killed as *Eden Lake* ends; while Marie in *Switchblade Romance* is ultimately revealed to be insane and homicidal (in a controversial plot twist that reveals the final girl as herself a brutal murderer).

It will not do to overstate the link between this kind of survivalist horror and the female werewolf film or to collapse significant distinctions between them. However, both do offer comparable aestheticisations of women transforming away from themselves into agents of body-centred violence. Together they evince a fascination with the increasingly beautiful shape-shifting female figure in terms of liminality and transience, positioned at what is perceived as the far edge of femininity, in a state where that which is feminine begins to give way to something else, something remarkably violent.

A twist in the tale

There is a sequence in the American anthology horror film *Trick 'r Treat* (2007, dir. Michael Dougherty) that offers a perverse contemporary restaging of the Red Riding Hood story. It takes place during a Halloween carnival and involves Laurie (Anna Paquin) wandering through a lonely wood while dressed as Red Riding Hood. It turns out that she is being stalked, not by a wolf but instead by what appears to be a vampire, although this figure is shortly to be revealed as a plain ordinary male serial killer in disguise.

The killer attacks ... At this point *Trick 'r Treat* takes particular pleasure in upturning our expectations through revealing that Laurie herself is a werewolf, part of a female werewolf pack that has come to the carnival to find male victims, and that she is more than capable of defending herself against any assailant.

Trick 'r Treat was made at the same time as the 'she-wolf' survivalist horrors discussed in the previous section and can be seen as playfully combining attitudes also evident there with more established female werewolf conventions. The idea of the female werewolf as plot twist connects the film back with the likes of *Dr Terror's House of Horrors* and *The Beast Must Die*. More importantly, the transformation scene that concludes this part of the film clearly replays the idea of the female werewolf attaining an intense beauty immediately prior to its becoming a violent, non-gendered beast. At the final moment of her change, the make-up on Laurie's face accentuates her eyes and the lines of her jaw and mouth in a way that denotes strength but which also retains the symmetry of the actor's features. Her bodily contortions, while extreme and stylised, are also controlled and balanced. In this, she is contrasted with one of her 'sisters' in full beast mode, who stands next to Laurie and displays no visible gendered characteristics at all.

It is not just Laurie we see transforming, however, but her pack as well. The scene's emphasis throughout is on transformation as pleasurable rather than painful, with this supported by some sensual slow-motion photography with a group of women excitedly casting off their skin as if it is merely a garment while Marilyn Manson's languorous cover version of the Eurythmics' 'Sweet Dreams are Made of This' plays on the soundtrack. There is no sense here of an unwilling subjection to biological process, and no sense either of lycanthropy as a curse. Yet as was the case with Martha in *She-Wolf of London* and Sarah in *The Descent*, we are presented with images that can speak of female violence only as something that exists elsewhere, with this applying even for women in contemporary horror films who, as we have now seen, are more than capable of ripping apart their unfortunate victims.

Bearing all this in mind, one might suppose that the female werewolf, at least as she has been developed in horror cinema, is something of a contradiction in terms. Even as one recognises this, one also has to acknowledge the fascination exerted by this figure as well as the way in which her presence seems to extend beyond those few films that actually feature a female werewolf. Much has been written in recent years about the female hero not just in horror but in other contemporary film genres. Looking at the female werewolf, or the she-wolf, within such a context forces us to consider some of the awkward and disturbing issues raised by the prospect of proactive female violence. The attitudes and approaches evolved in what might be termed 'she-wolf cinema' are not necessarily progressive in this regard but they do range over a contradictory and difficult field in ways that are troubling, but provocative and revealing as well. They also possess their own peculiar power.

Notes

1. Chantal Bourgault du Coudray, *The Curse of the Werewolf: Fantasy, Horror and the Beast Within* (London: I.B. Tauris, 2006), 112.
2. The line from *The Wolf Man* that establishes this lunar connection – 'Even a man who is pure at heart, and says his prayers by night, may become a wolf when the wolfbane blooms and the autumn moon is bright' – sounds like it might be an authentic folk saying but was in fact made up for the film by the screenwriter, Curt Siodmak.
3. Du Coudray, *The Curse of the Werewolf*, 121. For an interesting discussion of horror's different strategies for 'feminising' men and women, also see Aviva Briefel, 'Monster Pains: Masochism, Menstruation, and Identification in the Horror Film', *Film Quarterly*, 28:3 (2005): 16–27.
4. For examples of this, see Martin Barker, Ernest Mathijs and Xavier Mendik, 'Menstrual Monsters: The Reception of the *Ginger Snaps* Cult Horror Franchise', *Film International*, 21 (2006): 68–77; Briefel, 'Monster Pains'; April Miller, 'The Hair That Wasn't There Before: Demystifying Monstrosity and Menstruation in *Ginger Snaps* and *Ginger Snaps Unleashed*', *Western Folklore*, 64:3–4 (2005): 281–303; Bianca Nielsen, '"Something's Wrong, Like More Than You Being Female": Transgressive Sexuality and Discourses of Reproduction in *Ginger Snaps*', *thirdspace*, 3:2 (2004): 55–69.
5. Barbara Creed, *The Monstrous-Feminine: Film, Feminism, Psychoanalysis* (London: Routledge, 1993).
6. Robin Wood, 'An Introduction to the American Horror Film', in Bill Nichols (ed.), *Movies and Methods – Volume 2* (Berkeley, CA: University of California Press, 1985), 215.
7. Sunnie Rothenburger, '"Welcome to Civilization": Colonialism, the Gothic, and Canada's Self-protective Irony in the *Ginger Snaps* Werewolf Trilogy', *Journal of Canadian Studies*, 44:3 (2010): 96–117.
8. The film is not to be confused with the 1990 television series *She-Wolf of London*, which in itself is an interesting, if not very distinguished, treatment of the female werewolf.
9. 'The Screen', *New York Times* (6 April 1946), 10. The Rialto in New York was a key site for the exhibition of horror and horror-related films during the 1930s and 1940s, which might explain the passing reference to it in the review. For a discussion of this important horror venue, see Mark Jancovich and Tim Snelson, 'Horror at the Crossroads: Class, Gender and Taste at the Rialto', in John Cline and Robert G. Weiner (eds), *From the Arthouse to the Grindhouse: Highbrow and Lowbrow Transgression in Cinema's First Century* (Lanham, MD: The Scarecrow Press, 2010).
10. John Walker (ed.), *Halliwell's Film, Video and DVD Guide* (London: HarperCollins, 2005), 791; Phil Hardy (ed.), *The Aurum Film Encyclopedia: Horror* (London: Aurum Press, 1985), 93.
11. Hardy, *Aurum Film Encyclopedia*, 93.
12. In support of this, the British production *The Beast Must Die* featured the 'werewolf break', a moment in the film where the narrative was stopped and a sinister voiceover invited the audience to select the werewolf from a list of suspects including men and women.

13 Helen Hanson, *Hollywood Heroines: Women in Film Noir and the Female Gothic Film* (London: I.B. Tauris, 2007).
14 For a relevant discussion of US blaxploitation horror, see Harry Benshoff, 'Blaxploitation Horror Films: Generic Reappropriation or Reinscription?', *Cinema Journal* (2000): 31–50.
15 For the original critical formulation of the concept of the final girl, see Carol J. Clover, *Men, Women and Chainsaws: Gender in the Modern Horror Film* (London: British Film Institute, 1992).

11
Ginger Snaps: the monstrous feminine as *femme animale*

Barbara Creed

One of the most enduring faces of the monstrous-feminine is that of the *femme animale*.[1] Sphinx, gorgon, lamia, harpy, siren, echidna – these terrifying creatures who were part-woman and part-animal haunt the myths of the ancient world. In Greek mythology, the Sphinx possessed the face and breasts of a woman, a lion's body and the wings of a bird. Those unfortunate male adventurers who failed to answer her riddle were eaten whole. The gorgons, whose name meant 'dreadful' in Greek, were winged women with hair made of living snakes; they could turn men to stone with their deadly stare. The lamia was a monster who devoured children; in some versions she possessed a serpent's tail which extended from her waist. Harpies were hideous, winged bird-women. The sirens were bird-women who lured sailors to their death with their entrancing songs. A sea-dragon, the echidna, who was half-woman and half-serpent, ruled over the earth's corrupt substances such as fetid water, slime and disease.

The monstrous *femme animale* continues to haunt the modern horror film although in different guises from her ancient counterparts. She has starred in a range of films as female vampire, cat woman, leech woman, ape woman, *femme fatale*, spider woman, mother alien, and female werewolf. In a number of these narratives, the *femme animale* appears not just as a terrifying monster who must be destroyed, but also as creature who deliberately sets out to undermine the dominant norms of an anthropocentric and phallocentric symbolic order. With her question ('What goes on four legs?') the sphinx pointed not just to man's life as a crawling infant but also to man's animal origins – an interpretation that anthropocentrism (and conventional explanations of the riddle) seek to ignore. By turning into stone men who cast a voyeuristic gaze upon female sexuality (symbolised by writhing snakes), the gorgons pointed to a cultural fetishisation of the female body. The animalistic nature of these female monsters may have been designed to make them less than human, but at the same time it gave them the freedom to destroy their enemies – wandering heroes, such as Perseus and Oedipus, out to prove their manhood. In so doing the *femme animale* reinforces the phallocentric investment in the division of nature and culture, woman and animal while at the same time drawing attention to her subversive powers.

The female werewolf offers a perfect example of the symbol of the *femme animale* and her ability to explore new ways of being and knowing. Chantal Bourgault du Coudray examines this in her essay on the rise of the werewolf cycle in popular fantasy fiction since the 1930s and its 'preoccupation with the feminine experience of lycanthropy':

> Certainly, while by no means all explorations of the werewolf in fantasy are written by women or are explicitly feminist, nearly all fantasy narratives about lycanthropy explore themes that have been a consistent feature of feminist critical thought, and a high proportion trace a specifically female experience of lycanthropy.[2]

These themes include the equation of woman with nature in Western thought and the degradation of women and nature in patriarchal mythological and linguistic discourses. In *The Death of Nature: Women, Ecology and the Scientific Revolution*, scientist Carolyn Merchant investigates the impact of the scientific revolution of the sixteenth and seventeenth centuries, its exploitation of nature and subsequent denigration of women.[3]

One of the most notable offenders in women's oppression, and her negative alignment with nature, has been the Catholic Church. During the period of the Catholic Inquisition, the Church relied in part upon the *Malleus Maleficarum* (1484), which was written by two Dominicans, Heinrich Kramer and James Sprenger, in order to determine the nature of witches, how they might be identified, tortured and executed. Commissioned by the Church and in use for nearly three centuries, it was permeated by an extreme hatred of women. The *Malleus Maleficarum* was obsessed with the nature of female sexuality and the kinds of sexual acts witches were said to perpetrate. Forced to confess under torture to imaginary deeds, women were made to describe the exact nature of their supposed sexual acts with the devil as well as detailing information about his member – its size, texture and shape. Witches were also accused of causing male impotence and causing men's penises to disappear. The *Malleus Maleficarum* takes a dim view of sexuality, aligning it with the animal world. 'The animal nature of man' is something that must be 'cured' at all costs.[4]

Kramer and Sprenger also raise the issues of werewolves. They note that there were two kinds of werewolves: voluntary and involuntary. Individuals who voluntarily changed into a wolf were burned alive for 'the abominable crimes of lycanthropy and witchcraft'.[5] Kramer and Sprenger spent a great deal of time pondering the weighty question as to whether or not witches, through the use of a glamour, can change themselves and men into beasts: 'And again, that which seems to be, cannot really be; as in the case of a woman who seems to be a beast, for two substantial shapes cannot exist at one and the same time in the same matter.'[6] They conclude that such a metamorphosis occurs only through some glamour or illusion, which can be brought on by a witch, assisted by the Devil. In reality, they argued, only God has the power to change one creature into another.[7]

Nevertheless the Church did align witchcraft with lycanthropy and also accused witches of riding 'in the night hours on certain beasts with Diana, the heathen goddess, or with Herodias, and with a countless number of women, and that in the untimely silence of night they travel over great distances of land'.[8] By the sixteenth century it was written that witches arrived at Sabbats riding werewolves. Clearly in the mind of the Church – or, at least, in the minds of the writers of Inquisition handbooks – women enjoyed a special relationship with nature and the animal world, which explained their greater propensity for wicked and lustful behaviour. Because she was formed from a 'bent rib' she is an 'imperfect animal'.[9] 'You do not know that woman is the Chimaera, but it is good that you should know it; for that monster was of three forms; its face was that of a radiant and noble lion, it had the filthy belly of a goat, and it was armed with the virulent tail of a viper.'[10] Throughout, the *Malleus Maleficarum* aligns woman with nature, both of which are seen as degraded and base forms of existence. Although this volume was written in 1584, it was republished in 1971 along with an introduction by Montague Summers written in 1946 – immediately after the end of the Second World War. Summers describes both Kramer and Sprenger as men of 'genius', inspired by 'seemingly inexhaustible wells of wisdom'.[11]

In *The Open: Man and Animal*, Giorgio Agamben explores the ways in which Western thinkers have separated human and animal in their writings on the subject of human nature. He argues that the human has occupied a privileged place through the workings of the 'anthropological machine' of Western thought. The anthropological machine formulates this place by constructing an unassailable difference, 'a caesura' between human and animal. Man is not some kind of 'divine' creation but what is left over when human and animal are separated:

> Man exists historically only in this tension; he can be human only to the degree that he transcends and transforms the anthropophorous animal which supports him, and only because, through the action of negation, he is capable of mastering and, eventually, destroying his own animality (it is in this sense that Kojeve can write that 'man is a fatal disease of the animal').[12]

Agamben asks: 'What is man, if he is always the place – and, at the same time, the result – of ceaseless divisions and caesurae?' Agamben uses 'man' and 'human' interchangeably; he does not ask if the aporia or caesura between 'woman' and 'animal' might signify something different. This chapter will explore the boundary between woman and animal in popular discourse in order to analyse this difference.

The *Malleus Maleficarum* presents a particularly fine example of the anthropological machine at work and one which was still apparently exerting influence in religious discourse in the second half of the twentieth century. This unassailable difference between human and animal, however, does not hold as strongly when the gap is narrowed to one between woman and animal. This is because the anthropological machine of Western thought has also attempted to produce a caesura between man and woman by aligning woman with the animal and nature. Although Agamben does not consider the gendered nature of this caesura, it is crucial to an understanding of the workings of patriarchal ideology in cultural discourses. The negative pairing of woman and animal is particularly evident in publications such as the *Malleus Maleficarum*.

In Western patriarchal discourses, woman is associated more with the abject face of nature because of her role as mother of the human species. Like many female animals, she is impregnated, changes shape, gives birth, bleeds and lactates. While her prime function is to perpetuate the human species, man's duty is to regulate and rule over both the natural and human domains. In religious discourse, as discussed above, woman is the natural ally of the evil serpent. The Garden of Eden myth is frequently interpreted as a warning to man about woman's insatiable sexual and animal desires. Referring to ancient texts, the *Malleus Maleficarum* states that: 'In Rome … women copulated with bears, snakes and crocodiles.'[13] At the close of the nineteenth century, woman was associated with the animal world in the cultural imaginary as a result of a widespread fear of devolution. Influenced by a misinterpretation of Darwinian theory, many people believed that just as the human species had evolved into higher forms of life, it was capable of devolving to a more primitive form. Those most at risk were women, children and indigenous peoples. In his study of devolution in *fin-de-siècle* art, Bram Dijkstra argues that 'half-bestial creatures [such] as satyrs and centaurs' were used to depict men in danger of devolving. There was however 'no need to find a symbolic form to represent [woman's] bestial nature' as 'women, being female, were, as a matter of course, already representative of degeneration'.[14] Paintings of the time depict women sporting with satyrs and other animals in the depths of woods, outside the boundaries of the civilised world. The genre of hard-core pornography which specialises in bestiality frequently aligns woman with the animal. Women are posed in the 'doggy' position or depicted enjoying sex with animals such as dogs and horses. As Midas Dekkers has shown, however, bestiality is a complex and controversial subject which should not be dismissed as mere pornography.[15]

The alignment of woman and animal in myth and fairy tales, such as *The Frog Prince* and *Beauty and the Beast*, offers a refreshing and alternative view in which it is woman's ability to bond with the animal that brings about a new world order. In this context one could argue that Peter Jackson's remake of *King Kong* (2005) mourns the end of the creative union of woman and animal. This is emphasised in the scene in which the ape and the woman watch the sun set on Skull Island for the last time, just prior to Kong's capture and murder by so-called civilised man, who puts the great beast on display in chains for all the world to see. Although many narratives, which over the centuries have aligned woman with animal, denigrate woman it is not clear that they were always successful. In her discussion of ecofeminism and fantasy, du Coudray argues that the representation of the bond between woman and animal in literature offers new ways of thinking and being. She refers to the figures of the cyborg and the monster in the speculative genres of science fiction and horror as leading to new understanding of 'questions about subjectivity and identity'.[16]

The representation of the monstrous *femme animale* in the contemporary horror film, for instance, raises various issues designed to critique patriarchal forms of representation and to stimulate debate about woman's identity. In these films the various images of the monstrous-feminine are both terrifying and liberating. *Cat People* (1942, dir. Jacques Tourneur) offers a critique of man and his repressed sexual desire for dangerous animalistic women. *The Leech Woman* (1960, dir. Edward Dein) offers a critique of a society in which men cast aside older women for those who are young and beautiful. *The Ape Woman* (1964, dir. Marco Ferreri) tells the story of a man who puts a hirsute woman on display as if she were a creature in a circus.[17] A study of male cruelty, *The Ape Woman* is represented as both monstrous and sympathetic. The *Alien Quadrilogy*, particularly the second film, *Aliens* (1986, dir. James Cameron), represents female reproductive functions as both primitive and monstrous but not as horrific as man's desires to control the universe. The more recent black comedy, *Teeth* (2007, dir. Mitchell Lichtenstein), stars a female protagonist who unknowingly possesses a deadly *vagina dentata*. A study of male violence, *Teeth* represents woman's sexuality as both animalistic and liberating.

In recent decades the horror film has turned its attention to the *femme animale* as werewolf. The female werewolf stars in a range of films including: *The Company of Wolves* (1984, dir. Neil Jordan), *Howling II* (1985, dir. Philippe Mora), *Wolf* (1994, dir. Mike Nichols), *An American Werewolf in Paris* (1997, dir. Anthony Waller), *Blood and Chocolate* (2007, dir. Katja von Garnier), *Ginger Snaps* (2000, dir. John Fawcett), *Ginger Snaps 2: Unleashed* (2004, dir. Brett Sullivan); *Ginger Snaps Back: The Beginning* (2004, dir. Grant Harvey), *Cursed* (2005, dir. Wes Craven) and *Trick 'r Treat* (2007, dir. Michael Dougherty). *Trick 'r Treat* offers a new interpretation of the werewolf transformation scene in which the characters tear off their human skins to reveal the fur beneath. There is also the Italian classic, *La Lupa* (1996, dir. Gabriele Lavia), and the Mexican *La Loba* (1965, dir. Rafael Beledón), which was followed by a *La Loba* television series made in 1966, 1973 and 2010. The Italian rape-revenge film, *La Lupa Mannara* (1976, dir. Rino Di Silvestro), also known as *The Legend of the Wolf Woman* and *Terror of the She-Wolf*, has achieved cult status. More recently, the darkly humorous TV series, *She-Wolf of London* (1990–91), appeared on the small screen.

In many of these films, woman's metamorphosis into the werewolf draws on the powers of the uncanny to terrify audiences. In his 1919 essay 'The Uncanny' Freud defined the uncanny as 'that class of the frightening which leads us back to what is known of old and long familiar'.[18] The uncanny is that which is both *heimlich*/familiar yet *unheimlich*/unfamiliar. He was particularly interested in Schelling's definition of the uncanny as 'that which ought to have remained ... secret and hidden but has come to light'.[19] In this sense the uncanny describes the metamorphosis of the familiar into the unfamiliar, of bringing into the light that which should have remained hidden. The uncanny involves the dissolution of boundaries between familiar and unfamiliar, real and imagined. Rosemary Jackson argues that this gives an ideological or 'counter cultural' edge to the uncanny.[20] Films about the monstrous *femme animale* almost always involve a scene in which the protagonist encounters her dark, inner being – her familiar 'self' as an unfamiliar monstrous feminine. In *Ginger Snaps*, this encounter is both terrifying and liberating; it disturbs the boundaries that divide culture from nature and human from animal. The textual representations of woman as animal in cultural discourse and her physiology are varied and complex, but all draw on the concept of the uncanny in order to create a frightening image of woman which has the potential to explore new ways of knowing and being. It is what occurs in the uncanny space of this intersection that has the power to unsettle and disturb the notion of what it means to be human while simultaneously producing the human animal as central to more open discursive relationships. Films which feature the female werewolf, such as *Ginger Snaps*, also call gender and sexual boundaries into question, particular where the female grows a furry phallus of her own.[21]

Various theorists have explored the question of the human/animal divide and the 'othering' of the animal. In 'The Animal That Therefore I Am', Jacques Derrida questions all philosophers, from Aristotle to Lacan, who argue that 'the animal is without language' in that it is 'unable to respond':

> As with every bottomless gaze, as with the eyes of the other, the gaze called animal offers to my sight the abyssal limit of the human: the inhuman or the ahuman, the ends of man, that is to say the bordercrossing from which vantage man dares to announce himself to himself.[22]

Charles Darwin similarly questioned man's daring 'to announce himself to himself' at the expense of the animal. In rejecting the belief that man was central to the history of the Earth, the result of a divine act of creation, Darwin created a new voice and space for the non-human animal. 'It is absurd to talk of one animal being higher than another', he wrote in his notebook. 'People often talk of the wonderful event of intellectual Man appearing – the appearance of insects with other senses is more wonderful'.[23] In *Animal Lessons*, Kelly Oliver interrogates the 'continental' discourse on animals, and the way European philosophers have defined humanity in relation to animality in order to produce the human as apart from the animal and therefore superior. She concludes that animals teach us how to be human.[24] Margot Norris in *Beasts of the Modern Imagination* argues for a 'biocentric tradition' in art and literature in which writers create animals who not only speak in their own voice but do so to undermine the anthropocentrism of human culture. According to Norris the Darwinian revolution resulted in 'a subversive interrogation of the anthropocentric premises of Western philosophy and art'.[25] Agamben's concept of the privileged place of the human, produced through the anthropocentric machine of Western thought, similarly turns our attention to the representation of the animal whether in literature, painting or popular culture. But what of the place of woman and her relation to the animal? The monstrous-feminine as uncanny *femme animale* undermines Agamben's caesura and unsettles the traditional binaries of Western thinking in favour of more flexible discursive ways of thinking about the so-called human/animal and culture/nature divide.

Ginger Snaps

Ginger Snaps explores Agamben's caesura and its gendered structure through its narrative about a young girl who metamorphoses into a werewolf asserting that she derives greater pleasure from being animal than female. The two main characters are Ginger and her younger sister Brigitte. Events are told from Brigitte's point of view. Post-Romantics, the girls spend their time taking horrifyingly realistic but beautifully composed photographs of themselves in various stages of death and decomposition. This is a school assignment which they call their 'death project'. Their obsession with death represents an attempt to escape the boredom of everyday life in their hometown which announces itself to visitors as 'Bailey Downs: A Safe and Caring Community'. Terrified that they will end up like their parents, Brigitte tells Ginger: 'I hate our gene pool'. When the film commences neither of the sisters has begun to menstruate, much to the consternation of their mother, Pamela, who believes that her daughters are not normal because they are so late with their periods. In contrast to her difficult daughters, she eagerly awaits their entry into womanhood, which she sees as a cause for celebration. It almost seems as if the sisters have deliberately willed their bodies not to follow the normal path of womanhood. Ginger believes that suicide is the ultimate 'Fuck you' and has convinced Brigitte that they should 'go together' so that they can be 'together forever'. Although at the beginning of the film the sisters' close relationship suggests that this is a real possibility, as the narrative progresses and Ginger becomes the first to experience menstruation, the couple begin to grow apart.

The first sign that Ginger might be about to menstruate is a sudden back pain which attacks her when eating dinner with the family. Immediately Pamela suggests that this might indicate the onset of her period. 'Henry, the girls are both three years late menstruating. Ok. It's not normal!' Her husband is literally lost for words. Embarrassed by Pamela's intrusive comments, the sisters take pleasure in suggesting a range of fatal diseases which might be the real cause of Ginger's pain. 'Maybe it's cancer of the spine,' says Ginger wickedly. When the sisters leave the house at night they find the dismembered body of a dog on the road, which – despite their fascination with death – is far too abject for them. It is another victim of a strange creature which has been killing the local dogs and which has been dubbed 'The Beast of Bailey Downs'. Suddenly, Ginger discovers blood running down her leg. 'I just got the curse!' she announces. At the same time the frightening sounds of a growling beast fill the night air and Brigitte watches in horror as a screaming Ginger is transported into the forest. Brigitte can hear her sister's screams and the beast's howls but cannot see her sister through the darkness. Suddenly, Ginger rushes from the woods knocking Brigitte to the ground. The creature attacks, and gouges Ginger with its claws as it attempts to make off with the carcass of the dead dog. Ginger and Brigitte tear across the road pursued by the beast which smashes into a van driven by Greg, the young man who runs a plant nursery and also grows dope which he supplies to the students. A sudden glimpse of the creature reveals a wolf's head and hairy body with long legs and forearms which make it appear part-human. Brigitte manages to get Ginger home. She is crying hysterically, covered in blood, her shoulders marred by deep cuts. Brigitte suggests that perhaps it was a bear, as bears will come after a girl 'on the rag' because of the smell. 'It wasn't a fucking bear!' Ginger yells. Brigitte, who is touching her wounds, is astonished: 'That's impossible. They're already healing.'

Brigitte, who has managed to capture an image of creature's face with her Polaroid camera, stares in wonderment at its yellow eye and huge jaws. The scene cuts to school, where the students are watching a documentary on biology which is about the way a virus affects human cells. The voice-over explains that the virus is an intruder that 'devours the host from within' eventually consuming it completely. Because the film is screened just after Ginger is attacked by both her menstrual cycle and the monster, the implication is that both are capable of destroying their host or victim. Later when the girls are shopping in the supermarket for tampons, Jason, one of the boys from school, tells Ginger he has three sisters and he knows that nothing takes 'the edge off' like a good joint. Ginger replies defiantly, 'Well maybe I like my edge!' Shortly after, Brigitte bursts into the school toilets where Ginger has retreated. Something is wrong, she says – and it's 'like more than you just being female'. She sees blonde hairs sprout from the scars on Ginger's shoulders. 'Bitten on a full moon. Now you're hairy!' Ginger's bodily changes signal her metamorphosis into a monster. Bianca Nielsen states that, as Ginger takes such a long time to metamorphose, and as this is independent of whether or not there is a full moon, the implication is that she may never change back into her human self as does the conventional Hollywood werewolf: 'In this respect, *Ginger Snaps* differs from many other werewolf narratives, where those infected are able to control their animal side so long as the moon is not full.'[26] Woman's procreative functions signify a certain uncanniness denied the male that enhances her physical powers of mutability and transformation. They also align her very firmly with the animal.

As I have discussed elsewhere, Julia Kristeva's concept of the abject enables us to understand exactly what it is about woman that renders her monstrous in a way denied the male. The abject is that which does not 'respect borders, positions, rules', that which 'disturbs identity, system, order'.[27] The place of the abject is 'the place where meaning collapses', the place where 'I' am not. The abject threatens life; it must be 'radically excluded' from the realm of the living.[28] Human bodily wastes such as urine, mucus, blood and faeces are abject. The corpse, itself a waste, is the most abject of all things. All human societies however need the abject – in order to define what it means to be human. Hence the abject is an ambiguous entity – both repulsive yet alluring. Humankind explores the abject through representation and performance – ritual, art, poetry, popular culture. Ginger and Brigitte's death project represents an attempt to engage with the abject through artistic practice.

According to Kristeva woman occupies a different position from man in relation to nature and the abject. Because of her reproductive functions, woman's body is less discrete and stable. Woman's body bleeds, swells during pregnancy, subsides, lactates – fluids such as menstrual blood and afterbirth are part of woman's body and are ultimately expelled as waste. Because woman is in charge of toilet training, in teaching the infant about maintaining a clean and proper body, she is identified, more than man, with bodily wastes. In order to define itself as 'human' and not animal, human cultures have in varying degrees abjected the animal world. With the exception of certain domesticated animals, the human subject sees nature and the animal world as abject – dirty, diseased, mute. Yet, the human subject is drawn to myths and legends, fairy tales and literary narratives, painting and sculpture, film and media which continue to explore the fragile boundary between human and animal. As an abject being, the monstrous *femme animale* is both frightening and sympathetic, particularly as her rebellion involves a complete rejection of the proper feminine role. Ginger as female werewolf tears at the fragile suburban surfaces, exposing its abject depths, bringing that which should have remained hidden into the light.

The female werewolf is particularly abject because her body is even more unstable than that of the male. As a versipellous monster, the werewolf is a 'skin changer' that is, it is able to turn its skin inside out as it metamorphoses from human to animal and back again. The classic cinematic sign of this transformation is hair – the short hairs that sprout and burst through the inside of the skin to the outside. In the horror film, the scene of metamorphosis almost always points to the thinness of the human skin. The function of the skin, which Kristeva described as 'a fragile container' is to prevent the insides of the body from spilling to the outside.[29] On a metamorphosing body, these tiny hairs grow rapidly to cover the entire body. The female, whose body by its very nature is less stable (emitting menstrual blood, swelling with pregnancy, lactating) than the male body, signifies more powerfully the bond between human and animal. It is not by accident that Ginger starts to metamorphose into a werewolf at the very moment when she begins to menstruate.

When blood gushes from between Ginger's legs onto the floor, Brigitte takes her immediately to see the school nurse who is at her desk, a menstrual chart hanging behind her on the wall. She sits back grinning: 'I'm sure it seems like a lot of blood … it's a period.' Brigitte says it is more like a 'geyser'. The nurse says 'a syrupy, voluminous discharge is not uncommon'. In three to five days it will become lighter and brighter in colour but may change again at the end of the flow into 'a brownish or blackish sludge'. When Brigitte asks her about 'hair that wasn't there before', she replies 'comes with the territory'. In a perverse way she seems pleased that Ginger will be able to look forward to her period for 'the next thirty years'. Her description suggests that menstrual blood is basically an abject form of bodily waste. Nielsen suggests that this reinforces a particular medical discourse that sees menstruation as 'failed' reproduction.[30] The biology film combined with the nurse's account of menstruation both suggest that menstruation is an alien bodily function that is unwanted and repulsive. The fact that this scene takes place just after the monster's attack in the woods further associates menstruation with the dark side of nature.

In the classic werewolf and vampire film, the creature – male and female – almost always attacks on the full moon, that is, in accord with the moon's twenty-eight-day cycle, which is also the average length of the menstrual cycle. Both vampire and werewolf are blood creatures: the former sucks its victim's blood, usually from the neck, while the latter rips apart its victim's flesh. Once bitten, the victim either perishes or lives to repeat the cycle, becoming a monster itself. *Ginger Snaps* makes much of Ginger's menstrual flow, milking the moment for humour. When Pamela discovers Ginger's bloody underwear in the laundry she announces with clear pride: 'Our little girl's a young woman now!' To make matters worse, Pamela bakes a cake, smothered in red berries and dripping juice, for a family celebration. In a scene of black comedy, she congratulates her Ginger on her 'achievement'. One might expect that Ginger by now would be feeling deeply depressed. On the contrary, she tells Brigitte that the transformations that have taken over her body have made her feel 'so good'. Ginger as monstrous *femme animale* is revelling in her new identity and her power to rip apart and lay waste to the 'safe and caring community' of Bailey Downs that her mother holds so close to her heart.

A key menstrual reference in *Ginger Snaps* is the Little Red Riding Hood tale. Recent reworkings of the story in film focus on the themes of puberty and female werewolfism. In *The Company of Wolves*, based on Angela Carter's eponymous short story, Neil Jordan draws attention to this connection which Carter emphasises in her story. She informs the reader that Rosaleen's red cloak 'has the ominous if brilliant look of blood on snow', and that her body is undergoing important changes as her 'breasts have just begun to swell … her cheeks are an emblematic scarlet and white and she has just started her woman's bleeding'.[31] Carter draws attention to the girl's menstrual cycle as an important event and depicts her encounter with the wolf as a sexual one. In the cinematic adaptation, Neil Jordan goes further than the story by suggesting at the end that Rosaleen has become a wolf herself. Although Rosaleen's grandmother warned her never to trust men whose eyebrows meet in the middle, when she meets a woodsman whose eyebrows do just that she gives up her human shape for that of a wolf and we see her leaving granny's cottage in the company of a wolf. A number of cultural commentators have drawn attention to Little Red Riding Hood's 'red cape', interpreting it as symbolic of menstruation. Eric Fromm writes:

> Most of the symbolism in this fairy tale can be understood without difficulty. The 'little cap of red velvet' is a symbol of menstruation. The little girl of whose adventures we hear has become a mature woman and is now confronted with the problem of sex.[32]

In *Ginger Snaps*, woman's blood and the blood of the monster merges thus eroding the boundary or caesura between woman and creature. Once having been bitten there is no possibility of recuperation into proper womanhood for Ginger as the narrative documents her gradual metamorphosis into a wolf.

The dominant change that consumes Ginger's body is menarche. Images of Ginger bleeding, in which the blood runs down between her legs and covers her clothes, visually merge in the film with images of blood that accompany her metamorphosis into a female werewolf. In contrast to the male's metamorphosis into a werewolf, blood marks out Ginger's werewolfism as very different – a transformation that is intimately bound up with being female. The film's visual focus on woman's blood and reproductive cycle and on the female werewolf's bloodied attacks emphasise the close bonds between woman and animal. The abject side of this relationship is particularly evident in David Cronenberg's *The Brood* (1979). The film's most controversial scene occurs when Nola, the monstrous parthenogenetic mother, is in the process of giving birth. Her womb hangs at her side in the shape of a large sac. Having given birth to one of her misshapen brood, she bends over like an animal to lick away the blood and afterbirth. Her husband, who has been watching the birth, is filled with disgust: the woman is shocked at his response. Agamben's theory of the anthropological machine might explain the caesura between man and animal but it does not necessarily speak for woman.

As Ginger begins to change, becoming sexually provocative, the boys at school sit up and take notice. Brigitte is repulsed by Ginger's predatory behaviour, which she feels is a betrayal of their commitment to each other never to date boys and become 'average' like everyone else in Bailey Downs. 'You are doing drugs with guys. Something is definitely wrong with you.' Ginger accuses her of being jealous because she is growing up. It is Brigitte who is a green-eyed monster. Determined to save her beloved sister, Brigitte explores the werewolf legend. She marks the full moon on her calendar, reads up on werewolves and watches werewolf horror films. Ginger meanwhile is openly flirting with the boys at school. Brigitte is disturbed by other changes taking place on Ginger's body. One night she creeps across to Ginger's bed and peels back Ginger's pyjama pants. She is horrified – but not completely surprised – to see a small tail growing from her sister's tail bone. This scene brings to the fore the themes of sexual difference and otherness (bestiality, lesbianism, bisexuality, couvade) that haunt the narrative, strengthened by the fact that the werewolf is female. The werewolf as *femme animale* is hermaphroditic – a parthenogenetic phantasy.

Ginger's tail clearly resembles a penis. The scene could be a dream or nightmare. It takes place at night. Brigitte has been reading about werewolves under cover of the bedclothes and with the aid of a torch. Ginger lies perfectly still and doesn't even stir when her sister pulls down her pants and gasps out loud. Given the various references to an unspoken lesbian desire between the sisters, it is possible that Brigitte might like to dream of Ginger as a sexually predatory wolf. After all, Little Red Riding Hood was not at all afraid of the wolf, nor of the wolf dressed up in her granny's bonnet and nightgown. In her now famous comment on Little Red Riding Hood, Djuna Barnes said: 'God, children know something they can't tell; they like Red Riding Hood and the wolf in bed!'[33]

Freud's theory of the primal phantasies is central to an understanding of this scene. According to Freud, the primal phantasies involve three of life's major mysteries. Where did I come from? Whom do I desire? Why am I different? Laplanche and Pontalis point out that the primal phantasies directly address these three questions – questions that so often bewilder children in their formative years:

> If we consider the themes which can be recognised in primal phantasies (primal scene, castration, seduction) the striking thing is that they all have one trait in common: they are all related to the origins. Like collective myths, they claim to provide a representation of and a 'solution' to whatever constitutes a major enigma for the child [...] In the 'primal scene', it is the origin of the subject that is represented; in seduction phantasies, it is the origin or emergence of sexuality; in castration phantasies, the origin of the distinction between the sexes.[34]

Freud argues that the child may arrive at answers to these questions which themselves bear little relationship to reality. A frequent solution to the problem of origins is that the child imagines that it came from the mother's stomach – a concept explored in the Little Red Riding Hood fairy tale. The wolf swallows granny and the girl whole, and they both live in its stomach until the woodsman cuts the latter open and delivers them both back into the world. *Ginger Snaps* explores these three questions in relation to the possibility that the human is essentially a human animal – not the result of a special act of creation. In *Ginger Snaps*, the primal scene is imagined as the coupling of woman and wolf; castration is denied and woman is represented with a tail/phallus of her own; and sexual desire is represented as a bloody encounter between woman and animal. The effect of recasting the three primal phantasies in this way is to erase further the boundary between woman and animal. The sequel to *Ginger Snaps*, entitled *Ginger Snaps 2: Unleashed*, develops this erasure further.

Freud himself was very much aware of the human desire to become animal. In his most famous case study, 'From the History of an Infantile Neurosis' (1918), also known as 'The Wolf Man' case study, Freud developed his theory of the primal scene. He argued that the Wolf Man's wolf phobia, which he developed at the age of four, was based on an earlier episode in his life when as an infant he witnessed a scene of parental intercourse that greatly disturbed him. According to Freud, the infant witnessed a scene of coitus *a tergo* – that is, 'intercourse from behind'. He saw 'the man upright, and the woman bent down like an animal'.[35] He also interpreted this as a sadistic act in which the father was hurting the mother. Later in life when an adult, the Wolf Man himself could only derive pleasure from sex *a tergo*. As his wolf phobia developed, he suffered nightmares about wolves. He was particularly fearful of a picture from a book of fairy stories which depicted an upright wolf that would have suggested an uncanny merging of human and animal. Significantly, instead of exploring the significance of the collapse of boundaries between human and animal, Freud interprets the boy's nightmares as being about the castrating father and the institution of the patriarchal family. Yet, there are signs in Freud's account of the case history that the wolf that so terrified the boy might have been female. Freud states that as an infant he witnessed the mother on all fours, as if she were an animal, during the sex act with his father. The boy was also terrified of the wolf in the Red Riding Hood fairy tale, particularly of being 'eaten up', that is incorporated into the wolf's belly. In these two instances, the wolf assumes a female identity. This perhaps represents an instance of Agamben's caesura at work in Freud's interpretation of the Wolf Man's uncanny childhood trauma.

From the very beginning Ginger challenges so-called normal sexual conventions that dictate that the girl should be pliant and passive. During her first sexual encounter with Jason, she assumes the dominant role – her nascent werewolfism manifests itself as a rebellion against socially constructed gender roles that align femininity with passivity and masculinity with activity/ aggression. As Ginger takes the lead, Jason tells Ginger to 'take it easy'. She tells him to 'just lie back and relax'. Jason cries out: 'Who's the guy here?' Later she tells Brigitte that sex with Jason involved too much 'squirming and squealing'. Despite the fact that she was the dominant partner Ginger knows full well that he will be boasting to his classmates that he 'laid' her. Sex with Ginger, however, proves to be fatal. Shortly after he brags to his friends, they notice that blood is seeping through the front of his pants. They jeeringly ask him if he has his 'rag'. The suggestion that Jason is also menstruating suggests the ancient practice of couvade, in which men cut themselves to imitate women who are menstruating.[36]

Ginger tells Brigitte: 'No-one ever thinks that chicks do shit like this. A girl can only be a slut, a bitch, a tease, or the virgin next door.' As Ginger's metamorphosis into a werewolf intensifies, she discovers she has no room for sentiment. She is becoming animal. In Margot Norris's terms, the animal is autotelic. 'The beast has no sentiment, no room for love and memory of loved ones':

> However, in biocentric thought, animal violence is restored to its amoral Dionysian innocence: it functions as a discharge of power for its own sake, as an expenditure of superfluous, opulent energy and strength, and its therefore simply appropriative destroying its victims without malice or hatred[.][37]

For Ginger violence is both amoral and sexual. After killing the janitor she says:

> It feels so good, B. It's like touching yourself, you know, every move right on the fucking dot, and after, you see fucking fireworks, supernova, goddamn force of nature. I feel I could do just about anything. You know, we're almost not even related anymore.

Ginger's acknowledgement of the changes taking place involve a clear rejection of her human self and a recognition that she feels more like 'a force of nature'. There is no room for love – not even for Brigitte. Agamben writes: 'And perhaps even the most luminous sphere of our relations with the divine depends, in some way, on that darker one which separates us from the animal.'[38] In becoming a *femme animale*, Ginger's metamorphosis has enabled her to see very clearly what she has had to relinquish as a woman living in a phallocentric world and also enabled her to experience the exhilaration of overturning all of the roles she was destined to play. Although Agamben's anthropological machine works to separate humanity and animality in the film through Ginger's complete metamorphosis into a wolf, followed by her death as a wolf, the image that remains long after the film has ended is of Ginger as the monstrous *femme animale* tearing 'everything into fucking pieces'. The anthropological machine that makes woman monstrous through her reproductive and bodily functions does so by aligning biology with destiny. But when woman then elects to pursue her own pleasures and to align herself with the animal (even if only in representation) she exposes not just its androcentrism but also the inherent phallocentrism of the machine. Unlike Little Red Riding Hood, when Ginger strays from the path in the forest she decides to stay behind in the wilderness. To Ginger becoming wolf means embracing the darkness and erasing the endless divisions put in place by the anthropological machine.

Notes

1 I have used the term *femme animale* as it relates directly to the *femme fatale*, a figure who is central to film noir and some horror films. The English 'female animal', when signifying woman, is used predominantly in pornography. *Femme animale* will avoid unnecessary confusion.

2   Chantal Bourgault du Coudray, 'The Cycle of the Werewolf: Romantic Eulogies of Selfhood in Popular Fantasy', *Australian Feminist Studies* 18:40 (2003): 57–72 (61).
3   Carolyn Merchant, *The Death of Nature: Women, Ecology and the Scientific Revolution* (San Francisco: Harper & Row, 1983).
4   Heinrich Kramer and James Sprenger, *The Malleus Maleficarum*, trans. Montague Summers (New York: Dover Publications, 1971), 171.
5   *Ibid.*, 65.
6   *Ibid.*, 61.
7   Witches were accused of casting a glamour or a spell in order to carry out monstrous deeds. Today a beautiful woman is said to be 'glamorous' with the power to enchant.
8   Kramer and Sprenger, *Malleus Maleficarum*, 62.
9   *Ibid.*, 44.
10 *Ibid.*, 46.
11 *Ibid.*, viii–ix.
12 Giorgio Agamben, *The Open: Man and Animal* (Stanford, CA: Stanford University Press, 2004), 12.
13 Kramer and Sprenger, *Malleus Maleficarum*, 15.
14 Bram Dijkstra, *Idols of Perversity: Fantasies of Feminine Evil in Fin-de-Siècle Culture* (New York: Oxford University Press, 1986), 275.
15 Midas Dekkers, *Dearest Pet: On Bestiality* (London: Verso, 1994), 4.
16 Du Coudray, 'The Cycle of the Werewolf', 69.
17 *The Marvelous Hairy Girls* presents a compelling study of three sixteenth-century sisters, and their family, who had a rare genetic condition that made them very hairy. Wiesner-Hanks also explores sixteenth-century attitudes to the hairy girls which were remarkably accepting in comparison to those expressed in *The Ape Woman*. See Merry Wiesner-Hanks, *The Marvelous Hairy Girls: The Gonzales Sisters and Their Worlds* (New Haven, CT: Yale University Press, 2009).
18 Sigmund Freud, 'The Uncanny', in James Strachey and Angela Richards (eds), *The Pelican Freud Library*, vol. 14, trans. James Strachey (Ringwood: Penguin, 1975), 335–76 (340).
19 *Ibid.*
20 Rosemary Jackson, *Fantasy: The Literature of Subversion* (London and New York: Methuen, 1981), 69.
21 For a discussion of this phantasy, see 'Freud's Wolf Man, or the Tale of Granny's Furry Phallus', in Barbara Creed, *Phallic Panic* (Melbourne: Melbourne University Press, 2005).
22 Jacques Derrida, 'The Animal That Therefore I Am', *Critical Inquiry*, 28 (Winter 2002): 369–419 (375).
23 As quoted in Janet Browne, *Charles Darwin: A Biography*, vol 1, *Voyaging* (Princeton NJ: Princeton University Press, 1995), 373.
24 Kelly Oliver, *Animal Lessons: How They Teach Us To Be Human* (New York: Columbia University Press, 2009).
25 Margot Norris, *Beasts of the Modern Imagination* (Baltimore, MD and London: Johns Hopkins University Press, 1985), 5.
26 Bianca Nielsen, '"Something's Wrong, Like More Than You Being Female": Transgressive Sexuality and Discourses of Reproduction in *Ginger Snaps*',

thirdspace, 3:2 (2004), www.thirdspace.ca/articles/3_2nielsen.htm (11n). Accessed 19 November 2010.
27 Julia Kristeva, *Powers of Horror: An Essay on Abjection*, trans. Leon S. Roudiez (New York: Columbia University Press, 1982), 4.
28 *Ibid.*, 2.
29 Kristeva, *Powers of Horror*, 53.
30 Nielsen, 'Something's Wrong, Like More Than You Being Female', 7.
31 Angela Carter, 'The Company of Wolves', in Carter, *The Bloody Chamber and Other Stories* (Harmondsworth: Penguin, 1990), 12–118 (113).
32 Erich Fromm, *The Forgotten Language: An Introduction to the Understanding of Dreams, Fairy Tales and Myths* (New York: Grove Press, 1951), 240.
33 Quoted in Bruno Bettelheim, *The Uses of Enchantment: The Meaning and Importance of Fairy Tales* (New York: Vintage Books, 1977), 176.
34 J. Laplanche and J.B. Pontalis, *The Language of Psycho-Analysis* (London: Hogarth, 1985), 33.
35 Sigmund Freud, 'From the History of An Infantile Neurosis', in *The Pelican Freud Library*, vol. 9 (Ringwood: Penguin, 1979), 227–345 (270).
36 Some primitive societies practised couvade, in which men simulated the act of giving birth. In some rituals, they also cut their penises to simulate menstruation. See Sneja Gunew, 'Feminist Criticism: Positions and Questions', in 'Forum: Feminism and Interpretation Theory', *Southern Review*, 16.1: 149–73.
37 Norris, *Beasts of the Modern Imagination*, 10.
38 Agamben, *The Open*, 16.

12

Dans Ma Peau: shape-shifting and subjectivity

Laura Wilson

Dans Ma Peau (2002, dir. Marina de Van) is not your usual werewolf film, primarily as it features no werewolves to speak of. What it does feature is a woman named Esther who, while wandering alone in the dark, gets cut by an unknown object. This wound triggers a series of self-inflicted injuries of increasing severity as Esther mutilates and devours her own flesh in an attempt to define herself against others, while irreversibly losing herself to the beast within. Thus, *Dans Ma Peau* engages with a recognisable myth to construct a powerful way of thinking about selfhood. Esther is a representation of the shape-shifter as she contorts her body into insect-like positions and negotiates her way between the two worlds presented in the film: that of work, culture, rationality and relationships with others, and that of the desire and relationship of and with the self.

A striking aspect of *Dans Ma Peau* is the way it presents formal similarities between Esther the protagonist and her experiences, and the well-recognised werewolf narrative in cinema. From early films such as *Werewolf of London* (1935, dir. Stuart Walker) and *The Wolf-Man* (1941, dir. George Waggner), through to contemporary cult classics like *An American Werewolf in London* (1981, dir. John Landis) and *Ginger Snaps* (2000, dir. John Fawcett), the protagonist's journey is fairly predictable. For example, the destined-to-be werewolf gets injured, often by something unknown to them at the time. After this injury is incurred the victim begins to experience certain changes. The wound may heal unnaturally quickly, or the expected pain of such an injury may be absent. Then the victim begins to experience new and overwhelming urges: urges to harm, maim and devour human flesh. All of this happens to Esther in *Dans Ma Peau*. One noticeable difference between her and the werewolves of the silver screen is Esther's desire to harm, maim and devour her *own* flesh. It is not this difference, however, that calls into question the value of reading this film against the werewolf film narrative.

In spite of the number of formal similarities between Esther and the werewolf, I did not consider this connection until it was brought to my attention that Esther represented the shape-shifter through her bodily contortions and negotiations of various societal (and frequently contradictory) roles, including friend, lover and employee. Like the werewolf, what enables her to blur the boundaries of human/animal, adult/child, woman/girl, and navigate across domestic and professional spheres, is grounded in the body or, more specifically, *her* body. However, what initially led me to reject the idea of thinking about the film in tandem with werewolf film narratives was one difference against all other cues: the werewolf made popular by the types of films mentioned above – that which has the fur, the teeth, the claws, the label – is absent from *Dans Ma Peau*. Yet, I argue the werewolf is so powerfully present in this film in, perhaps, less immediately recognisable ways. It was this contradiction that led me to consider the limits of popular cinematic incarnations of the most famous and popular shape-shifter.

The werewolf is so rich in symbolic value because it potentially allows artists, theorists and philosophers to explore the outer limits and blurred boundaries of a number of dichotomies, frequently bringing into focus the less culturally dominant side of the binary, i.e. body (mind), nature (culture), animal (human) and woman (man). The female werewolf serves to complicate these categories further and provides a means by which we can think about female subjectivity through varied and fluid, rather than rigid and essentialist, modes of embodiment. However, the prevalence of werewolf and female werewolf imagery, and its importance in recognising their particular narratives, has reduced this shape-shifter to reductive notions of the body. In her book *Carnal Thoughts,* Vivian Sobchack argues that there is 'extensive contemporary literature' in the humanities that focuses 'objectively (but sometimes superficially) on "the body"'.[1] By this, Sobchack is referring to the way the body is often thought about in an abstracted fashion, that which always belongs to someone else other than me. Counter to this, Sobchack draws on phenomenology to focus on the lived body, that is, on 'what it means to be "embodied"'.[2] To be embodied, Sobchack explains, is to be an objective *subject* and a subjective *object* – 'sentient, sensual, and sensible'.[3] The reliance of a visual and/or linguistic signifier – in other words, werewolf as 'the body' – reduces the potentially liberating notion of the female werewolf to an abstract object, that which is other than myself, yourself, ourselves, and that which is defined by image and label.[4] This chapter aims to consider how *Dans Ma Peau* frees the female werewolf from the status of the body to allow it to be considered as a mode of embodiment.

Dans Ma Peau has been classed among a large number of films emerging from France that are aggressively difficult to watch. Film scholar Tim Palmer includes it in his category 'new French cinema of the body',[5] whereas critic James Quandt prefers the label 'New French Extremity',[6] and Martine Beugnet references the film in her book *Cinema and Sensation: French Film and the Art of Trangression.*[7] These studies and films alike show a turn towards a fascination with the evocation of visceral engagements between viewer and film. Exactly how an audio-visual medium is able to generate physical sensations is a large and varied topic; however, I argue that the way this is achieved in *Dans Ma Peau* is through the undermining of the dominance of the visual by the film's sound effects. Unlike films coming mainly from America that share with *Dans Ma Peau* the ability to create corporeal feelings in the viewer,[8] de Van's film is not preoccupied with the visual detail of mutilation. Although Esther's self-harm drives the narrative forward, its image is not capitalised upon. Instead, her gradual fragmentation is represented largely through sound which, arguably, has a greater capacity for generating anxiety in the viewer as there is no clear object onto which this disturbing sensation may be placed.[9] The omission of extensively bloody imagery therefore constructs a mode of spectatorship that constitutes an understanding of Esther's actions through embodiment.

Esther's actions of self-harm indicate a desire to define her own subjectivity, in effect drawing (or cutting) a literal line to separate her body, her flesh and her insides from the outside world of work, relationships and other bodies. As will be discussed further, this holds similarities to other werewolf narratives and the concept of the shape-shifter, in particular *female* werewolf narratives that use lycanthropy as a way for a woman to derive power and delight from the abjection that is so often pushed upon her. However, Esther is not given the freedom normally awarded a werewolf: the liberty to roam forests or high school corridors, the action of uncontrolled and frenzied murder free (if only temporarily) from a guilty conscience. Instead, she is often confined to cupboards, basements and bathrooms. More than this, she is confined to herself. Thus her access to 'nature, embodiment and the unconscious',[10] so praised in many female werewolf narratives, actually serves to *exclude* her from the very world in which she is attempting to define herself, leading ultimately to the death of the subject.

Like the werewolf narrative, *Dans Ma Peau* is a story of transformation. Whether it is represented by werewolves or by self-harm, the transformation is the same: the character must descend and lose themselves to the abject. Both the act of cutting into your skin and the event of transforming from human to werewolf represents the blurring and transgression of rigidly defined boundaries. The blurring of anything that is supposed to be separate – the inner and the outer body, human and animal – creates a place for the abject. Barbara Creed discusses Kristeva's notion of the abject in relation to horror films and feminist theory in her book *The Monstrous-Feminine*. She states that the abject is 'the places where "I" am not'.[11] The imagery of blood and gore (or fur and claws) shifts the subject into the realm of the unsubject where 'I' no longer exists. As long as the abject is forcibly present there is a danger of, albeit also a desire for, the subject to become lost in the abject. So on the one hand, we could argue that the werewolf and shape-shifter narrative that sees a subject being reintroduced to their carnal, pre-social and animalistic states is a liberating one, where the viewer can vicariously and safely enjoy the werewolf's or Esther's perverse desires from a distance. On the other hand, if the abject is not expelled, the werewolf, Esther and the viewer are in danger of becoming lost within it.

Dans Ma Peau: shape-shifting and subjectivity

This chapter will discuss similarities between *Dans Ma Peau* and werewolf narratives, such as the split-self, the split world within the film, representations of transformation, and how each have severe limitations for theorising female subjectivity. It will consider the limitations of a subjectivity that relies on the very dualisms it is attempting to transgress, such as animal and human, nature and culture, and irrationality and reason. Although it argues that, for Esther, self-harm represents an unsuccessful attempt to define her subjectivity and her self against others, it will also suggest that the werewolf image has little more success and has the added potential of providing a reductive and essentialist notion of female subjectivity that *Dans Ma Peau* avoids.

Dans Ma Peau begins with a sequence which, through the use of stills, shows a city that has been brought to a standstill. Cars and people are suspended in their commute along busy highways and crowded escalators. Isolated roofs of office blocks are set against a blue and white sky that is neither bright nor dull. Each of these shots leads into one another through a slow dissolve, and the pace is set by a steady repetition of chords on top of which plays a gentle and calming melody. The overall effect is of a city that is winding down, at rest from what would normally present a lively scene. In the midst of all this Esther is introduced. Her presence is indicated before her character is shown through a soft, but abrasive, sound that is matched by a medium shot of her sitting at a desk where she is writing something out of frame. Her character is presented as separate from the calm of the city shots that precede her. During her brief interaction with her boyfriend, Vincent, she barely takes her eyes off her work. The pace of her work is mentioned and it is implied she will be working all night while the rest of the city sleeps. Setting her at odds with her context, the discord between Esther and the outside world anticipates her future actions as her self-harm is read as an attempt, in part, to communicate and to connect to a world outside of herself. Yet, like the fate of the werewolf, it will end with her exclusion.

In a style which prefigures the later treatment of Esther's body, the camera explores the exterior of buildings and interior office objects to a point where they can no longer be recognised as anything intelligible. This use of close-ups serves to highlight the distortion that occurs when the desire to become closer to something, to delight in its detail, overrides and fragments the appreciation of the whole. It therefore predicts the result of Esther's obsession with her own body and her own flesh, as her self-harm can no longer provide a bridge between her two selves and the two worlds presented within the film. In the prologue, during a close-up of Esther's calf, the camera pans up to reveal its superficial imperfections. The lighting does nothing to flatter the skin as goose bumps and stretch marks are apparent. The skin appears abrasive, tough enough to bear the testimony of Esther's life so far. In *Dans Ma Peau*, the *feel* of skin and of flesh is strained against the overriding sense to look, as Esther must hide her self-harm away from others. This results in a sensory organ that has been stretched to its limits in regards to its ability to feel, yet is rendered something impossible to bear witness to. If Esther cannot be seen, if she must confine herself to hidden spaces just as the werewolf must be chained in cages or exiled to the forest; her self-harm will not and cannot allow her to define herself against others, leading to the death of the subject.

The prologue and the opening credits create a metonym for the journey Esther will embark on throughout the course of the film. The shots of the city are presented in split-screens and the image to the right is always a negative of the left. In line with the idea that the film, like the werewolf and shape-shifter narrative, acts as a metaphor for a world and a *self* that is split, Carrie Tarr suggests that these split images represent gender as 'the contrast between the hard (masculine) lines of the positive images on the left of the screen and the less differentiated, less well-focused negative view images on the right also suggests that sexual difference may be an issue'.[12] As the film's setting moves from the exterior to the interior of offices where folds of paper, collections of pens, and other stationery objects are shown in medium and close-up shots, they may speculate where in this public sphere Esther, as a woman, belongs. Her career becomes a motivation for her self-harm later on in the film and it is a part of the outside world that she is never able to fully connect to, since she is torn 'between the desire to perform the roles that others expect of her and the delicious but destructive pleasures of self-mutilation'.[13] Slavoj Žižek says of monsters generally that they bridge the gap of these numerous binaries – man/woman, culture/nature and so on – which in effect is exactly what Esther does as she descends into a monster of her own making.[14] And for her efforts, she is excluded from the very world to which she is trying to belong.

A dominant werewolf and shape-shifter narrative is that of the split-self. Often, the wolf represents nature and the animal within, whereas the clean and proper body of the human represents culture, rationality and reason. This, of course, has a clear gender split as women are very often associated with nature, whereas 'masculinity has been positively associated with the attainment of self through the *transcendence* of nature'.[15] This makes the female werewolf an incredibly interesting character to consider. Whereas with the male werewolf it may be argued that the man's animalistic alter-ego represents a part of his self ordinarily repressed, thus creating a literal metaphor for the beast within all mankind that must be kept in check in order for society to function, a female's journey into the mind of the wolf should, for want of a better phrase, come naturally to her. She is fulfilling her half of the binary making the female werewolf more inevitable, more uncontrollable, and more dangerous. This essentialist assumption is frequently signposted through the aesthetics of the female werewolf change scenes.

In Chapter 10, Peter Hutchings notes that very often the transformation sequence for the female werewolf is remarkable for its elegance. For example, in *An American Werewolf in Paris* (1997, dir. Anthony Waller), Julie Delpy's character Serafine Pigot looks up into the moonlit sky as her face seamlessly changes from human to werewolf. Further to this, the female werewolf transformation may be linked to sexual acts. In *Trick 'r Treat* (2007, dir.

Michael Dougherty), Anna Paquin, as Laurie, writhes in seemingly erotic pleasure on top of the person who will become her first victim; at the same time, her body begins its metamorphosis. Compare this to the excruciating and lengthy transformation scenes in *An American Werewolf in London* (1981, dir. John Landis) and *The Howling* (1981, dir. Joe Dante) where the pain for the male-turning-into-werewolf is undeniable and, although the special effects for these films are acclaimed and aesthetically impressive, they remain monstrous in their excesses. In the case of *Dans Ma Peau*, the entire film is arguably a transformation scene for Esther as she slowly and irreversibly loses herself to her desire for self-harm, yet there is one particular scene where she significantly represents the shape-shifter. After engaging in her most extreme act of self-harm where she removes a large section of skin from her leg, and covered in drying blood, she manipulates her body into strange and awkward positions, bringing her leg over her shoulder to rub her foot on her face. Potentially monstrous, this scene and Esther's elegant contorted physique retain a strange beauty that is absent from the male transformation scenes mentioned above. For a woman already on the outskirts of society, transforming into a monster is merely returning to a natural state. However, unlike the case of Laurie (*Trick 'r Treat*), this scene creates an alternative for the female transformation, one that undermines the erotic spectacle to find beauty in the abject.

One of the most notable examples of a female finding temporary sexual fulfilment and social freedom from her werewolf affliction is the character of Ginger from *Ginger Snaps*, who ecstatically informs her disgusted sister Brigitte that she is now a 'goddamn force of nature'. Another example is Veruca, the female werewolf revealed in the Season 4 episode of *Buffy the Vampire Slayer* (1997–2003), 'Wild at Heart' (1999). Veruca attempts to convince the male werewolf Oz that they are privileged in their affliction and that he, like her, should embrace the wolf within. For these women, the self that is werewolf is powerful and free. Yet as it is for these werewolves, as Esther explores and defines herself through cutting, biting and eating flesh, the power and freedom this affords her is limited.

Not only is the concept of the self frequently split in werewolf and shape-shifter narratives, so are the worlds within the texts. Although the werewolf is often associated with signs of nature such as the full moon, endless forests and frightening moors, more often than not it causes the most disruption when placed in civilisation. Such iconographies enable filmmakers to demonstrate the devastating impact of a werewolf as the antithesis of culture, rationality and reason. This is no different in *Dans Ma Peau*, where Esther first gets injured at a work-related party, first harms herself in the basement at work, first shows her desires to cannibalise herself at a work dinner, and is threatened by exposure at a work outing to a swimming baths. The significance of self-harm for Esther is similar to the significance of the werewolf for the female. The werewolf for the male threatens him with exclusion from a society in which he belongs first and foremost. The werewolf for the female is often also the *avenue* into this society, just as Esther turns to self-mutilation to cope with the demands her work and relationships place on her identity. In *Ginger Snaps*, Ginger is approaching puberty, the entry into 'womanhood', when she is attacked and begins her transformation. This is followed by increasing popularity and the desire for sexual relationships previously scorned. In 'Heart' (2007), an episode from the second series of the television series *Supernatural* (2005–), a female werewolf called Madison describes how her life changed for the better after a strange mugging during which the criminal bit her. She was then more confident, able to free herself from an abusive relationship, and able to re-evaluate her life. Yet for Ginger, Madison and Esther, this path has its toll.

Like the world of werewolves and shape-shifters, the world of *Dans Ma Peau* is split between what could crudely be referred to as a man's world and the world of the woman, but in the context of *Dans Ma Peau* it is more appropriate to think of this as a split between the outside world and Esther. This is because, although the film to an extent provides a way of thinking about female subjectivity, it does not provide any evidence that this is anything more than an account of an *individual*. Although the film and its director Marina de Van have been criticised for this lack of depth and apparent self-absorption,[16] in actuality by choosing to omit any details of the character's past and psychological development the film avoids presenting an essentialist and reductive representation of female subjectivity. Although the werewolf creates an avenue into the societies presented in each respective text, it ultimately redraws and redefines the boundaries that separate human from animal, man from woman, and culture from nature. The female werewolf provides an image of subjectivity that is dependant on, or re-inscribes, the dualism that connects women with nature and irrationality and therefore excludes them from culture and reason. Part of the outside world to which self-harm could have provided Esther an avenue is her workplace. As with the initial confidence with which female werewolves are rewarded when they are first afflicted (Ginger, Veruca, Madison), her acts of self-harm initially appear successful, but as the film continues it becomes evident that Esther is becoming more and more isolated to herself and her own abjection.

Esther commits her first act of self-harm in the basement at her work. Before this she is shown to be sitting at her computer, distracted and unable to think of anything to type. The film then cuts to her entering a dimly lit space, little bigger than a corridor, with concrete stairs and walls lined with files. The image is claustrophobic but the hollow and grating sound of her footsteps serves to create a space around Esther far bigger and more hostile than the *mise-en-scène* suggests. This has already been done earlier in the film where particular diegetic sounds are foregrounded to create a distance between Esther and the physical world around her, and to present this physical world as harsh and impenetrable. As she removes her trousers, her crouched foetal position is centrally placed in the one shaft of light coming into the screen. The wound on her leg is clearly visible and appears soft, malleable and very penetrable, unlike her surroundings. As Esther removes her shoe the tearing sound of its zip placed on top of the image of her gaping and vulnerable flesh anticipates what is to come.

This is the most physical detail of mutilated flesh that is shown in this scene. For most of the duration of Esther's self-harm the camera focuses on her face while the noise of ripping and tearing this time, we assume, of flesh is played on the soundtrack. This does not relieve the viewer from Esther's actions, however, as the sound of her tearing her skin and her heavy, grating breath affect the viewer physically as they *recall* the image of flesh. After this, the image cuts to her scrambling through a jumble of objects off-screen before choosing a blunt metal object with which she proceeds to push against her skin. Apart from the blood that has appeared on her wound between the two shots, the viewer sees nothing. The separation of image and sound creates a space which the viewer fills with the sense of touch. Esther's searching eyes, which look away from the image and appear detached from the sound, signal a loss of her own ability to feel. The viewer covers this loss with a physical response that both covers and reaffirms Esther's loss.

Esther's disintegration of self is marked by her fading ability to feel. That she cannot feel anything when she cuts herself is shown by her glazed and expressionless eyes that gaze off-screen, as if she is searching for another sense of self that transcends the millions of nerve endings in the skin. This is a physiological example of the fading ability to consider social morality that comes with most werewolf transformations. Just as Ginger's act of killing an innocent janitor negatively highlights (rather than celebrates) her loss of awareness of social norms, the physical response that *Dans Ma Peau* generates through the representation of self-harm, that renders the film almost unwatchable, is indicative of Esther's failing subjectivity. The film continues to present Esther with more examples of an extreme lack of physical awareness of her own body providing both herself and the viewer with further evidence that she is failing in her attempt to define herself. One scene shows her to have slept on her arm and she wakes up to find she has lost all feeling of it. She pulls it out from beneath her as if it is disembodied. Another arm reaches from behind her, a third arm within the shot while the audience can only see Esther. It is not until her boyfriend's head emerges from behind her that it is clear which arm belongs to which character. Extremities in *Dans Ma Peau* are detachable and interchangeable; like prosthetics, the human body becomes an object that can be broken down and rebuilt. This is played out to the extreme in the scene immediately prior to her second major act of self-harm.

The scene is set in a restaurant where Esther is having dinner with her business associates. The setting of the restaurant is introduced by low-level panning of the tables as if attributing the point of view to the hands that rest there. Later, as Esther eats her dinner, her hand begins to act as if it has a mind of its own, much like the hands in *Mad Love* (1935, dir. Karl Freund), *The Beast with Five Fingers* (1946, dir. Robert Florey) and *Idle Hands* (1999, dir. Rodman Flender). She has to use her other hand to stop herself from clawing at the food on her plate. As she does so the camera pans down her forearm to reveal it to be *actually* removed from her upper arm. She taps at this removed hand as if it has no feeling, and when it is once more connected she massages her elbow as if checking that she is again all in one piece and proceeds to stab at it with her steak knife, drawing blood. This forces Esther to confront her worst fear in a public setting and threatens her with the possibility that her lack of subjectivity will become apparent to others. In her article 'Carved in Skin: Bearing Witness to Self-Harm', Jane Kilby suggests that the act of self-harm serves as a substitute for a language that has failed.[17] For Esther, it is a substitution that remains unintelligible to her colleagues as they show no sign of noticing her actions. Thus the language is discounted, and her viability as a subject is called into question.[18]

Her actions that follow both in the restaurant and at the hotel indicate a primal desire that further connects Esther with the abject. The place of the abject to which Esther returns during her self-harm is a state of 'infantile pre-socialization' which, Tarr claims, 'is (momentarily) a source of nourishment, sensual enjoyment and solitary, erotic intoxication'.[19] The return to this state begins with the taste of her own blood. Once she does this, there are shots of her looking off camera that are cut with images of all the rich food around her. Moist surfaces of fruit are broken into by juice-covered fingers that dig into its soft, sticky flesh. Fat slices of steak are dipped and smothered in thick glutinous sauces. The images represent a decadence that Esther refuses. Esther's downfall is that her desires are turned inward; she has an overwhelming desire for herself. In the scene that follows she displays instead a desire for herself: her own blood, her own skin.

In the scene at the hotel, Esther is shown to continue to be drawn into the abject as she tears off her skin with her teeth and tastes her blood. She abjects herself and then devours her own abjection, drawing the other inside herself until the boundaries that separate them have all but disappeared. As she cuts her thigh and brings it towards her face, her leg, shrouded in black, takes the place of a lover coming down towards their partner in bed. There is an over the shoulder shot as she bites and sucks her arm, tearing away pieces of skin with her teeth. From this angle, her arm is again presented as detached. If a unified subject is represented on-screen as a 'clean and proper body' then Esther has regressed almost entirely into the realm of the unsubject, the 'inhuman, abject body'.[20] In what can be read as a defence against the desire for the abject, Esther keeps the skin she has removed as an object to cover her lack of unification. Through creating an 'other' to keep separate from herself, she attempts to retain the unification she has risked through her abjection. Yet this defence comes at a price: a piece of herself.

Like Veruca in *Buffy* and Ginger in *Ginger Snaps*, Esther comes to 'revel' in her actions. She becomes fascinated with herself: her image, her flesh, her taste. In the scene mentioned in the introduction to this chapter where she can most visually be likened to a shape-shifter, and where she contorts her body into shapes that, for Tarr, make her appear 'sub-human, even insect-like',[21] she displays an increased desire to see herself. Even as she looks out at the viewer, the use of shot-reverse-shot reveals the viewer to have been in the place of a mirror, reflecting Esther back upon herself. The scene that can be described as primal – the scene that one may be tempted to experience as a liberating display of regression, a metamorphosis into a creature that transcends the boundaries between technology and flesh, work and play – is instead a representation of a monstrous being, a fragmented woman that threatens the society within the film as she desires a unified self.

Esther, like the werewolf, *is* a monster for the very fact that she threatens society. She is the embodiment of the fear that the abject, the monster, the other, can never fully be expelled. She is not entirely 'other'; we as viewers cannot completely separate ourselves from her, as Esther fails to separate and define herself from others, and for this reason she *must* be expelled. Like the werewolf, Esther bridges the gap between more than just human and animalistic natures; she threatens the blurring of reason and irrationality, of culture and nature, of the conscious and the unconscious. As mentioned above, the split screens that introduce the film suggest that the viewer is entering a world where everything is 'slightly out of kilter'.[22] Although the use of split images may present a desire to separate one thing from another, it anticipates the imagery of split skin that subverts the boundary between inner and outer and causes them to bleed into one another. The representation of self-harm in *Dans Ma Peau* articulates its paradoxical nature. It can be read as a way for the subject to separate the self from the abject even though it increases the connection. Similarly, if it is used as a form of language it can only ever render the subject incomprehensible. Jane Kilby describes self-harm as a 'plea ... for social recognition'.[23] This can be seen in *Dans Ma Peau* as Esther tells her best friend Sandrine of her first act of self-harm, only to be met with confusion and ineffectual attempts of censoring; during one scene where Esther stays at Sandrine's house, the latter demands to be allowed into the bathroom with Esther and promptly removes all sharp objects. The 'voice' of self-harm is 'so sheer that it is virtually impossible for anyone to bear witness to'.[24] Kilby references Judith Butler's *Excitable Speech*, and its warning against the dangers of speaking in a language that is unintelligible to others, not the least of which is the erasure of the subject. Butler argues:[25]

> If the subject speaks impossibly, speaks in ways that cannot be regarded as speech or as the speech of a subject, then that speech is discounted and the viability of the subject called into question.[26]

The danger that lies in Esther's path is the death of her own subjectivity through its refusal by others as she loses herself to the abject. Once she begins to self-harm this becomes the only way with which she can both connect (through her own language) and draw a line between herself and others in order to define herself as a subject. As others pull away from her, questioning her viability as a subject, the only other she has is the abjection of herself. Yet it also serves as a constant reminder and eventual cause of her de-subjectivity.

Like many cinematic werewolves, Esther is a sympathetic character.[27] She is both victim and perpetrator of violence in this film, which prompts Tarr to comment on her link to both Creed's 'monstrous-feminine' and Carol Clover's 'post-feminine victim hero'.[28] As a victim of her own violence, Esther becomes an abject figure that must be expelled for order and structure to be restored in both the professional and personal spheres set up in the film. Esther as shape-shifter *must* be slain. Yet the viewer identifies with these spheres *through* the character of Esther, thus her expulsion would signal a loss of that which is restored. Whether she lives or dies (and by the end this is not made clear), a boundary has been crossed that can never be reinstated for Esther or the viewer. The abject remains and closure is denied. But Esther is still not afforded any of the freedom that very occasionally the female werewolf is allowed.[29] The part of Esther that can be likened to the werewolf, the part that both promises and denies entry into subjectivity, by the end of the film has devoured her completely.

The film ends with a repetition of a shot which begins as a close-up of Esther's face that slowly pulls out to reveal her lying stretched out on the hotel bed. Yet it is not the image of a 'body as a whole' as Tarr suggests.[30] If it were, the final image would provide closure for the film as a body that has been continuously fragmented is re-integrated and 'whole'. Instead the image is of Esther's face, hand and ankle dispersed over a black space. Surrounding her is the green of the wallpaper and the yellow of the bedspread: colours of sickness. The wallpaper is patterned with repeated vertical lines that create bars to hold Esther in her state of regression for which self-harm was her only cure and eventual downfall. These lines are continued by folds in the bedspread which reach out of the scene towards the viewer, yet Esther is pushed right back into the wall. She is a body that is not working as it should, a body cut up and off from itself. Her death-like stare is re-enforced by the camera that repeatedly pulls out from a close-up of her eye in a circular motion, referencing *Psycho*'s (1960, dir. Alfred Hitchcock) famous shower scene. She is caught in this repetition, an endless cycle of reaching for herself only to be pulled further away. She is dead to feeling, dead to the viewer, dead to herself.

According to Chantal Bourgault du Coudray, 'fiction about female werewolves, especially by authors sympathetic to feminism, has exemplified this process [non-exclusive construction of self] by celebrating lycanthropy as an ability that enriches rather than undermines the conscious experience of reasoning subjectivity'.[31] To the extent to which we can compare Esther to the female werewolf, we can see how here they dramatically part ways. While, according to du Coudray, certain female werewolves may be provided with choices (albeit limited) as a result of their 'curse', Esther has but one. She *must* continue down her path of mutilation for fear of disappearing entirely;

yet, since her accident, this has been the only possible outcome. Of course many female werewolves do not fare much better than Esther. Ginger and Veruca must be killed for their sin of embracing their affliction with relish. Madison accepts her fate so completely she sits and waits for her lover to kill her. The cost of subjectivity for the female in werewolf and shape-shifting narratives is often exile, or death.

Although the similarity between *Dans Ma Peau* and werewolf narratives comes superficially from the narrative of someone being hurt, and consequently undergoing extreme changes in behaviour and personality that leads to bloodshed, cannibalism and death, more interestingly the comparison goes deeper, as *Dans Ma Peau* and the figure of the werewolf provide powerful ways of thinking about the self and subjectivity, particularly female subjectivity. However, unlike many fictions about female werewolves that, for du Coudray, provide an 'access to nature, embodiment and the unconscious' that figures lycanthropy 'as a powerful resource for self-development',[32] Esther's self-mutilation and cannibalism become instead an exclusive construction of the self – a construction that is dependent on the exclusion of others – that descends into unintelligibility and the death of the subject. By the end of the film, Esther's attempt to attain subjectivity comes at a cost as the final shot suggests distance, exclusion and death.

Esther speaks to the concept of the female werewolf not because she is labelled as such, or because she turns into a wolf-like monster and/or exists in a predominantly supernatural narrative, but because she is always in the process of becoming something other than herself, internalising this other while at the same time subverting, critiquing and questioning previous notions of her 'self' as lover, as friend, as employee, as woman, as child, as whole, as fragmented, as human, as animal. Embodiment (hers, and ours, as viewers) is central to these transformations. Her attempts at defining herself are inscribed onto the skin of the viewer and blur the boundary between audience and film. Her transformations are far more affective than those of Laurie and Serafine, and yet less of a visual spectacle than those of David and Eddie (*The Howling*). Esther's transformations create a visceral engagement between viewer and film that is not reduced to bodily images, therefore Esther's subjectivity is not reduced to its corporal limitations and is instead understood through embodiment. It is from this engagement with the lived, rather than abstracted, body, that the female werewolf emerges.

Notes

1 Vivian Sobchack, *Carnal Thoughts: Embodiment and Moving Image Culture* (London: University of California Press, 2004), 2.
2 *Ibid.*, 1.
3 *Ibid.*, 2. Sobchack notes that 'vision, visuality, and visibility are as central to the subjective dimensions of embodied existence as they are to its objective

dimensions'; however, it is a vision that takes into account all senses through which we make sense of our being in the world.

4   The concept of the werewolf has been taken up enthusiastically on internet discussion forums, where website members profess to identify themselves with this myth. These communities represent a resistance against rigid definitions and signifiers of the werewolf through their extensive discussions regarding the kinds of terms they are willing to use to mould their identities and their, perhaps inevitable, refusal to provide visual evidence of their transformations. See, for example, www.experienceproject.com/groups/Am-A-Real-Werewolf/293509; www.lycanforums.com/. Accessed 7 January 2012.

5   Tim Palmer, 'Style and Sensation in the Contemporary French Cinema of the Body', *Journal of Film and Video*, 58:3 (2006): 22–32 (25).

6   James Quandt, 'Flesh & Blood: Sex and Violence in Recent French Cinema', *Artforum*, 42:6 (2004): 126–32 (127).

7   Martine Beugnet, *Cinema and Sensation: French Film and the Art of Transgression* (Edinburgh: Edinburgh University Press, 2007), 126, 158, 159.

8   For example, the *Saw* franchise (2004–10, dirs James Wan, Darren Lynn Bousman, David Hackl, Kevin Greutert) and *Hostel I*, *Hostel II* (2005, 2007, dir. Eli Roth) are the most famous examples; however, there are many more, including *Hostel III* (2011, dir. Scott Spiegel) and the *Wrong Turn* franchise (2003–12, dirs Rob Schmidt, Joe Lynch, Declan O'Brien).

9   Some theorists have suggested that sound has the greater potential to construct physicality. As Anthony Storr states, it is not possible to dispel sound as easily as an image; the latter can quickly be shut out with closed eyes. (Storr, *Music and the Mind* (London: HarperCollins, 1992), 100–1). Similarly, Reni Celeste identifies the interior and invasive nature of sound as it 'seems to originate from within. Vision presents the world at a distance, as outside your body, whereas sound penetrates into your body'. (Celeste, 'The Sound of Silence: Film Music and Lament', *Quarterly Review of Film and Video*, 22 (2005): 113–23 (115)) Kim Cascone's analysis of the soundscapes created by David Lynch and Andrey Tarkovsky inspires the same notion of interiority with a description of them as a 'viral contagion' with an ability to 'infect' (Cascone, *Viral Space: The Cinema of Atmosphere* (2003), www.acs.ucalgary.ca/~tstronds/nostalghia.com/TheTopics/Tributes/another_kind_of_insert_2.jpg. Accessed 7 January 2012.

10 Chantal Bourgault du Coudray, *The Curse of the Werewolf: Fantasy, Horror and the Beast Within* (London: I.B. Tauris, 2006), 8.

11 Barbara Creed, *The Monstrous-Feminine: Film, Feminism, Psychoanalysis* (Oxford: Routledge, 1993), 9.

12 Carrie Tarr, 'Director's Cuts: The Aesthetics of Self-Harming in Marina de Van's *Dans Ma Peau*', *Nottingham French Studies*, 45:3 (2006): 78–91 (88).

13 *Ibid.*, 90.

14 See du Coudray's summary of Žižek's argument in *Curse of the Werewolf*, 3.

15 *Ibid.*, 6. One possible exception to this would be the British 'kitchen sink dramas' from the 1950s and 1960s, notably *Saturday Night and Sunday Morning* (1960, dir. Karel Reisz) where women were often portrayed as a domesticating influence on the wilder and somewhat angry young male protagonists.

16 Stuart Jeffries, writing for *The Guardian*, completed a particularly offensive review of both the film and its director by suggesting to Marina de Van 'you're

a self-absorbed woman who's made a sickening film'. (Jeffries, 'Review: In the Cut', *The Guardian* (15 September 2004).)
17 Jane Kilby, 'Carved in Skin: Bearing Witness to Self-Harm', in Stacey Ahmed and Jackie Stacey (eds), *Thinking Through the Skin* (London: Routledge, 2001), 124–42 (125).
18 Judith Butler, *Excitable Speech: A Politics of the Performance* (New York: Routledge, 1997), 136.
19 Tarr, 'Director's Cuts', 84.
20 *Ibid.*, 81.
21 *Ibid.*, 82.
22 *Ibid.*, 87.
23 Kilby, 'Carved in Skin', 124.
24 *Ibid.*, 124.
25 *Ibid.*, 126.
26 Butler, *Excitable Speech*, 136.
27 Whether a werewolf is sympathetic or not is highly subjective; however, there are often a number of signifiers that enable us to recognise a character that is worthy of sympathy. This, more often than not, is centred on the werewolf's consciousness of their actions and their feelings towards them which is, in turn, represented by their willingness to endure pain and sacrifice their lives. Brigitte (*Ginger Snaps 2: Unleashed*, 2004, dir. Brett Sullivan) is disgusted by the thought of becoming a werewolf as she has already seen the kinds of misery and torture she will desire to inflict on others, and so she takes drastic measures to change her fate, including injecting monkshood (a poison derived from a plant that reverses the werewolf curse) and cutting off the tips of her wolf-like ears. David (*An American Werewolf in London*) seriously considers suicide and Madison (*Supernatural*) allows herself to be killed. In contrast, Veruca (*Buffy*) and Fenrir Greyback (*Harry Potter and the Half-Blood Prince*, 2009, dir. David Yates; *Harry Potter and the Deathly Hallows: Part 1* and *2*, 2010, 2011, dir. David Yates), both enjoy the freedom and power their affliction affords them and express no desire to change, thereby constructing an unsympathetic creature.
28 Tarr, 'Director's Cuts', 80.
29 This freedom, however, is usually coupled with a moral vacuity. Veruca and Ginger profess to feeling powerful and liberated, yet they are signified as unsympathetic (see n. 27).
30 Tarr, 'Director's Cuts', 81.
31 Du Coudray, *The Curse of the Werewolf*, 8.
32 *Ibid.*, 8.

Select bibliography

Publications

Agamben, Giorgio, *The Open: Man and Animal* (Stanford, CA: Stanford University Press, 2004)
Anwell, Maggie, 'Lolita Meets the Werewolf: *The Company of Wolves*', in Lorraine Gamman and Margaret Marshment (eds), *The Female Gaze: Women as Viewers of Popular Culture* (London: Women's Press, 1988)
Apo, Satu, '"Ex cunno come the folk and force": Concepts of Women's Dynamistic Power in Finnish-Karelian Tradition', in Satu Apo, Aili Nenola and Laura Stark-Arola (eds), *Gender and Folklore: Perspectives on Finnish and Karelian Culture* (Helsinki: Finnish Literature Society, 1998), 63–91
Apps, Lara A., and Andrew Gow, *Male Witches in Early Modern Europe* (Manchester and New York: Manchester University Press, 2003)
Archibald, Elizabeth, *Incest and the Medieval Imagination* (Oxford: Clarendon, 2001)
Bacchilega, Cristina, *Postmodern Fairy Tales: Gender and Narrative Strategies* (Philadelphia: University of Pennsylvania Press, 1997)
Baker, Martin, Ernest Mathijs and Xavier Mendik, 'Menstrual Monsters: The Reception of the *Ginger Snaps* Cult Horror Franchise', *Film International*, 21 (2006): 68–77
Baring-Gould, Sabine, *The Book of the Were-Wolves* (Forgotten Books, 2008 [1865])
Barnes, Jennifer Lynn, *Raised by Wolves* (London: Quercus, 2010)
Bayers, Peter L., 'William Apess's Manhood and Native Resistance in Jacksonian America', *MELUS* 31:1 (Spring 2006): 123–46
Beaugrand, Honoré, 'The Werewolves', *Century Illustrated Magazine*, 56.6 (1898): 814–23
Bettelheim, Bruno, *The Uses of Enchantment: The Meaning and Importance of Fairy Tales* (New York: Vintage Books, 1977)
Beugnet, Martine, *Cinema and Sensation: French Film and the Art of Transgression* (Edinburgh: Edinburgh University Press, 2007)
Black, Nancy B., *Medieval Narratives of Accused Queens* (Gainesville, FL: University Press of Florida, 2003)
Boguet, Henri, *Discours execrable des sorciers: ensemble leur proces, faits depuis 2 ans en ça, en divers endroicts de France* (Paris: D. Binet, 1603)
Bonvillain, Nancy, *Native Nations: Cultures and Histories of Native North America* (Upper Saddle River, NJ: Prentice-Hall, Inc., 2001)
Bowen, Carl, Rick Jones, James Kiley, Matthew McFarland and Adam Tinworth, *Werewolf: The Forsaken* (Stone Mountain, CA: White Wolf Publishing, Inc., 2005)
Briefel, Aviva, 'Monster Pains: Masochism, Menstruation, and Identification in the Horror Film', *Film Quarterly* 28:3 (2005): 16–27

Briggs, Robin, 'Dangerous Spirits: Shapeshifting, Apparitions, and Fantasy in Lorraine Witchcraft Trials', in Katherine A. Edwards (ed.), *Werewolves, Witches and Wanderings Spirits: Traditional Belief and Folklore in Early Modern Europe* (Kirksville, MO: Truman State University Press, 2002), 1–24

Burkert, Walter, *Homo Necans: The Anthropology of Ancient Greek Sacrificial Ritual and Myth*, trans. Peter Bing (Berkeley, CA: University of California Press, 1983)

Butler, Judith, *Excitable Speech: A Politics of the Performance* (New York: Routledge, 1997)

Bynum, Caroline Walker, *Metamorphosis and Identity* (New York: Zone Books, 2001)

Canepa, Nancy L., *From Court to Forest: Giambattista Basile's* Lo cunto de li cunti *and the Birth of the Literary Fairy Tale* (Detroit: Wayne State University Press, 1999)

Carey, John, 'Werewolves in Medieval Ireland', *Cambrian Medieval Celtic Studies* 44 (2002): 37–72

Carter, Angela, *The Bloody Chamber and Other Stories* (London: Gollanz, 1979)

——, *The Curious Room: Plays, Film Scripts and an Opera* (London: Chatto and Windus, 1996)

Castor, Helen, *She-Wolves: The Women Who Ruled England Before Elizabeth* (London: Faber and Faber, 2011)

Cavallo, Sandra, and Silvia Evangelisti (eds), *A Cultural History of Childhood and Family in the Early Modern Age* (Oxford and New York: Berg, 2010)

Charnas, Suzy McKee, 'Boobs', in Pam Keesey (ed.), *Women Who Run With the Werewolves: Tales of Blood, Lust and Metamorphosis* (Pittsburgh: Cleis Press, 1996), 25–42

Cininas, Jazmina, 'Beware the Full Moon: Female Werewolves and That Time of the Month', in Maria Barrett (ed.), *Grotesque Femininities* (Oxford: Inter-Disciplinary Press, 2010), 3–36

Clark, Elizabeth M., '"Hairy Thuggish Women": Female Werewolves, Gender, and the Hoped-For Monster', MA dissertation (Georgetown University, 2008)

Clover, Carol J., *Men, Women and Chainsaws: Gender in the Modern Horror Film* (London: British Film Institute, 1992)

Creed, Barbara, *The Monstrous-Feminine: Film, Feminism, Psychoanalysis* (London: Routledge, 1993)

——, *Phallic Panic* (Melbourne: Melbourne University Press, 2005)

Cremer, Andrea, *Nightshade* (London: Atom Books, 2010)

——, *Wolfsbane* (London: Atom Books, 2011)

——, *Bloodrose* (London: Atom Books, 2012)

Crofts, Charlotte, 'Curiously Downbeat Hybrid or Radical Retelling?: Neil Jordan's and Angela Carter's *The Company of Wolves*', in Deborah Cartmell, I.Q. Hunter, Heidi Kaye and Imelda Whelehan (eds), *Sisterhoods: Across the Literature/Media Divide* (London: Pluto Press, 1998), 48–63

Cross, Helen, 'Fur', in Hannah Kate (ed.), *Wolf-Girls: Dark Tales of Teeth, Claws and Lycogyny* (Manchester: Hic Dragones, 2013), 219–26

Curran, Bob, *Werewolves: A Field Guide to Shapeshifters, Lycanthropes, and Man-Beasts* (Franklin Lakes, NJ: New Page Books, 2009)

da Silva, Francisco Vaz, 'Extraordinary Children, Werewolves, and Witches in Portuguese Folk Tradition', in Éva Pócs and Gábor Klaniczay (eds), *Witchcraft Mythologies and Persecutions* (Budapest: Central European University Press, 2008), 255–68

Dayan, Daniel, 'Copyrighted Subcultures: Review of *Shared Fantasy: Role Playing Games as Social Worlds* by Gary Alan Fine', *American Journal of Sociology* 91:5 (March 1986): 1219–28

de Blécourt, Willem, 'A Journey to Hell: Reconsidering the Livonian "Werewolf"', *Magic, Ritual, and Witchcraft* 2:1 (Summer 2007): 49–67

——, 'The Werewolf, the Witch, the Warlock: Aspects of Gender in the Early Modern Period', in Alison Rowlands (ed.), *Witchcraft and Masculinities in Early Modern Europe* (Basingstoke: Palgrave Macmillan, 2009), 191–213

——, *Tales of Magic, Tales in Print: On the Genealogy of Fairy Tales and the Brothers Grimm* (Manchester: Manchester University Press, 2012)

Dekkers, Midas, *Dearest Pet: On Bestiality* (London: Verso, 1994)

Derrida, Jacques, 'The Animal That Therefore I Am', *Critical Inquiry*, 28 (Winter 2002): 369–419

Despain, Bree, *The Dark Divine* (London: Egmont, 2010)

Dijkstra, Bram, *Idols of Perversity: Fantasies of Feminine Evil in Fin-de-Siècle Culture* (New York: Oxford University Press, 1986)

Dinzelbacher, Peter, 'Lycanthropy', in Richard M. Golden (ed.), *Encyclopedia of Witchcraft: the Western Tradition*, vol. III (Santa Barbara, CA: ABC-Clio, 2006), 681

Douglas, Adam, *The Beast Within: A History of the Werewolf* (New York: Avon Books, 1992)

du Coudray, Chantal Bourgault, 'The Cycle of the Werewolf: Romantic Eulogies of Selfhood in Popular Fantasy', *Australian Feminist Studies* 18:40 (2003): 57–72

——, *The Curse of the Werewolf: Fantasy, Horror and the Beast Within* (London and New York: I.B. Taurus, 2006)

Dundes, Alan (ed.), *Little Red Riding Hood: A Casebook* (Madison, WI: University of Wisconsin Press, 1989)

Durbach, Nadja, 'The Missing Link and the Hairy Belle: Krao and the Victorian Discourses of Evolution, Imperialism, and Primitive Sexuality', in Marlene Tromp (ed.), *Victorian Freaks: The Social Contexts of Freakery in Britain* (Columbus, OH: Ohio State University Press, 2008), 134–54

Edwards, Lynne Y., Elizabeth L. Rambo and James B. South (eds), *Buffy Goes Dark* (Jefferson, NC: McFarland, 2008)

Emson, Thomas, *Maneater* (London: Snowbooks, 2008)

Evans, Walter, 'Monster Movies: a Sexual Theory', *Journal of Popular Film* 2 (1973): 353–65

Filimon, Eliza, 'Cinematic landscapes: Angela Carter's Movie Adaptations', *Romanian Journal of English Studies* 6 (2009): 47–59

Fine, Gary Alan, *Shared Fantasy: Role Playing Games as Social Worlds* (Chicago: University of Chicago Press, 1983)

Fissell, Mary E., 'Hairy Women and Naked Truths: Gender and Politics of Knowledge in *Aristotle's Masterpiece*', *William and Mary Quarterly*, 3rd Series, LX:1 (2003), 43–74

Ford, Patrick K. (ed. and trans.), *The Mabinogi and Other Medieval Welsh Tales* (Berkeley, CA: University of California Press, 1977)

Foster, Shirley, *Victorian Women's Fiction: Marriage, Freedom and the Individual* (London: Croom Helm, 1985)

Freake, Douglas and Carole Henderson Carpenter, 'Folklore and Literature: Canadian Contexts', *Ethnologies*, 21 (1999): 97–114

Freud, Sigmund, 'From the History of An Infantile Neurosis', in *The Pelican Freud Library*, vol. 9 (Ringwood: Penguin, 1979), 227–345
——, 'The Uncanny,' in *The Pelican Freud Library*, vol. 14 (Ringwood: Penguin, 1975), 335–76
Fromm, Erich, *The Forgotten Language: An Introduction to the Understanding of Dreams, Fairy Tales and Myths* (New York: Grove Press, 1951)
Frost, Brian J., *The Essential Guide to Werewolf Literature* (Madison, WI: University of Wisconsin Press, 2003)
Garland-Thompson, Rosemarie (ed.), *Freakery: Cultural Spectacles of the Extraordinary Body* (New York: New York University Press, 1996)
——, 'Narratives of Deviance and Delight: Staring at Julia Pastrana, the "Extraordinary Lady"', in Timothy B. Powell (ed.), *Beyond the Binary: Reconstructing Cultural Identity* (New Brunswick, NJ: Rutgers University Press, 1999), 81–104
George-Kanentiio, Doug, *Iroquois Culture and Commentary* (Santa Fe: Clear Light Publishers, 2000)
Gerald of Wales, *The History and Topography of Ireland*, trans. John J. O'Meara (London: Penguin, 1982)
Giacopasi, Caitlin B., 'The Werewolf Pride Movement: A Step Back from Queer Medieval Tradition', MA dissertation (Seton Hall University, NJ, 2011)
Gilbert, Sandra, and Susan Gubar, *The Madwoman in the Attic: the Woman Writer and the Nineteenth-Century Imagination* (London: Yale Nota Bene, 2000 [1979])
Grimstad, Kaaren (ed.), *Volsunga Saga: The Saga of the Volsungs* (Saarbrücken: AQ, 2000)
Gutenberg, Andrea, 'Shape-shifters from the Wilderness: Werewolves Roaming the Twentieth Century', in Monika Mueller (ed.), *The Abject of Desire: The Aestheticization of the Unaesthetic in Contemporary Literature and Culture* (Amsterdam and New York: Rodopi, 2007), 162–80
Halberstam, Judith, *Female Masculinity* (Durham, NC and London: Duke University Press, 1998)
Hanson, Helen, *Hollywood Heroines: Women in Film Noir and the Female Gothic Film* (London: I.B. Tauris, 2007)
Haraway, Donna J., *Simians, Cyborgs, and Women: The Reinvention of Nature* (New York: Routledge, 1991)
Harrison, Lisi, *Monster High* (London: Atom Books, 2010)
Herringer, Carol Engelhardt, *Victorians and the Virgin Mary: Religion and Gender in England, 1830–85* (Manchester: Manchester University Press, 2008)
Hertel, Christiane, 'Hairy Issues: Portraits of Petrus Gonsalus and his family in Archduke Ferdinand II's *Kunsthammer* and their contexts', *Journal of the History of Collections* 13:1 (2001), 1–22
Hirsch, Marianne, *The Mother/Daughter Plot: Narrative, Psychoanalysis, Feminism* (Bloomington, IN: Indiana University Press, 1989)
Hopper, Keith, 'Hairy on the Inside: Revisiting Neil Jordan's *The Company of Wolves*', *Canadian Journal of Irish Studies* 29:2 (2003): 17–26
Housman, Clemence, *The Were-Wolf* (London: Lane, 1896)
Hughes, Linda K., '"Fair Hymen Holdeth Hid a World of Woes": Myth and Marriage in Poems by "Graham R. Tomson" (Rosamund Marriott Watson)', *Victorian Poetry* 32:2 (Summer 1994): 97–120
——, *Graham R: Rosamund Marriott Watson, Woman of Letters* (Athens, OH: Ohio University Press, 2005)

Jackson, Rosemary, *Fantasy: The Literature of Subversion* (London and New York: Methuen, 1981), 69
Kilby, Jane, 'Carved in Skin: Bearing Witness to Self-Harm', in Stacey Ahmed and Jackie Stacey (eds), *Thinking Through the Skin* (London: Routledge, 2001), 124–42
Kilcup, Karen L., 'Writing "The Red Woman's America": An Introduction to Writing by Earlier Native American Women', in Karen L. Kilcup (ed.), *Native American Women's Writing 1800–1924: An Anthology* (Oxford: Blackwell Publishers, 2000)
Klause, Annette Curtis, *Blood and Chocolate* (New York: Delacorte Press, 1997)
Kramer, Heinrich and James Sprenger, *The Malleus Maleficarum*, trans. Montague Summers (New York: Dover Publications, 1971)
Kristeva, Julia, *Powers of Horror: An Essay on Abjection*, trans. Leon S. Roudiez (New York: Columbia University Press, 1982)
Krzywinska, Tanya, *Sex and the Cinema* (London and New York: Wallflower Press, 2006)
La Com, Cindy, 'Ideological Aporia: When Victorian England's Hairy Woman Met God and Darwin', *Nineteenth-Century Gender Studies* 4:2 (2008), www.ncgsjournal.com/issue42/lacom.htm.
Larbalestier, Justine, *Liar* (Crows Nest: Allen & Unwin, 2009)
Lau, Kimberly J., 'Erotic Infidelities: Angela Carter's Wolf Trilogy', *Marvels and Tales* 22 (2008): 77–94
Lesnik-Oberstein, Karín (ed.), *The Last Taboo: Women and Body Hair* (Manchester: Manchester University Press, 2006)
Lopez, Barry, *Of Wolves and Men* (New York: Scribner, 1978)
Lundoff, Catherine, *Silver Moon* (Maple Shade, NJ: Lethe Press, 2012)
McCann, Sharon, '"With Redundance of Blood": Reading Ireland in Neil Jordan's *Company of Wolves*', *Marvels and Tales* 14 (2010): 68–85
McGinley, Meghan, 'You Play Like a Girl', *RPGirl Zine* (August 2010): 30–3
Mackay, Daniel, *The Fantasy Role-Playing Game: A New Performing Art* (Jefferson, NC: McFarland, 2001)
Madar, Maia, 'Estonia I: Werewolves and Poisoners', in Bengt Ankarloo and Gustav Henningsen (eds), *Early Modern Witchcraft: Centres and Peripheries* (Oxford: Clarendon Press, 1990), 257–72
Magnanini, Suzanne, 'Postulated Routes from Naples to Paris: The Printer Antonio Bulifon and Giambattista Basile's Fairy Tales in Seventeenth-Century France', *Marvels and Tales* 21 (2007): 78–92
Marie de France, 'Bisclavret', in Karl Warnke (ed.), *Lais de Marie de France* (Paris: Librairie Générale Française, 1990)
Marryat, Frederick, 'The White Wolf of the Hartz Mountains', in Alexis Easley and Shannon Scott (eds), *Terrifying Transformations: An Anthology of Victorian Werewolf Fiction* (Kansas City: Valancourt Books, 2013)
Marvin, Garry, *Wolf* (London: Reaktion Books, 2012)
Mazzoni, Cristina, *She-Wolf: The Story of a Roman Icon* (Cambridge: Cambridge University Press, 2010)
Merchant, Carolyn, *The Death of Nature: Women, Ecology and the Scientific Revolution* (San Francisco: Harper & Row, 1983)
Meyer, Stephenie, *Twilight* (London: Atom Books, 2006)
——, *Eclipse* (London: Atom Books, 2007)

——, *Breaking Dawn* (London: Atom Books, 2010)
Miles, A.E.W., 'Julia Pastrana: The Bearded Lady', *Proceedings of the Royal Society of Medicine*, 67 (1973), 160–4
Miller, April, 'The Hair that Wasn't There Before: Demystifying Monstrosity and Menstruation in *Ginger Snaps* and *Ginger Snaps Unleashed*', *Western Folklore* 64:3–4 (2005): 281–303
Millar, Martin, *Lonely Werewolf Girl* (London: Piatkus, 2010)
Monter, William, *Witchcraft in France and Switzerland: The Borderlands During the Reformation* (Ithaca, NY: Cornell University Press, 1976)
Moore, Alan, 'The Curse', *Swamp Thing* 40 (September 1985)
Mulvey, Laura, 'Cinema Magic and the Old Monsters', in Lorna Sage (ed.), *Flesh and the Mirror: Essays on the Art of Angela Carter* (London: Virago, 1994), 230–42
Nielsen, Bianca, '"Something's Wrong, Like More Than You Being Female": Transgressive Sexuality and Discourses of Reproduction in *Ginger Snaps*', *thirdspace* 3:2 (2004): 55–69
Norris, Margot, *Beasts of the Modern Imagination* (Baltimore, MD and London: Johns Hopkins University Press, 1985)
Oates, Caroline, 'Metamorphosis and Lycanthropy in Franche-Comté, 1521–1643', in M. Feher (ed.), *Fragments for a History of the Human Body: Part One* (New York: Zone 1989), 305–63
Oliver, Kelly, *Animal Lessons: How They Teach Us To Be Human* (New York: Columbia University Press, 2009)
Orenstein, Catherine, *Little Red Riding Hood Uncloaked: Sex, Morality, and the Evolution of a Fairy Tale* (New York: Basic Books, 2002)
Otten, Charlotte F., *A Lycanthropy Reader: Werewolves in Western Culture* (Syracuse, NY: Syracuse University Press, 1986)
Palmer, Tim, 'Style and Sensation in the Contemporary French Cinema of the Body', *Journal of Film and Video* 58:3 (2006): 22–32
Porter, Tom, *And Grandmother Said … Iroquois Teachings as Passed Down Through the Oral Tradition* (Bloomington, IN: Xlibris, 2008)
Priest, Hannah, 'Pack versus Coven: Guardianship of Tribal Memory in Vampire versus Werewolf Narratives', in Simon Bacon and Katarzyna Bronk (eds), *Undead Memory: Vampires and Human Memory in Popular Culture* (New York: Peter Lang, 2014)
——, 'Bogeysliche as a Boye: Performing Sexuality in *William of Palerne*', in Robert Rouse and Cory Rushton (eds), *Sexual Culture in Late Medieval Britain* (Cambridge: D.S. Brewer, 2014)
Quandt, James, 'Flesh & Blood: Sex and Violence in Recent French Cinema', *Artforum* 42:6 (2004): 126–32
Raand, L.L., *The Midnight Hunt* (Valley Falls, NY: Bold Strokes Books, 2010)
Rein-Hagen, Mark, Robert Hatch and Bill Bridges, *Werewolf: The Apocalypse*, 2nd edition (Stone Mountain, CA: White Wolf, Inc., 1994)
Richards, Chris, *Forever Young: Essays on Young Adult Fictions* (New York: Peter Lang, 2008)
Robisch, S.K., *Wolves and the Wolf Myth in American Literature* (Reno, NV: University of Nevada Press, 2009)
Rosenwald, Lawrence Alan, *Multilingual America: Language and the Making of American Literature* (Cambridge: Cambridge University Press, 2008)

Rothenburger, Sunnie, '"Welcome to Civilization": Colonialism, the Gothic, and Canada's Self-protective Irony in the *Ginger Snaps* Werewolf Trilogy', *Journal of Canadian Studies* 44:3 (2010): 96–117
Ruthven, K.K., *Feminist Literary Studies: An Introduction* (Cambridge: Cambridge University Press, 1984)
Salisbury, Joyce E., *The Beast Within: Animals in the Middle Ages* (London: Routledge, 1994)
Scheckel, Susan, *The Insistence of the Indian: Race and Nationalism in Nineteenth-Century American Culture* (Princeton, NJ: Princeton University Press, 1998)
Schlegel, Alice, *Male Dominance and Female Autonomy: Domestic Authority in Matrilineal Societies* (New Haven, CT: Human Relations Area Files Press, 1972)
Schulte, Rolf, *Man as Witch: Male Witches in Central Europe* (Basingstoke: Palgrave Macmillan, 2009)
Sconduto, Leslie A., *Metamorphoses of the Werewolf: A Literary Study from Antiquity through the Renaissance* (Jefferson, NC: McFarland and Co., 2008)
Showalter, Elaine, *Sexual Anarchy: Gender and Culture at the Fin de Siècle* (London: Virago, 1992)
Silverman, Lisa, *Tortured Subjects: Pain, Truth, and the Body in Early Modern France* (Chicago: University of Chicago Press, 2001)
Sleeper-Smith, Susan, 'Women, Kin, and Catholicism: New Perspectives on the Fur Trade', in Rebecca Kugel and Lucy Eldersveld Murphy (eds), *Native Women's History in Eastern North American Before 1900: A Guide to Research and Writing* (Lincoln, NE: University of Nebraska Press, 2007), 234–74
Snell, D.L., and Thom Brannan, *Pavlov's Dogs* (New York: Permuted Press, 2012)
Sobchack, Vivian, *Carnal Thoughts: Embodiment and Moving Image Culture* (London: University of California Press, 2004)
Starr, Jason, *The Pack* (London: Penguin, 2011)
Stern, Rebecca, 'Our Bear Women, Ourselves', in Marlene Tromp (ed.), *Victorian Freaks: The Social Contexts of Freakery in Britain* (Columbus, OH: Ohio State University Press, 2008), 200–33
Stiefvater, Maggie, *Shiver* (London: Scholastic, 2009)
——, *Linger* (London: Scholastic, 2010)
——, *Forever* (London: Scholastic, 2011)
Summers, Montague, *The Werewolf* (London: Kegan Paul, 1933)
Takaki, Ronald, *Iron Cages: Race and Culture in 19th-Century America* (Oxford: Oxford University Press, 1990)
Tarr, Carrie, 'Director's Cuts: The Aesthetics of Self-Harming in Marina de Van's *Dans Ma Peau*', *Nottingham French Studies* 45:3 (2006): 78–91
Taylor, Paul and Steve Jenkins, 'Wolf at the Door ... Down in the Woods', *Monthly Film Bulletin* 51:608 (1984): 265–6
Toerien, Merran, and Sue Wilkinson, 'Gender and Body Hair: Constructing the Feminine Woman', *Women's Studies International Forum* 26:4 (2003), 333–44
Toivo, Raisa Maria, *Witchcraft and Gender in Early Modern Society: Finland and the Wider European Experience* (Burlington: Ashgate, 2008)
Toscano, Margaret M., 'Mormon Morality and Immortality in Stephenie Meyer's Twilight Series', in Melissa A. Click, Jennifer Stevens Aubrey and Elizabeth Behm-Morawitz (eds), *Bitten by Twilight: Youth Culture, Media and the Vampire Franchise* (New York: Peter Lang, 2010), 21–36
Vaughn, Carrie, *Kitty and the Silver Bullet* (London: Gollancz, 2008)

———, *Kitty Goes to Washington* (London: Gollancz, 2008)
———, *Kitty and the Dead Man's Hand* (London: Gollancz, 2009)
Velay-Vallantin, Catherine, 'Little Red Riding Hood as Fairy Tale, Fait-divers, and Children's Literature: The Invention of a Traditional Heritage', in Nancy L. Canepa (ed.), *Out of the Woods: The Origins of the Literary Fairy Tale in Italy and France* (Detroit: Wayne State University Press, 1997), 306–51
Vicinus, Martha, *Suffer and be Still: Women in the Victorian Age* (London: Indiana University Press, 1972)
Walker, Anne E., *The Menstrual Cycle* (London: Routledge, 1997)
Ward, Rachel Mizsei, 'Copyright, Association and Gothic Sensibilities: *Underworld* and *World of Darkness*', in Brigid Cherry, Peter Howell and Caroline Ruddell (eds), *Twenty-First-Century Gothic* (Newcastle-Upon-Tyne: Cambridge Scholars Publishing, 2010), 149–66
Warner, Marina, *From the Beast to the Blonde: On Fairy Tales and their Tellers* (London: Vintage, 1995)
———, *Six Myths of Our Time: Little Angels, Little Monsters, Beautiful Beasts and More* (New York: Vintage Books, 1995)
———, *Fantastic Metamorphoses, Other Worlds* (Oxford: Oxford University Press, 2002)
Waskul, Dennis and Matt Lust, 'Role-Playing and Playing Roles: The Person, Player, and Persona in Fantasy Role-Playing', *Symbolic Interaction* 27:3 (Summer 2004): 333–56
Watson, Rosamund Marriott, 'A Ballad of the Were-wolf', in Montague Summers, *Werewolf* (Whitefish, MT: Kessinger Publishing Co., 2003), 266–7
Weir, Alison, *Isabella: She-Wolf of France, Queen of England* (London: Vintage, 2012)
Welldon, Estela V., *Mother, Madonna, Whore: the Idealization and Denigration of Motherhood* (New York and London: Karnac Books, 1992)
Wiesner-Hanks, Merry E., *Women and Gender in Early Modern Europe: New Approaches to European History* (Cambridge: Cambridge University Press, 2008)
———, *The Marvelous Hairy Girls: The Gonzales Sisters and Their Worlds* (New Haven, CT: Yale University Press, 2009)
Wilson, Natalie, 'Civilized Vampires Versus Savage Werewolves: Race and Ethnicity in the Twilight Series', in Melissa A. Click, Jennifer Stevens Aubrey and Elizabeth Behm-Morawitz (eds), *Bitten by Twilight: Youth Culture, Media, and the Vampire Franchise* (New York: Peter Lang, 2010), 55–70
Wood, Robin, 'An Introduction to the American Horror Film', in Bill Nichols (ed.), *Movies and Methods – Volume 2* (Berkeley, CA: University of California Press, 1985), 215
Zipes, Jack, *The Trials and Tribulations of Little Red Riding Hood* (New York and London: Routledge, 1993)
———, *The Great Fairy Tale Tradition: from Straparola and Basile to the Brothers Grimm* (New York and London: Norton, 2001)
———, *The Enchanted Screen: the Unknown History of Fairy-Tale Films* (New York: Routledge, 2011)

Films and television programmes

Aja, Alexandre (dir.), *Switchblade Romance*, 2003
Annett, Paul (dir.), *The Beast Must Die*, 1974
Baledón, Rafael (dir.), *La Loba*, 1965
Being Human (UK), 2008–13
Being Human (US), 2011–
Brahm, John (dir.), *Undying Monster*, 1942
Browning, Tod (dir.), *Dracula*, 1931
Buffy the Vampire Slayer, 1997–2003
Cameron, James (dir.), *Aliens*, 1986
Craven, Wes (dir.), *Cursed*, 2005
Cronenberg, David (dir.), *The Brood*, 1979
Daniels, Rod (dir.), *Teen Wolf*, 1985
Dante, Joe (dir.), *The Howling*, 1981
Dein, Edward (dir.), *The Leech Woman*, 1960
de Van, Marina (dir.), *Dans Ma Peau*, 2002
di Silvestro, Rino (dir.), *La Lupa Mannara*, 1976
Dougherty, Michael (dir.), *Trick 'r Treat*, 2007
Fawcett, John (dir.), *Ginger Snaps*, 2000
Ferreri, Marco (dir.), *The Ape Woman*, 1964
Fitzgerald, Thom (dir.), *Wolf Girl* (aka *Blood Moon*), 2001
Flender, Rodman (dir.), *Idle Hands*, 1999
Florey, Robert (dir.), *The Beast with Five Fingers*, 1946
Fowler Jr., Gene (dir.), *I Was a Teenage Werewolf*, 1957
Francis, Freddie (dir.), *Dr Terror's House of Horrors*, 1965
Freund, Karl (dir.), *Mad Love*, 1935
Galindo, Rubén, and Jaime Jiménez Pons (dirs), *Santo versus the She-Wolves*, 1972
Harris, John (dir.), *The Descent Part 2*, 2009
Harvey, Grant (dir.), *Ginger Snaps Back: The Beginning*, 2004
'Heart', *Supernatural*, Season 2, 2007
Hillyer, Lambert (dir.), *Dracula's Daughter*, 1936
Jackson, Peter (dir.), *King Kong*, 2005
Johnston, Joe (dir.), *The Wolfman*, 2010
Jordan, Neil (dir.), *The Company of Wolves*, 1984
Khalfoun, Franck (dir.), *P2*, 2007
Landis, John (dir.), *An American Werewolf in London*, 1981
Lavia, Gabriele (dir.), *La Lupa*, 1996
Levin, Henry (dir.), *Cry of the Werewolf*, 1944
Lichtenstein, Mitchell (dir.), *Teeth*, 2007
Marshall, Neil (dir.), *Dog Soldiers*, 2002
——, *The Descent*, 2005
Mora, Philippe (dir.), *Howling II*, 1985
Nichols, Mike (dir.), *Wolf*, 1994
She-Wolf of London (1990–91)
Strachan, Craig (dir.), *Wild Country*, 2005
Sullivan, Brett (dir.), *Ginger Snaps 2: Unleashed*, 2004
Tourneur, Jacques (dir.), *Cat People*, 1942
von Garnier, Katja (dir.), *Blood and Chocolate*, 2007

Waggner, George (dir.), *The Wolf-Man*, 1941
Walker, Stuart (dir.), *Werewolf of London*, 1935
Waller, Anthony (dir.), *An American Werewolf in Paris*, 1997
Watkins, James (dir.), *Eden Lake*, 2008
'The Werewolves', *CSI: Crime Scene Investigation* 6:11, 2006
Williams, Paul (dir.), *The Furred Man*, 2010
Wizards of Waverly Place, 2007–12
Yarbrough, Jean (dir.), *She-Wolf of London*, 1946
Yates, David (dir.), *Harry Potter and the Half-Blood Prince*, 2009
——, *Harry Potter and the Deathly Hallows: Part 1*, 2010
——, *Harry Potter and the Deathly Hallows: Part 2*, 2011

Index

abjection 168, 187, 188–9, 198, 202, 204, 206
abortion 141
Aceves family 85
adultery 49
Agamben, Giorgio 182, 183, 186, 190, 192, 193
AIDS 130
Akwesasne reserve (Canada) 98
Aliens (1986) 184
alpha 18, 73, 138, 139–40, 141, 146n.59
Altered Beast (video game) 89
Ambras syndrome *see* body hair
American Werewolf in London, An (1981) 4, 63, 172, 196, 201
American Werewolf in Paris, An (1997) 171, 173–4, 184, 200
amputation
  of the foot 50
  of the hand 107, 108, 119–20, 122, 148–9, 151, 156, 157, 159, 160, 204
anorexia 90, 131–2
anthropophagy *see* cannibalism
Ape Woman, The (1964) 184
Artemis *see* Luna

banishment *see* exile
Baring-Gould, Sabine 12
Barnagoz, Marie 43
Barnard, Guillemette 44
Beast Must Die, The (1974) 169, 173–4, 177, 170n.12
Beaugrand, Honoré 16, 96, 97–100, 101, 102–8
Beauty and the Beast 89, 183
Being Human (UK TV) 10–11

Being Human (US TV) 14
berserker 66
bestiality 32, 49, 80–1, 83, 159, 183, 191
  pornography and 183
Black Werewolf (1974) *see Beast Must Die, The* (1974)
Blood and Chocolate (2007) 171, 184
Blood Moon (2001) *see Wolf Girl* (2001)
Bodin, Jean 54
body hair 8, 16–17, 77–95 *passim*, 172, 184, 187, 188, 189
  hypertrichosis 79, 83–4, 85, 87
  removal of 8, 9, 17, 77, 86, 87, 89, 91
Boguet, Henri 42–3, 48, 54, 55, 108, 111, 151, 157
breasts 78, 130–3 *passim*, 180, 189
breastfeeding 26, 37, 183, 188
Brisbane, Grace (character) 133–7, 142–3
Brood, The (1979) 190
Buffy the Vampire Slayer (TV) 14–15, 201, 202, 204, 206
Bulwer, John 77, 91
Burgundy (France) 41–58 *passim*
Butler, Judith 205

Calla (character) 138–40, 143
cannibalism 3, 42, 86, 100, 151, 152, 154, 159, 160, 175, 198, 207
  grave desecration and 12, 150
  infanticide and 13, 44, 46–7, 50, 180
  self-cannibalism 198, 201, 204
  for sexual gratification 49
  vagina dentata and 37
Carter, Angela 129, 150–1, 152, 154, 157–60

'The Company of Wolves' 125, 149, 154, 157
   Red Riding Hood 149, 159
   'The Tiger Bride' 89
   'The Werewolf' 149, 150–1, 157
   'Wolf-Alice' 125, 151, 157
Cat People (1942) 169, 184
celibacy 117
Champon, Oudette 45–6
Charnas, Suzy McKee 130–3
childbirth 190
   see also pregnancy
Chimera, the 182
Christianity 6, 100, 136–7, 145n.30
   allegory 114, 150
   Catholic Inquisition 43, 47, 181–2
   conversion of Estonia to 32, 34, 36, 37
   conversion of Mohawk nation to 101, 102
   original sin 72
   in *Werewolf: The Forsaken* 72
   see also Eucharist
Clearwater, Leah (character) 140–2
Clover, Carol 206
Company of Wolves, The (1984) 129, 148–9, 157–160, 184, 189
contagious bite 10, 16, 131, 134, 135, 187, 189, 202
contraception 87, 88
Cooper, James Fenimore 96, 97–8, 100–1
cosmetic surgery 90
couvade 191, 192, 195n.36
   see also menstruation
Creed, Barbara 166, 198, 206
Cremer, Andrea 137–40, 143
Cry of the Werewolf (1944) 171
Cursed (2005) 169, 171, 184
cyborg 184

Dans Ma Peau (2002) 196–207 *passim*
Darwin, Charles 81, 183, 185–6
   theory of evolution 82, 84
de Beauvoir, Simone 144
decapitation 43
Derrida, Jacques 185
Descent, The (2005) 175, 176, 177
Descent Part 2, The (2009) 175, 176

Despain, Bree 135–7, 143
Devil, the *see* Satan
devolution 183
Divine, Grace (character) 135–7, 143
divorce 33, 113, 123
Dog Soldiers (2002) 171
Dracula's Daughter (1936) 169–70
Dr Terror's House of Horrors (1965) 172–3, 177
drugs 131, 187, 190
   addiction to 90
du Coudray, Chantal Bourgault 2, 104–6, 125, 131, 166, 181, 184, 206, 207
Dungeons and Dragons (RPG) 62

echidnas 180
economic history 4–5, 53
Eden Lake (2008) 175, 176
Emson, Thomas 11
Erinyes, the *see* Furies, the
erotica 17–18
Esther (character) 196–207 *passim*
Estonian Folklore Archive 24–40 *passim*
etymology 3, 5, 21n.8, 49, 50
Eucharist 6, 9
   bread as symbol of 28
   desecration of 44
execution by burning 42, 43, 45, 108, 175, 181
exile 44, 47, 78, 207
   self-imposed 119, 125

fairies 66, 73, 132, 144n.7, 154
fairy tales 25, 26, 120, 152, 153, 154, 155, 183, 188, 190, 191, 192
Farini, Krao 82–3, 84
farming 4, 35, 38, 53
fatherhood 10, 14, 116, 155, 157
feminism 15, 36, 77, 117, 149, 166, 181, 198, 206
   ecofeminism 183–4
Fitzgerald, Ginger (character) 17, 131, 133, 186–93, 202, 203, 204, 206
folklore 106–7
   collecting of 24, 26, 27, 151, 152, 153, 160
   Estonian 24–40 *passim*
   Scandinavian 25
   Slavonic 25

forest spirit 35
Franche-Comté (France) 41–58 *passim*
Frayre, Guillauma 44, 48
freak shows 81, 84, 85–6, 184
Freud, Sigmund 112, 126n.7, 191–2
  'The Uncanny' 184–5
  'The Wolf Man' 192
Frog Prince, The 183
Furies, the 66, 73
Furred Man, The (2010) 21n.3

Gaia 64, 65, 70, 71, 73
Gaillard, Clauda 42–3
Gandillon, Perrenette 12–13, 41–2, 43, 48, 150
Garou (characters) 64–76 *passim*
genetic modification 90
genetic throwback 18, 83
  see also devolution
genitalia 11, 18, 181, 185, 191
  vagina dentata 11, 37, 133, 184
Gerald of Wales 5–7, 9–10, 68
Gervase of Tilbury 50
Gilbert, Sandra 112, 118–19, 120
Ginger Snaps (2000) 17, 131, 133, 166, 171, 184, 185, 186–93, 196, 201, 202, 204, 206
Ginger Snaps 2: Unleashed (2004) 133, 167, 184, 192, 209n.270
Ginger Snaps Back: The Beginning (2004) 167, 184
Glaon, Perrenette 44–5
Gonsalus sisters 77, 78–80, 81
Gorgades tribe 78
gorgons 180
Gothic
  aesthetic 62, 158
  in 1940s cinema 170
  in Victorian literature 7, 15, 150, 151, 160
Grimm, Jacob and Wilhelm 29, 152, 154
Gubar, Susan 112, 118–19, 120
Guillaume, Clauda 42–3
Guyenot, Jeanne 43

Halloween (1978) 175, 176
Halloween (2007) 175, 176
Haraway, Donna 90

harpies 180
Harrison, Lisi 7–10
Hiiumaa (Estonia) 31, 35
hirsutism *see* body hair
holy water 114
homosocial bonds 115
Horriel, Jeanne 45
Housman, Clemence 111–26 *passim*, 150
  and A.E. Housman 112
  and Laurence Housman 112–13
Howling, The (1981) 172, 201, 207
Howling II (1985) 184
Huron tribe 100–1

incest 49, 87, 154–7, 159
  and monstrous births 157
infanticide 12–13, 41, 42, 44, 46–7, 50, 52, 114, 118, 119, 122, 124, 150, 154, 156, 157, 159, 170, 171, 175, 180
  see also cannibalism
infertility 13, 69, 72–3, 142
Iroquois Confederacy 97, 98, 99–100
  mythology of 107
  role of women in 98
Isabella, wife of Edward II 7
I Was a Teenage Werewolf (1957) 129

Jackson, Andrew 98, 99
Jeanprost, Clauda 42

Kahnawá:ke settlement (Canada) 97, 98, 99, 100, 101, 102, 106
  expropriation of 99
Kanien'kehá:ka *see* Mohawk nation
Kelsey (character) 130–3
King Kong (2005) 183
Klause, Annette Curtis 13
Kristeva, Julia 188, 198

Labé, Louize 51
lactation *see* breastfeeding
La-Linotte-Qui-Chante (character) 97, 98, 99, 102–8
  illustration of 104–6
La Loba (1965) 172, 184
La Lupa (1996) 184
La Lupa Mannara (1976) 184

lamia 180
Larbalestier, Justine 77, 85, 86–8, 90–1
Leech Woman, The (1960) 184
lesbianism 14, 17–18, 22n.47, 86, 88, 169–70, 191
Lilith 118–19, 122, 125
Little Red Riding Hood 149–50, 151–4, 158, 159, 176, 189, 190, 191, 192, 193
Livonia 25
Luna 66, 70, 71, 72

madness 70, 71, 87–8, 136, 176
  and incarceration 154
maleficium see witchcraft
Malleus Maleficarum 15, 181–3
Marie de France 3, 49–50, 63, 111
marriage 11–12, 13, 33, 36–7, 102–3, 106, 108, 113, 119, 122, 123, 124, 138, 154–7
  arranged marriage 138
  and spousal murder 108, 123, 125, 153
Marryat, Frederick 7, 12, 15, 111, 150
Mary Magdalene 78, 86
masculinisation 16–18, 67, 118, 172
masturbation 156, 193
matrilineal inheritance 5, 98, 120
meningitis 136, 143
menstruation 71, 88, 130–1, 133, 142, 159, 167, 168, 183, 186–7, 188–90
  lunar cycle and 166, 189
  menarche 129, 130–1, 133, 144, 186–7, 188, 189, 190
  menopause 22n.47, 142
  menstruating man 160, 166, 192
  pre-menstrual syndrome 76n.26
Meyer, Stephenie 140–2
Middle Ages
  Estonia in 5, 33
  literature of 3–4, 5–7, 49–51, 63, 155, 156–7
  queenship in 7
  theology in 50, 114
Millar, Martin 11
miscarriage 13–14
miscegenation 32, 80–1, 83,
missing link 77, 82, 84
  see also genetic throwback

Mohawk nation 97, 98, 99, 100, 101, 103, 106, 108
  conversion to Christianity 101, 102
  language 98
Monster High *see* Wolf, Clawdeen
moon 70–1, 166, 173, 187, 190, 201
  lunar determinism 70–1, 131, 166, 187, 189
  tidal patterns and 70
Moore, Alan 12
motherhood 11, 31–2, 37, 80–1, 85, 120, 121, 122, 124, 130, 142, 156, 183
  see also pregnancy
Muhu (Estonia) 26–7, 31

Native Americans 96–110 *passim*
  image of 63, 65
  murder of Native American women 98
  in the Twilight series 140–1, 146n.46
  see also Iroquois Confederacy; Huron tribe; Mohawk nation
Nina (character) 10, 14
Norah (character) 14
Norville, Kitty (character) 13–14

Ösel *see* Saaremaa
Otten, Charlotte 114

pack 10, 11, 48, 63, 67–9, 74, 138, 139–40, 141, 177
  as familial unit 8–9, 22n.33, 68
Paget, Thivienne 42–3
Pastrana, Julia 81–2, 83, 84, 89
Perrault, Charles 152–3, 154, 158, 159, 160
Pinard, Colette 45
Pliny the Elder 78
pregnancy 11, 13–14, 32, 33, 72–3, 130, 141–2, 157, 188
  see also miscarriage
prostitution 80
puberty 17, 87, 129, 130–3 *passim*, 166, 189, 202
P2 (2007) 175

Raand, L.L. 17–18
Rabelais, François 51

rabies 52
race 23n.58, 63–4, 66, 82–3, 87, 173
  discourse of degeneracy and 106
  exoticism and 82–3
rape 49, 130, 132, 155, 158
  rape-revenge narrative 184
role-playing games (RPG) 13, 59–74 *passim*
Rosaleen (character) 148, 158–9, 189, 190

Saaremaa (Estonia) 24–40 *passim*
Sacred Hairy Family of Burma 83
sacrifice
  and Crucifixion symbolism 114
  personal 115, 116, 118, 130, 136–7, 138–9, 140, 143, 144, 156, 209n.27
  ritual killing 2, 5–6, 35, 138
  and suicide 140, 142
Saint George 34
Santo versus the She-Wolves (1972) 172
Satan 35, 119, 150, 154
  genitalia of 181
  pact with 42, 107, 156, 181–2
  sexual intercourse with 49, 181
Sécretain, Françoise 42
Sedgwick, Catharine Maria 96, 98–9, 100, 101
self-injury 196, 198, 199–200, 201–4, 205, 206
Seventh Book of Moses 28
severed paw *see* amputation
sexuality 80, 104, 106, 159, 167, 180, 181, 184, 190–1, 200–1, 204
  hypersexuality 14–16, 17, 49, 80, 145n.22, 183
  promiscuity 90
  see also lesbianism
Shakira 11–12
shamanism 65, 72, 73
she-wolf 171, 177
  and female violence 170, 174, 177
  totem of Rome 7
She-Wolf of London (1946) 168–71, 174, 176, 177
Showalter, Elaine 117, 125
silver bullet 27, 172, 173
Simon, Renoberte 47
sirens 180

smallpox 106
Society of Estonian Literati 27
sodomy 49
Sphinx, the 180
Stiefvater, Maggie 133–7, 142–3
subjectivity 199, 202, 203, 204, 205–6, 207
suicide 140, 142, 186
Summers, Montague 111, 182
Supernatural (TV) 202, 206
Switchblade Romance (2003) 175, 176

Talbot, Tara (character) 84, 85–6, 90
Teen Wolf (1985) 129
Teeth (2007) 184
telepathy 141–2
Thoreau, Henry David 96
Tomson, Graham R. *see* Watson, Rosamund Marriott
Tornier, Perrenette 43
transvestitism 118
Trick 'r Treat (2007) 176–7, 184, 200–1

uncanny, the 184–5, 186, 187, 192
Uratha (characters) 71–3

Valentine and Orson 89
Vampire: The Masquerade (RPG) 61, 69
Vampire: The Requiem (RPG) 71
vampires 73, 140–2, 146n.46, 150, 176, 180, 189
van Revestyn, Dirck 80
Vaughn, Carrie 13–14
Veruca (character) 14–15, 201, 202, 204, 206
Vichard, Pierrette 46–7
Victorian literature 68, 111–26 *passim*, 150, 151, 160
virginity 153
Volsunga Saga 155

Warner, Marina 89, 106–7, 120, 155
Watson, Rosamund Marriott 111–26 *passim*
Werewolf (card game) 13
Werewolf of London (1935) 169, 196
werewolf syndrome *see* body hair
Werewolf: The Apocalypse (RPG) 59–74 *passim*

Werewolf: The Forsaken (RPG) 71–3
'Werewolves' (TV) 84–5, 90
White Fell (character) 114–15, 117–19, 120–1, 123, 124–6, 150
White Wolf Publishing *see* World of Darkness
Wild Country (2005) 171
Wilkins, Micah (character) 77, 85, 86–8, 90–1
William of Paris 50
witchcraft 14, 34, 41, 43, 44, 46, 47, 48–9, 55, 100, 102, 107, 150, 151, 155 181–2
  fertility magic 36–7
witch trials 25, 26, 34, 36, 41–58 *passim*, 79, 92n.10, 153, 156, 159, 181
Wizards of Waverly Place (TV) 15–16
Wolf (1994) 184

Wolf, Clawdeen (character) 7–10, 15, 17
Wolf Girl (2001) 84, 85–6, 90
Wolfman, The (2010) 172
Wolf-Man, The (1941) 63, 84, 166, 196
wolves 1, 24, 29, 52, 53, 86, 96–7, 98, 134
  child raised by 151
  hunting of 4, 21n.10, 27, 35, 46, 52, 75n.17, 96, 107–8
  impregnation by 32
  sexual intercourse with 32, 191
  see also she-wolf
World of Darkness 59, 61–2, 66, 69, 71
World of Warcraft (video game) 61

Zipes, Jack 158
Žižek, Slavoj 200
zoophilia *see* bestiality

EU authorised representative for GPSR:
Easy Access System Europe, Mustamäe tee 50,
10621 Tallinn, Estonia
gpsr.requests@easproject.com

www.ingramcontent.com/pod-product-compliance
Lightning Source LLC
Chambersburg PA
CBHW021854230426
43671CB00006B/391